# Responsible Leadership
Global and Contextual Ethical Perspectives

# Responsible Leadership
## Global and Contextual Ethical Perspectives

Editors

Christoph Stückelberger / J. N. K. Mugambi

Globethics.net Series No. 1

Cover design: Juan Pablo Cisneros

© 2007 Globethics.net
150 route de Ferney
1211 Geneva 2, Switzerland
Web: http://www.globethics.net

Published by WCC Publications
150 route de Ferney, P.O. Box 2100
1211 Geneva 2, Switzerland
Web: http://www.wcc-coe.org
ISBN 978-2-8254-1516-0

Printed in France

# CONTENTS

## PART II: RESPONSIBLE RELIGIOUS LEADERSHIP

# INTRODUCTION

Each group of human beings has a leader or leaders. From the smallest entity of a family until international institutions like the UN, from companies to religious communities, from NGOs to parliaments and governments, from schools to the media. There are many leaders: parents, teachers, editors in chief, boards, presidents of associations, CEOs, pastors, deacons and bishops, men, women and children.

Many leaders act in a responsible way, but many others do not. Responsibility and responsiveness are directly related. A leader is responsible when he or she is responsive to the needs, concerns and interest of those whom one aspires to lead. At its best, leadership must be demonstrated in the responsible management of public and private resources for the common good. From this perspective, stewardship is an expression of responsible leadership. Responsible leadership also has to do with integrity, which in turn has to do with respectability and respectfulness. To be respectable, a leader must be respectful of those for whom that leader expects respect and compliance. Respect can only be deserved. It must not be demanded. Self-imposition evokes fear, whereas exemplary leadership wins respect.

Globalisation leads to a close interaction between different value systems. Different concepts and traditions of leadership are confronted with each other by media, trade, tourism, encounters, conferences and migration. This is enriching and challenging at the same time. How to come to a common understanding of leadership when one has to work together with others and has to find common decision-making processes? How to respect at the same time the diversity of values and leadership models?

These questions were the starting point for this book. Globethics.net, the global network for applied ethics, unites ethicists and practitioners from all continents. A first volume (Christoph Stückelberger, Jesse N.K. Mugambi (eds), *Responsible Leadership. Global Perspectives*, Nairobi, Kenya: Acton Publishers, 2005) collected 15 articles which are reprinted in this book. In September 2005, the International Globethics.net Conference in Bangkok, Thailand on the theme 'Responsible Leadership' brought together a broad variety of ethicists from five continents. A selection of revised keynote speeches and papers are presented in the second part of this publication. Some of these 23 contributions respond to and are in dialogue with articles from the first volume. At the end, 'Globethics.net Elements for Responsible Leadership' are published as a common result of the conference.

The contributions in this book cover four main sectors of responsible leadership: *family leadership* (including educational leadership), *religious leadership, business leadership and political leadership.* This fascinating and rich variety of 39 contributions from 21 countries shows the diversity of leadership concepts, e.g. family leadership models in the different cultures. The struggle between Confucianism, Socialism and Christian ethics in China, the conflicts between traditional and Christian concepts in Cameroon, the debate between conservative and liberal family ethics in Canada show the conflicts of values in almost all societies and show ethical argumentation to solve it. The articles also show the interaction between the different sectors so that e.g. family models are reflected in politics and the behaviour of their leaders. The contributions also show the strong influence of religious leadership on other sectors in its positive and negative sense.

Many of the authors argue from a Christian ethical background, some from a Muslim or a philosophical point of view. Leadership is also an important gender issue which is an explicit focus in different articles such as from South Korea, Argentina, Switzerland and South Africa. All authors are rooted in their own context and try, at the same time, to overcome it in situations of transformation and to confront it with the global challenges.

In the name of *Globethics.net*, we thank all the authors for their contribution, the Globethics.net secretariat and WCC publications for the good and efficient cooperation in the production of the book.

We hope that this collection contributes to sharpen the sensitivity for irresponsible and unjust leadership and the abuse of power. We hope that it strengthens the vision and values of responsible leadership in global and contextual perspectives. We hope that men, women and young people act as responsible stewards who understand leadership as a service to those in need and a service to human development in this one world.

*Geneva/Nairobi, Advent 2006*
*Christoph Stückelberger and J. N. K. Mugambi, editors*

# 1

# STEWARDS AND 'CAREHOLDERS'. A CHRISTIAN ETHICAL PERSPECTIVE

*Christoph Stückelberger, Switzerland*

## Introduction

To be a master? A king? A global player? A CEO? A guide? A pathfinder? A steward? A shareholder? A 'careholder'? What is the vision of responsible leadership which guides us and should guide us? Let us look at the biblical vision and Jesus' practice of stewardship. It is not an outdated concept, but highly relevant and feasible for the leaders of today and tomorrow.

Leaders have a specific responsibility.[1] But in order to find out, what responsible leadership means, we ask: What does responsible life as such mean? To act as leader is only a specific form of acting as human being. This leads us straight to the fundamental question of anthropology: What are we? What should human beings become? What is our role and mandate in human relations and in relations with the nonhuman creation?

Power is the ability to decide on one's own authority and to impose this decision on others. This classical definition of power from the famous sociologist Max Weber describes the mainstream understanding of leadership today: a leader is a master with the power to decide, direct and dominate. Not only as teachers or directors, but also as parents or as masters of our own free time. Most human beings want – in that sense – to be masters because nobody likes to be dependent on or 'manipulated' by others.

The same understanding is included in the vision to be a king. 'The consumer is king' means: he or she can decide independently what to buy or not to buy. The king seems to be responsible to nobody but himself. A modern expression for kingship in today's business world is 'global player.' Two top managers of (Swiss) companies, one from the nutrition sector and the other from the banking sector, told me independently from each other, that they are convinced that in future, only 'about ten big global players' will dominate the global market in their respective sector. They stated that they intend to be and remain one of them. They mainly think in categories of power and manipulation. World development is seen as a game and the aim is to define the rules of the game as global players and to influence them in their favour. That is the modern misunderstanding of *Dominium terrae* (to rule the world; to subdue it, Genesis 1,28). The word 'global players' underlines this world-view, like a 'religion of the market', which at the same time destroys the competition of the market through the monopoly of the big players.

This understanding of 'kings' and 'masters' is a model of dominion which is always accompanied by the other side of the coin: the people as 'servants'. It is a model of hierarchy which often leads to oppression, exploitation and humiliation.

The Judeo-Christian faith is based on a totally different world view of the role of humans on earth and of leadership: The 'good king', the 'good shepherd', to be a 'guest on earth', the 'good servant' and the 'steward' — are biblical anthropological models relevant for responsible leadership. Let us look at two of them, the good manager and the guest.

## 1. Biblical Model: The Good Manager

The New Testament model of responsible leadership which impresses me most is the one of the good manager. Its clearest expression is found in Luke 12:42-48:

> 42 Who then is the faithful and wise steward,[2] whom his master will set over his household, to give them their portion of food at the proper time? 43 Blessed is that servant whom his master when he comes will find so doing. 44 Truly, I say to you, he will set him over all his possessions. 45 But if that servant says to himself, 'My master is delayed in coming' and begins to beat the menservants and the maidservants, and to eat and drink and get drunk, 46 the master of that servant will come on a day when he does not expect him and at an hour he does not know, and will punish him, and put him with the unfaithful. ... 48 Every one to whom much is given, of him will much be required; and of him to whom men commit much they will demand the more.

The Greek word in this text for 'steward' is *oikonomos*, the 'economist'! Oikos means the house and the household. The oikonomos is housekeeper who keeps the house in order. It is the administrator and manager who cares for the economy of the household and for all people living and working in this community. It is the first servant. There are four characteristics in the text which distinguish the responsible and the irresponsible manager.

1. The good manager recognises that he is not the proprietor of the house or the shareholder of the company but responsible to maintain and develop it in the name of the owner. The bad manager

behaves as if he is the owner and sees the house or company as his own property.

2. The faithful steward cares for the people under his responsibility! He gives food, salary and social security at the proper time (v. 42). But the bad leader violates and exploits the people he should be responsible for (v. 45).

3. The good leader represents a solid work ethic. He works hard for the well-being of his collaborators and therefore serves as a good example. The irresponsible leader does not work, is corrupt, drunken (that means he is greedy and hooked on all kind of things). His exploitation and slavery is an expression that he regards not only the household but also human beings as his personal property.

4. The wise servant acts in a responsible way at every moment of his life because he knows that the 'master' could come and control every time. Business ethics and response to God are fully integrated in the daily life. But the stupid manager believes that no control will happen, that he can win every court case by bribing the judges, that it is enough to go to church and start to pray just at the end of life in order to be saved.

The story shows in a very simple and convincing way the meaning of responsibility: it means to respond to somebody (the word 'responsibility' comes from 'response'): the manager to the owner, the Christian to God. A bad leader wants to be autonomous, that means 'independent' from all responsibility towards others except himself. And by that, as a drunken person, he even loses control over himself. He is controlled by his greed for mammon and power. The good steward is theonomous, that means he gets his responsibility, respect and dignity from his dependency from God. And the more responsible he acts the more responsibilities he gets and can manage (v. 48).

This responsible behaviour is a vision for everybody, but especially for leaders. This model is convincing because it is not only a theory but a model practiced by Jesus himself in his life as a 'serving king', offering his own life for the benefit and salvation of the whole community. He preached, healed, danced and laughed, constantly responding to the neet of his 'clients' as his 'work ethics'. He served as a servant washing the feeds of his disciples, he gave orientation and guidelines by his challenging parables, he shared food. He remained faithful to God whom he called father, even on the cross. The disciples of the resurrected Christ are invited to become such good stewards of God's gifts.

## 2. Biblical Model II: The Guest on Earth

A second biblical model of responsible leadership and behaviour is God's invitation to humankind to live as guests in his house, which is the earth. This view is closely linked to the model of stewardship. It is meaningful for economic ethics as well as for environmental ethics.[3]

The message 'Bring the earth under your control' (Gen 1:28) in the younger of the two biblical Histories of creation written in the Babylonian exile 2500 years ago, is the biblical statement defining the relationship between man and the rest of creation that is still most known to the public. It is often misunderstood as an oppressive position of power and thus rejected. However, this *dominium terrae* is by no means an invitation to the unlimited exploitation of the earth. On the contrary, it means that we have a responsibility for our environment in the same way as a king should feel responsible towards his people or a good steward takes care of the goods that he has been entrusted with. The older biblical creation story in Genesis 2 shows God's generosity of allowing humanity to live on earth like in a fertile garden but combines it with the command 'to cultivate and to guard it,' or – in an other translation – 'to work it and take care of it.' (Gen 2:15).

God is the host and mankind is guest on earth. At the end of time and already in these times, God invites to the great banquet. He offers the abundant creation to his guests and lets them partake in the completion of creation. Mankind can only respond to this promise and this offer in the most appropriate way by showing joy, praise and thanks. At the same time, this offer represents the foundations of the ethical re-orientation: Because humanity has experienced God's promise it is possible to live on earth like a respectful guest. God himself is host. He is the one to prepare the banquet (Isa 25:6-8). The laid table is creation in perfection. And it is not up to the guest to choose his or her host, but the host invites his guests (John 15:16).

In the eschatological reconciliation, the mutual hospitality of all creatures becomes perfect: 'Wolves will be the guests of sheep' (Isa 11:6)! This means that to be God's guest and host of fellow-humans and fellow-creatures is a basic attitude including even the world of non-humans! To be a guest is also a model for leadership which leads to peace.

The eschatological direction of the image of mankind towards being guest in the New Testament has to be closely linked to the abundant comprehension of being guest on earth present in the Old Testament, being particularly influenced by the tradition of Exodus: 'My people went to live in Egypt as foreigners' (Isa 52:4). In the Old Testament, the concept of being a guest on earth develops into an anthropologically essential property of being human: The people of Israel experienced in Egypt and for a second time in the Babylonian exile what it meant to be foreigners. The attitude – that one's own life as well as the earth and its resources are not our property but only a loan – is closely connected to this (1 Chron 29:1). In economic and ecological terms, psalm 24 is also significant: 'The world and all that is in it belong to the Lord; the earth and all who live on it are his' (Ps 24:1). Thus, humans have no right of disposal, but a right of use upon the resources of this earth.

'I am a guest on earth for just a little while' (Ps 119:19) does not mean to long for the beyond while withdrawing from this world. This would not be responsible leadership but to escape responsibility. The invitation to be a guest on earth enables the guests to bare the burden of responsibility because they know that they must not bare the whole world on their shoulder but the light burden in joyful expectation of God's kingdom to come and in deep respect towards creation knowing that the guests cannot and must not possess it. Who behaves like a guest, leaves the guesthouse behind in good order for the next guests that will arrive after him/her.

The model of being a guest on earth lays also the foundation for a community oriented understanding of responsible leadership. Hospitality plays an eminent role in the gospel, especially in the gospel according to Luke. The community of guests around a table is the embodiment of hospitality and the anticipation of the eschatological reconciliation. The eucharistic community is an expression of God's hospitality and thus the visible banquet community of the guests that have been invited by God himself (1 Cor 10:16-18; Mark 14:22). The most important feature of the guests that are partaking in the banquet community is the sharing. Thus, the Eucharist turns into the starting point of the worldwide sharing among guests including fellow-beings and the environment.

The meaning of the model of the guest on earth for responsible leadership can be summarised as follows:

1. The guest is not the owner of the guesthouse but s/he is invited to use it for his/her well-being, joy and life in dignity. The *dominium terrae* (to rule over the earth) is replaced by the *servicium terrae*, serving the earth and all living beings on it.

2. Everything that has been created is placed at the guest's disposal, however, it cannot be possessed. Things which are on loan are treated with care, respect and sustainability. Every intervention into the 'goods on loan' is done with greatest caution and only on consultation with the host. Thus results a 'guest-economy'.

3. In the same way as God is not only host but also guest himself (and foreigner! John 1:11; Matt 8:20) on this earth, man is not only guest but mandated by God to take over the tasks of a host. To be host thus also corresponds to the *diakonos* of the New Testament, who serves the guests unselfishly for example at the banquet community. Jesus as a leader understood himself as such a serving *diakonos*. There is a close connection between the duties of the host, of the steward and of the deacon towards his guests and the poor, who may claim particular respect and protection! The host protects his guests. Responsible leadership includes the responsibility to protect!

## 3. The Christian Vision: Stewards and 'Careholders'

The two models of the faithful steward and the thankful guest can also be summarised in the word 'careholder'. The shareholder holds shares and therefore possesses a part of a company in order to make profit out of his invested money. The responsible shareholder, in addition, cares for the well-being of the company and its workers. The responsible leader as a 'careholder' holds responsibility and cares for values, goods and for people who are entrusted to him or her.

Responsible behaviour and its virtues are first of all valid for all human beings. Leaders 'only' have a higher degree of responsibility to care than the 'ordinary' people. The stronger has more responsibilities than the weaker because he has more power, competences and means to decide and to act. The steward and 'careholder' can be characterised by six virtues:

*To care:* 'The Lord God took the man and put him in the Garden of Eden to work it and take care of it.' (Gen 2:15). The shareholder cultivates and conserves, transforms and protects and finds the right balance between the two. To care for others as for oneself is a direct expression of the commandment to love the other as oneself. To care does not primarily mean charity, but to care for a life in dignity of all, to strengthen justice and to develop technological skills and political mechanisms for the well-being of the individuals as well as the community (see Luke 12:42: to care for food). To care includes to be attentive, present, near to those for whom the leader has to care.

*To protect:* the steward is among others, the watchman who recognises coming dangers, who takes protecting measures in advance, who intervenes in order to avoid damage and who – if a problem or a catastrophe could not be avoided – helps to restore and to heal the wounds. The good leader has an obligation to protect. That is valid for the leader as an individual as for institutional leaders such as a government or a multilateral institution like the UN. [4]

*To guide:* The steward is the pathfinder and shows the direction. He reminds the subordinate that they all together are not owners and to respond in their behaviour to the owner's – the Creator's – expectations. His or her guidance is based on values, filled with knowledge and know how. S/he has the skill to think ahead and to be in planning and vision always a step ahead of the others.

*To order:* To guide means also to bring an order and structure into unclear situations and confusing structures, to restructure where necessary in order to strengthen the strategy, the community, the efficiency and sustainability of the work and the orientation of the people entrusted.

*To serve:* The responsible leader as steward sees himself or herself not as opposed to the subordinate, but as *primus inter pares*, as the first among equals, as the first servant. This anthropological unity and equality of the leader with his or her employees is fundamental even if the task and responsibilities are very different.

*To share:* The 'careholder'-steward shares the entrusted natural, material human and spiritual resources with the subordinate according to needs and performance. Since the manager is not owner, s/he cares for a just distribution of goods and fair access to services.

The word 'oikos' today is present in three dimensions: the *eco*nomy, the *eco*logy and the *ecu*menism. The responsible steward cares for the economy as the material basis of life in the household; s/he cares for the ecology as the environmental basis of life in the household; s/he also cares for ecumenism as the spiritual basis for life and its interreligious and intercultural community in the global household. S/he cares, protects, guides, orders, serves and shares on all three levels.

## 4. Responsible Stewardship is Concrete

These principles and virtues of responsible stewardship are the basis for more concrete guidelines in applied ethics of leadership. The Ghanaian theologian Emmanuel Asante developed an 'Ethics of Stewardship' [5] for the stewardship of talents, of time, of wealth, of power, of sexuality, of poverty eradication etc. We concentrate on three examples:

## a) Stewards in Managing Natural Resources

A key challenge for responsible leadership is the management of resources:[6] natural resources such as energy, water, air, soil and forests, material resources such as property of goods and services, financial resources such as capital or insurances, structural resources such as administrative control mechanisms or human resources such as personnel. Let us take oil, the fundamental energy resource, as an example. What is the behaviour of the responsible steward of oil (as producer, politician, consumer or scientist) who cares, protects, guides, orders, serves and shares this resource?

First the un-renewable energy sources have to be seen not as property[7] but as a gift lent from God and given to today's but also to tomorrow's generations.

To care means to use it so carefully that something remains for future generations. Today's behaviour is not sustainable since we know that the oil reserves will be used between 2040 und 2060, that means within one to three generations.

To protect includes the protection of the interests of the indigenous population and the environment in a given area of exploitation of oil.

To guide includes information and education on careful use of oil resources and orientation on alternatives.

To order leads to involvement in an efficient management of the production and waste management of these resources and in a value-based energy policy.

To serve the responsible management of resources includes – among others – financial transparency, clear control mechanisms, anti-corruption programmes etc.

To share means fighting for fair distribution of energy resources in the perspective of poverty eradication strategies.

## b) Stewards in Managing Spiritual Resources

Religious leaders have a special responsibility in the management of spiritual resources. Christian literature on leadership concentrates, often one-sided, on this dimension.[8] Church leaders have to be faithful stewards in the management of natural resources, caring for God's creation, using material goods and church properties in a transparent way, managing church elections in a transparent way without buying votes or doing other corrupt practices.[9] But a special responsibility is to manage spiritual resources. Spiritual stewardship is based on the same six values and virtues as stewardship in other fields knowing that spiritual leadership is a gift and talent to work with as God's 'careholder': to care, to protect, to guide, to order, to serve and to share.

To care for the faithful interpretation of the Holy Scripture and not to instrumentalise it for proper interests and ideologies; to care for those who fall into religious depression provoked or at least increased by religious pressure; to protect the spiritual weaker in a religious community in order not to exclude him/her; to guide the community in developing the prophetic sensitivity to distinguish between good and false prophets, good and bad spirits, life giving and life destroying forces; to develop church orders on the basis of business principles which include spiritual criteria; to serve not only one interest group in a parish or church institution but to strengthen the unity of the community; to share spiritual power by acknowledging that the Holy Spirit is present not only in church leaders but as well in lay persons.

## c) Stewards in Responsible Use of Power

Power is a pejorative term for many, owing to the fact that it is often abused. Can power be used in responsible stewardship? According to Max Weber, power is the possibility of enforcing one's own will. As a capacity for the realisation and implementation of ethical values, power is positive; indeed, it is necessary. According to the theological definition of the World Council of Churches, power represents man's ability to participate in God's creation. This is not a question of as much power as possible, but about the power that is appropriate to the task and aims at every level of action. Ethically speaking, power and responsibility are inextricably two sides of the same coin. If you have no power, you cannot assume any responsibility, and if you exercise power without any responsibility, you will have to be divested of it because in such a case, the other fundamental values are in jeopardy. The more power one has the higher is his or her responsibility, as we quoted at the beginning: 'Every one to whom much is given, of him will much be required.' (Luke 12:48)

The measure of responsibility must be adequate to the measure of power given to a person or institution, and vice versa. Responsibility that is not shared and limited will make people feel responsible for things they are unable to influence, and this is almost as destructive as undivided power. A worker without power cannot be made responsible for the failure of the company. It is irresponsible to demand responsibility from others without granting them the corresponding authority and power. Power is a talent in order to serve the community and especially the weaker in this community. The steward sees his or her power not as property but as a gift and loan to work with. Power is tamed by responsibility, reinvested in an authority that is above the holder of power, and thus placed at the service of humanity. In Christian faith power is given by God to serve. If it is abused God takes it away as seen in Old Testament biographies such as the king Saul. Power/responsibility must be fairly distributed and democratically limited and controlled lest they be abused. The dictator claims unlimited and uncontrolled power. The steward accepts and even promotes the sharing/limitation and the democratic control of his or her own power knowing that even the best human being is tempted to abuse power once s/he has it and that this can only be avoided by internal and external control of power. [10]

## Conclusion

In summary, we have seen that the biblical Christian vision of responsible leadership is very clear and precise: The good manager behaves as steward, as 'careholder', as guest on earth, acting not as owner but on behalf of the owner. S/he cares, protects, guides, orders, serves and shares in the management of natural and spiritual resources, of power, of economic affairs as well as of the ecumenical community of denominations and religions in the service of peace.

NOTES

[1]   Responsibility is a key value in ethics. See e.g. Simon, René, *Ethique de la responsabilité*, Paris: Cerf, 1993; Jonas, Hans, *Das Prinzip Verantwortung*, Frankfurt: Suhrkamp, 1984.

[2]   The English New International Version translates *oikonomos* by 'manager'! In the modern business world the expression 'manager' – who is not the shareholder, but the head of the employees – is a precise translation and creates a direct bridge to business ethics. 'Steward' can be translated into French as *gestionnaire or mandataire*.

[3]   My view of environmental ethics is based on this anthropological vision of being a guest. See Stückelberger, Christoph, *Umwelt und Entwicklung*, Stuttgart: Kohlhammer Verlag, 1997, pp. 230-239 (see also the Chinese edition, a Korean edition is in preparation).

[4]   ICISS, *The Responsibility to Protect. Report of the International Commission on Intervention and State Sovereignty*, Ottawa, Canada: ICISS, 2001.

[5]   Asante, Emmanuel, *Stewardship. Essays on Ethics of Stewardship*, Accra, Ghana: Wilas Press, 1999.

[6]   Jena, Purna Chandra, *Masters or Stewards. A Theological Reflection on Ecology and Environment*, Delhi/Nagpur: ISPCK/NCCI, 2003; Stückelberger, Christoph, *Umwelt und Entwicklung, op. cit.*, pp. 27ff.

[7]   For theological and ethical reflection on property, see works by Ulrich Duchrow.

[8]   Sanders, Oswald, *Spiritual Leadership. Principles of Excellence for Every Believer*, Chicago, IL: Moody Press, 1994 (1967 for the 1st edition. Over half a million of copies sold).

[9]   Reflections on responsible church leadership in fighting corruption with concrete proposals such as codes of conduct can be found in: Christoph, Stückelberger, *Continue Fighting Corruption. Experiences and Tasks of Churches, Mission Societies and Aid Agencies*, Berne: Bread for all, 2003. Can be found as pdf on the website www.christophstueckelberger.ch.

[10]   Stückelberger, Christoph, *Global Trade Ethics*, Geneva: WCC Publications, 2003, Chapter 3.10 (available also in French and Chinese).

# 2

# ENGENDERING LEADERSHIP. A CHRISTIAN FEMINIST PERSPECTIVE FROM INDIA

*Evangeline Anderson-Rajkumar, India*

## Introduction

Several questions flooded my mind as I began to reflect critically on the theme of responsible leadership. *Who* is a leader? *What* is good leadership? What are the qualities that we expect or admire in leaders? What are those things that we would not an accomplished leader to be? Can an assessment of power-flow from the leader to the people be a marker to define responsible leadership? These questions are valid and necessary that one has to deal with, in order to critically and imaginatively weave a pattern of responsible leadership that would contribute to the enhancement of human dignity and wholeness in community at any given time.

## 1. Towards Non-Hierarchical Patterns of Leadership

What I shall do in this brief paper is to juxtapose two stories of women in leadership – one is a story from the past and the other a story from the present – to address the above questions as well as focus on engendered leadership that would lead to a transformed community. The first story is that of Miriam, the first woman in the Bible who was named as a prophet. The second story is a *collective* story of women who participated in the *Panchayati Raj* governance, in Karnataka, South India. An overview of these two stories brings to surface, issues concerned with power, control over resources, exercise of freedom with responsibility, agency over one's body, reclaiming of the power of voice and speech, and so on.

The women in these stories challenge dominant notions of leadership, and reconstruct the identity and selfhood of women in a decisive way through their leadership. These two stories present for us a challenge to search for non-hierarchical patterns of leadership, in a world where leadership if often equated with power *over* another. Let us now turn to the two stories as resource for our critical reflection on the major theme – responsible leadership.

## 2. The Story of Miriam

In the second chapter of the book of Exodus (Ex) in the Bible, we first meet Miriam as a young girl who stands guard for her baby brother Moses. She seems to be a smart and courageous girl who takes a bold initiative to link her mother with the adoptive parent (Pharaoh's daughter) in a novel way. She assumes a leadership role along with her mother Jochebed, Pharaoh's daughter, the two mid-wives Shiphrah and Puah in challenging the mandate of Pharaoh to kill all the newborn male Hebrew children. In Ex 15:20 of the same book, Miriam is referred to as a prophet who led the *people* to celebrate their journey of liberation from the hands of Pharaoh.

It is important to note the *masculine, plural* (them) in Ex 15:21 that underlines the fact that Miriam was not just a leader of the women's wing of Israel but of the *whole people*. The significance of her role, responsibility and leadership is however undermined as she is evaluated more against the book Number (Num) 12, where she is por-trayed as a power monger, as one jealous of Moses.

In most references, the names of Moses and Aaron figure as the leaders of Israel but not Miriam. Prophet Micah however does not forget to mention the name of Miriam along with Moses, and Aaron, as those sent by God to deliver the people of Israel (Micah 6:4). This is seldom uplifted as *history* that has to be celebrated. Micah who lived several centuries later than Miriam was being faithful and sensitive to the tradition that prevailed among the people who chose to remember Miriam as one among the leaders sent by God. Hence my interest to reconstruct the person and leadership of Miriam and creatively re-imagine some of the *turning point* decisions she must have made in order to challenge some of the prevalent patterns of leadership.

My feminist antenna often senses something amiss when I read in the Bible, of a woman who is either praised as wonderful or dismissed as a sinner. Both these actually reflect how far the praised women or the dismissed women chose to abide by or challenge the patriarchal social norms of that time. A good woman is often praised as one who does not transgress the boundaries of social expectations and values laid down by a patriarchal society. A bad woman is often identified as one who challenges the construct of a 'good woman' in that given cul-ture. My interest in Miriam was especially aroused when I read of Miriam as the first prophet, as one among the three sent by God, according to Micah on the one hand and to see the haste with which common women and men tried to dissociate from Miriam because she was punished with leprosy for her audacious, jealous voice. What was the intention of the writer who uncritically narrates that Miriam alone was punished for her question of audacity? With these prelim-inary questions, let us turn to the story of Miriam.

We read of a severe crisis that emerged in the community of Israel during their journey in the wilderness in Num 11 where the people of Israel complain to Moses that they have not had meat for several days. Perhaps there were several 'I told you so', 'never mind', 'Old is Gold' opinions shared openly among people and with Moses in particular. Moses cannot help but turn to God saying: 'Did I give birth to these people that I have to be responsible for them?' The daily menu is monotonous! An understandable need indeed for the people, considering how important food is, to keep one's body, mind and heart as fit as possible. Num 11 tells us of a 'stranger' that kills several hundreds of people overnight, even as meat was still between their teeth! One may probably visualise a case of food poisoning, or a sudden massacre of people, or a case of people breaking into sudden communal riot that saw several dead in a short time. What interests me most is the reference to 'plague' in Num 11 as well as in Num 25, which results also in the sudden death of thousands of people. Whereas it is vague and difficult to connect a reason for the 'plague' that robbed the lives of thousands of Israelites during their journey in the wilderness in Numbers 11, the reason for 'plague' is quite clear in Num 25. Moreover the reference to the Cushite woman in Num 12 (of whom Miriam and Aaron seem to have questioned Moses about) and the incident narrated in Numbers 25 seem to have a connection!

### 3. 'Has the Lord Spoken Only Through You, Moses?'

The reference to developing of sexual relationships between the people of Israel and Moab is looked upon as an abomination before God. The people of Israel had a deliberate negative construction of the Moabites as the 'other' – polluting, evil, irreligious, and idol worshippers – in order to create a pure, holy, good and religious 'self' before God. Those who dared to relate to the women of other religious communities had to be taught a lesson in monotheism and monoculturism. Zimri, an Israelite man tries to be bold and defies the order of Moses who wanted all the Israelite men to give up their relationships with women from other religious communities. He takes his Midianite woman Cozbi and declares that they will remain as a couple together and enter a tent. Phineas interprets this as a revolt *against God* and kills both Zimri and Cozbi. The narrator interprets this act of Phineas as that which propitiates the wrath of a jealous God! God also seems to approve of Xenophobia, a jealous ethnic narrow minded God fashioned according to the mind of the powerful, including Moses.

It is here that I imagine the role of Miriam, a senior leader, a woman, who probably challenged Moses very strongly on his stand on interrace, inter-caste, interreligious, inter-cultural marriage and relationship. Moses himself had chosen to marry a Midianite, and befriend also another woman of Cushite origin, a woman of colour. I can imagine Miriam as one who would have been terribly disturbed to see the fellow-women of other religious communities and cultural traditions bearing the brunt of violence because they were looked upon as source of evil and source of temptation for a normal Israel male Jew.

I cannot ignore the incident narrated in Num 25 when I read the story of a 'jealous' Miriam in Numbers chapter 12! Num 12 has such an abrupt beginning, citing Miriam and Aaron who were upset with Moses about the Cushite woman whom he had married. It shows *Miriam and Aaron* in a poor light as xenophobic individuals! It also offers a traditional patriarchal explanation of 'a woman against another woman' to legitimise the violence against women that occurs within a patriarchal society. I admire Miriam for the supposedly audacious question that she and Aaron put to Moses, namely, 'Has the Lord spoken only through you, Moses?' (Num 12:2) I consider this as a perfectly normal and necessary question to be raised within a democratic system. Then why was Moses upset? Why was it interpreted as Miriam kindling God's wrath and God's intervention being necessary to support Moses and punish only Miriam with leprosy? What is the implication of this message for women, especially for those in leadership? While it was all right for Moses to exercise his own choice to marry a Midianite and a Cushite (both foreign wives), why and how can he suddenly become so closed-minded and xenophobic when it comes to understanding other people's life, sex and sexuality?

## 4.  Five Markers of Responsible Leadership

Even though Aaron and Moses reportedly plead with God to be merciful and patient with Miriam, it seems that her irreversible punishment has to be borne in silence. She is shut out of the community for a week because of her leprosy, a social disease just as much as a physical disease. What fascinates me is the fact that the people of Israel refuse to move on in their journey without their leader Miriam. This is an affirmative action on the part of the people to acknowledge Miriam as truly *their* leader. I would like to list below, what I find as fundamental markers of responsible leadership:

1. Responsible leadership should always be rooted in justice: A good leader is one who is bold and courageous to raise his/her voice in the face of injustice done to a fellow-human in community. A good leader is empathetic in approach and feels the pain experienced by others as one's own. This sensitivity to experience the pain and

failures of others as one's own, is a rich gift from God. This response-ability is congruous with responsibility.

2. A responsible leader does not seek glory for oneself in the process of struggling with people for justice. Leadership is not a moment of exercising power over another. Neither is it an opportunity to prove one's selfrighteousness at the cost of the institution or of a community to which one belongs. A responsible leader does not seek one's own glory at the cost of a community. Rather s/he regards leadership as a God-given responsibility to enable every one in the community to mutually influence another to experience the richness of love and fellowship in community.

3. A responsible leader cannot be defined in terms of one's talents alone. Responsible leadership does not lie in the individual capability of a person to carry out tasks. It depends on the support and co-operation of people in the community. 'A Responsible Leader' is a *certificate* that *people* ought to give to a leader, based on the way they experience his/her leadership.

4. Responsible leadership means readiness to suffer ridicule, rejection or punishment for the sake of justice. At times, criticism and rejection may come from unexpected quarters. Rather than withdrawing from the scene of chaos and difficulties, a responsible leader is expected to bounce back with enthusiasm to sustain the spirit and resistance of the people.

5. A responsible leader does not hesitate to be open to criticism. Good leadership does not mean that there will be no opposition. A test of leadership means including the space for another to critique the leader as well as the structure and system. It is not easy for a leader to find the needed energy to be constantly open for criticism, while at the same time strive for newness and new vision.

Gleaning through the material in hand of the portrait of Miriam from the Hebrew Scriptures, we can identify the above characters and qualities that Miriam showed in her life as a leader and a prophet among the people of Israel. If the story of Miriam being punished with leprosy was used to condemn Miriam and shun her into oblivion, I see in this very story of punishment of Miriam, a bold Miriam, who did not hesitate to voice her question, plain and straight, to Moses, a fellow leader and a younger brother! The punishment she received from 'God', I see as a 'punishment designed by a patriarchal male' to caution any woman, every woman, about questioning a male about his status before God. I see in the punishment of Miriam a threat to all women, to abide by the limitations prescribed by the patriarchal society or be ready to face any punitive action.

That which makes me identify in Miriam a popular leader, is the act of the people following her experience of being alienated from them. The common people for generations together did not allow this incident of 'punishment with leprosy' to eclipse the service and leadership of Miriam which they had experienced. This long remembered tradition by the people is what Micah picks up and does not cut out her name as one of those God sent to liberate the people of Israel from bondage. Miriam thus stands tall as a responsible leader in her community and as an example for us who search for non-hierarchical patterns of leadership.

## 5.  Women in Panchayati Raj: Local Governance

The second story that I have to share is from my socio-political-cultural-religious-economic context of India. It is about common women who experienced a dramatic change in their life, when they were elected to become members and leaders in village governing councils or the *gram panchayats*. I am referring to the *Panchayati Raj* system that was introduced in India as an initiative to reserve at least 33 % of seats for women to participate in the local governance in villages. After experimenting on the process of getting 33 % of women into leadership and decision-making levels in southern state of Karnataka (1987-1992), the historic 73rd amendment to the Constitution of India was made on April 24, 1993 to initiate the same in every state in India. *Panchayat* means village and *Raj* means rule. Of the 14,000 women who were elected as members and leaders on the village councils, at least 80 % were new comers into politics. By 1994, the total number of women elected rose to 330,000! Truly a revolution was underway.

Following the election, the elected women were willing to be trained in leadership, in gender awareness, in learning to reconstruct their selves as women who had a task, a responsibility and a calling. They had to put up with nasty and snide remarks from women and men about their newfound identity. Deviramma, a 50 year-old woman from the 'Golla', or cowherd community, who kept cattle and sold curd for livelihood became a member of village council and subsequently, the president of her village council in December 1993. She narrates her experience thus:

> If we are outspoken, they – the men – call us brazen and dub us shameless. But now we don't care because we know we have access to people who will have to hear us. The day we have our *Gram Panchayat* meeting, the men and the people at home mock us – that's when we bring out books and show them what we know...[1]

Another woman named Sibamma, a Dalit woman who became an articulate leader in a village council, narrates her experience thus:

> The men have always ridiculed us, and perceived us as incapable of the management of public affairs. We now make up one third of the councils. This adds to our sense of strength. We must be 50 percent or more. We must overpower them with our numbers.[2]

Women have thus changed the political process. They have also reformulated the priorities of governance based on the needs of the community. It has converted grass-root leadership to state level leadership. At least 75 % of the elected women were below 45 years of age. Most of the women elected were illiterate and had no prior political experience. In some cases, these women defeated renowned, experienced politicians and one of them was even beaten up because it was too much of a humiliation for the party workers of the male politician. Ratnaprabha who was one of those beaten up for the 'crime' of outwitting a male politician says thus:

> Whenever there is any tension in the villages, they come to me and I have learnt how to sort out the problem. Many people have realised that it is indeed a waste of time to make a complaint to the police station…[3]

Ratnaprabha had studied only up to 7th grade in school. As an elected *panchayat* leader, she launched programmes for adult education, dug wells for drinking water and focused on repairing school buildings.

Thus the elected women joined together and worked as a team, across party lines. They changed the nature of local village governance and thus carried the spirit into the state governance. *Panchayati Raj* was a success story of grass-root women in Indian context. They gave priority to everyday issues of life, like access to clean drinking water, putting an end to the alcohol menace and liquor consumption of their husbands who did not bring their salaries home. The women together decided to close the door on every drunken husband! Women also realised that their health was also an important aspect. Such a linking between women's health, development, survival issues, addressing violence against women brought about a new perspective to life, to governance and the emergence of new self of a woman.

## 6. Engendering Leadership as a Faith Mandate

The two stories that I have shared above are powerful stories of life. If one feels threatened by the power of redefining leadership in these two stories, there is a possibility of the following accusations and responses: a) Scepticism; b) Making too much of too little; c) Romanticising of women's leadership; d) Faithful to the verbal inspiration of the Bible and hence no space for life-affirming interpretations. I can imagine a positive response, too from sections of a community who would be energised to hear these positive stories of women and their experiences in leadership, and would acknowledge the success story of women in grass roots as women who have a lot to contribute to this world. The experience of women elected to become important members and leaders of the *Panchayati Raj* may be identified as phenomenal and transformative followed by an affirmation that these women could be the agents of change who could offer us alternatives for a better and a new world.

Engendering leadership is not an option. It needs to be affirmed as a faith mandate. If only this could be applied to the situation of women in the Church, then women and men should first of all be given equal power and responsibility beginning at the grass local church level.

Engendering leadership means a fundamental affirmation in the equality of women and men as those created in the image of God, regardless. It is that critical faith response to put into practice the meaning of this core, non-negotiable principle that we, as women and men, are equal before God, and are called to various forms of ministry, irrespective of our gender, sex and sexuality. There should be no power on earth, or barrier, structure, individual or ideology to take away this basic gift of God to the whole humanity.

Engendering leadership is an opportunity to be a step closer to the heart of God who has created this world out of love. To recognise the image of God in the other, and respect the other to be truly equal is to live out the value in the reign of God. Someone once said, leadership is a verb. I do believe that leadership can only be a lived out experience. It is not a quality that one possesses. It is a gift from God that we can cherish, a gift that can be nourished and nurtured through relationships in community. Such a leadership can be best compared with the image of the body that St. Paul addresses in I Corinthians 12 where there is absolute equality of every single part of the body. An affirmation of the Body stands at the root of our struggles for justice and liberation. Exercising responsible leadership is yet another opportunity and an invitation that God extends to every member of humanity to mutually love and affirm one another.

NOTES

[1]   Rai, Sharita *et al.*, 'Grassroots women', in: *The Indian Express*, 5 March 1995.

[2]   *Ibidem.*

[3]   *Ibid.*

# PART I
# RESPONSIBLE FAMILY LEADERSHIP

# 3

# FAMILY LEADERSHIP SHIFT IN CHINA. PRELIMINARY PERSPECTIVES FOR A CONFUCIAN AND CHRISTIAN DIALOGUE

*Rachel Xiaohong Zhu, China*

## Introduction

This paper discusses the Chinese traditional family leadership and its transformation during the process of modernisation. Since Confucianism shaped and influenced Chinese society and cultural values, so main Confucian ideas on family leadership would be discussed in this first part. In particular, this part concentrates on the Confucian tradition on three relationships, i.e. the relationship between father and son, husband and wife, and younger and older brother.

Then, the second part will discuss the prodigious changes that have taken place in Chinese society in the last century, with an analysis of the three stages or elements which brought about these changes. In the third and fourth part of this paper, I discuss the main factors of the new family leadership and its main challenges in the face of Christian values.

## 1. Traditional Confucian Family Ethics

Family, the social structure based on wedlock and consanguinity, is the basic element of society. Confucian tradition always considered family as the core of social life. There is an old Chinese saying, which says that the family is the foundation of the state, and a state's harmony and prosperity depend on the stability of families. There are several historical reasons behind this tradition. Its founder, the great sage Confucius (551-479 BC), imitated the ancient tradition of the Zhou dynasty (1134-250 BC), which emphasised the importance of a virtuous rule through 'benevolence' *(Ren)* and a proper conduct according to the so called 'rites' *(Li)*. A patriarchal clan system and an echelon of aristocracy, on which the 'son heaven' is at the top and common people at the bottom, emerged during the Zhou dynasty. It also brought about the system of agnatic primogeniture, in which the succession goes from the first wife of the emperor to the eldest son (son of heaven, the royal and regional feudal authority).

In this system, the emperor was regarded as the father of the big family of the state, while feudatories as the parents of the smaller families of the counties. In this system, the government of the ruler is similar to the management of a family. It was believed that only when the family has been well managed, the state would be well governed. *Ren* represents mankind's cardinal virtue in the system of Confucian morality[1] for both the ruler and ordinary people. The essence of the virtue of *Ren* is for a person to love his/her parents, then extend the love to siblings, neighbours and then to everyone else. In other words, the love of parents is the beginning and premise of the loyalty to the ruler or emperor.

Family orientation is one of the main characters of Confucian ethics. Confucianism emphasises five cardinal relations, known as *Wu-Lun*, where power differences and responsibilities are prescribed: emperor and minister, father and son, husband and wife, elder and younger brother, and friend. From these five relationships, Dong Zhong-shu (179-104 BC) develops the formal Confucian teaching on the *three Gangs*,[2] namely, 'the emperor guides the minister, the father guides the son, the husband guides the wife'. It is obvious that these *Three Gangs* are hierarchical in nature, in each of them the first one holds pre-eminence over the latter. In a system based on the *Three Gangs* and *Five Changs*, family ethics and family leadership are the foundations of social ethics and leadership. Mencius said: 'Treat the aged in your family as they should be treated, and extend this treatment to the aged of other people's families. Treat the young in your family as they should be treated, and extend this treatment to the young of other people's families.'[3] The development of one's proper relationship with one's parents and the others around her/him is fundamental in life. Society is possible and stable when all the different relationships which imply different norms of interaction are appropriately maintained.

From a Confucian's perspective, a Chinese family should possess those three basic relationships of father and son, husband and wife, elder and younger brothers, as mentioned above. These three relationships are the origin of the generations and the nations. Now, let us discuss the traditional family leadership according to these three relationships.

### a)  *The Relationship Between Father and Son*[4]

The family instruction on domestic discipline existed for a long time in China. It stresses that every family should have a clear sovereignty, namely, parenthood. Compared with the other two relationships in the family, the relationship 'parents-offspring' is the most important one in the Confucian teaching. It is so fundamental that it becomes the model of all other relationships, such as that between emperor and minister. Parents carry the responsibility of cultivating their children, not only by raising them well and finding them good partners to marry, but also by teaching them to know *Ren* and *Yi*. According to *The Family Instructions of Master Yan*, the famous book by the Confucian scholar Yan Zhitui (born 531 AD), in order to be both strict and kind to their children, parents must behave very well and should not show their affections and sternness in an improper way. On one hand, parents should not be on too intimate terms with their kids, otherwise the children could be encouraged to neglect their parents; on the other hand, parent should take the needs of their children seriously and not treat them carelessly, otherwise the children will not know the filial piety and inherit their parents' benevolence. The parents' sternness will make the child more reverent and filial. Correspondingly, in terms of the development of the character of the human being, the most fundamental practice is that of filial piety *(Xiao)*.

Confucius believed that if people cultivated this innate tendency well, all other natural forms of human goodness would be positively affected. The children should show their filial piety, treat their parents with reverence, obedience and care, and not diverge from their teachings. 'When parents are alive, serve them with propriety; when they die, bury them with propriety, and then worship them with propriety.'[5]

Parents have absolute leadership over children. Confucius said: 'When your father is alive, observe his will. When your father is dead observe his former actions. If, for three years you do not change from the ways of your father, you can be called a "real son".'[6] In other words, children should not have any independent actions under parents supervision, so that a bystander can judge them from the observation of their will; moreover, when parents pass away, neither the way in which their parents lived nor the people whom their parents appointed could be replaced by children.

*b) The Relationship Between Wife and Husband*

There are a lot of muchtold tales of harmonious couples in ancient China, for instance, the *Book of Odes (Shijing)* portrays a couple's mutual respect, so that they live their life together as beautifully as the instruments play on a common chord. *The Family Instructions of Master Yan* also confirm that the wife should not only submit to her husband, but also the husband must respect his wife and treat her righteously *(Yi)*. However, generally speaking, most of the marriages in ancient times were only approved and arranged by the couple's parents, so there are few couples who have true love for each other as starting point. Especially after the Song Dynasty, since the Neo-Confucian master Chenghao (1032-1085) proposed that for a widow starving to death is the smallest issue, while losing the chastity is the biggest issue, the concept of maidenly chastity and chaste widowhood had played a central part in the life of Chinese women, but friendship between couples has hardly been guaranteed.

In the traditional Confucian culture, the husband is dominating, and the wife is submissive. Dong Zhongshu is the first Confucian thinker who justifies this relationship in this way: 'In all things there must be correlates... Here is nothing that does not have a correlate, and in each correlation there is the *Yin* and *Yang*. Thus the relationship between sovereign and subject, father and son, and husband and wife, are all derived from the principles of the *Yin* and *Yang*.'[7] The husband's dominant position and wife's compliant status are justified according to the natural order. This tradition not only advocates that 'the male is venerable and the female debased' *(Nan zhun nv bei)*, but also encourages women to become 'worthy wives and good mothers' *(Xian qi liang mu)* with many admonitions and instructions.

Besides the five constant virtues, the woman as a wife, in a family, has to follow the threefold obedience and the four virtues *(San Cong Si De)*, as her primary principles to protect the family honour. The four virtues refer to female virtue, female speech, female appearance and female accomplishment, which demand from the woman fidelity, propriety in speech, physical charm and proficiency with the needle and cooking. The threefold obedience refers to obedience to her father before marriage, her husband during marriage and her son during widowhood.[8]

## c) *Relationship Between Elder and Younger Brothers*

The third important element of family leadership exists in the relationship between elder and younger brothers. The principle of 'the elder brother must be friendly and the younger must be compliant' has a long history. It is the duty of the younger brother to show his respect and submission to the elder brother, the elder showing his friendship to the younger. It applies also to all the relationships between younger-elder siblings, although the male siblings would have the higher status than his sisters, no matter whether they are older or younger. Hierarchy also exists between elder and younger sisters.

The eldest son in a family inherits not only most of the estate of the parents, but also the patriarchal power, when the father resigns from the position of patriarch. According to the principle of priority, the elder brother must assume responsibility for raising the younger siblings, even when the mother lives. It is necessary to point out that the father-son relationship is the most fundamental dimension in the traditional family. The Chinese have been deeply influenced by the feudal ideology, based on sayings such as 'there are three ways not to be filial, and the greatest is having no descendents'.[9] In addition, Confucian teaching included: 'The more descendents, the more blessings'. The father-son dimension is superior, while the relationship husband-wife is subordinate. The result is that most couples work hard all their lives for their descendents, but fail to appease each other. However, the Confucian teaching on family leadership has been, in practice, modified during the process of modernisation.

## 2. Transformation and Modernisation in Family Leadership

In the ancient geoponic society, the society hardly changed, and so the family structure. However, rapid transformations took place in the past century. The three great historical events in China – the New Culture Movement (from 1915, climax with the May 4th movement in 1919), the establishment of the new system of socialism in 1949 and the commencement of the Reformation and Open Door Policy in 1979 – almost destroyed the traditional Confucian family leadership and family pattern. The lower status of the female partner and the patriarchal style were gradually abandoned as women were encouraged to demand equality. The 'clan-families' gradually disappeared and the nuclear family became the most popular pattern.

The new Culture Movement, which created the paradigm of anti-traditionalism and slogans such as 'down with Confucianism' changed very profoundly the concept of family. This movement introduced new ideas of science and democracy from the West and strongly criticised the Confucian ethical code, including the *Three Gangs, Five Constant Virtues* and family ethics. During the Movement, the Confucian 'rites' and teaching were dismissed as the tool for the rulers and patriarchs to oppress the inferiors. In the first issue of the leading periodical *New Youth*, the leader of this movement, Chen Duxiu, stated that Confucian ethics is only a way to enslave people and deprive them of their personalities. 'The reason why we can see no one of unattached individuals, but the minister, son and wife, is the *Three Gangs*'.[10] The famous writer Lu Xun generalised the conclusion that feudal Confucian ethics is 'a cannibal' *(Chi Ren)*.

This movement enlightened the common people to reflect intellectually on the Chinese family leadership and ethics, and indirectly influenced their family life. Fifty years later, with the 'Destroy Four Olds' (old ideas, old culture, old customs and old habits) program of the Cultural Revolution – which started in 1966 – and the Anti-Lin Piao Campaign (a competing political figure) and Anti-Confucius

Campaign (Pi Lin Pi Kong) in 1971, the Confucian familial ethics was intellectually and officially discarded.

Collectivism overthrew the foundations of the patriarchal system and cultivated equality between family members. The legal system regulated the family, as the constitution of the socialist system directly impacted the Chinese traditional family in many ways, for example in the case of parents-children relationship. In the old fashion, parents arranged their children's marriage and government seldom intervened in this family activity. In the new system, the government for bids arranged marriages and any other actions which interfere with the autonomy of matrimony. [11] The same China Marriage Law regulates the minimum age for the young people to be married, for instance, Article 6 provide that only men over 22 and women over 20 years have the right to marry, which guarantees the young people's capacity of autonomy of choice for their marriage partner. Parents were deprived of the power to arrange their children's marriage. The new system also remodels the family type and size. As the private ownership was gone with the old society, parents as patriarchs lost their economic power as a tool to command their children, most of the children would leave their parents and live separately when they got married and were, able to have their own house, although the government did not directly regulate how to dispose family property and live apart. Most Chinese clan-families disintegrated into nuclear families already with the small societies by the end of the 1960s, and the nuclear families increased, while the family size decreased very swiftly in both urban and rural areas. [12] The average urban family is today 3.1 persons and rural family 3.6 persons according to the 5th census of 2000, which is much lower than the 3.96 persons of the 4th census in 1990.

The beginning of the Reformation and Open Door Policy, by the end of the 1970s, ended the old ideology focused on class struggle and political movement which neglected the individual needs and personality. With the wider opening and the influence of Western values, the Chinese have now higher expectations on affection or sentiment in marriage and family. Moreover, the rapid developing productivity after the Reformation altered also the functions of the Chinese family. There was no essential improvement for the agricultural productivity from 1940 to 1970. [13] Owing to the low economic situation of the old days, the family first of all acted as a unit of production or economic complex, where the greater labour force would increase the income of the family. However, those functions of reproduction and procreation, which were considered to be very demanding, have been weakened after the Reformation, while the demands for care, affection and companionship became more demanding. At the same time, the centrifugal forces of economic, institutional and ideological changes, which tend to weaken emotional ties among family members, are often more powerful than the centripetal psychological forces which establish emotional bonds among family members. Hence an increasing divorce rate and affairs outside marriage challenge today's traditional familial relationships.

## 3. The New Familial Leadership

What are the consequences of modernisation and globalisation on family leadership? And how do these traditional cultural features shape this change? On the one hand, the nuclear family, which consists of two generations (wife/mother, husband/father and their child), became primarily a unit of residence and consumption. On the other hand, the different nuclear families in the same lineal relationships are still very close to each other and often live in the same district. Let us now select three profiles of the main relationships in the nuclear family: the couple to their child, the couple to their parents and the relation between husband and wife. We want to analyse how the family leadership in the loose extended family is organised and to see the vestiges of the Confucian mentality.

### a) Young Couples and Their Child

Since many changes have been taking place in the Chinese society, the nuclear family, divorced family, one-parent family and even dink family are much more accepted these days. However, most Chinese families are still under great pressure of procreation and cultivation of children, and they take seriously the Confucian code of 'giving birth but not to instruct is the parent's fault'. Since the one-child policy was implemented, from the end of the 1970s to the year 2000, over 55,780,000 families have had one single child, who is described as a 'little emperor'. It might not be exaggerated to say that the so-called 'little emperor' is today the main factor to influence a family in making decisions, and it is the focus of six adults' lives (four grandparents and two parents). It is said that the primary reason of conflict between a young couple is how to raise the kid. [14]

### b) More Equal Interdependent Eldership

Traditional Confucianism required that when the parents are alive, children should not travel far away, and when parents die, children should remain in mourning for three years. Now, in China, in rural areas, the rate of aged people is 7,35 % and 6,30 % in urban areas, according to the 5th census in 2000. More and more elder people choose to spend the last part of their life in a nursing home, something that was impossible before. On the one hand, due to the reform of the system of the registered permanent residence and to the phenomenon of urbanisation, many people leave their old parents and go to work elsewhere; they marry and settle down in big cities, so that these two generations become much more independent. On the other hand, filial piety is so rooted in many Chinese people that young couples are supposed to support both husband and wife's parents financially if the parents do not have a pension, while the grandparents would help to look after their grandchild. This interdependent relationship makes these two generations more equal than before.

### c) The Choice of the Spouse and Marriage

Nowadays young people are exposed to all kind of mass media and international social exchanges and have more channels and chances to meet partners than the old generations had, so the young people are increasingly choosing their spouses rather than submitting to arranged marriages. Most of the young people follow the principle of 'making decisions on his/her own and getting consent from parents' to choose their spouses. During the 1950s to 1970s, the best candidate for the spouse would be a member of the communist party or a military, a cadre or a model worker from a good family by political standards. Now, since the younger generation cares much more about the economic and educational background of the partner, the standard for the choice of the candidate is much more varied. On the other hand, a self-determined marriage seems easier to be dissolved, and the divorce rate in 2003 was 0,21 %, which was much higher than the 0,07 % in 1980.

The traditional teaching on the threefold obedience and the four virtues, as the submission to one's husband for the entire life, has been challenged by the increase of educated and working mothers in China. The last generation of Chinese urban women illiteracy rate was 55,3 %, now it is only 2,1 % ; the rural women illiteracy rate was 88,6 %, now it is 36,6 %. Nowadays, urban female employees are 38 % of the total, and rural female employees are over 47 % of the total employees. Compared to the traditional marriage lifestyle, the wife/mother figure has gained economic power, while the father has been losing his absolute control of the family. In the process of modernisation and globalisation, acculturation and enculturation have also affected the younger generation's marriage. A lot of young couples accept the western idea of marital agreement, premarital property notarisation, separate postnuptial financing, in order to keep equality and freedom even within the marriage. The establishment and development of the pension system generally lessen the economic dependence on their child, while the progress of high-tech alleviates the housework in a family, and the political and legal system confirms the equal status of women and men both in the family and the society. This is a novelty: the sexual equality, mutual respect and mutual assistance between husband and wife have never been deeply embodied in a society which was mainly predominantly Confucian.

## Conclusion: an Approach to the Perspectives of Christian Family Ethics

As discussed above, after the political, cultural and economic revolution and transformation of the 20th century, the features of the Chinese family have been totally different from those of the past. The traditional teachings of the Confucian ethics on family leadership are weakened or were even institutionally destroyed, opening a way to the present day moral vacuum. How to revive and to reform the traditional family ethics while reflecting on the prevailing contemporary phenomena has become a very important subject for many Chinese. Finding harmony without becoming uniform is the principle for the Chinese to approach different cultures. In a globalised world, where running a family is still a great responsibility, the dialogue between Confucian and Christian thought might contribute a lot for the reflection on family ethics.

According to Chinese official statistics, the Christian Protestants are today over 16,000,000 and the Christian Catholics are about 6-8,000,000. This is less than 1,5 % of the total population, but however, the population of the Christian Protestants increases about 500,000 annually. Since Christianity had been introduced in China, more than 1300 years ago and in five different periods, the dialogue between Christian teaching and traditional non-Christian Chinese culture is a challengeable topic also for the Chinese intellectual circle. It has been said that the feeling of finiteness is the same for the individual in both Chinese and Western society. One obvious difference in the origin of this feeling is that Chinese finiteness derives from the hierarchy, while in the Christian society it comes from God.[15] The way of Confucian salvation consists in an indwelling of the moral teaching in the individual and in his moral practice within society, the Five Constant Virtues being the aim of the behaviour of the individual. On the other hand, the salvation that comes from Jesus Christ is transcendent. It is a way through Faith. This makes the love of Christ and the love *(Ren)* in the Confucian sense quite different. Although both Christianity and Confucianism consider 'love' as the core of their teaching, love in the Confucian tradition *(Ren)* is still graded or strict hierarchal, while the love preached, lived and communicated by Christ is unconditional. In the Confucian way, *Ren* is to love people, and the strongest love is the love between father and son, then husband and wife and then to the others of the Five Relationships. Love is limited and should be regulated by the rite or rituals and by the wisdom which must be cultivated by the master or patriarch. For Christian Faith, we cannot love until grace comes into us. God's grace transforms family life and leads to new patterns of love including mercy and self-sacrifice. This is a wide and challenging topic, which would make this paper too long. It is enough to say, as a conclusion, that after all the changes and transformations undergone by the Chinese family, the meeting with the grace of Christ can open a new chapter, to be written not so much on paper but on the real life of the Chinese people.

REFERENCES FOR FURTHER READING

Fung Yu-lan, A., *Short History of Chinese Philosophy*, Taiwan: Derk Bodde, 1979.

Mencius, A., Translation in progress by Dan Robins:
http://www.hku.hk/philodep/courses/dr/mencius/mencius/mencius-06.html.

Confucius, *The Analects of Confucius* (I-III):
http://www.misericordia.edu/users/ DAVIES/RELIGION/conprint.htm

*The Four Books for Women: Ancient Chinese Texts for the Education of Women*:
http://nacrp.cic.sfu.ca/nacrp/articles/fourbookwoman.html

*On the Chinese Birth Control Policy*, by State Department News Release Office:
http://www.cpirc.org.cn/yjwx/yjwx_detail.asp?id = 2175

Shao Xiazhen, 'The Varieties in the Marriage of Chinese Agricultural Women During the Social Transformation': http://www.cass.net.cn/webnew/show_news.asp?id = 5778

NOTES

[1]  Later Mencius (371-289) proposes the four constant virtues, namely, *Ren* (humanheartedness, humanness or benevolence), *Yi* (righteousness), *Li* (propriety, rituals or rites), *Zhi* (wisdom). Dong Zhong-shu adds *Xin* (Good faith, fidelity) as the fifth *Chang* (five constant virtues).

[2]  The literal meaning of *Gang* is: a major cord in a net, to which all the other strings are attached. *Three Gang* means three guides (Fung:197).

[3]  Mencius, Ia,7, quoted from Fung:72.

[4]  To use solely the expression 'father-son' sounds limiting, since I believe that it would also apply to the female family members. It should be mother/father and daughter/son (or parentoff-spring). Although the mother would have a lower status than the father, there is still a hierarchy between mother and daughter, mother and underage son.

[5]  Analects, 2:5.

[6]  Analects, 1:11.

[7]  Quoted from Fung: 196-197.

[8]  Zhang Mingqi, *The Four Books for Women. Ancient Chinese texts for the education of women* on http://nacrp.cic.sfu.ca/nacrp/articles/fourbookwoman.html

[9]  Mencius: 4A/26.

[10]  *The Duxiu' s Reader*, Hefei People Press, 1987, p. 34.

[11]  Article 3 in the Chinese Marriage Law.

[12]  Even though the numbers of nuclear families are increasing, they still live very close with their kin, psychologically and geographically.

13 Cf. the research by Wang Yuesheng, *Social transformation and family shift: based on a study of Southern Hebei Area during 1930-1990*, http://www.npopsscn.gov.cn/cgxjwzh/sh/rkw1.htm.

14 Housework and economic problems are the second and third causes of conflicts between couples. Cf. Shao Xiazhen, *The varieties in the marriage of Chinese agricultural women during the social transformation*, in http://www.cass.net.cn/ webnew/show_news.asp?id = 5778.

15 Qian Mansu, *Emerson and China*, Beijing: Sanlian Press, 1996, p. 212.

# 4

# RESPONSIBLE FAMILY LEADERSHIP. TRADITIONAL AND CHRISTIAN APPROACHES IN CAMEROON

*Richard Ondji'i Toung, Cameroon*

## Introduction

This paper will examine family leadership in our cultural setting, identifying its limitations and offering solutions in the light of Christian ethics. Why reflect on the subject of responsible leadership in families today? It is clear that we are experiencing a kind of social crisis, a crisis that has affected the family and resulted in the dislocation of the family unit in our villages and in our cities. For us, this raises the question of who exactly carries responsibility in the sociopolitical units which these families represent. Specifically, to use our own language, we want to know what it means to be the *Nya mbôrô* in our families and in our villages today, and who fulfils that role. Taking Southern Cameroon as the cultural context for our study, and bearing in mind the task assigned to us as part of the Globethics.net study programme, the question is: 'What is the family leader responsible for, and what is he not responsible for, in the traditions of Southern Cameroon, and from the perspective of Christian ethics?' This is the question that makes this study relevant and of interest. Our intention is to contribute to resolving and healing the crisis mentioned above.

## 1. Definitions

First I would like to give a working definition of the content of what seem to me to be essential concepts: family; clan; tribe; Cameroonian tradition; leader and leadership; responsibility; responsible leadership; Christian ethics.

*Family*: in a broad sense, the family may be considered as a group of people linked together by marriage and filiation, or, exceptionally, by adoption. It can therefore be understood as a succession of individuals descended from one another, from one generation to the next.

In the Fang setting, the family is described by the term *Nda bôt*, which literally translated means: the 'men's house'. This definition points to two things: first, the people dwell in a place, the house, which refers to a geographical and cultural criterion; second, it emphasises the dynamic nature of family through the people that comprise it and who represent life. So, there can be no family without a house, that is, a place to live and hence a cultural context, just as there can be no family without human life. This makes the family a social institution in constant evolution.[1]

*Clan and tribe:* for the purposes of this study the clan may be understood as a group of families with a common ancestor. The tribe is defined as a social and political group based on real or supposed ethnic kinship among peoples with a primitive organisation. The notion of kinship is central to the three concepts defined above and forms their common denominator. In this study the family will be raised to the status of clan, for two reasons. First, in theoretical and practical terms it is a social and political unit, and second, the tribes in Southern Cameroon do in fact live and conceive of themselves as families. The *Esakoran*, for instance, can be spoken of as a tribe and as a family because marriages are prohibited within them and their members are known by the same name.

*Cameroonian tradition:* is there such a thing as a Cameroonian tradition? Given the many ethnic groups that make up our country, one would have to say that there are numerous Cameroonian *traditions*. However, these micro-traditions are moving towards one macro-tradition for Cameroon, even though there is still a long way to go. For the purposes of this study we shall draw on traditional elements in the south of Cameroon. Southern Cameroon belongs to the large Fang group, of which the Ntumu are a sub-group, to which I belong. Tradition will be used in its meaning as a way of thinking, acting or behaving which is inherited from the past of a particular human group.

*Leader and leadership:* by leader is meant the head, the spokesperson of a political movement, the person who takes the lead in a movement or a group, and to whom others refer. Leadership therefore refers to the function and position of leader, taking command and setting direction, the ability to direct.

*Responsibility and the person responsible:* responsibility here is understood as an intellectual obligation or moral necessity to make good an error, fulfil a duty, meet a commitment and bear the strain. The person responsible is then the one who is charged with leading and taking the decisions in any human group. Responsible as an adjective indicates someone who is accountable for his/her actions, someone who is thoughtful, reasonable and serious and who considers the consequences of his actions. Responsible leadership then means fulfilling the function of leadership in a considered, reasonable, accountable way. It is the capacity to lead a human group, taking into account individual and collective worries, and with a concern for humanity, organisation, equity and discipline.

*Christianity and Christian ethics:* generally speaking, Christianity is considered as the religion that is founded on the teaching, person and life of Jesus Christ. The ethic deriving from it is to be found in the moral teaching of the Old and New Testaments. It is a morality which sees itself as a faithful response to God's summons, in terms of human behaviour. The norms and rules of behaviour here have their basis and legitimation in the holiness, will, love and omnipotence of God. The ultimate purpose of life is the blessed participation of human beings in the salvation which is God himself and which God alone can effect. Consequently, the Christian ethic is an ethic of responsibility, because human beings must account for themselves before God who summons them, and before the community into which they are sent. This central value of responsibility is accompanied by others such as love of God and of our neighbour, justice, freedom, solidarity, to name only those.

*Theoretical ethical interest:* confrontation or encounter between two cultures in relation to the concept of responsible leadership: debate, exchange of ideas, enrichment, production, broadening or development of concepts and methodologies (ways of becoming, being and experiencing a responsible leader).

*Practical interest:* provide the public with a tool to help them understand intercultural relations (tradition and Christianity, Africanity and westernity…) on the basis of universal values. Contribute to building a universal culture.

## 2. Leadership Among the Fang of Cameroon

### a) In the Family

The *Mmé nda* (the owner of the house) is the head of the family (family = *Nda bôt*), the father of the family whose duty is to protect his wife and children and watch over what becomes of them. The latter in turn recognise his rights, which include the right to give a name to every new-born child in order to preserve the memory of an ancestor or some other living member of the paternal or maternal clan, and the right to educate, judge, congratulate or censure his people. For Mbala Owono, the head of the family 'is conscious of his vocation to ensure that the members of his family live in respect for customs and habits, for their best possible future. In other words, the authority of the head of the family coexists with the full participation of all the members of the family. This is how power is structured.'[2]

At this level, the author tells us, there are three conditions for exercising power. The person must:

– be male (principle)

- be a legitimate son born of a proper marriage. Illegitimate sons and the children of slaves are thus excluded.
- be able to marry (have at least one wife) and to procreate. This is essential.

One might say that here leadership is expressed in terms of biology, matrimonial status and property.

*b) In the Village Community*

The organisation of the village community corresponds to that of the *Nda bôt*, so that the family and the villages have the same ethical and, above all, political concerns.

For the *Nya mbôrô* (true man) both biological and ethical considerations count: a man is a *Nya mbôrô* according to age, the *Nya mbôrô* being the oldest of the group *(Nto mbôt, Mvéngômô)*. From the ethical point of view, a man is a *Nya mbôrô* if he is wise, mature, upright and responsible. This ethical criterion is the most important because, in our society, younger men are sometimes classed among the *Be nya bôrô* while older people who are immature or irresponsible are placed among the *zeze bôt* (useless men).[3] It is this ethical consideration that concerns us here. By virtue of his wisdom, the *Nya mbôrô* is the judge, the mediator, the one who finds a solution to individual and collective problems. In this capacity he is called *Nyaamemviè*. Having moral authority, he may also assume the duties of village chief *(Mbi ntum, Evet)*, which are purely political, but alongside him there may also be a village chief who today is not chosen on account of his moral authority but because it is the will of the sub-prefect representing the modern political authorities, themselves a product of the colonial regime.[4]

The duty of the village head or *Ndzoé* (the verb *dzoé* means to order or command) is to direct, inform and mobilise the members of the village community for a specific purpose or goal, as decided by the village council, which is a deliberative gathering. In agreement with Mbala Owono, it should also be noted that the notion of giving orders strikes a false note in the ears of the Fang, who abhor subordination and any word that seems to refer to it. They prefer the art of persuasion and negotiation demonstrated by the *Nya mbôrô*, whom they recognise as having moral authority. This is why the political sector needs to use the ethical language if its authority is to become more familiar, more 'natural' and more acceptable. Our study will examine the ethical aspect of the traditional leader. On the traditional level, a man is a *Nya mbôrô* if he can meet the following criteria:

- moral integrity
- sense of responsibility

- credibility
- sensitivity towards his people and his country
- wisdom
- tolerance
- generosity
- strictness and concern for propriety
- justice
- humanity
- matrimonial status (married to at least one wife) and procreation
- competence
- balanced material situation
- mental maturity.

This list of criteria is not exhaustive; it is the outcome of our investigations through conversations and talks in churches, and among friends and families. Apart from the general considerations outlined above, the *Nya mbôrô* is to be found in certain specific fields. The *Nya mbôrô*, or true man, who is a reality in the community, can emerge or assert himself in different domains, such as:

- speaking
- knowledge *(Nnem)*
- practical achievements (his actions)
- war (when he is called *Asuzo'o*)
- games
- health *(Ngengan)*
- the arts
- religion *(Zingui)*
- the political/legal/social sphere *(Mbi ntum, Ntyik-Ntol)*

## 3. Responsibility of the Traditional Leader

In what concerns us here, the notion of the responsibility of the traditional leader refers on the one hand to the duties incumbent on him (this is the theoretical aspect, i.e. what the *Nya mbôrô* should do and what he should be) and, on the other hand, his capacity to assume those duties (the *Nya mbôrô*'s experience of life today). The latter may be rendered by the German word *Verantwortlichkeit*.

Generally speaking and according to Father Jean-Samuel Zoie Obianga the *Nya mbôrô* fulfils the role of 'repository and transmitter of a founding figure' (the original ancestor). 'He is the leader who activates the original forces, contributing to perpetuate certain values and enduring powers that guarantee the integrity of the ideal of the human being, humanity and society, of which the archetype is to be found at the time of the creation'.

Above all, the *Nya mbôrô* is the man who guarantees the equilibrium of the village and of the family. As the referee in differences among the members of the community, he personifies justice and impartiality. He is the one they can turn to for the right advice, a solution to their problems, peace of mind. Another distinguishing feature is his capacity to sacrifice his own interests to those of the group and to forego certain privileges on account of his reputation as a *Nya mbôrô*. He is surrounded by an element of mystery and it is all these things together that give him the status of patriarch.

In practice, experience with those who are called to be, or are considered as the *Be Nya bôrô* today has been mixed. Here and there we have noted some confusion in identifying who is a *Nya mbôrô*, as well as an inability on the part of the latter to assume their responsibilities, whether because of the material pressures around them, or delusions of grandeur or simply a misunderstanding of the times. So we have some *Nya bôrô* who are out of step with the times and who cannot understand and cope with their world today. Many of them complain of a lack of respect and understanding among the young, which gives rise to a generation conflict. Moreover, in the midst of rampant individualism, today's *Nya mbôrô* finds it difficult to fulfil his tasks in the community and, above all, in the family.

The answers to the question of who is a *Nya mbôrô* in our societies, in our villages and families today will be varied, contradictory, partial and biased. Some will say the *Nya bôrô* are the elite of the village or the family because they enjoy a degree of material prosperity that allows them to maintain a group of individuals in their pay or because they act like *griots* in maintaining a personality cult. Others will consider the oldest member of the family as the *Nya mbôrô*, even though he does not assume that role. Yet others will say it is the rich man of the village, or the village chief appointed by the sub-prefect, or the chairman of the local committee of the party in power. Some informed people will have the courage to say who are not *Nya mbôrô*, and be bold enough to say who, in the light of the traditional criteria listed above, can be considered as a *Nya mbôrô* according to that scale of values. In other words, the conceptual limitations to the notion of

*Nya mbôrô* can be seen as deriving from difficulties of definition, and the complexity and extreme rarity of the personality in question. This explains the empirical limitations.

Because such a personality is rare and because the definition of the *Nya mbôrô* is so broad and diverse, people will experience only certain aspects of the person and will therefore have a partial or distant view of him: experiences of this personality are often contradictory, depending on whether the contact is close to or from a distance. So it is difficult to find unanimity on the subject of the *Nya mbôrô*. However, when such a person does exist in a community, he dominates by his natural authority and his legitimacy is seldom called in question.

In the last analysis, the *Nya mbôrô* is a human being with all his capabilities and limitations. He is a rare species which has existed in the past and still does exist, for the history of our families and villages records a number of figures who have been outstanding in their time and place. In our reflection we have sought to theologise the concept, assuming that the *Nya mbôrô* is basically a product of God himself. His formation continues in the training school of the family, popular wisdom, educational institutions and religious confessions. But despite this basic hypothesis about the concept and the life of the *Nya mbôrô*, the latter remains a creature exposed to the fall and subject to failure: this is what makes him human. Some propositions of Christian ethics may help to overcome these human limitations of the *Nya mbôrô*.

## 4. Implications for Christian Ethics

### a)  *Leadership from a Christian Perspective*

The principle or criterion of responsibility may be understood in terms of Christian ethics as the duty of each individual to conduct his or her life in a way that takes into account the wellbeing and life possibilities of others. [5] The notion of responsibility here may be seen as summarising the reality of Christian ethics applied in the life of society. [6] Professor Christoph Stückelberger, a Swiss theologian and ethicist, links the concept of responsibility to that of power *(Macht – Verantwortung)* [7] showing the correlation between these two values. In his view, responsibility should correspond to the power an individual or an institution effectively has. Likewise, if a person or a group of people has responsibilities, then that person or group should also have the power necessary to assume the corresponding responsibilities. Here responsibility is expressed before God and before the community served by the individual (or the group), the people who are affected by the action in question. Thus, from the Christian point of view, we may say that the power/responsibility/service correlation describes the chain of human relations in society.

On closer analysis, this relation is set on three levels: the person responsible, the area of responsibility (individuals, duties, actions, attitudes, character) and the authority before which one is accountable (e.g. a tribunal, the people concerned by a decision, one's conscience, God). In short, responsibility will be understood here as the capacity to answer for and assume one's actions and their consequences vis-à-vis others and society, on the one hand, and this awareness of being at the service of others, the wider community and God, on the other. This is a requirement of community life which is part of the I-me, I-you, I-we, I-it relationship.[8] Consequently, the responsible person or the responsible leader from the Christian point of view, is the one who is concerned for the balance of the community. He is called to serve and to which he must answer, just as he is accountable before God, on whose will all his decisions and actions are based.

What is central for the responsible Christian leader (in theory) is the sense of service and of accountability to the community and to God. Such a leader is motivated by:

- fear of God

- God's will

- faith

- love

- solidarity

- service

- justice

- humility

For the Christian leader, the model is Jesus Christ crucified, obeying the will of his Father, the humble servant, sacrificed for the sake of humankind and for others. In some respects, the responsible leader from the Christian point of view, resembles the responsible traditional leader, theoretically at least, for both are meant to render service to society and, to do that, they have to abide by certain principles such as moral integrity, credibility, justice, solidarity.

The theoretical difference appears when it comes to the authorities to which each is accountable. While the conception of the traditional leader sees him as accountable only to society, when possible,[9] the conception of the Christian leader makes it clear that he must give account of himself both to God, to whom he is answerable as God's envoy, and to the society into which he is sent. At the purely conceptual level one might say that the difference is that, on the one hand, we have the leader as seen in sociological terms and on the other, the leader as seen in the christological approach applied to society, for which Christ is the model.

## b)  Christ as the Model of the Responsible Leader

Son of God, Lamb that takes away the sins of the world, Rabbi, Master, Messiah, Christ or Saviour, Son of Man – these basic names attributed to Jesus Christ personify the responsible leader according to the New Testament. And although other examples are quoted in the Old Testament, Jesus remains the paradigm of the responsible leader for the whole of the Bible. This can be understood with the help of the dogmatic principle of the trinity which sees Christ as the second person of the Triune God. He is the Father's equal, he is God, and so is responsible for creation.

From the historical and practical point of view, the life of Jesus as it is recounted in the Gospels, is a responsible life. He was there for his disciples and the crowds who flocked to meet him and follow him, and he was sensitive to the problems brought to him by others. We can list a number of attitudes, characteristics and behaviours that marked him out:

- he did nothing wrong

- obedient and humble unto death

- the servant of his disciples and the crowds

- love, loyalty courage

- tolerance, solidarity

- human and humane

- honest, sincere, just, truthful

- strict and with a strong sense of what is right

- open to criticism and discussion

Conceptually speaking, Jesus makes service the basis of responsible leadership. [10] Speaking of this, he says to his disciples, 'And whoever wishes to be first among you must be your slave; just as the Son of Man came not to be served but to serve, and to give his life as ransom for many' (Matt 20:27-28). This concept of responsible leadership is fundamental for Christian political ethics, because it places the emphasis on the leader's duty, humility (the slave of others), sense of sacrifice expressed in the idea of 'giving his life as ransom for many'. Here the leader is thus present for and attentive to those around him who are his main concern in all he does.

## Conclusion

Responsible family leadership between tradition and Christianity: there is a need for dialogue and complementarity, moving towards a culture of responsible leadership centred on Christ and rooted in positive and universal traditional values. In short, we would urge that we set about developing a practical concept of responsible family leadership of a general and integral type, i.e. a leadership model that incorporates both positive traditional values and Christian principles. A model of this type would enjoy a wide measure of legitimacy in different cultural settings because it would be the outcome of encounter, dialogue and complementarity among cultures. It would also be useful in our families today and could be used by them in their search for authority, reference points and a model to follow.

The approach based on inter cultural dialogue would form the basis of family political ethics worldwide and would thus contribute to the world ethic proposed by Hans Küng in his Projekt Weltethos. This is challenging from the practical point of view, but it is not impossible.

REFERENCES FOR FURTHER READING

FTPY, Eglise et éducation, Yaoundé: *Collection Semaine Interdisciplinaire*, 1987. *Handbuch der Christlichen Ethic*, Band 3: Wege Ethischer Praxis, Basel: Herder, 1982.

IPAM, *Histoire: le monde, des premiers hommes au 6 ème siècle après J. C.*, Tours: Mame, 1977.

Kesteloot, Lilyan, *Anthologie négro-africaine*, Verviers: Marabout université, 1976.

Matateyou, Emmanuel, *Les nouveaux défis de la littérature orale africaine*, Yaoundé: PUY, 1999.

Mbala Owono, Rigobert, *Education traditionnelle et développement endogène en Afrique Centrale*, Yaoundé: Ceper, 1990.

Mvé Bekale, Marc, *Piere Claver Zeng et l'art poétique fang: esquisse d'une herméneutique*, Paris: l'Harmattan, 2001.

Ondji'i Toung, Richard, Contribution de l'éthique économique à l'examen de l'endettement extérieur et de la pauvreté dans les pays de la C.E.M.A.C., thèse, Université de Bâle, 2003.

Quéré, France, *L'Ethique et la vie*, Paris: Odile Jacob, 1991.

Rich, Arthur, *Ethique économique*, Genève: Labor et Fides, 1994.

Stückelberger, Christoph, *Global Trade Ethics*, Geneva: WCC publications, 2002.

Tsira Ndong Ndoutoume, Le Mvett, *épopée fang*, Paris: Présence Africaine, 1983.

NOTES

[1]   On the family as an evolving social institution, cf. Rigobert Mbala Owono, *Éducation traditionnelle et développement endogène en Afrique Centrale*, Yaoundé: Ceper, 1990, p. 24.

[2]   For what follows, cf. *Ibidem*, p. 46

[3]   For further information on the 'Nya mbôrô', especially with regard to procreation, cf. Mbala Owono, *op. cit.*, p. 45, where having male children is a criterion in identifying the true man. We shall come back to this.

[4]   It is rare for the population's choice to take precedence over the will of the administrative authorities.

[5]   For more on the different areas in which responsibility is expressed, cf. Richard Ondji'i Toung, *Contribution de l'éthique économique à l'examen de l'endettement extérieur et de la pauvreté dans les pays de la C.E.M.A.C*, doctoral thesis, University of Basel, 2003, p. 277 ff.

[6]   cf. *Handbuch der Christlichen Ethik*, vol.3: Wege ethischer Praxis, Basel: Herder, 1982, p. 117 ff.

[7]   Stückelberger, Christoph, *Global Trade Ethics*, Geneva: WCC publications, 2002, pp. 66-67.

[8]   Rich, A., *Éthique économique*, Geneva: Labor et Fides, 1994, p. 61 ff.

[9]   Our limited knowledge of our tradition precludes us from saying categorically that account did not also have to be given to the relevant authority in the domain of the sacred, i.e. the universe of God or the gods.

[10]   As mentioned above, service was also a constitutive element in the traditional model of the responsible leader and so is the common denominator in the two approaches.

# 5

# WOMEN LEADERSHIP IN THE KOREAN SALIMIST[1] CONCEPT

*Un HeyKim, South Korea*

## Introduction

The topic of family has received much attention since the 1980s, both inside and outside the churches. Particularly, Korean churches in the 21st century have been perplexed by the phenomenon of a fast deconstruction of the traditional nuclear family and the emergence of various types of families. Most Korean Christians feel uneasy about the frequent breakdown of marriages, the seriously low birth rate, and the weakening of the conventional nuclear family. Therefore many Korean churches have been concerned about family issues and invested their energy in various family recovery programmes that focussed on the traditional family concept.

Recent discourses on the issue of family can be divided in two groups. Both agree that family forms are changing, but diagnose the cause and results of this phenomenon very differently. On one side are those who are concerned about widespread family disintegration caused by a rising divorce rate. On the other side are those who view newly pluralistic family forms as liberation from the patriarchal nuclear family. Diversity in families is a welcome change, and it should not be judged as socially and morally inferior.[2]

In the Korean society, a male dominant culture with patriarchal structures has been operating in many families where values of control and a powerful, dominant and authoritarian leadership can be observed. Hence families are contexts in which male violence against women and the abuse of children are still increasingly found. Families are criticised for having confined wives to the private domestic sphere where they are subservient to the needs and demands of husbands and children. Conservative Korean Christians are very concerned about the need to restore what they say is the biblical view of the family: a male-dominated nuclear family consisting of a working husband, a non-working wife who is a full-time mother, and several dependent children. From the conservative stance of a Korean church, therefore, the weakening of the leadership of the father in the family must be faced determinately.

However the hierarchical pattern of power in patriarchal structures fails to show God's grace and love to all members of the family.

It also fails to show the original Christian vision of radical equality in Christ. This pattern of leadership is paternalistic and authoritarian and thus not reciprocal. It is hardly to be transformed by family practice. The exhortation to the husband to love your wife as Christ loves the Church, is not paralleled by the exhortation to the wife to love her husband likewise, but rather by a command to submit to her husband as the Church submits to Christ. A similar pattern is suggested in the relationship of slaves to masters and subjects to the emperor.[3] The family is the basic unit of society and it is the place where people can learn and practice the primary skills and attitudes of leadership among the mother, the father and the siblings.

The notion of 'family' has become a moral and political symbol, it is ideologically charged. Theological reflection will need to begin with the experience of families and family members who are impoverished, marginalised, victimised or violated. Families can be life-enhancing or life-destroying, and the Church has colluded oppressively and uncritically with the family by endorsing versions of it which are patriarchal, sexist and marginalising. The family must be a place where God's grace is experienced and where people can find nurturing and healing, but in these times, the family has been a place where people have experienced the deepest wound and suffering, which is the most difficult for the victims of domestic violence. Whether families are channels of God's grace has a lot to do with the way in which power is exercised in the family group.

Therefore, life in abundance for all people and life as central affirmation of the Gospel of Jesus is impossible in today's world. The culture of death and violence has been developed in close relation with the patriarchal system and a Western civilisation focused on growing and competing values. The patriarchal culture and the corresponding structure deeply and systematically affect the constitution not only of beliefs and ideas but also of emotions, the subconscious and unconscious dimension of both men and women which allow to affirm male domination and women's oppression. It seems to me that we, Christians and theologians, have not sufficiently developed and honoured our understandings of a life witnessing Jesus' teachings in the challenges of our day.

This paper tries to examine how we create new family leadership models for a radical transformation of the hierarchical, authoritarian, violent and patriarchal values in Korean families and churches. How do we fulfil life in abundance through families as we resist the culture of violence and death in our daily life? How do we develop women leadership to create an alternative family leadership through the critique and the transformation of the current patriarchal domination? In order to develop women leadership, how do we have to change our way of thinking in concrete as much as we criticise the culture of violence and its cultural domination in the patriarchal system? These are the questions I want to deal with in this essay.

In Korean society and in the Korean Church, the issue of leadership and especially of women's leadership as an alternative has received much attention from the late 1990s to the present. In the various areas where the issues of leadership have been discussed – such as political leadership and business leadership – people seriously re-evaluate female characters and values in order to find alternative leadership patterns responding to the paradigm shift of the contemporary Korean society. Within the contemporary discourse on the family, it is a particular issue as to how to create a new model of Christian women's leadership: Korean Christian women need to change inherited patterns of family leadership which has been represented by the males only, such as the fathers, sons, and husbands.

To find a new model of family leadership, I explore the Korean concept of Salim and feminine values of Daoism.[4] Religious plurality necessarily plays a central role for Korean Christianity and many Korean feminist theologians are acutely aware that they are rooted in several religious identities such as Shamanism, Buddhism, Daoism and Confucianism. I think that Korean thought and Daoism can be the philosophical and cultural soil in which we should develop the new values and meanings of women's leadership as an alternative pattern of family leadership.

## 1.  The Cosmic Salim Model of Leadership as a Model of Family Leadership

One of the significant problems of family leadership is, for East Asian women, the strong division between the private and the public spheres as well as the male domination in the relationships between husbands and wives or sisters and brothers. This patriarchal hierarchy has produced values of power and competition, rather than caring, sharing, serving and emptying. Those values produced by the hierarchical patriarchy closely related to distortion of spirituality have easily controlled people's lives, thoughts, minds, and spirits. We must concretise all the ideas and concepts for new models of family leadership in response to how to live and practice with faith in God. We must create a new way of life that enables all members of the family to be blessed by God.

In the traditional Korean way of life, people believe that a human being is part of nature and that economy and ecology must therefore be in a harmonious relationship making all life in abundance possible. These two words – economy and ecology – share a same Greek root, 'oikos' (house, habitation). The Korean word corresponding to this meaning is *Salimsali*. This word consists of two different parts, *Salim* and *Sali*. The first one is derived from household economy and the latter from house management. *Salimsali* means all the work and spirit which make things alive. I want to suggest Salim leadership as a new model of family leadership: the goal of good family leadership is to make things alive.

*Salim* refers to a Korean woman's everyday household chores, e.g. gathering wood, water and food, cooking, cleaning, washing, raising children, healing the sick. These tasks also include caring for the old and the weak, as well as for plants and trees. Salimists make things alive again, especially dying things and wounded things like the Earth. When Korean people say about a particular woman that 'she is a *'Salim-kun'* (a Salim expert)', this means that she has perfected the skill or art of making things alive. This includes feeding and nurturing everybody (so that they are all full and happy), creating peace, health, abundant living and a beautiful environment for the family (the very large extended family of all forms of life).

A Salimist also embraces a vision of fundamental social change, she gets involved in movements and develops strategies. She is an 'inclusivist,' or 'embracist.' A Salimist, in other words, is a peace activist. In Korea, some Salimists are married. Their husbands call them *'An-Hae'*, which means 'the sun of the household.' Salimists promote conflict resolution, non-violent resistance, peace, reconciliation and harmony wherever they go.[5] Salimists, therefore, are leaders for peace and life.

## 2. The Principles of Salimist Leadership

### a)  Shift from a Male-Centred to a Life-Centred Way of Life

The new model of Salim leadership can emerge through a paradigm shift from reason-centred, human being-centred and material-centred reasoning and behaviour to a life-centred and spirit-centred approach. This perspective leads us to the future of cosmic community and to recognise even our responsibility of maintaining and preserving our planet Earth, which goes beyond individualistic and nationalistic worldviews. This is what we may call 'cosmic Salimsali'. This shift produces new values of Salim culture such as keeping alive *(Salim)*, serving, emptying and sharing to find new ways of life.

### b)  A New Women Leadership Through Interaction Between Human Beings and Nature

Through inter-feeling between people and nature for building an ecological community, which respects all life on earth, we can learn from earth and nature to correct the destructive and wounded way of life. Facing, in particular, the ecological crisis in relation with the growing economical injustice, many Western Christian theologians concede that Christianity has a great responsibility in this problem. To fix it, Daoism suggests the recognition of a deep connection between nature and human beings. The core beliefs of Daoism are relationality, mutuality, and wholeness between humans.

In Daoism, the law of nature is not dualistic, in the sense of opposing, for instance, life to death. Rather, it is the circulation of all existence. The human being is part of nature and follows the natural cycle. An Eastern Asian philosophy such as Daoism, originally does not contain any concept of dualistic domination. It emphasises the balance and unity of nature, which includes the human being as a part of it. The Eastern epistemology has a potential to provide schemes and models for a new way of life. Nevertheless, the original principle of Daoism is hard to be found in contemporary society even in Eastern thinking. It is our responsibility, both in the East and in the West, to revise the life style for the future.

The inherent characteristic of nature is the constant flux of life. This flux, in the Salimist concept, depends on the female, which means on the life-giving and life-nurturing role women are able to fulfil. Throughout history, women have struggled with the natural resources such as food, land, water and energy. Nevertheless, unlike the dualistic view that puts the nature/culture in antagonistic relation, women do not objectify nature, but are rather embedded in it, embrace it as part of their life, and nourish it. Therefore, it is very natural that feminists are radically participating in movements of non-violent resistance against the ecological crisis. Thus, the Earth and the land are often symbolised as the mother or the women's womb, which is the metaphor of creation and product as we can particularly see it in Daoism.

## c) *Female Leadership Focused on the Values of Sharing, Emptying, and Serving*

According to Mother Teresa, there is no peace without sharing. The reason of poverty and oppression in present days is not a lack of resources but a failure of adequate distribution and sharing. Economical injustice and ecological destruction cannot be resolved through a change in our ways of thinking or through reforms of the system only; they require a change in every individual's way of life. If we can transform values of life according to Salimist principles such as sharing, emptying, serving, people will know that wealth and possession cannot guarantee life and peace, and that changing values, styles and attitudes of life can give life and peace for all living beings on Earth. Serving others and sharing with others is very difficult for everyone. But persons who live with sharing and serving can be persons who know the art of living and who experience a real happiness of life. They are often happier than those who receive help from others. Therefore, persons who never experience sharing, never experience the joy such sharing creates. The way to overcome the divisions in this world is only sharing and emptying.

### d)   The New Leadership in Re-evaluating Feminine Values Such as Nurturing, Caring, Accepting, and Life Giving.

In some Western epistemologies, which are based on hierarchical dualism, the image of the female is often connected with a negative concept such as body, feelings, myth, spontaneity, darkness, weakness, death, etc. These concepts support a hierarchical social structure, and the ideology of gender control has been established on this. However, Daoism suggests different methods of looking at and understanding our contemporary society. In what follows, I will evaluate these female images to enrich the concept of women leadership presented thus far.

There are several female images in the *Dao Te Ching*, such as giving birth, nurturing, softness, darkness, etc.[7] These notions are often used to explain the Dao and the principle of nature. The notion of Dao does not contain any negativity, and more important, any notion of domination. Thus the female image in Daoism does not contain and yield negativity or oppression; rather it presents very positive and embracing aspects. Before discussing the female image in the *Dao Te Ching*, it is necessary that the two different images of the female in modern society be classified. One category is the mythical, irrational image of the female characterised by chaos, spontaneity, darkness, fluctuation, weakness, etc.[7] The notions in this category support male domination over women in hierarchical society. Some former Western ethics or concepts of nature, that is, the exploitation and monopolisation of resources, are also placed in this category because symbolically nature and women have been considered to be in the same image. Most contemporary Western environmental ethics look at it critically.

The other category is the image of the mother; it entails nurturing and devotion and is often considered in a very positive way in contemporary society. However, the fact cannot be ignored that the positive outlook embraced by the mother image has also been used for manipulation and for the advancement of the ideology of gender control.

The mother image in Daoism represents the Dao,[8] which is life-giving and nurturing. Lao Tzu said: 'The Dao is called the Great Mother: empty yet inexhaustible, it gives birth to infinite worlds.'[9]

He also said that 'the Dao gives birth to all beings, nourishes them, maintains them, cares for them, comforts them, protects them. [...] That is why love of the Dao is in the very nature of things.'[10] Therefore, this mother image cannot be restricted to the women's reproductive role or the domestic work only. It is an immense and profound image. The Dao as the female image creates all things, human beings and nature. At the same time, it is immanent in its creation. The metaphor-image of the Great Mother is the harmony and unity of the creator and the creation.

Daoism presents other concepts, which can be categorised in the female image, such as softness and flux, in an affirmative way. As Lao Tzu said: 'The gentlest thing in the world overcomes the hardest thing in the world.' The softness and weakness as the female image are usually regarded to be inferior to the rigidity and strength of the male image. But Lao Tzu saw it reversed. He said: 'Thus, whoever is stiff and inflexible is a disciple of death. Whoever is soft and yielding is a disciple of life. The hard and stiff will be broken. The soft and supple will prevail.' The emphasis on the superiority of the female image illustrates the emancipation of life. All things die when the circulation of life is blocked, but all things live if they are let to flow with their own circulation.

## Conclusion

Women leadership includes feminine, female, and feminist perspectives altogether. To create a new model of leadership focused on life and peace, I think that it is important to rethink and re-evaluate various kinds of women's ways of seeing, thinking, and acting which have been silenced, marginalised, and considered as inferior concepts for a long time. I think that women leadership oriented along the lines of the concept of Salim and inspired by the Daoist principles summarised above, could restore and revitalise all families which are suffering, wounded and broken.

NOTES

1   'Salimist' is a term derived from the Korean word *Salim*, which means literally 'to make things alive'. The word *Salim* is one of the important concepts through which we can understand Korean thought. Initially, the Association of Korean Feminist Theologians used this word in 2001.

2   Cahill, Lisa Sowle, *Family. A Christian Social Perspective,* Minneapolis: Fortress Press, 200, p. 9.

3   Radford Ruether, Rosemary, 'An Unrealized Revolution. Searching Scripture for Model of the Family', in: Stuart, Elizabeth/Thatcher, Adrian (eds), *Christian Perspectives on Sexuality and Gender*, Grand Rapids: Eerdmans, 1996, pp. 442-450, especially p. 449.

4   Daoism and Confucianism are the most important and dominant factors, which formed the spiritual aspect of both Chinese and Korean culture. While Confucianism was usurped by the rulers

and became the political ideology of the dynasties, Daoism remained the metaphysical soul of East Asia.

[5]    The Korean feminist theologian, Hyun Kyung, presented a 'Salimist Manifesto' at the 2005 World Life-Culture Forum in Gyeonggi, Korea.

[6]    Lao Tzu, *Tao Te Ching. New English Version*, transl. by Stephen Mitchell, New York: Harper & Row, 1988, chap. 1-5.

[7]    See e.g. Graham, Angus C./Chuang-Tzu, *The Seven Inner Chapters and Other Writing from the Book Chuang-tzu*, London: George Allen and Unwin, 1981.

[8]    Dao, as the word is used in China, Korea, and Japan, is not limited to Daoism; in all major Chinese systems it refers to the right way (the Way) or cosmic order even though different schools have different interpretations.

[9]    Lao Tzu, *op. cit.*, chap. 6.

[10]    Lao Tzu, *op. cit.*, chap. 51. For the following quotes, see chap. 6-13.

# 6

## LEADERSHIP IN ETHICAL FAMILIES.
## A NORTH AMERICAN PERSPECTIVE

*Christopher Lind, Canada*

In this paper I have been asked to respond to two papers presented at an earlier conference. Both deal with the ethics of leadership in families. The first paper, by Rachel Xiaohong Zhu from the People's Republic of China, reviews the concept of family relationships and duties in the Confucian tradition and compares that with the changes going on in China today as a consequence of westernisation and modernisation and also as a consequence of China's one child policy.[1] The second paper is by Richard Ondji'i Toung from Cameroon.[2] He reviews the concept of the family, as is understood by the Fang people of southern Cameroon. He is particularly concerned with the breakdown of assumptions about how traditional leadership roles should be carried out and what resources Christianity may have to offer in this situation. Both papers pay very close attention to the questions that emerge from their geographic and cultural context and both take for granted that families are biological.

I want to respond by paying close attention to my context and the questions that emerge there. I am a Canadian academic theologian with special expertise in Christian social ethics, specifically ethics and economics, born of English and American immigrant parents. I am a lay Anglican, who worked for almost 20 years for the United Church of Canada, a 20th century denomination formed from the Congregational, Methodist and Presbyterian traditions.

### 1. Biblical and Historical Forms of the Family

In North America the form of family life is contested terrain. One of the fields of contest is whether the concept is reserved for the biological family or whether it can encompass a larger variety of social forms. Especially in the United States of America, conservative evangelical Christians like James Dobson, founder of Focus on the Family demand a return to the traditional Christian family. Focus on the Family is an evangelical organisation dedicated to 'helping to preserve traditional values and the institution of the family.' It runs a radio program broadcast on 3500 radio stations in the USA and in 163 other countries including Canada, China and Southern Africa.[3] It is opposed to divorce, abortion and homosexuality as social practices that undermine the family which is considered one of the three institutions (alongside the Church and the government) ordained by God for the benefit of all humankind. Its publications approvingly quote and publicise others who promote the concept of the natural family which is defined as 'married mom and dad, with children.'[4]

That is to say, the traditional or natural family is a two-generation family in a monogamous marriage. Is this the kind of family promoted by the Bible and the early Church?

Well, it is not the kind of marriage that Abram had with Sarai, who encouraged him to sleep with their Egyptian slave Hagar in order to have children (Gen 16:1-6). Yes, Abraham eventually renounced Hagar and sent her and Ishmael away, but only after Sarah produced her own child and started worrying about his eventual inheritance. It is not the kind of family Jacob had. In Genesis (46:26) we read that his household numbered 66 persons. Indeed scholars tell us that the average Hebrew household numbered closer to 50 or 100 people. This contrasts with the average American household, which consists of 2.63 people according to the U.S. Census.[5] Canadian families have a similar character.

It is not the family of the early Church. The family structure typical of the society of the early Church is vastly different from the family structure of contemporary North America. As Lisa Sowle Cahill pointed out, 'the family of [first century Palestine] is decidedly not the nuclear family of today. Parents and children never function as a social unit in isolation. The latin *familia* can refer to all those related through the male line; it can also denote all those under the authority of the *paterfamilias* in a household, the membership of which is not limited to kin. The household *(domus)* includes a married couple and their children but also incorporates slaves, clients, unmarried relatives, freedmen or freedwomen, and other tenants of the property.'[5] I note in passing that some clergy friends of mine in Canada now make a point of referring not to families but to households, in order to include all those with whom people live and on whom people depend.

It is not the family of Roman society in this period which was far from a social arrangement freely entered into. In Rome there is an ancient church dedicated to an early Christian martyr. It is called the Church of Sant'Agnese, or the Church of St. Agnes who died in 305 C.E. Her story goes like this: 'Agnes had aroused a burning desire in the son of a Roman prefect, who had seen her coming home from school. Agnes was twelve or at most thirteen years old, the age at which Roman women could be engaged to be married. He begged her to marry him, offering her houses, riches, and luxury, as well as the power of being a member of the prefect's family, if she would agree... Agnes replied that she was engaged already, to someone far better than he, and who loved her more... She had chosen Christ over the son of a Roman prefect... The law gave Agnes a fiendish choice if she would not marry: either to be made a vestal virgin and spend the rest of her life sacrificing to Roman idols, or to be exposed naked... in a brothel. She chose the brothel, but was miraculously saved from rape. In the end she was stabbed in the throat... The story also tells us that they tried to burn her alive because she would not change her mind, but the flames divided and went out.'[7] Agnes' story is matched by the story of many virgin martyrs. Victoria refused a marriage and died in a prison in Carthage. Lucy and Agatha refused their suitors and were sent to brothels as well. Lucy was stabbed to death and Agatha tortured. Cecelia was beheaded and Vivian was beaten to death.[8]

Is the family being imagined by North American conservatives, the family endorsed by the New Testament? In the New Testament St. Paul considers singleness to be a higher estate than marriage (1 Cor 7:38) and Jesus envisages a family far different from a biological relationship. It appears as though his disciples are required to hate their fathers and mothers (Luke 14:25). Indeed he declares as his closest relatives anyone who 'does the will of my father' (Mark 3:35). Some people actually consider the traditions of the gospels and early Christianity to be 'anti-family.'[9]

In response to the claims of people like Dobson, many scholars have begun to critically examine this concept of the traditional Christian family. What they have found is that 'what evangelicals call the "traditional family" is in fact the bourgeois or middle-class family, which rose to dominance in the nineteenth century – not accidentally alongside capitalism and, a little later, America as the ascendant world power.'[10]

In the discourse of conservative, evangelical America, what is being imagined is a family made up of a married father and mother with children where the father works outside of the home and is the head of the household and the mother is devoted to the religious and moral education of the children and the nurturing of affective bonds in the family.

It is a patriarchal family model that emerged in the late nineteenth century within the growing urban North American middle class. It was an urban model because agriculture was still being organised in the north and west of the continent around the model of the family farm where all family members participated in production.[11] It was a middle class model because the upper class had servants to perform domestic labour and the working class provided servants at the expense of their own family bonds. This model peaked in the early twentieth century in North America when the agricultural population peaked. The patriarchal model was enshrined in social policy in Canada until about 1970.[12]

## 2. A Christian View of Socially Constructed Families

Even from this brief review we can see that forms of family life are socially constructed, that is, they can change over time and across cultures according to economic, political and social needs. The nineteenth century North American patriarchal model was partly a response to the economic forces of the day. That does not make it better or worse; just a creature of its time. Today in North America, the single parent family is also in part a response to contemporary economic forces. People are less likely to live in the same place they grew up and so lack the supports of an extended family in close proximity. When both parents work outside the home, there is increased stress involved in child rearing. An intentional but not biologically related extended family is one contemporary response to these pressures.

In Canada there is an influential research institute called the Vanier Institute of the Family, named after the first Canadian born Governor General, George Vanier. The Vanier Institute defines the family as 'any combination of two or more persons who are bound together over time by ties of mutual consent, birth and/or adoption or placement and who, together, assume responsibilities for variant combinations of the following:

- physical maintenance and care of group members;
- addition of new members through procreation or adoption;
- socialisation of children;
- social control of members;
- production, consumption, distribution of goods and services; and
- affective nurturance – love.[13]

This definition of the family is not a biological definition. It is characterised by freedom (mutual consent), mutual responsibility (maintenance and care of group members) and legal obligation (in Canada, procreation and adoption automatically generate obligations in law). To fit this definition you do not have to be married, though it allows for that. You do not have to have children, though it allows for that, too. Finally, you do not have to be a heterosexual couple, though, of course, it allows for that. You can still be a family without those qualifiers.

### 3. Christian View: Family More Than Biological

The question now is: does this definition fit with our Christian tradition? The Old Testament is also full of examples of families that are not biological families, in the narrow sense of that term. For example, do Naomi and Ruth not constitute a family? Naomi is a widow, and Ruth, also a widow, was married to Naomi's son. They are related by marriage but not by biology, especially after the death of their common parent. In many cultures the expectation is that when a woman marries a man she leaves her father's household and joins her husband's. In this arrangement she has an obligation to her mother-in-law. In the story of Naomi, Ruth and Orpah, Orpah is obedient by returning to her people, the Moabites, as she is commanded to do by her mother-in-law Naomi. Ruth is disobedient and refuses to leave. In the story she emerges as disobedient but faithful. Can we not say they are a family despite biology? In the text we find one of the most famous and moving declarations of devotion and loyalty when Ruth says to Naomi:

'Where you go, I will go;

Where you lodge, I will lodge;

Your people shall be my people,

And your God will be my God.'[14]

If Ruth had not married Boaz, would not Naomi and Ruth still have been a family?

Let me use another example. In 1 Samuel we find a narrative establishing the rise of great leaders, Kings, in Israel. In this story the mantle of leadership passes from Eli to Samuel to Saul and finally to David. In the New Testament, Jesus is described as having descended from the House of David (Luke 1:69). We are accustomed to the mantle of kingship being passed through blood lines, that is biologically, from father to son. And yet in 1 Samuel, that is emphatically not what happens. There we find leadership being passed, not from Eli to his sons Hophni or Phinehas, but to Samuel who is like a son. Indeed Eli calls Samuel 'son' (3:6,16). In turn, leadership then passes not from Samuel to his sons Joel or Abijah, but to Saul. Finally, leadership passes from Saul. Again, it does not pass to his son Jonathan but to David. Once again, David is like a son to Saul and Saul is like a father to David. David calls Saul 'father' (24:11) and Saul calls David 'son' several times (24:16; 26:17,21,25).[15]

In each case one leader functions as a surrogate father to the next. Their relationship is not biological but is it not a family relationship? Families are social units characterised by obligation and entitlement, responsibilities and rights. We use the language of biological relationship to describe the various roles we play but that does not mean families should be normatively defined by biology. It is common in cultures around the world for families to have extensive networks of people identified as aunts and uncles, without there being a biological tie through the brother or sister of one's father or mother.

So, two people can form a family by mutual consent. They may or may not procreate. We would surely have said that Zechariah and Elizabeth had formed a family during all those years that they were childless (Luke 1:7). They did not become a family only when John (the Baptist) was born! (In China a family is commonly thought to be made by marriage, not by procreation.) A family is characterised by love and the physical care of one another. On this ground Ruth and Naomi are also a family.

Some scholars use the term 'fictive kin' to describe relationships that are familial but not biological. They provide relationships that are supportive and caring, responsible and communal. The church has made extensive use of these relationships in the institution of godparents through baptism. In the medieval period these relationships were taken so seriously that European laws of incest were extended to cover relations between godparents and godchildren. In many parts of the world today, the godparent relationship is an integral part of the family system. [16]

I do not know of any culture where parents do not have an obligation to care for their child, though responsibilities may be divided unevenly between father and mother or shared with village members or an extended kinship group. These obligations are matched by the rights of the child to receive such care and we have various enforcement mechanisms to ensure such care. So, family members have both rights and responsibilities.

Children, upon reaching the maturity of adulthood, must choose to assume these mutual responsibilities in their own right in order to maintain their membership in the family. I recall a story I heard from a friend who was born into the Cree First Nation of western Canada. A friend of his had grown up on a poor, rural reserve and moved to the city where he received a European style education, married a woman who was not Cree, and was employed in a high status government job. Members of his extended family felt entitled to spontaneously come to his house in the city and stay for months at a time, eating his food without making any financial contribution to the household. This was very stressful for his wife and eventually he asked his family to stop doing this. His family returned to the reserve and held a funeral for him. He had violated a norm so central to their understanding of family relationship that they no longer considered him a part of their family.

So, families can take many forms and I do not believe any one form is mandated by God for all time and in all places. One of the questions this raises is: how do we derive ethical norms from Scripture? This is too big a subject for this small paper.[17] However, we should not derive them by isolating some texts from others and applying them uncritically to contemporary life. Rather we must apply the tools of reason to all the biblical texts taken together in the same way we apply our critical faculties to contemporary society. In addition we must critically appropriate Church teachings in the same way as we critically appropriate our own experience of God and the world. Only then can we begin to say what ethical norms can be derived from Scripture and how they relate to the Christian life.

## 4. Four Criteria for Ethical Families

One implication of the idea of multiple family forms is that it is possible to distinguish between ethical and unethical families. The Vanier Institute definition already implies some ethical criteria since it characterises families by mutual consent, mutual responsibility and legal obligation. Families that are not characterised by freedom cannot be ethical. So, forced marriages would not be ethical but arranged marriages might be if the participants were truly free to consent. Families where members refuse to care for one another are also unethical. So, where parents refuse to care for their children or adult children refuse to care for their dependent parents, they are acting in an unethical manner. Where legal obligations are not met, society will enforce sanctions (I do not assume here necessarily, that all laws are ethical. Some laws can be unjust). Obligations exist in both given families and constructed families. It is not the presence or absence of obligations that determine whether or not a family is ethical. Relationships of mutual support freely entered into will always entail obligations.

To the criteria of freedom and mutuality I would also add the criteria of peace and justice. Families have always had the potential of being unsafe places. Abraham's threat to sacrifice Isaac is not the only example in the Bible of violence being threatened by a parent against a child. We also read of examples where a father is allowed to have his son stoned (Deut 21:12-21) or his daughter burned (Gen 38:24), and instructed to execute them if they lead the father to serve other gods (Deut 13:6-9). In Judges (11:34-40) we read the horrific account of Jephthah slaughtering his daughter.

Today in Canada, some families continue to be unsafe places, primarily for women and children. Studies have shown that '29 % of [Canadian] women who have ever been married or lived common law with a partner have been assaulted by their marital partner and 45 %

of these cases resulted in physical injury to the woman... 39 per cent of all women have experienced at least one incident of sexual assault since the age of 16.'[18] So, a violent family is an unethical family.

Finally, there is the criteria of justice. This includes care for the poor and right relationship. A family where one member (a man for example) uses all the resources of the family for his own purposes without regard to the needs of the other family members would be an unethical family. Here I am in agreement with the American Catholic ethicist Lisa Sowle Cahill who redefines 'family values' as care for others. 'The Christian family, Cahill writes, defines *family values* as care for others, especially the poor; it appreciates that truly Christian families are not always the most socially acceptable or prestigious ones; it values and encourages all families who strive earnestly to meet the standard of compassionate action; and it encourages both personal commitment to and the social structuring of mercy and justice.'[19]

A family of whatever form, characterised by freedom and mutuality, peace and justice is an ethical family in the Christian tradition of ethical discourse, even if it is not explicitly Christian. As Rosemary Ruether has written, 'Today we face the breakdown of this Victorian pattern of the idealised family, with its segregation of male and female in separate spheres of work and home. The question now becomes: Is there some new way or reading marriage, family, sex and procreation theologically that can support a more just and sustainable harmony of women and men, home and work?' The response of James Dobson and his ilk is not to re-imagine the family but to reinforce its Victorian patriarchal form. For Ruether, by contrast, 'A new vision of family, of home and work, needs to be based on the mutuality of whole human beings, not on the truncation of such beings into separate parts, home for women and work for men... Theologically, this requires first of all a clear and explicit rejection of the doctrine that holds that the patriarchal family of male headship and female subordination is the "order of creation", mandated by God. The patriarchal family in its various forms, from the slavocracy of antiquity to the Victorian nuclear family, is a human construct, not a divine mandate.'[20]

I can summarise this form of family, characterised by freedom and mutuality, peace and justice by saying that it is a democratic family. My early nineteenth century ancestors would have been appalled by such a suggestion. An American Church newspaper from the early 1800s described the idea of 'pure family democracy' as 'most alarming.'[21] Even today, within the United Church of Canada there are dissenters who agonise about the direction their Church is taking with regard to a theological interpretation of the family.[22] However, I would define a democratic institution as one where all the adult members can participate in the decisions which affect them. Does that mean constructed families are more moral than given families? No, even democratic institutions can be unethical. One of the character-istics that makes a democratic institution ethical is that it cares for and protects the rights and interests of its dependent members.

So, in North America, the form of the family is contested. I advo-cate for ethical democratic forms as those which come closest to the gospel message of freedom and mutuality, peace and justice.

## Conclusion

Having successfully inverted the question of the ethics of leader-ship in families into the question of leadership in ethical families, I will now conclude as follows. The question of the ethics of leadership in ethical families is the same as the question of leadership in all democratic institutions. Formal leadership must emerge from just processes that ensure the possibility of participation of all qualified members. Ethical leadership will encourage participation in decision making, protect the rights and interests of dependents members and minorities, avoid self-interested behaviour and conflicts of interest, and seek the common good.

As always, the problem with Christian ethics is that it sets a high bar!

NOTES

[1]  Xiaohong Zhu, Rachel, 'Family Leadership Shift in China. Preliminary Perspectives For A Con-fucian and Christian Dialogue', in: Stückelberger, Christoph/Mugambi, J.N.K. (eds), *Responsi-ble Leadership. Global Perspectives*, Nairobi, Kenya: Acton Publishers, 2005, pp. 34-45. See also Chapter 3 in this volume.

[2]  Ondji'i Toung, Richard, 'Responsible Family Leadership. Traditional and Christian Approaches in Cameroon', in *op. cit.*, pp. 46-58. See also Chapter 4 in this volume.

[3]  Focus on the Family Mission Statement at www.family.org (last accessed 5 September 2005).

[4]  'But for too long, Carlson and Mero say, traditionalists have been more divided by distractions than united in defending their common base: the natural family – married mom and dad, with children – as society's bedrock.' http://www.family.org/cforum/fosi/marriage/nac/ a0036244.cfm (last accessed 10 September 2005).

[5]  Clapp, Rodney, *Families at the Crossroads. Beyond Traditional and Modern Options*, Leicester: InterVarsity Press, 1993, p. 35.

[6]  Sowle Cahill, Lisa, *Family. A Christian Social Perspective*, Minneapolis: Fortress Press, 2000, p. 19.

[7]  Visser, Margaret, *The Geometry of Love. Space, Time, Mystery and Meaning in an Ordinary Church*, Toronto: HarperCollins, 2000, pp. 96-97.

[8]  These stories are also recounted in *op. cit.*, p. 242.

[9]  See Radford Ruether, Rosemary, *Christianity and the Making of the Modern Family*, Boston: Beacon Press, 2000.

[10]  Clapp, Rodney, *op. cit.*, p. 11. He relies heavily on Brigitte and Peter Berger's *The War over the Family*, Garden City, NY: Doubleday, 1983.

[11]  In the east and south, especially prior to the American civil war, agriculture was organised around a plantation model based on slave labour.

[12]   See Eichler, Margrit, *Family Shifts. Families, Policies, and Gender Equality*, Toronto: Oxford University Press, 1997, p. 7.

[13]   http://www.vifamily.ca/about/about.html (last accessed 11 September 2005).

[14]   Ruth 1:16, New Revised Standard Version.

[15]   This relationship pattern is explored in detail by Jobling, David, *1 Samuel*, Collegeville, MN: The Liturgical Press, 1998, chapter 5.

[16]   See Radford Ruether, Rosemary, *op. cit*, p. 231, note 3.

[17]   For a fuller discussion of this question see Birch, Bruce/Rasmussen, Larry, *The Bible and Ethics in the Christian Life*, Minneapolis, MN: Augsburg Fortress, 1989, rev. ed.

[18]   Eichler, Margrit, *op. cit.*, p. 63.

[19]   Sowle Cahill, Lisa, *op. cit.*, p. 135.

[20]   Radford Ruether, Rosemary, *op. cit.*, p. 228.

[21]   'Second-generation American Episcopalians carried an almost proprietary view of leadership in a "world turned upside down" by the Revolutionary War; indeed, the prospect of "pure family democracy" was … "most alarming" [according to an 1807 author in a church magazine].' Bowen Gillespie, Joanna, 'Episcopal Family as the Nursery of Church & Society', in: Airhart, Phyllis D./Lamberts Bendroth, Margaret (eds), *Faith Traditions and the Family*, Louisville, KY: Westminster John Knox Press, 1996, p. 143.

[22]   See Anderson, Daphne J./Anderson, Terence R., 'United Church of Canada: Kingdom Symbol of Lifestyle Choice', in: Airhart, Phyllis D./Lamberts Bendroth, Margaret (eds), *op. cit.*

# 7

# FAMILY LEADERSHIP IN AFRICA

*Muteho Kasongo, Democratic Republic of Congo*

## Introduction

The main issue to be dealt with in this paper is the dynamic of leadership in the family and its relationship with leadership in society. The attempt in this study is to reflect on the way the family leadership model can influence leadership in society. Focusing on the model of family leadership, the objective of this study is to call upon a responsible family leadership in the process of the establishment of democratic and more responsive leadership in all societies. Analysing the model of family leadership, our intention is to challenge the model of leadership in Africa, and to awake people's consciousness to the need of reviewing the established leadership models towards more participatory leadership. In what follows, the topic will be developed from an African point of view.

The guiding assumption in this essay is that it appears clearly that the family represents the basic nucleus or the foundation of society. Since all members of society come from families, this implies that the leaders of societies are formed – at least partly and among other influences – in and by families. Given this, the family has a strong influence on society in various ways. Its power is the power of the whole society. Its weakness impacts on the whole society as well. In talking about leadership, it is important to note that all types of leadership start in the family. Therefore, if a family enjoys good leadership, it is more likely that children raised in such a family have acquired a culture of good leadership and that they might become themselves good leaders. This is also expressed in one of the Chinese sayings that the state's harmony and prosperity depend on the stability of the families.[1] Generally, if a leader in society emanates from a family where the father is tyrant, dictator, or battering his wife, he more likely becomes a tyrant, dictator and oppressive leader. The opposite may also be possible if the leader comes from more cooperative, respectful, loving, compassionate and humble parents. Children, in short, tend to imitate their parents' way of doing things, including their modes of acting as leaders. This sounds logical and inevitable, indeed, since psychologically speaking, the child learns from adults.

Therefore, the main questions are the following: 'What type of leadership is commonly carried out in families? What type of family leadership is suitable as a model for society leadership?' I will try to respond to these questions below.

## 1. Participatory Family Leadership

First of all, it should be noted that the African family is composed of father, mother, children as well as all members of the large family on both the father's and the mother's sides. It is an extended family, in which uncles, aunts, cousins, nephews and nieces are all included.

Secondly, the concept of 'leadership' shall be understood in this paper as the skill or the capacity of taking responsibility for matters that encompass all areas of life in society, i.e. the economic, the social, the political and the religious. All these aspects are reflected in family life. Daniel Arap Moi defined leadership as 'the dynamic and catalytic ability of an individual or a group to liberate, engage and direct the constructive endeavours of a people for betterment of individual and/or whole communities, for their material prosperity and for their social-cultural uplift, spiritual peace and mental productivity.'[2]

Practically, as a social group, a family needs leadership for its own development and for all its members'. No family can stand without a leader. In this dynamic, husband and wife within their parent-hood capacity are the main leaders of the family. They have a primary capacity and a responsibility to sustain the life of their family members. Their main task is to ensure the welfare of all members of the family.

Good family leadership takes responsibly and engages its power for the welfare of all family members. This welfare include many elements such as good education for the children and the provision of housing and food supply to the family, but also that needs such as health care, economic, political and social development be responded to. Through their leadership, the parents play the role of a good shepherd whose commitment is the protection of the members of the family, just as the shepherd does secure his flock.

This requires love, caring, self-respect and the respect for others, loyalty, wisdom, etc. Without love, parents cannot sacrifice themselves and cannot carry out their responsibility. Likewise, the parents' self-respect and their respect for the members of the family would help them establish a more respectful family leadership. This respect is supposed to be more inclusive, without any discrimination based on gender and age. Boys and girls would be taken as equal and given the same opportunity to develop their respective capacities and exploit them equally for the development of the family. They should be given the same opportunity to speak, to be heard, to be educated and to use their abilities in the interest of the whole family group.

It should be noted that parents are assisted in their responsibility by their children in the sense that the education they provide is not passive. It is a participative education in which the children learn how to do things in a practical way. It is thus through a process of 'learning by doing' that the children are taught how to become responsible persons capable of managing their own life and their surrounding environment.

Besides this, each family member has a responsibility to contribute to the common good within the family. The development of the family is the result of the participation of all its members. In this sense, family leadership cannot be the monopoly of one person, but needs to be a participative leadership where the wife, the father, the children as well as all other members join hands, each one on his level, to sustain the life and the development of the family. For instance, parents have power over all family members. They give them orders, direct, advise, and instruct them, and look after them in all ways. In the African context, children, too, have on their own level some responsibility in the management of the family. The elder son or daughter watches over the younger brothers or sisters, they help their parents to achieve some works in the house, in farming, in fetching water, in grinding the grains; they even participate in the upbringing of their younger brothers or sisters in ruling over them, giving orders, in imitation of their own parents. None can deny the fact that the elder children somehow influence the behaviour of the younger ones. This is somehow a participative leadership in which the children are being prepared for leadership. When they become mature, they have already acquired the necessary preparation to take on some responsibilities.

## 2. Patriarchal and Exclusive Family Leadership

Since most African societies are patriarchal, however, and despite the fact that both parents are the main leaders of the family, the father is always the head of the family. His power is predominantly submitting the power of women. This appears clearly in most families in which one can observe a tendency of men keeping the leadership as their monopoly to the point that women have been excluded from their 'natural' guiding roles in the family. For instance, in most families, men take decisions without consulting their wives. This is due to a culture where women are considered inferior and as secondary citizens, incapable of making any mature decision. This leads, in the long run to an oppressive family leadership in which women have simply to implement the decisions taken by men. This has affected women, who developed an inferiority complex and a tendency to be passive *vis-à-vis* all leadership.[3] Very often, women are even excluded from decisions affecting their own life and that of the family. The following examples are necessary to illustrate the type of exclusion of women from family power. For instance, in most traditional tribal families in the Democratic Republic of Congo, the woman could not own any property, even if she was the one who worked hard to avail it. If she is still single, her property will be on her father's or brother's account. If she is married all her properties will be subscribed on her husband's account. She could not open a bank account, neither buy or sell any valuables such as land or goats without her husband's permission, whereas men can do that without informing their wives. Women can also not own some important properties such as lands. Women are also requested to present a written marital authorisation for job application while this is not required from men. Despite her education, a man can decide whether his wife could work outside of her household in office or not; yet the opposite is not always obvious. This translates the fact that a woman cannot decide for her own job. However educated they may be, women in some traditional African societies are not given the power to take some important decisions. This prevents many women from going for some important position in society, especially since some men are reluctant to allow their wives to do so. As we can read in this statement of the World Council of Churches: 'Patriarchy makes us think in hierarchy that puts the male at the top, privileged or superior position.'[4] This has been strongly highlighted by Nkiru Nzegwu who pointed out the fact that 'Women's limited participation in politics has been sought in family structures.'[5] In order to bring any possible change in such way of excluding women from decision-making in the family as well as in society, the new constitution of the Democratic Republic of Congo has been amended so that women could be given the rights to be treated like any human being with all the corresponding rights.

Not only women are excluded from family leadership; children are also affected by patriarchal family leadership. Boys especially would like to rule over girls by simply following the example of their fathers. They also consider girls as inferior. This attitude is strengthened by proverbs teaching that a boy has more power and is stronger than a girl. In African cultures, boys are considered as more responsible than girls in the family. They are more involved in decision-making than their sisters. They are treated as the successors of their fathers, and can therefore inherit their fathers' properties. Their power and strength is translated in various attitudes, as shows in the following example: if a boy falls and if he wants to cry, the parents just simply tell him that he should not cry like a girl. If a girl achieves a wonderful work, they often congratulate her saying that she has acted like a man. With this type of education, African girls and women have been weakened in terms of leadership and men have been reserved the monopoly of power. This is apparent in the Congo government where the women are under-represented.[6] Thus, for some women in Africa, the family power has been generally patriarchal, oppressive and exclusive.

This type of dictatorship present in the family influences the position of women in the government leadership. Not only are most African governments dictatorships, but they only feature – as a commonplace – an under-representation of women. Talking about the consequences of the exclusion of women from power, Amoako declared in a statement to the United Nations General Assembly that: 'As we come to understand the links between responsive and effective governance and development more fully, we learn that the governance that does not represent both sexes, is neither participatory nor inclusive and this cannot move a society forward.'[7] This has been the source of conflicts and wars in some African societies. The example which stands for this is the genocide in Rwanda: when one ethnic group is excluded from leadership, it ends up to genocide. In Congo also, the many civil and political conflicts and wars are also due to long periods of dictatorship. This excluded the potential power of various social groups. The same thing is happening in African societies where development is imbalanced due to the fact that the talents and skills of women could not benefit to societies because of their exclusion. Many conflicts ended up in wars where males have decided alone – without women – to use their strength and weapons to settle conflicts.

## 3. Family Leadership and the Scriptural Model of Leadership

It is in the family that people can learn how to become honest and responsible. This requires the good role model that can be played by the parents. The latter should serve as good examples for their children and the other members of the family. Usually, as already mentioned, the children follow the model of their leaders. In their life, they try to reflect the pattern of people who shaped their lives. It is in this sense that the Scriptures declare that none should make the little one stumble. If he does, he should be tied a heavy stone on his neck and be thrown away in the sea (Matt 18:6).

According to the Scriptures, the parents' leadership originates from the creation. It is God's will that parents become co-creators with him by procreating and participating in the management of the whole creation in giving direction and a sense to the life of all creatures as well as of the whole creation (Gen 1:26-28).

Within this responsibility, parents' leadership is identified with God's leadership. In several scriptural books like the Proverbs, the children are summoned to obey the parents' teaching and leadership for their good life as they obey God (Prov 3:1-3, 5-7, 12; 4:1-4, but see also Eph 6:1-4). To faithfully carry out this responsibility, parents should therefore play the role of servants as God, through the incarnation, became the perfect servant of the whole creation in Jesus Christ. Jesus confirmed this when he said that 'The son of man did not come to be served, he came to redeem many people' (Matt 20:28). In his life, he made this declaration a reality by being on the service of those who sought help such as the sick people, the paralysed, the marginalised or those rejected because of their sins, in order to help them recover their full life. In this ministry, Jesus did not seek his own protection and glory. He humbled himself to humiliation so that he may provide for the welfare of humanity. He offered his life to a shameful death because of his leadership. His leadership appeared as a servanthood instead of being served like actual leaders who prefer to be served and who enrich themselves at the expense of the populations they lead. He himself identified leadership with the service to others by declaring that if someone wants to be the greatest he should be the servant of all (Mark 9:35). Jesus did it and at the end of his mission, he was revealed to the humanity as the king of kings who has the power over everything in heaven as well as on the earth. This happens after the resurrection (Matt 28:18).

To successfully fulfil his missionary leadership, Jesus complied with some important criteria which we cannot overlook in this model of leadership. These are criteria such as obedience to God, humility, love of the humanity, compassion, faithfulness to his mission, patience, perseverance, purposive self-giving, sacrifice, life giving, justice, equal consideration of all people without discrimination, etc. Besides, Jesus liked to share his life with many others for their welfare.

Jesus associated the disciples to his ministerial leadership. He gave them the power of healing the sick and of casting the demons as he himself did. He even included women in his ministry – as it becomes apparent, Jesus' leadership was truly participatory. Following this model of leadership, parents should respect these criteria if they are to be successful in carrying their responsibility as family leaders. The confidence they place in God, and the faithfulness to his command, will enable them to carry out this mission of family leadership according to God's will.

## 4. Family Leadership and Decision-Making

Within the family important decisions are taken in all aspects of life. Parents are those responsible for taking decisions in the family. However, it is also their responsibility to train their children on decision-making. In the line of what Jesus did, this can be done by involving them in some deliberations. Instead of excluding them, parents can consult the members of their family and enquire about their opinion regarding matters to settle jointly, thus enabling them to participate freely without any restriction. Everyone should be given the opportunity to be heard. Good family leaders should not be tempted to impose they decisions on others without considering whether it is helpful for them or whether it brings upon a dislocation of the group. The members of the family can also make suggestions that can enlighten the decisions of the parents. Good family leaders should not neglect the point of view of children pretending that they are all childish. This has been the tendency in many traditional African families, in spite of good proverbs that illustrate how a child can also give good advice to his/her parents. One of those proverbs says that the chick can also give advice its mother hen. [8]

In their leadership, men should learn how to value the gift of women and should involve them in decision-making. They should realise that the unity of working together with women is the strength of the family and the whole society.

## 5. Family Leadership and Conflict Management

As in every group interaction, good leadership is affirmed by its capacity of creating harmony in the case of conflicting interests among the various group members. As the family is composed of many members with different ways of perceiving things, there also exist conflicting interests, which correspond to the diversity of needs. The lack of good management of these conflicting needs can create conflicts and disharmony among the family members. This implies that one of the tasks of the family leaders is to know how to find the ground on which all these various needs can be met in a peaceful way so that the harmony in the family can be safeguarded.

On the other hand, good family leadership must think of preparing the children to peaceful conflict management. This is important in as much as by peaceful conflict management, the children learn how to settle the matters that bring divisions in the community and open new ways for each to give a chance to others and give space to a harmonious community life. This is important in training the children for future leadership. Women should be allowed to use their feminine experience of conflict management to the benefit of the family groups as well as of the whole society.

## Conclusion

From this reflection, let us note that family leadership is a God-given responsibility to the parents. Through this role, parents fulfil God's work as intended in humanity to create order and to ensure empowerment of people for the human and environmental development. Family leadership, understood in this biblical sense, could serve as a model for government leadership. That is the reason why parents should be watchful in their responsibility in order to serve as good models in the preparation of children for future leadership. Likewise, the leaders in power today have a responsibility to initiate a more participatory leadership.

NOTES

[1]   See Zhu, Rachel Xiaohong, 'Family Leadership Shift in China. Preliminary Perspectives for a Confucian and Christian Dialogue', in: Stückelberger, Christoph/Mugambi, J.N.K. (eds), *Responsible Leadership. Global Perspectives*, Nairobi: Acton Publishers, 2005, pp. 34-45. See also Chapter 3 in this volume.

[2]   *Ibidem.*

[3]   AACC & CETA: 'La violence domestique', in: *Lève-toi et marche. Matériel ressource sur la violence faite a la Femme,* p. 4.

[4]   World Council of Churches (WCC), 'Changing the World: An Interfaith Consultation on Gender Justice, June 2004', in: WCC (ed.), *Streams of Grace*, 2005, pp. 25-27, also on www. wcc-coe.org/wcc/what/jpc/streams_of_grace_the_book.pdf (last accessed 13 July 2006).

[5]   Nzegwu Nkiru, 'African Women and Fire Dance', in: *West Africa Review* 2 (1), 2000, also on www.africaresource.com/war/vol2.1/nzegwu2.html.

[6]   Study made by Butembo Coteder under the guise of the 'Parlement écoles des femmes' in Nord-Kivu.

[7]   Declaration of Amoako, K.Y., Executive Secretary of the Economic Commission for Africa, in the Report to the UN General Assembly Hall, July 28, 1997, New York.

[8]   This is a Nande proverb. The Nande are a tribe living in the North Eastern part of the Democratic Republic of Congo.

# 8

# MARRIAGE RESPONSIBILITIES.
# AN ORTHODOX VIEW
# FROM THE MIDDLE EAST

*Sleiman Gebran, Lebanon*

'Husband and wife are one body in the same way as Christ and the Father are one.'

'If we regulate our households by seeking the things that please God, we will also be fit to oversee the Church, for indeed the household is a little church. Therefore it is possible for us to surpass all others in virtue by becoming good husbands and wives.'

'Whenever you give your wife advice, always begin by telling how much you love her.'

*St. John Chrysostom*

'Just as God blessed the first family, commanding Adam and Eve to be fruitful and multiply, so the Church today gives its blessings to the union of man and woman. Marriage is not only a state of nature but a state of grace. Married life, no less than the life of a monk, is a special vocation, requiring a particular gift of the Holy Spirit; and this gift is conferred in the sacrament of the Holy Matrimony.'

*Bishop Kallistos Ware*

'The very notion of marriage as sacrament presupposes that man is not only being with physiological and social functions, but that he is a citizen of God's Kingdom, i.e. that his entire life and especially his most decisive moments involve eternal values and God Himself.'

*Fr. John Meyendorff*

## Introduction

Orthodox Christianity is a way of life that is a whole coming together of habits and attitudes, ideas and actions: a lifestyle. Many Orthodox Christians do not live in monasteries: they are married; they have homes, children, and jobs. But all Christians, whether monastic or not, are equally called by Christ to repentance and eternal salvation.

There are no classes of Orthodox Christians; all are equal and all are expected to be followers of Christ, regardless of their position in the church. However, it is very difficult for Christians to live an Orthodox lifestyle. 'Behold, I send you out as sheep in the midst of wolves; be wise as serpents and innocent as doves.' (Matt 10:16)

Marriage and family life are a tremendous bastion of strength for Orthodox lay people, a state that has been blessed by God for the salvation of each individual member of the family. In order to fully understand this, we must look at the doctrinal foundations of marriage found in the Scripture (God's Holy Word) and the Sacred Tradition (the wisdom of the church through the ages).

## 1. The Biblical View: Marriage as Covenant

When we look at the practice of marriage, family life, and the multiplication of the human race as described in the Old Testament, we immediately see the great emphasis placed on the continuation of the Hebrew race. Marriage was not the only way by which the race was continued at that time. Children were also begotten through the custom of concubinage and of one's marriage to his brother's widow, even though he might have already a wife. Many of the great personages of the Old Testament had multiple wives and concubines. The primary reason for this mating was not the gratification of lust, but the desire for descendants.

But during Old Testament times, God began to reveal His expectations to man. Gradually we see that God condemned polygamous marriages, concubines, and the practice of marrying one's brother's widow. He began to shift the focus of marriage from procreation to a higher, spiritual level. God emphasised that He, not the physical union of a man and a woman, was the ultimate source of life. And where God is, there can be only holiness, and mystery. And holiness and mystery must be protected, guarded, and preserved.

With the coming of Christ, marriage's primary goal was no longer the reproduction of human beings and the perpetuation of a family line, although procreation was still regarded as an important part of marriage. But Christ had come to the world and brought with Him the proof and guarantee of the resurrection of the dead, therefore giving to Christian marriage a new primary goal: the attainment of eternal life by husband, wife, and all children.

What gives meaning to a marriage from a spiritual standpoint? Marriage is the setting up, by two people, of a miniature church, a family church, wherein people may worship the true God and struggle to save their souls. It is also a family church that is in obedience to

Christ's church. Thus we see that in New Testament times the focus of marriage was switched from the primary purpose of producing children to the primary purpose of providing a way for human beings to save their souls. The wedding ceremony itself is filled with rich symbolism that makes this whole aspect of marriage very clear.

The Covenant that the Lord God seals with Israel engages each party in mutual responsibility and mutual commitment. God commissions the first man and woman to 'be fruitful and multiply, and fill the earth and subdue it,' thereby granting them dominion over God's own creation. This commission confers blessing and responsibility, the basic component of a 'covenant'. Throughout Israel's history the Lord establishes various covenantal relationships with Noah, Abraham, Moses and David. Each involves unconditional commitment to fulfil a promise or an obligation that has enduring value.

Finally, the church, as the true 'Israel of God' that unites Jew and Gentile into the one Body of Christ, is the inheritor of 'a new covenant, not in a written code but in the Spirit.' This is the new covenant or 'New Testament' in the blood of Christ, which is poured out for the life of the world. In each case, the two parties of the covenantal bond commit themselves to unconditional faithfulness toward the fulfilment of a pledge or promise that will last forever.

Thus the Covenant that the Lord establishes with Israel and with the church engages each party in mutual responsibility and mutual commitment. To be chosen by God involves both God and ourselves in an eternal commitment, one in which God remains unconditionally faithful. While we can betray that commitment through acts of sinful rebellion or wanton negligence, and the covenant bond can be broken, it is nonetheless intended by God to endure into eternity.

The sacrament of marriage is the clearest and fullest expression of what covenantal commitment is. The very purpose of the marriage is to provide between two parties – two persons – a bond of covenant responsibility and faithfulness that represents and re-actualises the eternal bond established by God with his chosen people. The covenantal bond within which God works out our salvation is in essence a nuptial bond. Conversely, the nuptial relationship achieves its true purpose and attains to its true fullness only insofar as it is based upon an eternal covenantal commitment.

Christ's love for the members of his Body has both a sacramental and an eschatological dimension. This sacred intention serves as a model for conjugal love. For man and woman become 'one flesh' in the sense intended by God, they need to assume toward one another the same kind and quality of faithfulness and self-sacrifice that Christ assumed and continues to assume on behalf of his people. The telos, or ultimate end of conjugal union, is then salvation of the other, the beloved, with whom one is eternally united in a covenant bond of faithfulness and self-giving. This teaching about the marriage needs to be affirmed in churches.

## 2. The Symbolism of the Eastern Orthodox Marriage Service

The marriage ceremony in the Orthodox Church is steeped in symbolism which proclaims that a husband and wife are crowned to each other, and that the two become one flesh. Physical actions and images are signs of the spiritual realities of marriage. The rite of marriage contains two parts: the 'betrothal', and the 'crowning'. These two rites are celebrated together as one whole rite of matrimony which strengthens the mutual responsibility of the couple.

*The rings:* from ancient times, rings have been a symbol of betrothal, agreement, authority, and stewardship. They are sign of wealth and bounty. The bride and groom exchange the rings three times, in honour of the Holy Trinity, to symbolise that in marriage their gifts, talents, and bounties are shared between each other. The exchange of the rings gives expression to the fact that in marriage the spouses will constantly be complementing each other. Each will be enriched by the union.

*The procession:* after the exchange of the rings the priest leads the couple in procession into the middle of the church. The priest chants Psalm 128, one of the 'Psalms of Ascent' sung by Jewish pilgrims on the way to the Jerusalem Temple. This point in the service most clearly reveals the action of the sacrament. The couple brings themselves, each other, their lives, and all that fills their lives, to the altar as an offering to God.

*The candles:* the bride and groom are then handed candles which are held throughout the service. The candles symbolise the light of hope and vigilance. They represent the couple's constant readiness to accept Christ into their home and their marital relationship.

*The white running cloth:* the couple stands on a white cloth throughout the rite if crowning. This cloth represents the road of life, which, from this day forward, they will walk as one.

*The crowning:* the crowning is the central act of the Orthodox wedding service. The bride and groom are crowned king and queen of their family which is viewed in Orthodoxy as a micro Kingdom of God. They are expected to rule over their kingdom with wisdom, justice, integrity, and, above all else, selfless love. The crowns have two meanings. First, they reveal that the man and woman, in their union with Christ, participate in His Kingship. Second, as in the ancient Church, crowns are a symbol of martyrdom. The word martyr means witness. The common life of the bride and groom is to bear witness to the presence of Christ in their lives and in the world. Martyrdom is usually associated with death. So the reality of God's Kingdom in the life of the husband and wife will necessarily take the form of dying to one's self, to one's will, and of giving one's life totally to the other, and through the other, to Christ.

*The Scripture readings:* a) the Epistle: Ephesians 5:20-33. In his letter to the Church in Ephesus, Saint Paul describes the marital relationship as being symbolic of the relationship between Christ and the church. It represents the cornerstone of the Christian vision of marriage; b) the Gospel: John 2:1-11. It is understood that Jesus blesses the matrimonial relationship through performing the first of his miracles at the wedding banquet. Marriage becomes more than a mere human institution, existing for whatever purpose a society assigns it. It becomes, like the Church herself, a sign that God's Kingdom has already begun in our midst.

*The common cup:* the drinking of wine from the common cup serves to impress upon the couple that from this day on they will share everything in life, both the bitter and the sweet, joys and sorrows, successes and failures, hopes and fears.

*The dance of Isaiah or the triumphant procession:* it is the triple procession around the central table: the dance of Isaiah. The priest leads the couple in a procession around the table, on which the Gospel (containing the word of God), and the Cross (the symbol of redemption through Jesus Christ) have been placed. Husband and wife take their first steps as a married couple, and the Church in the person of the priest leads them in the way they should walk. Their life will be a journey in which Jesus Christ, His Word and His Salvation, is at the centre. The hymns return once more to the theme of martyrdom and union with Christ. Since ancient times, the Church has used these hymns to emphasise God's blessings. They are also sung at ordinations into clergy orders, and signify that this couple has been set apart from the mundane world to live a life in Christ.

*Removal of the crowns:* at the end of the service, the crowns are removed and the priest prays that God will receive these crowns into His Kingdom. The reality of the Kingdom into which the bride and groom have entered is not completely fulfilled, but has only begun. Completion and fulfilment will come when Christ returns in power and glory to complete the establishment of His Kingdom in this word by filling all things with Him.

*The greetings of the couple:* at the end of the service, the couple stands at the foot of the altar. Only the eternal Kingdom of Jesus Christ, as signified by the altar, remains ahead of them. Their final act is to turn and face the assembled Church. Through this sacrament, they have become an icon of the Church and icon of Christ and the assembly comes up to congratulate them and share in their joy.

### 3. The Responsibility of the Husband

The husband is the head of the wife (Saint Paul). This does not mean that he is superior to his wife. In Christ's sight, all are equal. Saint Paul's declaration, 'in Christ there is neither male nor female,' means that the socially and culturally conditioned inequality between the sexes is abolished; it does not exist in the mind of God and has no place within the church communities.

It also means that in Christ men and women bear equal responsibility for upholding a moral ethos conductive to preserving the integrity of family life.

In fact, marriage is a partnership of equals. Let there be no misunderstanding: there is no room for chauvinism of any kind in Orthodoxy. Nor does a husband's position as head give him any kind of dictatorial, tyrannical, arbitrary or absolute authority over his wife and children. But as with every position of importance, responsibilities go with this one, and they are very heavy and difficult, but also very challenging and potentially creative responsibilities.

The Scripture tells us that a husband must love his wife even as Christ loved the Church and gave Himself for it; 'Greater love hath no man than he lay down his life for his friend.' (Eph 5:25) Love, then, from the Christian standpoint, means sacrifice and self-denial. A husband must take as much care, concern, thoughtfulness, attention, regard and precautions for his wife as Christ takes for the Church. The husband's attentiveness might even have to extend to death itself.

Again Saint Paul says the husband is the head of the wife as Christ is the head of the church. We know what kind of head Christ was: He washed the feet of His disciples. According to our Saviour, to be head, to be first, means to serve, to be the first in giving love, in giving understanding, in giving patience, in providing his family with protection.

Consequently, the husband is no less responsible than his wife for preserving the familial structure, stability and nurture necessary for the proper raising of their children. A husband is also as responsible as his wife for fulfilling the prescriptions of Ephesians 5. The key to this mutual relationship is provided in Ephesians 5:21, which introduces the entire passage: 'Submit yourselves to one another out of reverence for Christ.' The submission is reciprocal. This is the kind of head the husband is called to be. And when he is this kind of head, he is a real man, a true man, faithful to his divinely ordained nature. A husband's duty to give love to his wife and family does not allow him to intimidate his wife. He then cannot treat his wife as a hired servant. And remember that love is not only a noun, but also a verb.

## 4. The Responsibility of the Wife

Saint Paul says: 'Wives, submit yourselves unto your own husbands, as unto the Lord… As the Church is subject unto Christ, so let the wives be subject to their own husbands in everything.' (Eph 5:22, 24).

Within the church, hierarchical relations are established both by origin (divinely conferred baptism and ordination) and by function (the specific ministry to be assumed by the fourfold hierarchy of bishop, priest, deacon and layperson). Hierarchy presupposes, and in fact requires, the essential equality of its constituent members, and equality that derives from the fact that each member is created in the image of God and that each one is called in equal density to attain to the divine likeness. The same is true within the family for the specific roles of father, mother and offspring. As the 'house tables' in Eph 5:21-6:4 and Col 3:18-22 indicate, those roles concern duties and responsibilities of those who share equally the new life in Jesus Christ. They in no way suggest that any one role is ontologically or spiritually superior to any other.

## 5. The Characteristics of a Successful Marriage

The aim of Christian marriage is eternal life in Heaven with Jesus Christ. The obedience is actually a catalyst for Christian perfection. Christ Himself is the most perfect example of obedience, for it was through His obedience to the will of His Father that He went unto suffering and death for our sakes, and led us from sin to freedom and salvation. In the most mature, highly developed and spiritual marriages, the relationship of a man and a woman evolves into one of mutual obedience.

Experience tells us that two people get married and immediately begin to discover how very different they are. We do not really even begin to know ourselves until we are married. We live too close to ourselves. It really takes someone else to help us to see ourselves what we really are.

In a good marriage, husband and wife share their burdens with one another without reservation, without having to worry about how the other person will react, and without having to keep up a front. True love does not force itself on anyone, and it does not force change; it evokes growth. How? By accepting one's spouse as he or she is. When we marry, we do not sign up to change the other person; we just agree to love him as he is. The best thing a husband can do to change his wife, or vice-versa, is to change himself, to correct his own faults, in keeping with Christ's instructions to His followers. Anyone who is not ready to place his spouse ahead is not ready for marriage.

If you fit the first button into the first hole of your suit, all the other buttons will fall in their proper place. But if the first button is placed in the second hole, nothing will come out right. It is a matter of putting first thing in first place, of keeping priorities straight. Husbands, if you put your wives first, everything else will fall into its proper place in the marriage relationship. Wives, if you put your husbands first, everything else will fall into its proper place in the marriage relationship.

A successful marriage has many characteristics. The three most important are these:

*Praise:* no marriage can be proper if there is no praise. Everyone in life needs to feel appreciated at some point by someone. And nothing can kill love faster than continual criticism.

*Forgiveness:* forgiveness is essential for a happy marriage. It should be there every single day.

*Time:* a successful marriage takes time. It does not happen overnight. It must grow. It comes through considerable effort and struggle.

No marriage is so good that it cannot be better, and no marriage is so bad that it cannot be improved, provided that the persons involved are willing to grow together by God's grace toward the maturity of Christ, who came not to be served but to serve.

An absolutely essential requirement for a good marriage is the capacity to grow up. When I was a child, observed Saint Paul, I thought as a child. I spoke as a child, I understood as a child. But when I became a man, I put away childish things. How essential it is to a happy marriage to put away childish things. How important it is to pray every day: 'O God, help me to grow up, to look beyond myself, to realise the needs and feelings of my wife/husband and to accept the responsibility God has laid upon me.'

# 9

## RESPONSIBLE LEADERSHIP IN EDUCATION AND DEVELOPMENT. AN AFRICAN PERSPECTIVE

*J.N.K. Mugambi, Kenya*

### 1. Conceptual Clarifications

This paper explores the themes of responsible leadership in 'education' and 'development' from the perspective of applied ethics. In philosophical discourse, ethics deals with values, norms and attitudes. Applied ethics has to do with the practices derived from these three ingredients of ethics. The words 'education' and 'development' are two of the most over-used, misused and abused labels today. Too often, 'education' has been used as a synonym for 'schooling' and 'literacy', especially with reference to the so-called 'developing' countries. At the same time, 'development' has been commonly used as an indicator of the extent to which a former colony has adopted the North Atlantic mode of industrial production, economic organisation and political governance. In this era of 'globalisation,' there is great need for open discussion and critique on these words, and the processes they are intended to describe. Unfortunately, these words are often taken for granted in discourses on 'education' and 'development,' while they presuppose a wide variety of meanings and connotations. In the following pages it will be shown that 'education' is a cultural process through which individuals are socialised to become responsible adults within the community.

The goals of 'education', as defined here, are latent and presupposed within the community's self-understanding. In contrast, 'schooling' is an institution-based process of inculcating knowledge and skills to achieve specific objectives. Schools, colleges and universities are the places where 'schooling' is provided. The veracity and validity of those objectives is not open to question by the teachers and the learners. It is structured within the policy formulation.

From an African perspective, these two words ('education' and 'development') as commonly used are externally defined and superimposed. For this reason, African countries are often described as 'developing' while those of the North Atlantic are described as 'developed'. It is never specified when a country becomes 'developed' because the pace-setters and referees of 'development' are always changing the goal-posts. It appears that with this kind of rhetoric, former colonies will never become 'developed,' unless and until they become synchronised with the dominant economies. It is in this context that the former colonies of Africa, Caribbean and the Pacific (ACP) are economically tied to the European Union, whose dominant members are the respective former colonial powers.

The GNP and GDP indicators of 'development' are macro-economic statistics which do not portray the micro-economic and the local cultural specifics of the peoples in each country. In the annual UNDP *Human Development Report*, countries are grouped in clusters, as if 'development' means one thing to 'developed' countries and another to the 'developing' countries. The categorisation also groups the countries of northern Africa together with the Arab countries of West Asia. The phrase 'Sub-Sahara' Africa has become part of the UNDP vocabulary. No other region is labeled on the basis of a desert, a forest, or a prairie! What is the significance of the Sahara Desert in international economics and politics? The logic of this categorisation is inconsistent. Some countries are grouped together by race; others are grouped together by religion; while the rest are in one category because they are 'developed'. Such inconsistency in categorising the world's nations betrays the prejudice of those responsible for labeling the nations and peoples of this world. If the poor and the weak nations of the world had the power to name and label the world, they certainly would use different labels. But the power to name the world is vested in those who are able to exert themselves over the rest. Thus the poor and the weak cannot name themselves. They have to be named by others!

During the 2002 World Summit on Sustainable Development (WSSD) in Johannesburg, a set of 'Millennium Development Goals' were formulated and proposed with targets and indicators to be reached by 2015. These goals are not derived from the thinking of ordinary men and women in villages and towns across Africa and elsewhere. Nor are they the result of debates in the parliaments of the world. They are objectives for lobby groups, most of which are from Europe and North America. One of those goals is 'alleviation of poverty'. There are no Millennium Development Goals for the 'developed' countries to meet. Are they expected to continue developing? Or are they to 'slow down' and stagnate waiting for the 'developing' countries to catch up? If the only requirement is for them to make donations, grants and loans to 'help' the poor 'reduce' or 'alleviate' poverty, the chasm between the affluent and the destitute will continue to increase. Most of the rhetoric about 'alleviating' or 'reducing' poverty has more to do with charity than with equity.[1]

## 2. Historical Background

The constitutions of former African colonies that became sovereign nations during the 1960s, stated in the Preamble that the main objective of the State was to 'eradicate poverty, ignorance and disease.' By the year 2002 (when the WSSD was convened) nearly forty years later, this objective had not been achieved. On the contrary, poverty increased rather than decreased. Now the 'global agenda' under the 'Millennium Development Goals' is to 'reduce' or 'alleviate' poverty, rather than to 'eradicate' it. When, and why, did the 'developers' give up? Why did the first attempt fail? What are the guarantees for the success of this second attempt? One of the conditions for the success of this second initiative is that the 'developed' countries should honour their commitment to contribute 0.7 percent of their respective Gross Domestic Product (GDP) towards the 'poverty reduction' strategies. This target of 0.7 percent was set in the 1970s within the context of the UN Conference on Trade and Development (UNCTAD). It was never fulfilled by any of the industrialised countries which form the Organisation for Economic Cooperation and Development (OECD). There is no indication of any willingness or readiness on the part of these nations to meet the target even this time. Nor are there any coercive mechanisms to compel any nation to comply.

It seems that the rhetoric in international forums is often as distant from actual local realities as to be an irrelevant luxury, for a rather small globe-trotting elite. The 'Millennium Development Goals' are a 'dead letter' even before the strategy is launched. It is an open question whether these goals can be internalised in thought and action among ordinary individuals and communities across the world. Ordinary people do not have the statistical vocabulary to quantify and qualify the discourse on Millennium Development Goals.

The economic and technological achievements of the nations of Europe and North America (and those of Japan, India and China) were neither induced nor accelerated by external forces and agencies. They were not the result of a Declaration in an international conference. Nor are they the fruits of donations and grants by affluent nations to destitute ones. Rather, those achievements are the result of internal cultural responses to needs, challenges and problems of ordinary people. The eighteenth century industrial 'revolution' in Europe was internally propelled. In the twentieth century, China has had to institute cultural self-isolation in order to consolidate its internal capacity for technological innovation. During that period, a process of national reeducation for self-reliance helped the Chinese build the technical capacity which has proved an important asset after the 'globalisation' of trade and industry. Owing to that earlier strategy, China has now one of the fastest national economies in the world.

Likewise, in the 1940s India began with cottage industries which were intended to serve local communities in meeting their technical requirements for basic needs such as food, shelter, clothing, footwear, fuel, water, transportation and health. The national education policy was deliberately designed to promote local creativity and innovation for local consumption.

After the Second World War, the Marshall Plan was launched to facilitate the reconstruction of the destroyed infrastructure of the nations of Japan and Europe (especially West Germany). Under this plan, those nations received massive support for rebuilding their cities, infrastructures, industries, agricultural and social systems. They were guaranteed markets for their manufactured goods to Europe and North America. Their security was also guaranteed against any external threats that might result from the Cold War. In contrast, the decolonisation of Africa in the 1960s was not accompanied by any such special arrangements. Instead, loans were heaped upon the young sovereign nations at exorbitant interest, making it impossible for any of those nations to repay. The nations of South America suffered the same fate from the 1950s. The loans had to be repaid in 'hard' currencies, while the 'soft' local currencies were arbitrarily devalued making it impossible for these fragile and vulnerable economies to grow.[2]

These countries were destined to continue producing raw materials for the industries of the OECD. They would have to pay for imported manufactured agricultural and industrial inputs with poorly priced raw materials. Policies of import substitution did not work, because it was assumed that these countries were, of necessity, created to be producers of raw materials and importers of manufactured products. The producers could not set the price for their raw materials; nor could they dictate the price of their imports. They remained losers, both ways. After forty years, these countries had become much poorer than they had been under colonial rule. Thus the pauperisation of the nations of Africa, Caribbean and Pacific (ACP) was by design, not by accident. The 'Millennium Development Goals' will not change the relative distance between the affluent and the destitute. The strategy is not intended to reduce that distance, but to increase it. By 2015, the chasm between the industrialised and the destitute nations will be much deeper and wider than it was in 2002, when the 'Millennium Development Goals' were proposed. This is because there is no determination on the part of the affluent nations, to fundamentally change the relationship between the so-called 'developed' and the so-called 'developing' nations of this world. As long as *economic apartheid* is practiced, the chasm will continue to increase. Thus the ostensible rhetoric to 'alleviate' or 'reduce' poverty has the impact of increasing dependence and indebtedness on the part of the already destitute nations and peoples. Fair trade is a much more realistic and effective means of dealing with poverty than charity.[3]

## 3. National Debts and Poverty-Reduction Strategies

The campaigns launched by some North Atlantic voluntary agencies to persuade their respective governments to 'cancel' the debts owed to the industrialised countries by the poor ones have shown that there is hardly any readiness or willingness to remove the yoke of indebtedness on the necks of the same poor people whose poverty is to be 'alleviated'. Thus the poor must remain poor. The 'best' that can be done is to make their poverty a little 'bearable'. Under the World Trade Organisation's (WTO) rules and regulations, the poor countries are required to open their markets for manufactured goods from the industrialised countries at the same time that high tariffs are imposed on both their agricultural and manufactured products, making it impossible for them to compete in the global marketplace. The huge profits reaped by the industrialised countries from this unfair global trade regime are used to finance charity and relief disbursements within the global strategy of 'alleviating poverty'. Such disbursements help to mop up excess liquidity in the OECD, rather than to increase wealth in the destitute nations. Mopping up excess liquidity is a prudent tool of financial management. But it is not a tool for creating wealth among the poor. It risks increasing dependency among the recipients and destroying the capacity of individuals and communities to survive under difficult local conditions. The disbursements create artificial 'needs' and 'wants' which are external to the local economy. When the disbursements dry up, the communities find themselves destitute.

Here is an illustration. In central Kenya, coffee prices slumped in the late 1990s. The local farmers' co-operative societies through which coffee berries were processed had formed Savings and Credit Cooperatives (SACCO) to help the farmers. In the context of the collapse of the coffee industry, these credit bodies continued to lend the farmers money to meet such basic needs as payment of school fees and hospital bills. Since there was little or no income from the coffee produce to service the debts, the farmers became increasingly indebted. By the time the coffee prices rise again, many of those peasants will be so heavily indebted that they will find it difficult to recover economically. In the meantime, many of the peasants became disillusioned by the coffee industry, and abandoned their small coffee plantations. It would have been logical for the peasants to diversify their agricultural activities away from coffee production, and refrain from reliance on the credit facilities without any guarantee of adequate incomes from coffee to support comfortable livelihoods.[4]

International banking ensures that the affluent will become opulent, while the poor will deteriorate to destitution. Already, the cost of banking in the transnational banks in a country like Kenya is so high that a poor person finds it cheaper to bury his money in the ground or put it in a box. One needs huge minimum deposits which the poor people can neither meet nor sustain. At the same time, the cost of borrowing is so high that the terms of repayment make it almost impossible for the borrowers to create wealth and get away from poverty. Many borrowers spend the most productive part of their lives servicing the debts they have contracted for mortgages and other needs. It is ironic that loan interest rates are much higher in African countries than in the countries where the transnational banks originate. Even in the micro-credit schemes intended to help poor people, the interest rates are much higher than in the countries from which the funds are disbursed. Thus the 'alleviation of poverty' has become big business. The poor have to remain poor, for the rich to get richer.

In the mean time, offshore and private banking makes it possible for the elite across the world to instantaneously transfer funds across borders without any consideration of the impact of such transfers on local economies. The financial crisis in South East Asia in the late 1990s is a clear illustration of this point. The world is occasionally treated to media clips of political leaders who, after their death, are ostensibly reported to have stashed huge sums of money in private and offshore banks. Why is the disclosure done after death when no action can be taken? What is the ethical justification of such accounts? It would make sense to institute an international Convention to require that leaders should bank their money within their respective borders. Such a convention would ensure that national taxes and incomes are not surreptitiously transferred to other countries while the local citizens are left struggling with inflation. Such measures are much more effective in 'alleviating' or 'reducing' poverty than charity and relief disbursements.

## 4. The African Context

Today, 'education' and 'development' are defined in terms of adjustment to 'economic globalisation,' a concept which has no conceptual equivalent in many local languages. In tropical Africa, for example, colonial rule and the Christian missionary enterprise both undermined the traditional ways and means of socialisation. Through indoctrination these forces superimposed European values, norms and attitudes and practices on African individuals and communities. The colonial administrators' objective in this strategy was to form an African elite to facilitate subjugation. For many missionaries, on the other hand, traditional African values, norms, attitudes and practices were considered repugnant to their understanding of 'Christian' life, thought and belief. Preparation for salvation in heaven was measured in terms of the extent to which an African individual or community adopted the cultural norms of the missionary in charge. To missionaries, 'conversion' was another word for 'civilisation'. Thus the missionary curriculum for prospective African converts portrayed the imperial metropolis as the gateway to 'heaven'.

The impact of this combined onslaught on the African cultural and religious heritage was devastating. Schooling became the means through which Africans should be alienated from their own selves, their history, cultural and religious heritage. This colonial and missionary legacy has lingered on and persisted long after the attainment of national sovereignty. The curriculum at all levels of schooling has placed emphasis on ideas, beliefs and theories developed mainly in the North Atlantic, while denigrating the heritage of the majority of people who still live according to traditional values and norms. Textbooks and reference works, especially in secondary and tertiary levels, continue to be imported from Europe and North America. Through schooling, the African cultural and religious heritage is portrayed as a hindrance to 'development'. An African becomes more and more alienated from one's culture and history as one rises in academic achievement. Thus the most 'schooled' African individual is also the most alienated from one's own culture. [5]

In contrast, most societies which are considered 'developed' place great emphasis on their respective cultural and religious traditions. No society can be 'developed' unless and until its education system takes seriously its people's long history, culture and religion. To emphasise this insight, John Garang in his Address on 9 January 2005 during the Signing the Comprehensive Peace Agreement for Sudan, traced the history of the Sudanese from the biblical story of Creation at the Garden of Eden. [6] While it is possible to dismiss such an interpretation of national history as 'myth,' it is also possible to appreciate the power of myth in providing a people with reference points and signposts in their history. Factual accuracy is not essential for myths and legends. Yet without myths and legends a nation cannot sustain its identity. Cultural development begins when a people becomes conscious of the necessity to critique its own past and present. Constructive cultural and religious self-criticism should be the foundation of progress. This fact applies to all peoples, irrespective of race, place, religion or historical period. The former colonies of Africa, Caribbean and the Pacific cannot be an exception.

Development cannot be superimposed from outside a culture. The European Renaissance, which is the foundation of European modernity, evolved from within the cultural and religious self-critique. It did not abandon European traditions. Rather, the European Renaissance was a revival and re-interpretation of the European cultural and religious heritage. Likewise, Japan's technological prowess is based on a re-affirmation of the cultural and religious heritage of that nation's peoples. The same could be said of the newly industrialising countries, such as India, China, South Korea, Indonesia, Thailand and Malaysia. Perhaps one of the factors hindering technological progress in tropical Africa is the failure to incorporate African values, norms, attitudes and practices in the 'development' planning processes. If this analysis is correct, then the technological crisis in tropical Africa may be viewed as primarily ethical, rather than financial. It is not the lack of a resource base that causes technological stagnation or retrogression. Africa is rich in a wide diversity of resources. The colonial legacy has ensured that these resources are extracted for the benefit of the industries mainly, though not exclusively, in the North Atlantic. Fair trade, rather than massive 'aid' holds the key to prosperity in the former colonies of Africa, Caribbean and the Pacific.[7]

## 5. Education as a Process of Cultural Socialisation

All people in every culture have evolved a process (education) through which their members of the younger generation are socialised to understand and appreciate the values, norms, attitudes and practices of the community to which they respectively belong. This process involves transmission of the knowledge, skills and experience accumulated over generations for the survival of the community. Colonial subjugation interferes with this process as the invaders impose their own 'education' process on the conquered subjects. Such subjugation was experienced in various parts of tropical Africa, which were occupied by various European imperial powers following the Berlin Conference of 1884. Without any regard to the cultural unity and integrity of various African communities, the colonies were arbitrarily established in accordance with the clout wielded by various claimants to African territory. Britain and France took the largest share, followed by Germany, Belgium, Portugal, Spain and Italy. The USA continued to wield influence in Liberia, which had been established as a home for former slaves which were no longer needed as industrial machinery replaced manual labour in plantations and factories. Literacy skills are important but not essential to the process of education. It is possible to be 'highly schooled' and 'poorly educated'. This seems to be the situation applicable to the African elite today. Many have acquired high academic knowledge but are unable to relate it to the cultural and religious heritage of their respective communities and nations. At its best, the process of education is the responsibility of parents, teachers, priests, peers and the society generally. Education is multi-faceted, multi-dimensional and multi-disciplinary, concerned with the ends for which an individual ought to live. On the other hand, schooling is often specialised, narrow-minded and means-driven. Formal school examinations are intended to ensure that the learner has acquired the knowledge and skills specified in the syllabus. Effective 'education' is best achieved through informal learning. It is long-term and ends-driven.

It is unfortunate that in tropical Africa 'schooling' has been substituted for 'education'. In that substitution, the roles of parents and priests have been relegated to the background, while those of teachers and rulers are elevated. Most children and young people enrolled in school and college spend nine months every year under the instruction of their teachers and tutors. During the remaining period neither the parents nor the priests have adequate time to interact with the youth. Consequently, young people join peer groups which greatly influence the shaping of character and personality. The advertising industry promotes individualism and consumerism in a cultural context where there is little or no purchasing power. Urban norms are commended while rural life is condemned. Consequently, many young people flock to urban centers, where there is no infrastructure to absorb them. Informal urban settlements have become the rule rather than the exception in Africa's towns and cities. The majority of dwellers in these informal settlements are young people. Many of them have received basic schooling in rural areas, in a curriculum which praises urban lifestyles and shuns rural norms. From an ethical perspective, it is important to appreciate the role of schooling in the rural-urban influx. Likewise, corruption can be explained with reference to the lack of coherence between the knowledge and skills acquired at school on the one hand, and the moral values inculcated at home and church, on the other.

## 6. Schooling as an Instrument of Cultural Alienation

The following Table outlines some of the indicators of cultural alienation which arise from the substitution of 'schooling' for 'education.' The left column represents traditional African education, while the right column represents post-colonial African schooling. The details are self-explanatory, and the contrast is clear. The bottom row shows corruption as one of the logical consequences of schooling. By implication, corruption can best be eradicated through education, not through legislative and punitive measures. The reason is that as long as schooling portrays public goods and systems as external to individual values and interests, individuals will be tempted to take advantage and extract as much as they can from public resources and convert it for private use. Although *legislation* against corruption is important, it should supplement rather than substitute for *education*. Raising awareness against corruption should be presupposed in the values, norms and attitudes of the entire education system. Hard work should be praised and rewarded while laziness and underhand deals are condemned. Individualism, which schooling encourages, works against the common good in a social environment whose legacy is divisive. Communalism, which traditional education presupposes, operates as an alternative social security apparatus and as a sub-stratum of the official, formal social structure. Under these circumstances, it is very difficult to eradicate corruption. Many members of the elite do not recognise as corruption the strategies often used to by-pass the established bureaucratic procedures in various sectors of governance and industry.

Goran Hyden in his book *No Shortcuts to Progress* observes that it is difficult to synchronise tropical Africa into the global market while the majority of the population presupposes rural communitarian norms and operates a mode of production and consumption which he calls the *economy of affection*. Campaign against corruption in tropical Africa has not yet taken seriously the fact that the norms and values presupposed in economic globalisation are incompatible with those of local economies which have no terms of reference for corruption. Cheating, disguised as profit, seems to be the foundation of the market economy. There are no limits of how much profit should be made. The market economy values a person only as a customer who purchases goods and services. In contrast, the market-place in rural Africa is very different from the main shopping centre in the heart of a town or city. In addition to the exchange of goods through monetary transactions, a village market is the place where the villagers meet to exchange views and sustain their social identity. A prosperous businessman who exploits his customers and makes huge profits is likely to be regarded as an enemy of the people, rather than a 'patron' of the village.

| **Traditional African Education** | **Post-Colonial African Schooling** |
| --- | --- |
| Place of Learning: Home | Place of Learning: School and College |
| Teachers: Parents and Relatives | Teachers: Professionals |

| Traditional African Education | Post-Colonial African Schooling |
|---|---|
| **Knowledge Content:** Distilled from the African heritage | **Knowledge Content:** Imported from Western culture |
| **Skills:** Ways and means of survival | **Skills:** For salaried employment |
| **Techniques:** Apprenticeship | **Techniques:** Theory and experiment |
| **Pedagogy:** Oral and practical | **Pedagogy:** Textual and theoretical |
| **Quality Assurance:** Rites of passage | **Quality Assurance:** Examinations |
| **Values:** Self-esteem and integrity | **Values:** Upward mobility |
| **Beliefs:** From African religious heritage | **Beliefs:** From secular philosophies |
| **Norms:** Co-operation & diligence | **Norms:** Competition and opportunism |
| **Attitudes:** Caring and sharing | **Attitudes:** Individualism and exploitation |
| **Practices:** From each according to ability | **Practices:** According to job-description |
| **Impact:** Mutual responsibility | **Impact:** Selfishness and self-centredness |
| **Consequence:** To each according to need | **Consequence:** Corruption and inefficiency |

Schooling pedagogy tends to presuppose and inculcate the idea that 'modernity' is preferable to 'tradition.' In fact, there is nothing virtuous about modernity, and nothing vicious about tradition. Within every culture there is a creative tension between the past and the future. This creative tension provides the key to innovation. When the transformative tendencies predominate over conservative tendencies, change becomes the acceptable norm. Conservationism is normative whenever the conservative tendencies predominate. It is difficult to induce constructive change through externally imposed values, norms, attitudes and practices. The illustration above shows the negative consequences of externally superimposed schooling which fails to blend traditional values with new ideas and insights.

There is great need for schooling systems in post-colonial Africa to take seriously the traditional values, norms, attitudes and practices as a prerequisite for endogenous development. Such an approach will guarantee that epistemological and technological innovation emanates from the accumulated wisdom and expertise of local communities. All industrialised and industrialising countries have each a national ethos derived from national culture and history, on the basis of which the national curriculum is designed and implemented. Without a national ethos, it is impossible for citizens to evolve national goals and ideals. Globalisation is not a substitute for national and local aspirations. Rather, it is a distraction which fragments local and national initiatives in response to the pressures of advertising and propaganda from the more powerful nations and transnational corporations.

It is ironic that while African countries lag further and further behind in technology, they have become exporters of highly trained personnel, at the same time that they continue to import 'experts' from the industrialised countries. Hundreds of thousands of doctors, nurses, engineers, architects, professors, agriculturalists, economists, accountants, lawyers — continue migrating to the North Atlantic where they can earn higher salaries and enjoy higher standards of living. The campaigns for 'alleviating' or 'reducing' poverty will in the long term be futile, until African countries can train and retain their own experts. The so-called 'brain-drain' is directly related to the content of academic and professional training provided in African schools, colleges and universities, which is almost identical with that provided in the imperial metropolis. The African graduates who take employment abroad find it easier to fit in low-level employment in the host countries, than to become responsible leaders at home. Yet there has been no international Protocol to compensate African countries for the loss they suffer whenever a trained person takes up employment abroad after long and massive investment in education and training. The brain-drain has sometimes been rationalised with the argument that African professionals find it difficult to find employment within the public and private sector of their respective countries. Such an argument proves the point that the academic and professional curriculum is in dire need of reform, so that African academics and professionals can contribute meaningfully and effectively towards wealth creation and technological advancement in their respective nations of their birth. Reliance on expatriates will not, in the long term, 'alleviate' or 'reduce' poverty in Africa.[8]

## 7. Education as Custodian of Tradition and Schooling as Promoter of Modernity

The illustration shows how transformative and conservative tendencies pull against each other in every society. In tropical Africa, schooling has represented the transformative tendencies whereas traditional education has been primarily conservative. In industrialised countries, both the conservative and the transformative tendencies have comparable literary and technical competence. Within the governance structures both tendencies are creatively and constructively present. The tragedy of Africa's social transformation is that cultural resilience is sustained primarily by those with little or no schooling, while the schooled elite associates itself with 'modernity' and alien values, norms, attitudes, tastes and practices. It will be difficult to 'reduce' or 'alleviate' poverty in a context where the tension between tradition and modernity is ultimately destructive rather than reconstructive. Whenever and wherever external forces enter into a culture, a conflict inevitably arises between the foreign and local advocates of the new culture on the one hand and the custodians of the old culture on the other. Such a scenario is evident in most of tropical Africa. The traditional forms of education co-exist with the post-colonial norms of schooling. At home, children are exposed to traditional ways of thought and belief, while at school and church they are indoctrinated to adopt new ideas, creeds and practices.

Unfortunately, schooling and churching are given higher rating than traditional upbringing, even though the latter has cultural roots extending far back into history. One consequence, among others, is the continuing conflict between traditional values and norms on the one hand, and those associated with modernity, on the other. Although the tension between tradition and modernity is typical of all cultures, it is much more acute in those contexts where modernity is associated with imported values and norms that are superimposed upon the traditional ones. [9]

The nations most adversely affected by liberation of trade in cultural services are those whose institutions of schooling are rooted in cultural alienation. Thus countries of Europe and North America are managing to sustain their cultural values and norms at the same time that they import entertainment and leisure services from elsewhere. In Asia, the same can be said of Japan, India and China.

The rites of passage are a dramatic illustration. In central Kenya, since the 1920s there has been conflict between the church and the State on the one hand, and the custodians of traditional norms on the other. This conflict came to the surface over the practice of initiation of adolescents into adulthood. Missionaries wanted the youths to be released by their parents to undergo schooling. Many parents insisted that their traditional norms and practices of socialisation were essential to the preservation of their cultural identity. The missionaries involved colonial authorities to prohibit the practice and enforce the ban. In response, the practice was driven underground, and became one of the grievances in the nationalist struggle against colonial rule. More than seventy years later, a conference was convened in August 2004, at the International Conference Centre, Nairobi specifically to condemn female initiation. Why has it taken so long to eradicate the practice? Although many women participated in the conference on invitation and at the expense of non-governmental organisations, the campaign can hardly succeed until there is readiness and willingness to appreciate the perspective of those communities that find some value in the practice. It should not be surprising if a century after this conflict erupted there will still be campaigns against it. Cultural tradition cannot be eradicated through schooling. It requires a process of re-education. Another illustration is urbanisation. In Europe, rapid urbanisation was the result of the industrial revolution. People flocked into the towns to work in factories, and abandoned the farms which were increasingly mechanised. In tropical Africa, most urban centres during the twentieth century began as colonial administrative stations. Since the colonial economy required Africa to be a source of raw materials, the industrial sector remained undeveloped.

This colonial legacy was inherited by the new sovereign African nations. In the meantime, the school and college curriculum continued to give prominence and preference to the urban mode of life against rural habitation. The consequence has been an influx of schooled young people to the towns and cities, where they have found inadequate infrastructure to accommodate them. Today, most urban centres in tropical Africa contain large informal settlements characterised by shanties within and at the periphery of municipalities. Thus schooling has tended to uproot the African youth from the rural areas in an economy which is primarily agricultural. Reversing the influx from the urban centres back to the rural areas is impossible. Strategies will have to be devised to make rural areas more attractive for habitation, through improvement of infrastructure such as potable water, electricity, telephones, mechanised farming, food-processing and all-weather accessibility. In the long term, rural habitation may be more luxurious than life in urban centres. This is already the case in industrialised countries, where it is prestigious to live in the suburbs. Investment in basic infrastructure in rural Africa can contribute immensely towards the reversal of population flow from urban to rural areas.

## 8. Urbanisation without Secularisation

In Europe and North America urbanisation encouraged secularisation. With migration from the farm to the city, the individual became free from the communal values, norms, attitudes and routine practices which were reinforced by community. As the population became increasingly urban, the communitarian ethic was replaced by individualism. Religion ceased to be the basis for morality, and the employer became more important than the priest. Anonymity became a positive value and norm – as the way of life in town and city. In tropical Africa, informal settlements within the urban centres have more places of worship compared to the rural areas from which the schooled youth are migrating. These places of worship are much more diversified than in the rural areas. In addition to the older Christian denominations introduced by the missionary enterprise, there are independent churches dating from the colonial period, local independent churches initiated by self-styled preachers, and new Pentecostal, Charismatic and Congregational churches exported especially from North America. For example, in Kibera (one of the largest informal settlements in Nairobi) there are more churches than water supply points. Many of these churches are personal 'kiosks' started by enterprising young people who try to provide comfort and a sense of belonging to displaced individuals.[10] The localities within the informal settlements are often concentrations of people from the same rural area, trying to replicate rural norms within the city. Traditional norms, with some improvised modification, are trans-located into the informal settlements. Thus the process of secularisation, as described by such authors as Harvey Cox and Peter Berger, is hardly applicable in the urban centres of tropical Africa.[11]

High church attendance among the urbanite African elite confirms that religiosity does not decline with urbanisation, irrespective of social status and ethnic identity. New denominations of the Congregational, Charismatic and Pentecostal types continue to attract followers from all social strata especially in urban areas. Faith-based organisations both foreign and local participate in the provision of social services in both urban and rural areas. A large proportion of local popular music has religious lyrics and instructions, derived partly from sacred scriptures and partly from religious pedagogy. Thus religion spontaneously permeates the whole of the African social environment. Whereas modernity in the North Atlantic implies a shift form religiosity towards secularism, in Africa it provides new and diverse ways and means of responding to the sacred. Four Abrahamic faiths co-exist with varying intensity from region to region across the whole continent: African religion; Christianity, Islam and Judaism.[12]

| Urban centers in tropical Africa | Urban centers in north Atlantic |
|---|---|
| High religious adherence | Low religious adherence |
| Welfare associations the norm | State social security the norm |
| Small urbanite population | Predominantly urbanite population |
| Strong attachment to ancestral homes | Little or no attachment to ancestral homes |
| High unemployment rates | Low or medium unemployment rates |
| Small industrial sector | Large industrial sector |
| Administered by central government | Administered by autonomous authorities |
| Poor infrastructure | Sophisticated infrastructure |
| Huge gap between richest and poorest | Small gap between richest and poorest |
| Low telephone connectivity | High telephone connectivity |
| Low electric connectivity | High electric connectivity |
| Low water connectivity | High water connectivity |
| Poor transportation infrastructure | Advanced transportation infrastructure |
| Shanty housing for the majority | Permanent housing for the majority |
| Low schooling for the majority | High schooling for the majority |
| Low monthly income for the majority | High monthly income for the majority |
| Poor medical care for the majority | Advanced medical care for the majority |
| Poor leisure industry | Advanced leisure industry |

It is difficult to predict the future of Africa's urban informal settlements. Some countries (such as Tanzania, Nigeria, Malawi and the Ivory Coast) have tried to establish new capital cities, where modernity can become the mode of life. It is instructive to note that the rural-urban influx can be reduced only through educational processes which give prominence and preference to the rural mode of life.

## Conclusion

In this paper it has been shown that endogenous education and development are the most effective means through which individuals and communities can constructively respond to the challenges facing them in an increasingly globalised world. Responsible leadership in education and development demands re-training and re-orientation of all those invloved in preparing the youth for responsible adulthood and responsible citizenship. Schooling and skills training is important but inadequate. Inculcation of moral values, norms and attitudes must become an integral part of the process of education. Only in this way will responsible leadership be enhanced and sustained in the long term. Thus parents must play their full part in education, together with priests and other religious leaders. At the same time, educational and training institutions must include in the core of their syllabi the values, norms and attitudes which are consistent with efficiency and effectiveness in all sectors of the society. I have dealt with this theme in greater detail in my books *From Liberation to Reconstruction* (Nairobi: East African Educational Publishers, 1995) and *Christian Theology and Social Reconstruction* (Nairobi: Acton, 2003). One of the greatest pedagogical challenges in Africa today, is how to reform schooling so that it affirms traditional African values, norms and attitudes while at the same time encouraging innovation, inventiveness and creativity. In the knowledge-based global economy of the future, successful nations will be only those nations whose culture promotes education.

Synchronisation of local African economies with the dominant global capitalism will increase rather than reduce the chasm between the affluent and the destitute. Education as the process of socialisation for responsible citizenship can best be achieved when citizens have a national ethos to bind their social consciousness. The cultivation of such national social consciousness is the primary task of national leaders. Factional and sectarian leadership is ultimately destructive, even when it is intended to promote marginalised sectors of population. Education, at its best, should help the learners to understand and appreciate their actual and potential capabilities in the context of the wider society. In tropical Africa, schooling has tended to emphasise diversity rather than unity, even when unity is self-evident.

The decision to emphasise unity rather than diversity is an ideological choice, not a technical one.[13] The colonial regimes emphasise diversity and differentiation because it helps the colonial administrators to 'divide and rule'. Post-colonial education systems have to consolidate national consciousness through curricula that are designed to emphasise national unity and national destiny without undermining individual and community interests. Global capitalism thrives through transnational advertising and competition. Thus it runs counter to national economic strategies. Ideally, education should help learners at all levels to understand and appreciate the tension between local and national interests on the one hand, and global capitalism on the other. [14]

It is a matter of ethical concern when, under the pretext of 'reducing' or 'alleviating' poverty pauperisation becomes more the rule than the exception in most of the world. All statistical indications at the macro and micro levels suggest that the poor sectors of populations are becoming poorer, relative to the more affluent. In the long term, the world has to face the ethical challenge of choosing between charity and equity. [15]

NOTES

[1]   On Millennium Development Goals see Stein Villumstad, *Reconstruction of Africa. Perspectives from Without and Within*, Nairobi: Acton, 2005.

[2]   Escobar, Arturo, *Encountering Development: The Making and Unmaking of the Third World*, Princeton, NJ: Princeton University Press, 1995, pp. 29ff.

[3]   On this point see Stückelberger, Christoph, *Global Trade Ethics*, Geneva: WCC, 2002.

[4]   Oral interviews, January 2005.

[5]   The conflict between Traditional African Education and Christian Missionary Schooling is one of the enduring themes for African novels, plays and poetry since the 1950s. This point is amply illustrated in novels, plays and poetry authored by prominent African creative writers such as Wole Soyinka, Chinua Achebe, Mongo Beti, Ngugi wa Thiong'o, Okot p'Bitek, John Ruganda, Ayi Kweyi Amah, and others. (See African Writers Series, London: Heinemann Publishers).

[6]   The event was covered live on Kenyan Television and Radio channels.

[7]   For a documentary elaboration of this point see Ghai, Dharam (ed.), *Renewing Social and Economic Progress in Africa*, London: Macmillan, 2000; Devarajan, S. *et al.* (eds), *Aid and Reform in Africa*, Washington DC: The World Bank, 2001.

[8]   On this point see Paul Tiyambe Zeleza, *Manufacturing African Studies*, Dakar: CODESRIA, 2002.

[9]   For further discussion of this point see Mugambi, J.N.K., *Christianity and African Culture*, Nairobi: Acton, 2002, pp. 111-126.

[10]   Kibera Centre for Urban Mission, Carlile College, Nairobi, January 2005.

[11]   Cox, Harvey, *The Secular City*, New York: Penguin, 1965; Berger, Peter, *Rumor of Angels*, New York: Doubleday, 1969.

[12]   The phrase 'Abrahamic Faiths' refers to the common denominator of Judaism, African Religion, Christianity and Islam – all of them base their teachings and practices on what seems to be a 'synoptic' pool of tradition, rooted in ancient Upper Egypt (present Sudan). See Bernal, Martin, *Black Athena*, Vol. 1, New Brunswick: Rutgers University Press, 1987.

[13]   On this point see Makgoba, M. W. (ed.), *African Renaissance*, Cape Town: Tafelberg, 1999.

[14]   Nurnberger, Klaus, *Beyond Marx and Market: Outcomes of a Century of Economic Experimentation*, London: Zed Books, 1998.

[15]   For further discussion of this challenge see my two books, Mugambi, J.N.K., *Christian Theology and Social Reconstruction*, Nairobi: Acton, 2003; *From Liberation to Reconstruction*, Nairobi: EAEP, 1995.

# 10

# HOLISTIC LEADERSHIP IN EDUCATION. AN AFRICAN CALL

*Emmanuel Asante, Ghana*

## Introduction

Education in traditional Africa was, by and large, adapted to local needs. 'The older generation passed on to the young the knowledge, the skills, the mode of behaviour and the beliefs they should have for playing their social roles in adult life.'[1] In that sense education in traditional Africa was both preservative and conservative.

This traditional conception of education, however, was supplanted with the introduction of formal education, particularly the introduction of the Western type of education in Africa by the early Christian missionaries. 'Whereas continuity and survival of the community and its culture were the primary motivations lying behind and goals of Africa traditional education, Western missionary education sought to inculcate European ideals and values that were considered superior.'[2] Western education, in that sense, was negatively transformative. It led to the alienation of the schooled from their people and culture. Western education was by and large used as a tool to replace the 'backward' African culture. This assumption is reflected in the colonial education policies which were largely unsympathetic to the African culture and its values.

Needless to say, education has several reference points. It may refer to:

- what parents, teachers, and schools do, i.e. the activity of educating – what is at stake here is the teaching process;
- what goes on in the learner, i.e. the process of becoming educated – here one is touching on the learning process;
- what the learner gets as the end product, i.e. the content of education; or
- what the discipline of education is about, i.e. the study of above.

## 1. Different Philosophies of Education

Underlying any conception of education is a philosophy of education. A people's philosophy of education depends on what they have in mind, in respect of the objective of education as well as the first principle from which their philosophy of education derives. This first principle, normally, includes the people's theories of values (axiology) as well as their theories of reality (ontology) and of knowledge (epistemology). The traditional African conception of education, on the one hand, borders on somewhat idealistic and pragmatic philosophies of education. The educational goals of idealism and pragmatism may be presented as follows:

- the preservation of cultural, social and spiritual excellence;
- the promotion of things of the spirit;
- the development of ideal humanity and ideal society;
- the organisation and reorganisation of experience as adaptation to life and its environment;
- practical adaptation of needs rather than intellectual excellence alone.

*Pragmatism* holds that knowledge is relative, instrumental, practical and problem solving. As we shall see, in traditional African conception education was relative, practical, and instrumental. In that sense education in traditional Africa was pragmatic.

## 2. Idealism and Realism of Western Education

The Western conception of education, on the other hand, borders on idealism but it goes beyond that in that the Western conception of education also reflects realistic philosophy of education. In addition to what we have already observed in respect of *idealism* in relation to Africa, idealism holds the following principles which are highlighted and emphasised in Western education:

- the world is dependent on the mind or intellect;
- the truth is objective and discovered.

These principles of idealism are ignored or given less emphasis in the African conception of education.

*Realism*, which also informs Western education, holds that the goal of education is the transmission of the following:

- universal truths independent from minds or points of view (the intellectual emphasis);

- cultural values or excellence – education should make one aware of the real world including values and potentialities of life;
- truth is objective and discovered. The rational man is the one who discovers truth. [3]

Whereas both the African and Western conception of education are informed by idealism as a philosophy of education, as we have noted, they differ in terms of where they place the emphasis. African idealist philosophy of education places the emphasis on intuition, subjectivity, preservation and conservation of culture and values. The Western idealist and realist philosophies of education place the emphasis on precision, intellect, objectivity, discovery, transformation, exploitation, conservation, globalisation and assimilation of culture and values of the educator.

The African traditional philosophy of education tends to be *essentialist*. Here education is seen as the transmission of cultural essentials with a view to perpetuating the culture and one's identity. Personal identity is more important than the factual and self-knowledge more important than world knowledge. Education is geared towards practical adaptation to needs and the realisation of the self as a community entity.

In contrast, the Western philosophy of education, though also essentialist, tend to be dominated by *perennialism* and *progressivism*. Here education is not only seen as the transmission of perennial or absolute and universal truths, it is also seen 'as the process of intelligent problem solving, with emphasis on precision and method.' [4] What is emphasised in respect of Western education is intellectual excellence and universal or representational education. Thus there is a big gap between the Western and African conceptions of education. The Western education which is experienced in Africa in terms of schooling is hardly sympathetic to the values, norms, attitudes and practices of traditional Africa. In the words of J.N.K. Mugambi, 'schooling pedagogy tends to presuppose and inculcate the idea that "modernity" is preferable to "tradition".' [5]

In spite of this, the general outlook of post colonial Africa is still traditional. This means that, in spite of its transformative tendency, schooling, understood in terms of the Western conception of education, unsympathetic to African traditional values as it is, has hardly succeeded in facilitating authentic social change among traditional Africans. Thus one agrees with Mugambi that 'it is difficult to induce constructive change through externally imposed values, norms, attitudes and practices.' [6] This goes to stress 'the negative consequences of externally superimposed schooling which fails to blend traditional values with new ideas and insights.' [7]

## 3. The Way Forward

In the face of the problems outlined above in respect of Western education and its negative impact on traditional Africa, what should be the way forward? Mugambi, in his paper, called for 'schooling system in post colonial Africa to take seriously the traditional values, norms, attitudes and practices as a prerequisite for endogenous development.'[8] According to Mugambi, 'one of the greatest pedagogical challenges in Africa today is how to reform schooling so that it affirms traditional African values, norms and attitudes while at the same time encouraging innovation, inventiveness and creativity.'[9]

One could not agree more with Mugambi on this. The option is not the rejection of Western education. Indeed, it does post-colonial Africa no good to reject Western education. The issue is how to use Western education, what Mugambi has referred to as schooling, to enhance traditional African values, norms and practices in the context of dynamism of culture and globalisation. In other words, the issue is not to choose between traditional African education and post-colonial African schooling with their different pedagogical approaches and epistemologies. The issue is how to blend the two in the nexus of post-colonial education that will be both critically transformative and conservative, and holistic.

What philosophy of education will facilitate such a blend of education?

## 4. Pragmatism

In my view, the philosophy of education that will best facilitate the blend of education we have in view is *pragmatism* critically appropriated within the context of educational *holism*.

In the context of *pragmatic* philosophies of education, the goal of education is:

- the successful organisation and reorganisation of experience as adaptation to life. Here science will not be seen as a means to a detached end but as that which leads to the holistic becoming of the human;
- the promotion of the growth of a life which is fruitful and inherently significant – critically appropriated, one would say that this calls for the knowledge of God as well as the knowledge of the human and the natural order;
- the process through which the needed social transformation may be accomplished;
- the practical adaptation to present needs rather than intellectual excellence alone.

Pragmatism as we noted earlier holds that knowledge is:

- relative and instrumental rather than universal or representational – the value of knowledge of the past lies in its usefulness for the present;
- experimental problem-solving inquiry, a practical activity: knowing how, rather than knowing that or correct intellectual judgment or idea as such.

In pragmatism 'truth is a "thing done" (pragmatism), a function of practical value, made to happen, i.e. brought about rather than discovered to be the case.' [10]


## 5. Holistic Education

All of this, in my view, boils down to what has been observed by some contemporary scholars as holistic education. Writing on the subject of holistic education, a commission of the World Council of Churches (WCC) observed as follows:

'The concept of holism and holistic education refers to a worldview or theoretical position that opposes reductionism, positivism, and the Cartesian dualism of self and world with an emphasis on the ultimate unity, relatedness, and inherent meaningfulness of all existence. Holism draws upon newly emerging ecological and systems approaches in science as well as the "perennial philosophy" – the core wisdom of most of the world's spiritual traditions. Holistic educators attempt to address the fragmentation, alienation, competition, violence and gross materialism that pervade much of life in the late twentieth century. A holistic education seeks to heal the many divisions our civilisation has induced between mind and body, intellect and emotion, rationality and intuition, science and art, individual and community, humanity and the natural world.' [11]

As the above statement indicates, holistic education is intended to serve a number of purposes:

- as a critique of the dominant paradigm of education informed and defined by a mechanistic worldview, which is a paradigm of education which continues to 'instrumentalise and dichotomise people and their relationship with each other, with the earth and the divine.' [12]
- as an alternative to the existing paradigm of education, holistic education affirms the different ways of living and acting by embracing 'the quest for meaning and knowledge, rooted in the values of wholeness and healing'; it 'affirms individuals as persons in the context of community and communities as a whole.' [13] In

that sense, holistic education seeks to be all encompassing, drawing from a variety of traditions while affirming the centrality and unity of all creation in God.

Holistic education as espoused by the WCC operates on the following eight principles:[14]

1. 'Belief that it is God who is the Creator and Sustainer of life.' This principle forms the basis of the affirmation of the centrality and unity of all creation in God.
2. 'Education is for transformation.' Education must facilitate social transformation – transformation of persons and communities. It also requires 'the transformation of educational institutions, policies and activities resulting in holistic practices at all levels; multi-disciplinary perspectives; a focus on wholeness in human development.'
3. Education should aim at 'the development of the whole person in community.' 'This includes physical, social, moral aesthetic, creative and spiritual aspects as well as intellectual and vocational.' Holistic education, in this sense goes beyond the cognitive dimension which dominates conventional education and 'encourages the quest for meaning by introducing a holistic view of the planet, life on Earth, and the emerging world community.'
4. Education should honour 'the uniqueness and creativity of persons and communities on the basis of theft interconnectedness.' Here, holistic education 'affirms that we can build true learning communities in which people learn together from each other's differences, learn to value their own personal strengths, and are empowered to help one another.'
5. Education should enable 'active participation in a world community.' Holistic education, as indicated by this principle, 'promotes ways of mutual understanding and respect of the existing diversity of cultures and religions...' It seeks to understand how this diversity can enrich us but also how diversity can cause conflict. Thus 'holistic education includes methods of conflict management to establish conditions for peace and justice at all levels.'
6. Education should affirm 'Spirituality as being the core of life and hence central to education.' Holistic education focuses on 'those human depth dimensions that account for a spiritual basis of reality.' Spirituality, according to the WCC document 'is a state of connectedness to all life, honouring diversity in unity. It is an experience of being, belonging and caring. It is sensitivity and compassion, joy and hope. It is the harmony between the inner life and the outer life. It is the sense of wonder and reverence for the mysteries of the universe...'
7. Education should promote 'a new praxis (reflection and action) of knowing, of teaching, and of learning.' Under this principle, the

document affirmed that teaching is a vocation 'requiring artistic sensitivity and scientifically grounded practice.' Holistic education, in that sense, calls for mutual attentiveness in respect of teachers and learners. Both 'teachers and learners are mutually accountable, above all, to seeking a meaningful understanding of the world.' Here both teachers and learners are seen as partners in the project of education.

8. Finally the document affirms that 'holistic education relates to, and interacts, with differing perspectives and approaches' of education. The understanding here is that holistic education draws from the diverse educational approaches: 'Critical pedagogy, traditional pedagogy, feminist pedagogy, constructivism and transformative learning theories and global education.'

All the above-mentioned educational approaches and theories raise some fundamental questions with respect to us as human beings in communities. Thus a holistic approach to education can hardly ignore any of them. Hence holistic education, understood as an all-encompassing educational approach, brings the different educational approaches together in the nexus of holism.

A comparison of the holistic educational paradigm with the prevailing mechanistic educational paradigm brings out the following (again we draw critically from the WCC document): [15]

| Mechanistic education paradigm | Holistic education paradigm |
|---|---|
| *Interdisciplinary* <br> Attempts to integrate accumulated knowledge according to the logic of mechanistic science. | *Transdisciplinary* <br> Argues against isolated scientific disciplines and integrates within sciences and within a broader scale of fields of human knowledge such as art, customs, traditions, and spirituality. It is a global integration of knowledge. |
| *Fragmentation* <br> Knowledge is broken into parts. | *Integration* <br> Knowledge is interconnected. |
| *Systemic* <br> Emphasises structure. Manifestation of an underlying process. | *Holistic* <br> Emphasises process. Stresses the dynamism of the entire web of relationship. |

*Empirical-analytic*
Ascertains the simple elements or components of a given reality and studies the simple elements on their own. Everything exists in isolation.

*Empirical-analytic holistic*
Integrates science and spirituality in an expanded framework of human experience. Everything exists in relationship, in a context of connectedness and meaning.

---

*Development of thought*
Accumulation of knowledge and information. Emphasis is on literature and content knowledge.

*Development of intelligence*
Sees the essence or truth of things. Sees things holistically. Recognises the limitations of thought. Experience of things.

---

*Scientific-dogmatic*
Search for the external order in our world (objectivism). Elimination of non-scientific knowledge as false or inappropriate in an educational setting.

*Secular-spiritual*
Search for the inner-order within consciousness (subjectivism). Deep respect for diversity and the inner experience of individuals.

---

*Reductionist*
Rejects subjective knowledge or the inner experiences of people. Reduces knowledge to unrelated components.

*Integral*
Affirms an inherent interdependence of evolving theory, research and practice. Integration of knowledge. The interface of science, art, spirituality and traditions.

---

*Focused on teaching*
Teaching is transmission of knowledge or an assimilative tool. Learning is imbibition of knowledge.

*Focused on learning*
Teaching is a transformative tool, a tool for the enhancement of being. Learning is a creative and artistic process involving the emotional, physical, social and spiritual levels of human awareness.

---

*Paradigm of simplification*
Emphasises atomism in education.

*Paradigm of complexity*
Emphasises holism interconnectedness of knowledge.

---

*Predatory conscience*
Promotes exploitative life style. Discriminating. Assimilative.

*Ecological conscience*
Cares for the whole of the cosmos. Affirms the intrinsic values of all beings of whatever species. Interconnect, integrative.

The characteristic nature of the holistic education paradigm in contrast with that of the prevailing mechanistic education paradigm, as presented above, clearly indicates that 'holistic education creates the pedagogical conditions for an unfolding of the inner potential of the [learner]'.[16] We can hardly know the outer world, the planet, if we did not have an internal knowledge of ourselves. Mechanistic education affirms that we can know the planet without knowing ourselves. Holistic education affirms the contrary view. 'Only by knowing ourselves we can know the planet.'

## Conclusion

It is obvious from the foregoing that we have no other option in respect of ethical education than that of the holistic paradigm.

As Christians committed to ethical leadership in education, we naturally assume a fundamental commitment to peace, justice, integration, freedom and solidarity as an integral part of our educational commitment. The ethical values must be connected to the concrete educational actions we promote.

In our educational leadership, we must engage the whole person and not only the mind, given that the deepest learning is that which involves the whole person. The whole person can hardly be a whole person without the community which informs and defines the person. Human beings are gregarious. It means that a person's wholeness is defined by the community as the context of the individual human being into consideration.

'Holism asserts that everything exists in relationship, in a context of connection and meaning and that any change or event causes realignment, however slight, throughout the entire pattern.' Holistic education, in the sense of education informed by holism, promotes the quality of human relationship within a community characterised with diversity and individuality. Embedded in holistic education are ethical values that transform the educational process with a view to human responsibility. Tampered with ethical commitments, our educational projects must be holistically inclusive, and intolerant of the discrimination evident in mechanistic education, especially in the area of gender, race, religion, sexual orientation, physical and material limitations and economic inequalities.

John Dewey, one of the United States' most famous pragmatist educators, is reported to have said : 'The objective of a progressive education is the correction of unfair privilege and unfair deprivation.'[17] According to Henri Levi, 'the most complete application of this principle is to create an educational system that intervenes in Lire social system so that there is no systematic relation between a person's social origins or gender and his or her ultimate social attainments.'[18] The task of holistic education is formidable but is not insurmountable.

NOTES

[1]   Busia, K.A.A., *Purposeful Education for Africa*, The Hague: Mouton, 1996 (3rd ed.), p. 13.

[2]   Asante, Emmanuel, 'Toward An African Christian Theology of the Kingdom of God', in: *The Kingship of Onyame*, Lewinston/Queenston/Lampter: Mellen University Press, 1995, p. 16.

[3]   Hunnex, Milton D., *Chronological and Thematic Charts of Philosophers*, Grand Rapids, MI: Zondervan, 1986, p. 36.

[4]   *Ibidem*, p. 37.

[5]   Mugambi, J.N.K, 'Responsible Leadership in Education and Development. An African Perspective' in: Stückelberger, Christoph/Mugambi, J.N.K., *Responsible Leadership. Global Perspectives*, Nairobi: Acton Publishers, 2005, p. 25. See also Chapter 9 in this volume.

[6]   *Ibidem*.

[7]   *Ibid.*

[8]   *Ibid.*

[9]   *Ibid.*, p. 31.

[10]  Hunnex, *op. cit.*, p. 36.

[11]  Schreiner, Peter *et al.* (eds), *Holistic Education Resource Book. Learning and Teaching in an Ecumenical Context*, New York/Munich/Berlin: Waxmann, 2005, p. 18.

[12]  *Ibid.*, p. 19.

[13]  *Ibid.*

[14]  *Ibid.*, pp. 20-22.

[15]  *Ibid.*, p. 23.

[16]  *Ibid.*

[17]  Quoted in Bull, Vivian A., 'Economic Justice,' in: *Education for Human Responsibility in the Twenty-First Century. Third International Conference of the International Association of Methodist-Related Schools, Colleges and Universities at the Methodist College in Belfast, Northern Ireland, July 16-20, 2001*, Nashville, TN: General Board of Higher Education and Ministry, 2003, p. 62.

[18]  *Ibid.*

# PART II

# RESPONSIBLE RELIGIOUS LEADERSHIP

# 11

## PARISH LEADERSHIP.
## A PROTESTANT MINORITY PERSPECTIVE
## FROM EASTERN EUROPE/ROMANIA

*Árpád Ferencz, Romania*

### Introduction[1]

To write about the responsibilities of a pastor, of a minister, from a perspective of serving in a post-communist country is nearly one 'impossible possibility' – to quote Karl Barth's words. In a society of permanent transition, values such as responsibility or even responsible leadership are not highly regarded. In this particular area theological ethics has a monumental task to accomplish in the people's mindset.

In this article I will proceed as follows: I will initially discuss the minister's responsibility in general and the viewpoint of serving in a minority protestant church. Second, I will present various types of pastors ('leaders') based on one of my empirical studies. While this empirical study may not be representative for all post-communist environments, it does reflect the reality of such a society in Romania. Finally, I will formulate some conclusions to ponder. Prior to the first section, I must provide background, clarification, and context. The Reformed Church in Romania (RCR) is a protestant church with very strong Calvinistic and Presbyterian traditions. Thus, the RCR is in fact part of the Western Protestant world. This contact, the tradition of the church, as well as the very close contact with the Reformed Church in Hungary (the RCR was part of the Hungarian Reformed Church until the First World War) determine this situation.

The RCR functions in a country in which more than 80 percent of the population are members of the Romanian Orthodox Church. This creates both a relationship of conflict and, surprisingly, of dialogue with the Orthodox Church. In addition, due to their standing in Romanian society, the members of the RCR are not only a minority from a religious point of view but also from one based on nationality and culture as well. This special situation then determines the nature of the life and work of our church in Romania. For example, some tasks which, in a Western society, would be assumed by the State, are expected to be assumed by the church. As such, the RCR has developed one eminent political theology which has as its foundation the tradition from the Reformation.

## 1. Theological Foundation of Responsibility

What are the sources of the understanding of ministerial responsibility in the RCR? Ministerial responsibility as the responsibility of pastors, is not a primary theme in Hungarian Reformed theological ethics. The most often cited theological works on ethics do not mention the issue of responsibility. One can wonder how this is possible?

One possible explanation is that theologians of the past (especially in the 20th century) argued that responsibility is solely God's responsibility. This is not my view. Though it is a fact that the ancient Greeks considered responsibility to be an essential attribute of the gods, Aristotle writes in his *Ethics* extensively about this theme.[2] As we study the history of ethics and its development across centuries, the connection between the notion of responsibility and freedom is changing in an interesting manner. In humanism the notion of freedom started to be linked more and more to the one of responsibility. The different forms of ethics of responsibility are based on this link between responsibility and freedom.

However, in regards to theological ethics, we should ask whether this link between responsibility and freedom is the most important one. The RCR ethics has been very much influenced by the Swiss reformed theologians Emil Brunner (1889-1966) and Karl Barth (1886-1968). They link responsibility with sin. Barth speaks about responsibility in the context of an existential sin – a specific element of Christian ethics. In Brunner's understanding, by committing the original sin, man did not lose his/her freedom, but personal freedom was changed into formal freedom.[3]

Brunner gives three definitions of responsibility in his anthropology. The first: responsibility is the definition of human existence. His argument originates from the responses humans need to give to God's questions – responses that form the foundation of Christian love. The second: responsibility is an obligation of man, after falling into sin. The third definition of responsibility is related to the experience of freedom in Christ, and has an eschatological dimension.[4] This eschatological dimension of responsibility and its close connection with the responsibility to God, is also underlined in the theology of Karl Barth, the other main source of the RCR's ethics. He speaks in his main work about the man who has to be responsible in God's 'court of law'. The man who needs to stand in God's 'court of law' – and he calls him the 'Real Man' is in fact in his interpretation, Jesus Christ. This, however, does not absolve us from the duty of every-day self-examination in our lives.[5]

Barth and Brunner as the two main sources indicate the direction of understanding of pastoral responsibility in the theology of the RCR.

In conclusion, pastoral responsibility in the understanding of RCR theology is strongly connected with the issue of self-examination.

## 2. Pastoral and Political Responsibility of Pastors

The self-understanding in the RCR stands on strong biblical foundation. This biblical foundation is obviously the source of moral and ethical judgement. As we look closely at the biblical message, we are faced with a certain form of the prophet's responsibility in pastoral care.[6] The classical biblical witness is Num 18:23 about the special responsibility of the Levites. They have received a special mission from God and at the same time, a special responsibility. In the same sense, we face the problem of responsibility in 1 Sam 3:11: Responsibility is in all situations linked to God. In this sense we read about the special responsibility of the prophets in 2 Sam 12, Lam 2:14, Ezek 3:16-21.

The same understanding of responsibility is described in the New Testament, specifically in Matt 16:11-12, 18:17-18,28; Luke 10:17 and also in many verses in the Corpus Paulinum. The Bible gives us a special model of pastoral responsibility, which is strongly linked to God. It is very important in this context, that the priest/prophet has to know and to utilise the special experiences of his own community. This essential element of the biblical message is characteristic for the understanding of the responsible parish-leadership in the RCR.

In the RCR there are two confessions of faith that are mandatory for the Church: the *Heidelberg Catechism* and the *Second Helvetic Confession*, both from the times of Reformation. Due to the Calvinist tradition, Calvin's main publication *Institutio Christianae Religionis* also plays an important role in defining the role of pastoral responsibility. In the first document we cannot find any special remarks about human responsibility. Only the classical form in question 83 speaks about the 'power of the keys', meaning in the Churches of the Reformation the work of the whole congregation, not just of the pastors. In the second document we find a chapter (§ 18) about the 'servant of the Church'. In this context we also face the problem of the special responsibility of pastors. This responsibility is given from God and strongly connected to His grace. The same idea can be found in Calvin's *Institutio Christianae Religionis* (IV/3,6;3,8;3,12). The biblical message was strongly emphasised during the Reformation and it became the foundation for the understanding of responsible pastoral leadership in the RCR.

Until now I spoke about the responsibility of parish-leadership and sources that determine the understanding of the church in the reality of the post-communist Romania. We also have to mention the obvious political responsibility of the pastor in this context in the RCR. The RCR has always viewed itself as the keeper of our Hungarian culture and national traditions. This fact has determined the life of our Church in the past fifteen years, after the Romanian 'revolution'. If we look at the recent history of Romania, we can see that protestant churches have played a very important role in the different political movements. For example, the Romanian revolution in 1989 was initiated by the RCR. This is the consequence of our understanding of responsibility towards our parishioners as members of an oppressed minority. If we speak about responsibility, we have to mention the only article about this issue in the thirties of the 20th century in Romania. In his very important article, professor Tavaszy speaks about the responsibility of the Church in the society. To date, this article (with minor changes) is in fact determining the RCR's basic standpoint in the above issues.

Given the communist historical background of the country, our Church has developed a special way of understanding itself in a variety of roles. In my doctoral thesis I call it *Intellektuelles Gegensystem*,[7] an 'intellectual alternative' to the existing system. I mean by this that the Church has developed its own theological system that allowed us to eliminate the disturbing factors of surrounding political changes and oppression. The development of the post-communist society in the last fifteen years has opened many possibilities for the churches and this also leads to a change of paradigm in the understanding of leadership in parish work. The post-modern society in Romania, in the 21st century, is characterised by a special phenomenon which the German sociologist Ulrich Beck calls 'risk society'.[8] This risk society means that the old structure of society will rapidly change and the individuals will have to take decisions in new situations they may not have faced in the past. It also means that in risk society people need a much more critical view of old values and understandings in their daily lives and also of theological ethics. Old values and traditions are challenged from one minute to the other, and parishioners expect the pastor's leadership to provide answers and solutions in a responsible and ethical manner to questions and problems arising in this ever-changing society. This decision-maker role of ministers makes pastoral responsibility one of the most important features of pastoral work in the RCR today and tomorrow.

## 3. Typology of Leadership in Parish Work of RCR

The following typology was presented and discussed in two different deaneries ('dioceses') of the RCR. I spoke with many different colleagues about this topic. Their comments are integrated in the 'final' version of this typology. I am very grateful for the comments I have received. On the basis of the same theology, different pastors have developed different types of leadership, and the interpretation of responsibility has also changed in small ways from one pastor to another. That means that in the RCR we can see a variety of understandings about the role of pastors in society and in the congregation. This situation was generated by the RCR's special situation in history as a minority and by self-examination.

I now concentrate on the personality of the pastor, because on the basis of its special historical development, the RCR has a very pastor-oriented hierarchical structure. I will not speak about the possibilities of the special theology of the RCR and neither about the critical ideology specific to our theological view. I will only mention that the very positive role of pastors and the Church in the life of the national minorities in Romania builds the foundation of the following typology.[9]

### a) Type A: Classical Pastor

The work of this type of pastor is the so-called 'classical' pastoral work and responsibility. The main stream of the understanding of the work, and the self-understanding of this pastor is determined by the spiritual heritage of the theological liberalism and by the heritage of the cultural Protestantism mixed with one special understanding of service. This type of pastor fulfils the traditional pastoral work with traditional methods in full consciousness of his/her responsibility for pastoral care. S/he works in the traditionally oriented communities (the majority of RCR parishes) and has little time for theoretical reflections about the type of responsibility s/he carries. Theoretical problems linked to pastoral leadership are not reflected in this type of work.

This type of leader serves in a 'one-parson-parish'. Even though this kind of pastor is the most traditional type, s/he at the same time has the most difficult work form of parish leadership. One can ask if s/he can provide responsible leadership, and one can answer: yes, of course – it has been like this for centuries. The problem though arises when this pastor has to carry the full responsibility of leadership by him/herself in lack of persons with whom s/he could share the burdens and blessings of the pastoral work. Of course, we should also see the advantages of this type of leadership: the stability of decisions (if the system works, but what if it does not?) and the power of this historical type in the life of the RCR. But we also have to consider that the risk society needs other decisions and another form of leadership. This form of leadership is still a shadow of the past. I am sure that it is not the type of ministry of the future.

### b) Type B: Evangelical Pastor

The second type of leadership that I would like to present is the leadership in which the traditional elements of parish leadership are completed by additional elements. I only mention one element: a very profound evangelical orientation of the pastoral work. This type of leadership looks for a divided leadership responsibility on the basis of the universal priesthood. In this form of pastoral care and leadership, unconventional methods are very much favoured and it emphasises the necessity of personal conversion. This type of pastoral care and leadership includes the danger that it can very quickly become a closed system. On the other hand, shared responsibility is very seriously taken into consideration. In my observation the power and fascination of the closed system that can give answer to all types of questions has fascinated many people. The question that we should answer is whether the vision of a patriarchal church (or a patriarchal pastor) is the vision of the future. Due to the communist past in Romania it is a realistic danger, that this type of leadership will dominate the life of the Church in the future.

### c) Type C: Managerial Pastor

The third type of pastor is the 'manager-pastor'. Leadership is understood as management. It may well be that this type of leadership can be one of the future. I, however, have ethical questions. In this type of pastoral care the responsibility for society becomes a major part of the parish work. This means that the manager-pastor is involved in several economic and political activities and pastoral work as such occupies little space in his/her agenda. It is to be seen how the problems (mainly economic and political problems) in society can be solved by a pastor, meaningfully and in a sustainable way. We also have to examine how this type of leadership changes the relationship between the Church and society. In this type of leadership, the responsibility is in most cases a divided responsibility. This is a positive element of the model. Naturally, we cannot find these three models in their pure form in the real world, but we see elements of them in the contemporary life of the RCR, mixed and in many sub-types.

## Conclusion

Theoretically the idea of responsibility is so strongly connected to the self-understanding of the Church that theologians do not feel the necessity to formulate a special teaching about it. In the new postmodern and post-communist society, this issue becomes one of very significant importance.

For my personal understanding it is very important to see how we can define the responsible self of the pastor in his/her parish work. In order to understand the meaning of the responsible self (in the parish work, too!!) it is helpful to distinguish between wishes of first and second level, [10] taking into consideration lower or higher values. In the philosophical tradition of the 20th century, we also meet the idea that we have to distinguish between values of first and second level, with strong and not so strong value judgements. [11]

In the traditional understanding of responsible leadership (Type A) responsibility includes a very strong value judgement. The development of the Romanian society has changed the judgement of the parishioner and also the self-understanding of the pastor. It means that, in the work of the manager-pastor (Type C), the responsibility becomes mixed with other elements that create a weaker value judgement and values belonging to the first level. This understanding follows the changing of the society, but we have to ask if this is the way of responsible parish leadership. This society-oriented model of leadership has to remain constantly strong, especially in the situation of transition in our society today.

The biblical foundation of the RCR can be a control mechanism in the building of moral judgments. Some may ask for how long we can work with a model based on biblical values, but the fact is that they are strong components of the identity of the RCR. Responsible parish leadership has to know the connection of the responsibility with God and with the freedom, which is given in the work of Christ. From this point of view, responsible parish leadership has to integrate people in the community and cannot be a closed system. Responsibility means also that the parish shall not be against the world, but in the world with another possibility of moral judgement, based on theology and theological ethics. This makes it possible to build moral judgements not closed but open, not condemning others but sincerely wishing to change something for the best in the world.

We should not forget, in this conclusion, the importance of our own traditions and the eminent political sense of responsibility in the testimony of the RCR. Both are elements from a protestant/minority perspective which can be important for a global ethics of responsibility, not only in the parish work.

NOTES

1   This article is dedicated to my colleague and friend Christoph Ammann with thanks for the discussion about this topic – and much more.

2   On Aristotelean Ethics see, for example, J. P. Wogaman, *Christian Ethics: A Historical Introduction*, London: SPCK, 1993, pp. 86-88.

3   Brunner, E., *Gott und sein Rebell. Eine theologische Anthropologie*, Hamburg: U. Berger-Gebhardt, 1958, p. 74f.

4   *Ibidem*, p. 14f.

5   Barth, K., *Kirchliche Dogmatik* II/2, Zürich, 1942, p. 707, 713f.

6   In the following I will present a selection of a few biblical testimonies, knowing that this is only a very small part of the richness of texts.

7   To be soon published in English.

8   Beck, Ulrich, *Risk Society, Towards a New Modernity*, trans. from the German by Mark Ritter, and with an Introduction by Scott Lash and Brian Wynne, London: Sage Publications, 1992. [originally publ. 1986].

9   I would like to mention here that the types have a model-function, and as such they are excessive.

10  Frankfurt, H., *Freedom of the Will and the Concept of a Person*, in: *Journal of Philosophy* 67/1, p. 5-20. The author says in his article that most human beings are able to build wishes not only of first level, but also wishes of second level. This means human beings are able to estimate values. In my view, from the postmodern perspective responsibility should be considered in relation to the different values.

11  Taylor, C., *Negative Freiheit? Zur Kritik des neuzeitlichen Individualismus*, Frankfurt am Main, 1988, p. 10f. He speaks about 'soft value judgements' *(schwache Wertungen)* and 'strong value judgements' *(starke Wertungen)* with a difference in quality.

# 12

## THEOLOGICAL LEADERSHIP
## IN CHRISTIAN-MUSLIM ENCOUNTERS.
## AN INDONESIAN PERSPECTIVE

*Yahya Wijaya, Indonesia*

### Introduction

Indonesia is the country with the largest Muslim population in the world (160-180 mio); yet it is also home for more than 20 million Christians. The most well-known of its islands, Bali, is characteristically Hindu. There are also adherents of Buddhism, various folk religions and Chinese popular religions in a significant number. Such plurality has been made a part of the identity of the modern nation of Indonesia since its inception, as demonstrated in the national motto: *Bhinneka Tunggal Ika* (Unity in Diversity). The founding fathers were well aware that when this reality of plurality is denied, it is the existence of the nation is be at stake. To accept that fact, however, is not easy for religious groups having a history of conflict and rivalry, notably those of Islam and Christianity. In Indonesia, attempts to overcome the difficulties in accepting the reality of plurality can be seen in three areas: theological reinterpretation, political consensus, and interreligious dialogue and relationships.

### 1. Christian Reinterpretation of Uniqueness

Many religious leaders in Indonesia realise that one obstacle in accepting the reality of plurality are the particularistic perspectives developed from religions. For instance, both Islam and Christianity are strong enough in emphasising their own truth claim, the claim that the real truth or salvation is exclusively related to the belief of that community. Such claim motivates energetic and ambitious mission works of those religions, which contributes to their global expansion. Despite their constructive achievements, mission works of both Islam and Christianity, aiming at the conversion of other believers, create uneasy relationships between adherents of the two religions. The truth claim also fosters a sense of pride in believers, which drives them, to a certain degree, into a situation of conflict when meeting with people of other religions.

Reinterpretation of the truth claim has been attempted by Christian as well as Muslim theologians. The works of John Hick and Paul Knitter, among others, have provoked discourses regarding the need to develop a theology of religions which is more sensitive to the context of plurality. Knitter's typology of exclusive, inclusive and pluralist positions has helped many theologians to self-evaluate their theology of religions. There is a tendency among theologians of mainline Christian communities to leave behind the exclusive position and take either an inclusive or pluralist one. Having been aware of the difficult social and moral consequences of the exclusive position in the experience of Indonesian society, several Indonesian theologians are enthusiastic in contributing to the development of a more sympathetic theology of religions.

E.G. Singgih, biblical scholar at Duta Wacana Christian University in Yogyakarta, Indonesia, is one of those theologians who participate in the reconstruction of a Christian theology of religions, by suggesting a reinterpretation of the biblical concept of the 'chosen people'. Singgih affirms that the concept of the chosen people contradicts the recently growing spirit of 'interreligious ecumenism', since the first shows a particularistic attitude whilst the later is universalistic in nature. [1] He also agrees that the traditional interpretation of the chosen people implies a superiority feeling, which results in creating prejudices toward the others. To show historical evidences proving the negative implications of that concept, Singgih points to the experience of the people of South Africa. According to him, South Africa's apartheid system is a fruit of the idea of the chosen people which was developed among the white ethnic group, the Boer. That idea was generated by this Dutch descendant group who called themselves reformed Christians, but also enhanced by their unhappy encounters with the indigenous ethnic groups and the British in their attempt to control the rich natural resources. [2]

Singgih notes that the concept of the chosen people in the Old Testament reflects a paradox in the way Israel defined its identity. On the one hand, the concept indeed shows exclusivity as an expression of the feeling of being loved by God. The chosen people is thus meant as a subjective language of love, to be understood in terms of the relationship between the people and God. The reason of being the chosen people has nothing to do with either the moral quality of Israel or their spirituality. God's unconditional love is the only reason. There is therefore no reason for being superior. However, since a loving relationship can be exclusive, its expression in practice includes rejection and intolerance against other peoples. On the other hand, it is obvious that the status of the 'chosen people' is not to be taken for granted. Rather, it works only when Israel lives a faithful life, showing good conducts and responsible morality. There is also a notion that the election of the people is not for the honour of that people, but for their service. Referring to Isaiah's picture of the Suffering Servant of God, which suggests the suffering experience of Israel as a model for other nations, Singgih contends that there was a stream of spirituality in the Old Testament that challenges the emphasis of the dominant tradition on exclusivity and superiority of Israel.

From an exploration of the Old Testament's idea of the chosen people, Singgih goes on to investigate the concept of *ecclesia* (church, community of Christians) in the New Testament. According to him, the concept of *ecclesia* is parallel to the Old Testament's chosen people, in the sense that it points to a group of people who claim to be elected because of the love of God. Yet, *ecclesia* is far from the notion of exclusivity, superiority or intolerance, since it is related to the major themes of justice and service to the poorest in Matthew's Sermon on the Mount. However, later as recorded in Revelation, this service-oriented *ecclesia* was reinterpreted, under the experience of persecution, to reflect the desire of the people to gain justice and ultimate victory at the expense of punishment of the persecutors. For Singgih, this shift should be carefully recognised in order that the original idea of *ecclesia* is not left behind.

Reinterpretation of the concept of the chosen people has also been suggested by Wesley Ariarajah, a Sri Lankan Methodist theologian, whose work *The Bible and People of Other Faiths*[3] has been translated into Indonesian by a well-known Indonesian theologian and ecumenical leader, Eka Darmaputera.[4] Ariarajah argues that the 'chosen people' idea should not be understood apart from a theology of creation, in which God is the God of all creatures. This implies that there is no history, culture or spirituality which is isolated from the creation and providence of God. As with Singgih, Ariarajah points to several biblical stories that, he believes, correct the exclusive concept of Israel's God as a God with no relationship with people of other nations.

Ariarajah goes even further by discussing 'sensitive issues' such as the concept of Jesus as the only way of salvation. He contends that the claim of the uniqueness of Jesus in terms of salvation should be understood as a language of faith rather than as a social statement. That language of faith is originally meant as a defence of the Christian community against the pressure to prove the authenticity of their faith. That claim, according to Ariarajah, also indicates a shift in the community's centre of faith from God to Christ, which is parallel to the Buddhists' adoration of Gautama. For Ariarajah the claim of the uniqueness of Jesus thus is not relevant in the context of dealing with other religions. The real call for Christians, he believes, is not to make exclusive claims, but to show a clear commitment to open their lives to other people.

Another reinterpretation of the concept of Jesus as the only way of salvation is suggested by Iones Rakhmat, a minister of the Indonesian Christian Church and former lecturer in New Testament at Jakarta Theological Seminary.[5] Rakhmat suggests an 'interrelation approach' which joins the uniqueness claim with the Christian belief that the One God works with God's grace and speaks in all areas of human religions. Underlining the Christian belief in the uniqueness of Jesus as a true confession based on the Word of God, he calls Christians to realise the fact that God allows non Christian beliefs to exist. According to Rakhmat, this means that the uniqueness of Jesus does not imply any idea of negating other beliefs but that Jesus Christ, the unique revelation of the Word of God, is basically the same Word who reveals himself as the Creator God, 'the light of humans who enlightens every human being' (John 1:4,9).

Rakhmat goes on to argue that the Word's revelation in the human flesh of Jesus does not at all reduce his status as the universal God. Indeed, after the events of the cross, resurrection and ascension, he returns to his status as the Word with 'the glory he had owned before the world existed' (John 17:5), and with 'all power in him both in heaven and on earth' (John 17:2; Matt 28:18). The Christian belief in Jesus as the only saviour, Rakhmat suggests, does not reduce the inclusive work of the Word in the universe before and after the age of the New Testament.

## 2. Muslim Reinterpretation of Uniqueness

From the Muslim side, a group of theologians have produced an extensive theological reinterpretation in a collaborative work, *Fiqih Lintas Agama* ('Interreligious Dogma'), published by Paramadina Foundation in cooperation with the Asia Foundation.[6] Paramadina is a scholarly Islamic organisation led by a prominent Muslim figure, Nurcholis Madjid. *Fiqih Lintas Agama* (FLA) challenges uncritical uses of traditional Islamic dogmas that overlook their relatedness to particular social and cultural contexts. According to the authors, such non contextual dogmas lead to narrow-minded social and political concepts. The attempt to return to the Jakarta Charter (which requires Indonesian Muslims to practice Shariah as positive law) is an example of such narrow-mindedness.

According to FLA, Islam assumes that the core of all religions is the same, and all prophets are like children of one father but different mothers. The differences between religions are part of the nature of God's creative work, which dislikes total sameness. The authors argue that the Koran celebrates plurality as an opportunity to compete in doing goodness, living peaceful coexistence, struggling for justice and working for fairness. The Koran, thus, is unique in the sense that it contains 'all inclusive' teachings respecting other religious beliefs and their prophets.

FLA suggests an understanding of the terms 'Islam' and 'muslim' as first of all in their generic meanings, not in the spirit of sectarianism or communalism. In this sense, Islam means total submission to the One God, and muslim means the attitude of total submission to the purity, holiness and truth of God. Such an attitude is basically in accord with natural law, and therefore is not necessarily related to a particular religious institution. The terms Islam and muslim thus cover all people, who show total submission to God, regardless of religion. The origin of the terms, according to the authors, should be traced back to the story about the debate regarding the religion of Abraham. In that story, the Koran asserts that Abraham is neither Jewish nor Christian. The Koran employs the terms *'hanif'* and 'Muslim' for Abraham in their generic sense, precisely to reject sectarian and exclusivist claims raised by some Jews and Christians regarding Abraham. In this generic interpretation, the term 'Islam' refers not to a particular religious institution, but to all religions, since the call to submission and obedience to God is at the heart of religions. FLA's authors thus argue that the Koran's claim that Islam is the only true religion must be understood in this generic sense.

In Indonesia, Christians use the term 'Allah' for God. Some groups of Muslims as well as a particular group of Christians have raised their objections, arguing that the term refers exclusively to the Muslim God. They ask (some even warn) the Indonesian Bible Society and Christian leaders to stop using the term 'Allah' and find instead another term consistent with the biblical accounts. The term 'Yahweh', for instance, is suggested. FLA, however, rejects such a sectarian interpretation of the term 'Allah'. The authors assert that the term 'Allah' is nothing but the Arabic word referring to the idea of the true God, namely the Only One God, on whom all religions centre their worships and praises. The core meaning of that term is a rejection to the worship of false idols, not necessarily a rejection of a particular religion.

FLA challenges many rules *(fatwa)* issued by the Indonesian Council of Clerics, such as that of 1980 which leads Muslims to a difficult situation when encountering followers of other religions. According to the Council's *fatwa*, it is forbidden for a Muslim to greet Christians with the Islamic greeting *Assalamu'alaiku,* let alone to say 'Happy Christmas' or to come to a Christmas party. That *fatwa* is based on a sacred story *(hadith)* by Abu Hurairah, a friend of the prophet Mohammad, in which the prophet urged his followers not to start greeting Jews or Christians, but rather to push them aside when they meet these people on their ways. Similar stories are found in some other *hadiths* told by Bukhari, another friend of the prophet. FLA explains that the reliability of Abu Hurairah's *hadiths* are doubtful since he is known not only for his carelessness, but also his laziness.

Hurairah's *hadiths* also contradict many *hadiths* told by other friends of the prophet, including those by his most beloved wife, Aisyah. FLA contends that Hurairah's *hadiths* do not fit well with the basic character of Islam, which emphasises peace, hospitality and tenderness. In the case of Bukhari's *hadiths*, FLA explains that those *hadiths* reflect the situation when several Jewish people tried to humiliate the prophet by manipulating greeting words. There are many other *hadiths*, reflecting more principle characters of Islam, which advise Muslims to greet other people nicely, and treat them with hospitality and respect. FLA's authors thus believe that to greet 'people of the book' (meaning Jews and Christians) is not only allowed but also suggested and could even be compulsory.

### 3. Political Consensus: Indonesia's Pancasila

One of the most fundamental questions faced by the concept makers of the modern nation of Indonesia was: 'On what ideology would the new nation be based?' Two major options were suggested: Islam or Western-like secularism. Each was supported by a significantly strong camp. The debate on that issue in the Committee set up for preparing the independence of Indonesia had lasted for 3 days, when Soekarno offered a compromising draft in his speech on 1 June 1945. The draft offered was called *Pancasila* (The Five Principles) as the foundation of the nation. *Pancasila* covers both democratic principles implied in Western-like secularism and the most basic religious interest, which is belief in God. Soekarno therefore suggested that with *Pancasila* as the ideological foundation, Indonesia would be neither a secular country nor an Islamic one. Soekarno's draft was accepted to be followed up by an appointed committee, which then produced the second draft. This committee's draft, named as the 'Jakarta Charter', not only made the principle of Belief in God the first in order, but also added a phrase to that principle, namely *'with the compulsory to implement the Islamic Syariah* [Shariah] *for its adherents'*.

The addition was obviously made to accommodate the aspiration of the Islamic camp, who was not satisfied with the first draft's neutral description of religious belief. However, non Muslim groups raised their objection, arguing that such a principle of the national ideology should have not contained a reference to a particular religion, be it the majority one or else. The final draft, therefore, dropped the reference to the implementation of the Syariah [Shariah], and the formula of the religious principle became: *Belief in the Most One God.*[7] The formula, together with the other four principles *(a just and civilised humanity, the unity of Indonesia, democracy led by the wisdom of consensus and representation, and social welfare for all people of Indonesia)*, was widely accepted. Since then *Pancasila* has been made the basic reference for maintaining the unity and accepting the plurality of the nation.

Since the consensus to accept *Pancasila* has been crucial in preventing the state from being formed as an Islamic one, Christians face no problem at all in following that consensus. For the Christian minority, an idea of a more Christian-coloured state is obviously unrealistic. It is therefore not difficult for them to understand *Pancasila*, which implies a notion that religious freedom is guaranteed, as the best available option. Many Christian leaders even emphasise the importance of *Pancasila*, not particularly for the protection of the Christian community, but for the continuing existence of the modern nation of Indonesia. T.B. Simatupang, a former army general turned church leader, urged Christians to subscribe to *Pancasila* wholeheartedly, since there is no contradiction between *Pancasila* and the Christian faith. Rather, the relations between the two could be synergetic: Christians should be inspired and motivated by their faith to participate in the life of the nation according to the norms embedded in *Pancasila*.[8]

Simatupang's insistence has been reasserted by Eka Darmaputera, who wrote his PhD dissertation in Boston College on *Pancasila*. Referring to Simatupang, Darmaputera believes that *Pancasila* is the only option for Indonesia to maintain its unity and plurality.[9] Despite the fact that Islam is the religion of the majority in Indonesia, he argues, any attempt to replace *Pancasila* with a concept of an Islamic state would put the existence of the nation at stake. The same can be said about the idea of replacing *Pancasila* with a concept of a secular state, as has been attempted by the Indonesian Communist Party.[10]

The belief that maintaining Pancasila is crucial for the existence of the nation is also common among Muslims, despite the attempt to establish an Islamic state of Indonesia by certain groups of Muslims. Azyumardi Azra, professor of history and the rector of Syarif Hidayatulah State Islamic University in Jakarta, observes that 'overwhelming Muslims have accepted *Pancasila* as the final ideological basis of the Indonesian state'.[11] Considering the groups proposing the Islamic state as 'either splinters or fringes', Azra shows historical evidence proving that such groups have never been supported by the dominant Muslim community. According to him, the reasons of the Indonesian Muslims for not supporting the idea of an Islamic state are not merely political, but first of all related to the nature of Indonesian Islam itself,

which 'has a number of distinctive characters *vis-à-vis* Middle Eastern Islam'.[12] What Azra means is the tendency of Indonesian Islam to
moderation and embrace, as a result of its mixture and amalgamation
with elements of the indigenous religious traditions in the early history of Islam in Indonesia.

Rejection of the idea of an Islamic state has also been asserted by
Abdurrahman Wahid, a prominent leader of the largest Islamic organisation, Nadhlatul Ulama (NU), and former president of Indonesia.
Wahid's rejection is based on his analysis of the broader Islamic tradition, in which he does not find strong evidence that Islam provides
a blue print of an Islamic state.[13] Wahid argues that the place of Islam,
and religion in general, in relation to the state should be in the area
of social ethics. For Wahid, the idea of an Islamic state degrades the
dignity of religion. Relying on the power of the state in achieving religious aims, he argues, is a real process of secularism, which implies
permission for the state to become more powerful than religion.[14]

Wahid sees two trajectories in recent development of Islam in
Indonesia. The first is the *exclusivist trajectory*, which offers Islam as
a total life system covering a uniquely Islamic civil law, economic
system and institutions, and other elements of social and personal
lives. According to Wahid, this trajectory is not originated in the early
history of Indonesian Islam. Instead, it emerges as a reaction to the
challenge of modernisation promoted by the West to the whole world.
It is such a trajectory which leads to the formation of Islamic states in
countries like Iran, Sudan, Libya and Pakistan.[15] Among the advocates
of this trajectory in Indonesia are the Association of Indonesian
Muslim Intellectuals (Ikatan Cendekiawan Muslim Indonesia:
ICMI),[16] and a number of Islamic mass and youth organisations that
Imdadun Rahmat and Khamami Zada call 'new Islamic movement',
namely those having characteristics of 'militant, radical, scripturalist,
conservative, exclusive, hardliner and making politics part of religious
faith'. It is important to note that a new Islamic party, Partai Keadilan
Sejahtera (PKS), which gained a dramatic increase of votes in the
recent General Election, is rooted in that movement. Rahmat and Zada
suspect that despite its campaign for humanitarian issues, the PKS is
the political channel for the groups committed to that movement.[17]

The second trajectory is that of the *pluralist*. The pluralist trajectory emphasises universal values of humanity and recognises the
rights of minority groups to a treatment and status equal to those of
the majority. Consequently, the advocates of this trajectory see a
uniquely Islamic social system, such as formalised Syariah [Shariah],
irrelevant for a plural society like Indonesia.[18] It is obvious that
Wahid himself represents the advocates of the pluralist trajectory.
Indeed, his leadership in Nadhlatul Ulama contributes much to the
development of this organisation into an enhanced tolerant and

inclusive position. Another prominent figure of the pluralist group is Nurcholis Madjid, the founder of the Paramadina Foundation. Madjid, who received his PhD from the University of Chicago under the supervision of a well-known Muslim scholar, Fazlur Rahman, provokes a strong reaction from the exclusivist camp when delivering his speech in 1970, in which he states his disagreement with the existence of Islamic parties. In that speech, he asserts his political motto: 'Islam yes, Islamic party no.'[19]

The pluralist trajectory can also be seen in the emergence of 'a new generation of pluralist Muslims', working particularly in various non-governmental organisations (NGOs).[20] One of those organisations is Jaringan Islam Liberal (the Liberal Islam Network), which promotes its mission through the media. Jaringan Islam Liberal (JIL) is led by young Muslim scholars, including Ulil Abshar Abdalla and Luthfi Assyaukani, and focuses its mission on four major agendas: political maturity for determining an appropriate state system; theological development appreciating plurality and equal rights for all human beings; women emancipation; and freedom of opinion.[21]

Despite the fact that the attempt to establish an Islamic state of Indonesia has failed to attract enough support from Indonesian society, the exclusivist groups are far from dying. As has been stated above, one of the Islamic party representing those groups, PKS, has gained significant votes in the 2004 General Election, an achievement that led to the instalment of the president of PKS, Hidayat Nurwahid, as the chairperson of the People's Consultative Assembly, the highest legislative body. Yet, such an achievement would have not been made without a shift in the themes promoted by that party. The success of PKS has depended heavily on its policy to leave behind the mission to return to the Jakarta Charter, and to emphasise instead moral issues such as clean governance and simplicity. As such, PKS appears at least an exterior form similar to that of the pluralist. Many observers are, however, afraid that PKS just changes the strategy, not the ideology or the core mission, which is to establish an Islamic state.[22]

## 4. Interreligious Dialogue and Practical Relationships

Although personal and social relationships between people of different religions have long been a daily experience in the level of the common people, systematic interreligious dialogue in Indonesia had not been developed before the 1960s. It was the New Order (Suharto's regime) government which initiated the first formal dialogue between leaders of different religions in 1967, after a series of conflicts broke out between Muslim and Christian groups as a result of their enthusiasm in doing their proselytising missions.[23] The government's motivation was obviously political, namely to establish political stability needed for economic development of the country. Although that government-initiated programme failed to reach an agreement on the issue of religious mission, it sparked the spirit to carry out a further, more developed dialogue. Leaders of different religions, particularly those of Islam and Christianity, started to explore more fundamental basis for dialogue, realising that political reasons are not strong enough for establishing a constructive dialogue. Whilst the government continued its programme for reinforcing interreligious harmony in a more institutionalised form, e.g. by founding the interreligious Consultative Forum[24] in 1980, various civil society forums on interreligious dialogue and relationships are set up by religious scholars and leaders. An institution specifically dedicated to interreligious dialogue is the Institute of Interfidei, which has not only conducted seminars and conferences on interreligious themes, but also produced a series of publications on such themes.

The spirit of dialogue also drives churches and Islamic communities to review their concepts and practices of mission. This meets the ongoing passion within the Christian community to develop a contextual, post-colonial theology. Although the evangelical wing of Indonesian Christianity is still unaffected, the Communion of Churches in Indonesia (CCI), the umbrella of more than 80 percent of the Protestant denominations, gives a clear sign of shifting the traditional, proselytising concept of mission into a more plurality-sensitive one. The annual Seminar on Religions conducted by CCI provides rich resources for churches to practice new forms of mission.

Better relationships between Muslims and Christians are also attempted at the level of local communities. Although local conflicts between groups of Muslims and Christians do sometime happen, particularly in certain areas of Indonesia, their solutions involve mutual support between religious groups of both religions. It is not rare that a group of young Muslims, particularly those belonging to the youth organisation of Nadhlatul Ulama, do voluntary work to protect churches against the physical threat from Muslim extremists. A recent case (2004) happened in a suburb of Jakarta, where a group of people, claiming to represent the local community, built a wall to block the entrance access to 'Sang Timur', a Roman Catholic school campus. The group objected to the use of a building in that campus for Sunday mass service. Asserting the right of the Catholic community to do the worship, Abdurrahman Wahid came to the location and warned the government to demolish the wall, or he would bring the case to the court. After the local government cleared the access, a Muslim youth group, on Wahid's order, guarded the Catholic campus for several days.

Islamic and Christian theological institutions make important contributions to the progress of interreligious dialogue and relationships in Indonesia. The practice of exchanging lecturers and sharing resources between Islamic and Christian academic institutions have become quite common. For instance, the Faculty of Theology at Duta Wacana Christian University and Sunan Kalijaga State Islamic University, both in Yogyakarta/Java, have established a long-term formal cooperation in both teaching and research activities. It can be said that the reputation of the study of religions in those institutions depends heavily on the maintenance of their mutually constructive cooperation. Indeed their cooperation has attracted several universities abroad, not only to learn from them, but also to participate in the relationships.

Relationships between Muslim and Christian academic institutions have also transformed the approach of the study of religions employed in those institutions. Sunan Kalijaga State Islamic University, for instance, has been a pioneer in introducing the critical textual study of the Koran and the phenomenological study of religions. Figures such as Prof. Mukti Ali, a former rector of that institution, and Prof. Amin Abdullah, the present rector, contribute much to the development of such approaches within the Islamic academic circle. In the case of Duta Wacana Christian University, its Centre for the Study of Religions not only conducts collaborative research projects involving Muslim partners, but also the annual 'Studi Institut Tentang Islam' SITI (Institute of Studies on Islam), aiming at equipping Christian leaders with fresh knowledge on Islam learnt directly from Muslim scholars and leaders. In 1996, the centre conducted a seminar, inviting other Christian theological schools in Indonesia, in which curricula regarding religious studies in Christian theological seminaries were reviewed, with a perspective on interreligious dialogue in mind.[25]

## Conclusion

Leadership in the context of Muslim-Christian encounters should take account of the need to reinterpret theological resources of both religions, since the early constructions of those resources contemplated a situation with a lesser degree of plurality than that of today. Theological reinterpretation is not only necessary to make those resources meaningful for the present communities, but it is also crucial for the different religious communities to reach political consensus. Although a moderate, tolerant attitude may have been rooted in the traditional culture of the people, political consensus is still needed to prevent political interests from contaminating the culture.

Theological reinterpretation and political consensus should not be merely matters of the elite, but rather be practised on the level of local communities.

In an age badly affected by terrorism and the rise of religious fundamentalism, genuine dialogue and relationships between communities of different religions, based on a thoughtful theological reinterpretation and fair political consensus, would be an alternative to prejudice and self-centred mission practices.

NOTES

1   Singgih, E.G., 'Idea umat terpilih dalam Perjanjian Lama: Positif atau negative?', in: Sumartana, Th. *et al.*, Dialog: *Kritik dan Identitas Agama*, Yogyakarta: Dian/Interfidei, pp. 32-53.

2   The World Alliance of Reformed Churches (WARC) excluded this church from the alliance because WARC called the justification of apartheid a sin and heresy.

3   Ariarajah, Wesley, *The Bible and People of Other Faiths*, Geneva: WCC publications, 1985.

4   The Indonesian title is *Alkitab dan Orang-orang Berkepercayaan Lain*, Jakarta: BPK Gunung Mulia, 1987.

5   Rakhmat, Ioanes, 'Adakah Firman Allah di luar Alkitab?', in: *Penuntun* 1:2, 1995, pp. 130-149.

6   Sirry, Mun'im A. (ed.), *Fiqih Lintas Agama: Membangun Masyarakat Inklusif-Pluralis*, Jakarta: Paramadina, 2004.

7   For a short history concerning the 'birth' of *Pancasila*, see Darmaputera, Eka, *Pancasila: Identitas dan Modernitas, Tinjauan Etis dan Budaya*, Jakarta: BPK Gunung Mulia, 1987, pp. 104-117. The English version of this book is titled *Pancasila and the Search of Identity and Modernity. A Cultural and Ethical Analysis*, Leiden: E.J. Brill, 1987.

8   Simatupang, T.B., *Iman Kristen dan Pancasila*, Jakarta: BPK Gunung Mulia, 1985, p. 206.

9   Darmaputera, Eka, *op. cit.*, p. 130.

10   *Ibidem*, p. 131.

11   Azra, Azyumardi, 'Recent development of Indonesian Islam', in: *The Indonesian Quarterly* XXXII:1, 2004, pp. 10-18.

12   *Ibid.*, p. 12.

13   Wahid, Abdurrahman, *Mengurai Hubungan Agama dan Negara*, Jakarta: Grasindo, 1999, pp. 63-66.

14   *Ibid.*, p. 76.

15   Wahid, Abdurrahman, 'Hubungan antar agama: Dimensi internal-eksternalnya di Indonesia', in: Sumartana, Th. *et al., op. cit.*, pp. 3-12.

16   *Ibid.*, p. 10.

17   Rahmat, M. Imdadun/Zada, Khamami, 'Agenda politik gerakan Islam baru' in: *Tashwirul Afkar* 16, 2004, pp. 26-43.

18   *Ibid.*, p. 10.

19   See Liddle, R. William, *Leadership and Culture in Indonesian Politics*, Sydney: Allen and Unwin, 1996, p. 276.

20   See Suaedy, Ahmad, 'Muslim progresif dan praktik politik demokratisasi di era Indonesia pasca Suharto', in: *Tashwirul Afkar* 16, 2004, pp. 6-25.

21   *Ibid.*, p. 22-23.

22   Rahmat, M. Imdadun/Zada, Khamami, *op. cit.*, p. 41.

23   See Taher, Tarmizi, *Aspiring for the Middle Path. Religious Harmony in Indonesia*, Jakarta: CENSIS, 1997, p. 40-41.

24   *Ibid.*, p. 17.

25   For the proceedings of the seminar, see Duta Wacana's theological journal *Gema* 52, 1997.

# 13

## RELIGIOUS LEADERSHIP OF A MAJORITY CHURCH. THE CASE OF THE ORTHODOX CHURCH OF GREECE

*Nikos Dimitriadis, Greece*

### Introduction

A religious leadership can take place in two aspects of life: (a) in spiritual; and (b) in non-spiritual matters (secular), the latter being in relation with the State, administrative matters within the church, and so on. Inevitably they are both on a parallel road, but as in mathematics where parallel lines intersect in infinity, by the same token spiritual matters and non-spiritual matters need to be seen as connected. When I was first given the theme of this presentation 'Responsible leadership' and the sub-theme 'Responsible Religious Leadership', the latter sounded strange, not to say paradoxical, to me. My first thought was 'How can religious leadership not be responsible?' Anything spiritual certainly implies the sense of responsibility. Religious leadership is by definition responsible! There are no prerequisites for a religious leadership. Simply we recognise its principles. A religious leader's nomination is a result of the intervention of Divine Grace. Or at least this is how things should be...

Due to the diversity of societies and variety of beliefs, I believe that there is no *one single model* of responsible religious leadership applicable to all. Rather, what is ideally beneficial is an exchange of information, an analysis of the existing benchmarks and lastly, a mutual understanding. Therefore, I have decided to approach the subject of the ethical criteria of religious leadership from a specific perspective; that of my denomination, i.e. from the Greek Orthodox perspective, making special reference to the situation I live in (Greece), a case of a majority church, where approximately 97 % of 10.2 million inhabitants are Orthodox Christians.

My paper is divided into three parts. In the first part I briefly sketch a picture of the structure of the Orthodox Church, with due reference to the synodical system of the Greek Orthodox Church. In the second part I concentrate on three issues: the relation between the Church and its liturgical life and religious leadership; the relation between religious leadership with the State and politics; and the relation between religious leadership and society. The third part focuses on interreligious and ecumenical relations, which ought to be primary concerns of any religious leader in a pluralistic society.

## 1. The Structure of the Orthodox Church

The Greek Orthodox Church is built on the synodical system which is also the foundation of its administrative structure.[1] The synod of the bishops is 'the ultimate criterion of ecclesiastical affairs'.[2] This demands the obligatory participation of all diocesan bishops in the administration of the Church for the joint handling of its daily problems as well as the proportional allocation of responsibility to all participants.

Nevertheless, the synodical system in the Orthodox Church demands conciliarity (and/or synodality) to extend not only to the synods of bishops but also to all levels of the ecclesiastical life, from local parishes to diocesan councils and further on to regional and universal ones. In all these levels – according to the 34th Apostolic Canon – the 'one' should always cooperate with the 'many' (and *vice versa*). Unfortunately, this is still a *desideratum* in most *autocephali* churches in the Orthodox world.

## 2. Religious Leadership in the Church's Life

### a) Church Hierarchy, the Church and its Liturgical Life

The ordination of a new bishop and his placement by the Church at the helm of a diocese constitutes a historical ecclesiastical act, not only because it ensures apostolicity in succession, but primarily because it is the continuation of an important ecclesiastical service *(diakonia)*. For the new bishop, the concept of service and sacrifice are identical, as are the elevation of a bishop in his throne and his connection with the local church.

The elevation to any rank of the Church does not constitute an occupation of privilege or power, but an undertaking of service *(diakonia)* and sacrifice. The hierarchy that constitutes the ecclesiastical ranks has not the meaning of handing-over authority and rights, but distribution of ministries and services.

The picture of an 'upside down' pyramid represents clearly the elevation to the top in the hierarchy of the Church. Therefore, this elevation in the ecclesiastical pyramid has a 'self-emptying' *(kenotic)* character. The clergy, and especially the bishops, exist in the Church, not only *in persona Christi (eis topon Christou)*, but also in imitation, i.e. as a 'type of Christ' *(eis typon Christou)*; they are called to 'empty' themselves in order to carry the burden of others and render visible the presence of Christ among the faithful.[3]

Christ is at the top of the pyramid. Those who choose to follow him must aim to reach this top. Christ is the *High priest*[4] and even though in the liturgical life of the Orthodox Church *priesthood* he is sometimes erroneously identified only with the ordained clergy, all the baptised faithful are understood as priests (the so-called *royal priesthood*).[5] Of course the *higher orders* (bishops, presbyters, deacons, to be distinguished from a great number of lower orders)[6] existed from the very beginning, but their duty was to *preside*, not to *exercise* a priestly function.[7] The priestly function is exercised by Jesus Christ, and the priest (or bishop), when celebrating the Eucharist, is not a mediator between God and humanity, but acts *in persona Christi*. So the primate in the Church is a primate of service and sacrifice.

'If any human being wants to be first, he shall be last of all and servant of all.' (Mark 9:35) This action of unselfish love stands in opposition to any secular understanding of order, power and authority: 'You know that the rulers of the nations exercise power over them, and their great ones exercise authority over them. It shall be not so among you, but whoever desires to become great among you shall be your servant. Whoever desires to be first among you shall be your bondservant, as the Son of Man came not to be served, but to serve, and to give his life as a ransom for many.' (Matt 20:25-28)

The hierarchical structure of the Orthodox administration is rooted in the *trinitarian theology*,[8] which George Florovsky, John Meyendorff and Alexander Schmemann have so beautifully illustrated. And so, the hierarchy in the Church of Greece is justified by the order of the trinitarian structure, shown by the role of the Father, the Son and the Holy Spirit in the economy of salvation. This is particularly apparent in the eucharistic celebration and secondly in the collegial Synod of the Bishops.

In the *eucharistic ecclesiology*,[9] firstly developed by N. Afanassieff, emphasis is placed on the role of every local church – the expression of the whole (catholic) Church. That ecclesiology contrasts with *universal ecclesiology*, which favours the supremacy of the bishop and has until very recently been the dominant ecclesiological theory in the traditional churches. This has been the source of great debate. Afanassieff declared that 'where there is a Eucharistic gathering, there lives Christ; there lives also the Church of God in Christ.'[10]

In contrast to *eucharistic ecclesiology*,[11] *universal ecclesiology* exclusively attributes the catholicity of all local communities in the world to the one universal Church (and by extension to the first ecclesiastical see, Rome) and not from the individual local eucharistic community.

This way of addressing ecclesiology supports the sovereignty of *'bishop centralism'*. The theory of *universal ecclesiology* is based on the well-known position of Saint Cyprian of Carthage, according to whom 'The bishop is in the Church and the Church is in the bishop and who is not with the bishop does not belong to the Church'. [12]

In eucharistic ecclesiology the priority is given to the Eucharist, which is the only expression of unity in the Church, and in addition the eschatological (in opposition to the historical) dimension of the Church is emphasised. What is very important in this respect is that all clergy are understood as images of the authentic eschatological Kingdom of God, and not as higher offices within the Church *(in a secular hierarchical perspective)*. [13]

This eucharistic understanding of the Church leads also to a two-fold understanding of the liturgy: as a gathering of the people of God, and their mission as a *meta-liturgy*, i.e. as an authentic witness to the world.

## b)  Religious Leadership, State and Politics

Even though religion and politics are two entirely different matters, this does not mean that religious people should disassociate themselves from political matters. Politics are a major aspect of everyday life, and for that reason religious authorities, the Church in our case, should not remain voiceless. Of course the Church should not act as an institution which tries to offer solutions and find formulas for political debates, but it can help in a different way. It could help *politics to be more thoughtful and less confident*. [14]

In Greece the recognition of the Church as a social institution considerably influences the integration and keeping of people in her body. The Church is considered not only as an ark where the faithful receive the Grace of God and collaborate for their salvation and restoration, but also as an element of society. However, we cannot transform faith into political action.

The quotation from Matthew: 'Give therefore to Caesar the things that are Caesar's, and to God the things that are God's', [15] certainly separates religion from politics. But those are regulations with a deontological character and that means that they cannot form the social reality since actions by religious leaders sometimes have political consequences. Even dialogue between religion and the State can have positive or negative results, depending on the nature of their intentions. [16] Similarly, as with the aforementioned *eucharistic ecclesiology*, when a religiously committed person realises the ecclesiological dimension of the Church connected with *eschaton*, namely in its eucharistic approach, then safe political solutions to social problems can be provided.

In conclusion I will draw on the accurate observation by Prof. Vassiliadis that specifies the relation between church and State as follows: 'The Church as a religious institution does not counter act against the secular State, because it is not actually a secular authority, but the eschatological and charismatic people of God that is peacefully integrated in its social environment, aiming at sanctifying and transforming it'.[17]

*c) Religious Leadership and its Public Role in Society at Large*

In civil society, religion in its social dimension indicates how people should relate to each other. However, one of religion's main characteristics is that it is a private affair. Some of its principles are private and some are generalised cultural principles. But both should play an important role in achieving common and personal good. The link between those two aspects is inextricably linked to how religion connects private and public life. And this connection is only possible if its role can be understood and if it relates to the field of a religious leader.

As I have previously mentioned, a religious leader should not dictate resolutions on certain political issues. What he can do is to guide and to arm the faithful with the principles of love and concern for the other and to realise the *transformative power* of the Church that empowers their lives in history.[18]

To summarise, the Church should dare to address the multitude of critical and controversial issues of everyday life in a fast-changing world. This is a great challenge. And the witness of the Church to society is testified in two aspects: moral and social. The Church should find solutions to connect those two aspects. Many scholars[19] suggest that one possible way could be a synthesis of Eastern and Western spiritualities. Let us explain this a little further.

The Orthodox Church raises awareness about the ecclesial identity of Christianity focused on an eschatological dimension. On the other hand, Western theology reminds the world of the responsibility of the church, stressing the historical element in ecclesiology, theology and ethics. I fully agree that a *synthesis* between the two dimensions, historical and eschatological, cannot only enrich Eastern and Western traditions, but is also essential and can prevent serious dangers facing Christianity nowadays like religious isolationism and the desacralisation of the Gospel.

## 3. Religious Leadership and the 'Neighbour'

The great issue to which a religious leader is confronted is that of *negotiation of diversities*.[20] In a multireligious and multicultural society people of different historical and national backgrounds live with concrete cultural identities that everybody has to respect. This diversity is increasing. This raises the question: 'How can one face this diversity?'

As I previously mentioned, Greek religious reality does not have to face different faiths and different religious backgrounds. But nowadays under the light of universalism, the fact that we are also citizens of one world cannot be ignored. So, it is not a question of majority and minority in an Orthodox dominated society. It is a question of facing the other as God's creation. This 'chosen people' idea that Prof. Yahya Wijaya refers to in his article[21] quoting Wesley Ariarajah, can be a start of fundamentalist and nationalistic behaviours. The church *(ecclesia)* is not identified with the Kingdom of God, but is directed to it. And the church institutions do not constitute the utmost point of the faithful, but they are symbols of the Kingdom of God in the world that is offered to all as a result of their free will.

That great opening of the church to the world is based on freedom. And the reference to the *eschaton*, which is the essence of the liturgical life[22] of the church, is a characteristic of religious freedom. We see it clearly in the last verse of the Bible: 'He who testifies these things says, 'Yes, I come quickly'. Amen! Yes, come, Lord Jesus.' (Rev 22:20)

However, religious freedom should not be confused with religious tolerance, which some times can serve as a mask for unjust behaviour and promote social inequality. There is also a need for a more active leadership that will raise awareness that *diakonia* is not an optional action, but a duty. It is the praxis of the Church that authenticates its message, not vice versa.[23] An example of such a *life in community* is presented clearly in the *trinitarian theology*. The same hypostasis of the divinity is a paradigm of *life in community* and the intervention of God in history aims to lead humanity and all creation to be one with the very existence of God.

Also, the concept of the *liturgy after the liturgy*[24] that was first introduced by Ion Bria offers the opening of Christian life for public and political realm in a unique way. As Bria notes, 'The church has to struggle for the fulfilment of that justice and freedom which was promised by God to all men. It has constantly to give account of how the kingdom of heaven is or is not within it. It has to ask itself if by the conservativism of its worship it may appear to support the violation of human rights inside and outside the Christian community.'[25]

The struggle to comprehend the relation between Christianity and other religious traditions has engaged the church since the early centuries of Christianity. Christian mission has already passed through many phases. I shall refrain from referring to the historical development of the church's understanding of mission[26] because this is not the focus of my presentation. I simply maintain that Christian theology nowadays has a more holistic view of the *oekoumene* and should continue like this, abandoning old paradigms of proselytism which were detrimental not only to people of other religions but also to Christians of other denominations.

In Orthodox Christianity, mission does not aim primarily at propagating or dictating truths, doctrines, moral commands and so on, but rather at making *life in community* inherent in the trinitarian divinity visible and active. The 'sending' *(pempein)* of mission (John 14:26)[27] is the mission of the Holy Spirit that constitutes substantially the revelation of life of God as *koinonia*. And this *life in community* is characterised by the values of God's Kingdom that can be seen to all people of good will,[28] even the non religious!

## Conclusion

In modernity, despite the challenge of post-modernism, a person's life in religion is a private affair. That means it is optional and based on one's own free will. Leadership, all over the world, should promote the idea that the witness *(martyria)* of the church is mainly directly related to the internal individual local churches. It is a matter of identity of each concrete ecclesiastical community: 'For even as we have many members in one body, and all the members do not have the same function, so we, who are many, are one body in Christ, and individually members one of another' (Rom 12:4-5).

When we address issues of personal identity and cohesion of society, religion, as part of a cultural system,[29] plays an important role. No one can talk about probable models of a multicultural society without taking religion into consideration.

The academic analysis of the religious phenomenon has shown that the study of religious data is not only useful but also essential to social matters.[30] The history of religions and academic interreligious dialogue aids the effort to achieve mutual understanding and the exchange of religious knowledge. Both mutual understanding and the exchange of religious knowledge are vital devices necessary to approach the world religious experience.

The formulation of the structure of an ecclesiastical community[31] is related with the face of the leader and how this had gradually developed in the political systems and the cultural regulations that emerged in the long-lasting course of various Christian communities.

Nowadays, the pressing issue that arises in a continuously transforming society is how religious leadership can respond to the new demands and face the new challenges.[32] In the words of Saint Paul: 'Don't be conformed to this world, but be transformed by the renewing of your mind, so that you may prove what is the good, well-pleasing, and perfect will of God.' (Rom 12:2), *transforming* then seems to be the key rather than *conforming*.

It is a widely accepted historical fact that in the past religion provided a motive for bloody conflicts and animosity between people. At the same time, it is also acknowledged that religion has the internal dynamics to heal the traumas and tensions caused by errors of the past. Religion cannot remain indifferent to the anxieties and needs of people today.

Of course, many people believe that the church is betrayed by its leaders every time they abuse their leadership role and position, and every time they show an arrogant conviction that they are the only bearers of God's grace. They have to keep in mind that it is God who reconciles, and human beings actually participate in God's Mission. We are living in the new era of globalisation which has brought people together and at the same time pointed to the diversities of the several pluralistic environments. It is our duty to create safe places and reconciling (and reconciled) communities. Our vision must be to form such communities, in other words to make again the church what it really is.

NOTES

[1]   About the hierarchy of the Greek Orthodox Church, see the official website of the Church of Greece: http://www.ecclesia.gr.

[2]   Nicodemus of the Holy Mountain, *To Pidalion* (in Greek), Athens: Astir, 1976, p. 120. English translation: *The Rudder* (trans. D. Cummings), Chicago, 1957.

[3]   Mantzarides, G., *Christian Ethics*, Thessaloniki: Pournaras, 1995, p.166.

[4]   Meyendorff, Paul, *The Priesthood of the Laity*. From his April 2005 presentation at the Theological Faculty of AuTh. 'The notion of Christ as "high priest" is developed in the epistle to the Hebrews – cf. Heb 2:17; 3:1; 4:14; 5:1-10; 6:20; 7:26-28; 8:1-3; 9:11-22; 10:21'.

[5]   *Ibidem*, p. 6. Paul Meyendorff argues that in the Orthodox liturgical life, priesthood is typically identified with ordained clergy, particularly bishops and priests, who have the authority to preside over the eucharistic liturgy and other sacraments and services.

[6]   More about the concept of order in Schmemann, Alexander, *Introduction to Liturgical Theology*, Crestwood, NY: St. Vladimir's Seminary Press, 1966. Translation into Greek by Fr. Demetrios Tzerpos, 1991.

[7]   'All things should be done decently and in order'. (1 Cor 14:40)

[8]   I draw the following footnote from my personal notes, which in turn may come from some reading I have done: 'Within the Trinitarian hierarchical order each one of the three Persons *(hypostases)* have an entire divine role. On this basis, the three divine persons dwell in one another *(perichoresis)*: inter-dwelling, co-inherence. Each one of the three acts together with the other two; however, each of them relates to the creation in a personal way: the Father conceives the plan of creation (and of restoration of Creation in His Christ); the Son of God makes the Father's plan of creation (and the salvation of creation) a reality; the Holy Spirit leads God's (the Father's) plan of creation (and restoration of creation in Christ, the incarnate Logos of God) to its perfection.'

[9]   Almost concomitantly with the present conference, several thousand miles away in the small village of Assisi in Italy, another conference is taking place with the title: 'L'Eucaristica nella tradizione orientale e occidentale con speciale riferimento al dialogo ecumenico', Assisi 4-7 September 2005. There Prof. Stamoulis argues that the ecclesiastical body of the Church does not consist of bishops and clergy. Everyone that takes part in the Eucharist is part of the ecclesias-

tical body *(royal priesthood)*. He adds also the fine remark that the 'Eucharist and practice *(askhsh)* are not magical actions that automatically transform insufficiency in sufficiency, sickness in health, pain in comfort'. There are signs of the existing unity.

10 Afanassieff, N., 'Una Sancta', in: *Irenikon* 36 (1963), p. 459. 'Là où est une assemblée eucharistique, là demeure le Christ et là est l'Eglise de Dieu en Christ.'

11 Vassiliadis, Petros, 'Eucharistic Theology, the consensus fideliun, and the contribution of theology to the ecclesial witness', delivered at the Ecumenical symposium in Bari, December 1999. 'The eucharistic theology was not exclusively an Eastern theological product; it was rather the child of the ecumenical era'.

12 Carthagene, Cyprianus, *Epistle* LXVI, 8, 3: 'Scribe debes episcorum in ecclesia esse et ecclesiam in episcopo et si qui cum episcopo non sit in ecclesia non esse'.

13 Vassiliadis, Petros, *op. cit.* About the notion of universal ecclesiology he argues that 'The universal ecclesiology, having as its point of departure the historical dimension of the Church, understands unity, truth and other related aspects the Church, such as e.g. the apostolic succession, in a linear and not in an eschatological way that is why the bishop, even when he is understood as a type and/or image of the Christ, has a clear priority over the eucharistic community, and even over the Eucharist itself. The Sacrament, therefore, of Priesthood theoretically surpasses the Sacrament of the Eucharist.'

14 Clapsis, Emmanuel, *Orthodoxy in Conversation*, Geneva: World Council of Churches, 2000, pp. 221-224.

15 Matt 22:21.

16 More about the distinction of religion and politics in Greece in Petrou, I., *Multicultularism and Religious Freedom*, Thessaloniki: Paratiritis, 2003, pp. 181-184.

17 Vassiliadis, Petros, *PAUL. Trajectories into his Theology*, Thessaloniki: Pournaras, 2004, p. 232. In the same book he notes four bible passages that in the past were held as principles for constituting a religious leadership.

18 More about the public role of religion in Clapsis, Emmanuel, *Orthodoxy in Conversation*, Geneva: World Council of Churches, 2000, pp. 131-136.

19 See Vassiliadis, Petros, 'Orthodoxy and Ecumenism,' in *Eucharist and Witness. Orthodox Perspectives on the Unity and Mission of the Church*, Geneva/Brookline, MA: World Council of Churches/Holy Cross Orthodox Press, 1998 and 'Eucharistic Theology, the consensus fideliun, and the contribution of theology to the ecclesial witness' delivered at the Ecumenical Symposium in Bari, December 1999.

20 I prefer the term 'diversities', than the term 'differences'.

21 Wijaya, Yahya, 'Theological Leadership in Christian-Muslim Encounters. An Indonesian Perspective' in: Stückelberger, Christoph/Mugambi, J.N.K (eds), *Responsible Leadership. Global Perspectives*, Nairobi: Acton Publishers, 2005, pp. 71-84. See also Chapter 12 in this volume.

22 Eucharist does not draw its content just from the remembrance of the resurrection of Christ, but also from the expectation of the final resurrection (1 Cor 11:26).

23 Clapsis, Emmanuel, *op. cit.*, p. 224.

24 Bria, Ion, *The Liturgy after the Liturgy. Mission and Witness from an Orthodox Perspective*, Geneva: World Council of Churches, 1996.

25 Raiser, Konrad, 'The Importance of the Orthodox Contribution to the WCC', in: *The Orthodox Church and the Ecumenical Movement, Thessaloniki: Apostoliki diakonia* , 2003, p. 49.

26 Vassiliadis, Petros, 'Reconciliation and the Holy Spirit. The Theological Dimension of the Christian Mission' in *IRM* 2005.

27 John 14:26, 'But the Counsellor, the Holy Spirit, whom the Father will send in my name, he will teach you all things, and will remind you of all that I said to you.'

28 In the press release of WCC on 26 August 2003 the moderator of the Central Committee, His Holiness Aram I, Catholicos of Cilicia, has called for 'dialogue, relations and collaboration with other religions' to have a 'high priority' in the Council's ecumenical witness. Among other things he suggests that 'the implication for missionary strategy is that, particularly in pluralistic environments, it is inappropriate to attempt to add new members.' Instead, 'we should seek to identify the Christic values in other religions'.

29 Hock, Klaus, 'Beyond the Multireligious. Transculturation and Religious Differentiation', in: 'Search of a New Paradigm in the Academic Study of Religious Change and Interreligious

138 Responsible Leadership: Global Perspectives

Encounter', in: Mortensen, Viggo (ed.), *Theology and the Religions. A Dialogue*, Grand Rapids, MI/Cambridge: Eerdmans, 2003, pp. 46-63. 'Furthermore, the cultural turn in the humanities has had its impact on the academic study of religions, inasmuch as religious studies are now more and more understood as a 'social/cultural anthropological discipline' dealing with religions as cultural phenomena', p. 55.

[30] McCutcheon, Russel T./Braun, Willi, *Guide to the Study of Religion*, London/New York : Cassell, 2000. Also in the book of Russel McCutcheon, *Critics, not Caretakers. Redescribing the Public Study of Religion*, New York: SUNY Press, 2001. The same author argues that we should examine religion only as a social phenomenon, p. x.

[31] About the evolution in the ecclesiastical structure through the ages in East and West see more in Petrou, J., *Christianity and Society*, Thessaloniki: Vanias, 2004, pp. 80-105.

[32] Many scholars had proposed a 'liturgical renewal' and a renewal of theology, in order to correspond to the requirements of the modern cultural environment, but also with the needs of the church.

# 14

## GENDER RESPONSIBILITY
## IN RELIGIOUS LEADERSHIP

*Heike Walz, Germany/Argentina*

## 1. Leadership in Argentina

Leadership is in crisis in Argentina. It is not only about politicians, who have been criticised for showing lack of moral authority and integrity in recent times, but also about religious leaders, mainly from the Roman Catholic Church, which traditionally has had a significant impact on religious life in Argentina.[1] On the one hand, trust in politicians, political organisations and the State is lacking, and the credibility of institutions such as political parties, members of the judicial system, trade unions, educational institutions and religious institutions is in crisis. On the other hand, human rights organisations of civil society such as the Mothers of Plaza de Mayo or the ecumenical movement for human rights (MEDH) are still active and publicly respected. Argentina is going through a transformation process from a 'defective democracy' to a 'consolidated democracy', to use categories of political science. A lack of confidence in democracy as a political system as well as in representatives of democracy is part of the crisis of leadership.

However, as we have noted, there are also actors of civil society such as neighbourhood organisations, NGOs, social and church networks, which, in many cases, are experimenting with participative and horizontal democratic structures themselves, or are accompanying those developing them, with the aim of enabling and fostering citizenship participation. Diaconal projects against poverty see *enabling participation* as a key goal because almost half of the population is suffering from some kind of non-participation, especially with respect to basic needs and citizenship. One of the most urgent problems all leaders of the country are facing is the high rate of poverty and of pauperisation.[2] A sort of social ecumenism already exists between members of different denominations, sometimes extending to other religions, together with NGOs and social movements, e.g. in empowerment projects to help women and men develop basic competencies in citizenship (e.g. in the so-called *escuelas de ciudadanía*, schools of citizenship), and projects focused on education and literacy.

Those working in such projects are observing *gender differences* in terms of participation. Women and men are participating or *not* participating in economy and society in different manners. They are also participating differently in the struggle for citizenship. Generally speaking, groups of women are often the first to organise for social change in contrast to the many men who leave their family, become addicts or violent. The concept of masculinity is at stake here since without a job and money men lose self-esteem. There is little evidence of men finding constructive solutions to their problems. Generally, women are those left alone with the responsibility to care for the children. As they have to struggle for their own survival and the survival of their children, many women have been taken to sharing their crisis, often creating neighbourhood organisations. While women also feel shame, depression and loss of self-esteem, they seem to have to loose less than men, so that many of them are able to share their crisis with others and to mobilise themselves. The concept of femininity is also a factor here. Though the economical crisis has increased, and in spite of their vulnerability (e.g. women earn 48 % of the wages of men in the informal economic sector), women have been organising themselves and developing leadership qualities within these participation projects.

A specific gendering in churches and in society can either enable women or men to participate in the struggle for a better life, or prevent and negate their participation. The question is how religious leadership can contribute to solve this problem of lack of participation. What I would like to suggest in this paper is that leadership implies *enabling participation* of everybody in church and society; and therefore that religious leadership should include *gender responsibility*.

With regard to this, I will (1) explain the idea of *religious leadership* as enabling participation; demonstrate (2) the need for *gender responsibility* and (3) the necessity of developing *gendered ethics* of religious leadership; (4) explore the idea of how *body vulnerability* as a 'material principle' (Enrique Dussel) serves as a critical principle; (5) argue that the model of leadership as enabling participation is based on Christian understandings of *God's Trinitarian participation* in the world that enables the church's mission in the world, before (6) ending with some conclusions.

## 2. Religious Leadership as Enabling Participation in Life

In this paper I will focus on religious leadership from a Christian perspective. I will refer to internal church leadership, clergywomen and clergymen and lay leaders as well as to the *public and prophetic mandate* of churches within society, noting that Christians are called to be like salt of the earth (Matt 5:13). It is a diaconal perspective of leadership, as it puts emphasis on serving the community, as a testimony that God's Kingdom is already present on earth. This christological concept of leadership is based on Mark 10:35-45 where Jesus presents himself as deacon of all human beings. Leadership as service means here that leadership is understood as *enabling women and men participating in life.* [3]

Some people on the margins of Argentina criticise the idea of 'participation' as utopian. In the Province of Buenos Aires new generations of children are growing up without schooling, a stable family life or job prospects and in a context of violence and crime. Participation in civil life seems to be a utopian vision. [4] At the same time leadership as a public and prophetic mandate of the churches deals with responsibility. Generally speaking, responsibility can be understood as the will or obligation to deal with the consequences of one's actions. [5] Applying this on the proposed concept of leadership, gender-conscious ethical reflection is a result. Naivety or ignorance with regard to gender must be transformed.

## 3. Gender Responsibility in Ethical Discourses

Gender neutrality is not possible, because everybody is dealing with social constructs of gender and accompanying prejudices in personal relationships and the wider society. This becomes clearer when we look at the history of philosophical and theological ethical discourses. There have been various hermeneutics with which the discourses have faced the question that human beings are considered either female or male. The gender question is either explicitly or implicitly dealt with, and the relation between women and men is valorised in a specific way.

The first hermeneutic presents itself as *gender neutral*, since it fails to talk about men and women explicitly. Most of the historical protestant theologians kept silent about gender. Perhaps some considered women and men as equal and thought that there was nothing more to say, yet working with a concept of abstract humanity that ignores concrete reality that all human beings are declared either female or male in the first seconds of their life. Taking a closer look at this type of discourse, it becomes clear that it is operating *implicitly* with gender constructions that are also asymmetrical in many cases.

The second method is talking about women and men *explicitly* and in an *asymmetrical way*, as it had been present in much philosophical history. The female is viewed in comparison to the 'general human', which is considered as male. As a consequence of the feminist movements, Women Studies, and Gender Studies this discourse has been criticised, but – depending on the context – has not completely disappeared.

The third hermeneutic is the concept of *complementarities* of women and men, which is very common (explicitly or implicitly) in theological discourses and church life as well as in many cultural contexts. In many cases this discourse puts emphasis on the different 'nature' and social position of women and men, but states that this difference means equality. It argues that women and men have different destinies in the world. Looking at the lived reality it becomes clear that this discourse is instrumentalising the concept of difference in order to hide inequality. This discourse confuses two concepts: it is not difference that should be eliminated in favour of a more equal society, but inequality. All people are different from each other (by age, nationality, sex, ethnicity, etc.) and this difference is part of the interdependency of identity and alterity in humanity, but differences do not have to result in inequalities. The discourse of complementarities mixes up the antinomy of equal/unequal and identical/different.

This brief overview on gender hermeneutics in philosophy and theology shows that in most cases implicit and explicit gendering of ethical discourses does not manage to overcome gender asymmetries. As a result, ethical discourses tend to be accomplices in devaluing women while failing to meet the needs of men, too. Gender responsibility in ethical discourses about religious leadership needs gender reflection, which deals with the concrete realities of women and men, instead of operating with an abstract concept of humanity that is supposed to talk about 'man'.

## 4. Gender Ethics as Responsibility for the Concrete 'Other'[6]

Gender ethics are not just another theory of ethics, but offer a specific perspective on ethics intending to transform ethical theories and moral practices. In the same way as feminist ethics are considered to be a specific form of *political ethics*,[7] gender ethics can be understood as a form of critical theory that questions the very concept of politics (including the conceptualisation of the private and the public) and of democracy, arguments legitimating power, the concept of subjectivity, autonomy, etc. In addition to this, I want to suggest that the moral subject should not be conceptualised as an abstract subject without body and without relationships, because this tends to result in a white male moral subject with property and social status. Gender ethics is dealing with a situated person living in a concrete historical situation, with a body and emotions.

At this stage it is helpful to consider Seyla Benhabib's ethical theory. In her concept of the *ethics of the concrete Other*,[8] she proposes a way of dealing with the concrete reality of women and men. She makes a distinction between the standpoint of the generalised Other and the standpoint of the concrete Other. Moral theories based on autonomy in a universalistic perspective normally deal with the standpoint of the generalised, but in order to attempt to understand one's own subjectivity, as well as others' points of views, people need to interact with specific others. Benhabib states: 'Neither the concreteness nor the otherness of the "concrete other" can be known in the absence of the voice of the other. The viewpoint of the concrete other emerges as a distinct one only as a result of self-definition. It is the other who makes us aware both of her concreteness and her otherness'.[9] She proposes an interactive universalism in which the generalised Other always is a concrete Other. The difference between the generalised and the concrete Other is not meant in a prescriptive way, but in a critical perspective: the intention is to respect the dignity of the generalised Other in order to accept the moral identity of the concrete Other.[10] Benhabib developed this idea by discussing the controversy between Carol Gilligan and Lawrence Kohlberg.[11] It is obvious that she does not want to give up entirely universal and general perspectives in ethics, but she wants to include the standpoints of the concrete subjects of moral decisions.

Benhabib's concept is very close to the *ethics of responsibility* developed by Dietrich Bonhoeffer,[12] Hans Jonas,[13] Hans-Eduard Tödt,[14] and others. In this article I want to refer to the ethics of responsibility developed in Latin America and the Caribbean. Since the 1970s, during the Cold War, responsibility has become a central topic in Latin American moral reflection. 'Neoliberal' economic politics excluding wide sectors of the population, corruption in politics, ecological problems, marginalisation and discrimination led to an ethic which began with historical realities.[15] Enrique Dussel underlines that responsibility includes three aspects: responsibility for something or somebody; responsibility for action; and responsibility for consequences. His ethics of responsibility from the Latin-American context is individual and social at the same time, as persons and social structures are concerned.

Benhabib's concept of the concrete Other and an ethics of individual and social responsibility in Latin America lead to an *ethics of gender responsibility for the concrete Other and the social structures* of the society and the churches. Therefore it is important to make a shift from feminist ethics[16] to gender ethics[17] in the sense that the gender problem has to engage both women and men to transform the stereotypes of masculinity and femininity and in order to change the established gender order with its asymmetries.[18] Creating equal opportunities for women and men in all institutions (in law, politics, churches, etc.) will always be the base of gender ethics. I call this an *ethic of equality*. The struggle for equality should not assimilate women to men, this is an ethic of *equality in differences*, but it should also not repeat the classical gender order, in which women have to care for everybody and men have to exercise power. Hence, I prefer to combine an ethic of care with an ethic of justice, as various feminist ethicians are arguing.[19] Often women and men seem to use different strategies to cope with economical and life crisis. If we do not reduce this 'female' and 'male' ethics on biological reasons, the ethic of care and the ethic of justice are a result of gendered social practices and not a result of biological essence. Consequently we can suggest changing gender behaviour, and if we have a closer look at the concrete life of men, we observe that not every man is able to make profit of the 'patriarchal dividend'.[20] There are also specific gender barriers that sometimes prevent men from contributing to life, especially from caring for life. Still other barriers (ethnicity, class, age, etc.) interfere with gender.

Hence, what I am proposing here is a *constructivist* perspective on *gender ethics*. Gender does not automatically refer only to women, as women and men are constructors of their gender and of the gender of others. Furthermore the constructivist perspective includes critical men's studies on gender. One of the main protagonists of the critical men's studies, Robert W. Connell from Australia, shows how the 'hegemonic concept of masculinity' creates hierarchies between men.[21] Concepts of hegemonic masculinity and also classical femininity are interrelated. In the long run, changes in gender constructions will only be put in practice, if not only women are changing themselves and transforming the society, but if men are actively working on changing the gendered society as well. In most places, men who question the established masculinity are considered as 'dangerous' and meet a lot of resistance. Gender ethics including critical men's perspectives has to start with a *theological dialogue about gender between women and men who are taking over gender responsibility*. A sort of ethical code for this dialogue has to be worked out.[22]

This constructivist perspective on gender ethics takes into account differences between women and between men. The impact of gender on the life of persons and institutions can differ from one context to the other, as there are also other categories building up inequalities (class, race, ethnicity, sexuality, age, etc.). The interdependency of these categories should be taken in account by gender ethics. Therefore a constructivist perspective questions whether we can really talk about *one* female or *one* male moral behaviour; and we also have to ask if there is one female ethic and one male ethic. If we radicalise this position, the consequence is the deconstruction of the binary construction of female and male gender. This is the so-called *deconstructivist* perspective which says that social gender *and biological sex* are historically, socially, and culturally constructed. By questioning the established gender order and the very concept of gender itself, this position is causing *gender trouble*.[23]

There is an ongoing debate on the question whether it is a better strategy to claim 'female' values and a specific 'female morale' (as e.g. care ethic is doing it) or to put in question the category of female and male in itself (as deconstructivism is doing it) to overcome asymmetries. I think the only way to change the gender order is to question its very construction. It is not sufficient to value femininity, if the whole gender order is not challenged. Clear notions of what is female and what is male gives provides stability. But women pay a high price for this stability and, as highlighted above, men do, too, but in a different way. The idea is to accept and motivate more *fluid* gender conceptions, which enable women and men to enter in zones that have been closed for them. Therefore I suggest combining a *gender differentiated analysis* and a creative way of *gender troubling*.

Before concluding this section, I would like to make a critical observation. Deconstructivism tends to concentrate on symbolical and verbal recognition of different gendering. It risks forgetting the material, embodied, and institutional dimensions of gender. This leads to two consequences. Gender responsible ethics have to work both on the transformation of socio-economic and political gender barriers as well as on the transformation of symbolical gender constructions. This is the reason why I will introduce a critical principle in the next section – that of 'body vulnerability'.

## 5. Body Vulnerability as Critical Principle

There are two reasons for choosing body vulnerability as critical principle for gender ethics. The first has to do with the *Latin American context*. It is not accidental that in recent years the body has been central to Latin American liberation theologies and feminist discourses in general.[24] Vulneration of bodies prevents women and men in difficult conditions of life from real participation in life. Liberation theology has always considered the suffering of the people as the starting point of theology.[25] Therefore various *body theologies* have been developed; some concepts by male theologians, others within ecofeminist body theology. This focus on the body is related to the politics of violating bodies and making bodies disappear during the dictatorships of recent Latin America[26] having rigid reproduction laws, irresponsible sexual ethics and polluted body of the environment, which disproportionally impact on the bodies of poor people. Body theologies emerge in a context of pauperisation and male violence against women as well as in the context of violence of men against men.[27] Thus, bodies have been vulnerated by political powers, by consequences of rigid reproduction moral, by sexual moral teaching, by lack of ecological responsibility, and by violence. Caring for the body and the bodies of the concrete Other, responsibility for my body and the bodies of the concrete Other (individual perspective) should be combined with social ethics of justice for all embodied selves (social perspective) and with caring for the body of the earth (ecological perspective). Vulnerability is a fundamental of all life on earth. All human beings are facing body vulnerability, be they poor or the rich.

The second reason has to do with *anthropological aspects* of theology. The concrete gendered human being leads to the perception of human beings as *gendered embodied selves*. Thus gender discourse has focused on *body discourses* during recent years. Since reflecting on gender, questions about corporeality are automatically part of the problem. Body politics concern private and intimate aspects of life and yet are present in public, political and theological discourses. Including body discourses in ethical reflections changes the perception of the subjects of doing ethics. It becomes clear that these subjects are not abstract, but embodied selves. [28]

What I am suggesting here is a gender-differentiated perspective on the concrete body vulnerability of women and men. The intention is to overcome gender stereotypes in order to be responsible women and men. Thus care, responsibility, and justice for embodied selves do not picture care as female and justice as male, but gives value to such concerns as vulnerability, care giving, nurturing, mothering – not in the biological sense, but as a social activity – while disconnecting them from biological femininity, so that they are not exclusively female. The aim of this deconstructive position is to overcome these limitations in order to build up a society who takes over responsibility as a whole.

## 6. Theology of the Triune God's Participation in Life

Responsibility for gender and the body in religious leadership is based on a *Trinitarian participation theology*. God's wisdom participates in the life of creation, as it says in Wisdom 7:27: 'Although she is but one, she can do all things. And while remaining in herself, she renews all things; in every generation she passes into holy souls and makes them friends of God, and prophets.' [29] This participation can be seen in the history of salvation: the Triune God is the giver of life, creating the world as vulnerable. God incarnate in the body of Jesus Christ participates in the vulnerability and suffering of humanity, but overcomes suffering in the resurrection of Jesus Christ. The Spirit of God has been present since the creation of the world and is a gift to the world, participating in the lives of embodied selves of women and men. The community of women and men in the Church is nurtured by this participation of God in the community. This concept of *par-*

*ticipation in Christ* is part of Paul's theology, particularly through the metaphor of the mystical union with Christ ('to be in Christ', 'Body of Christ', see in 1 Cor 12:14, Rom 12:4-8, 1 Cor 6:15-15). This has consequences for ecclesiology and church leadership. The community of women and men celebrate and preach God's participation in bodily selves in the Church and in the world. The body of Christ as community of real embodied selves has received the mandate to be responsible to enable participation in God's life for every woman or man, within the Church and within the political community. It is obvious that there would be a more equal Church.[30]

## 7. Final Remarks

God's participation in the world in salvation history enables women and men to see themselves as enablers of participation in life. Leadership means to engage oneself in enabling of participation. Religious leaders have to take over gender responsibility, as gender constructions can either facilitate or prevent women and men's participation in life. Responsible leadership needs to develop gender ethics, which have been described above as ethics of gender responsibility for the concrete Other and the social structures of communities. Starting point of gender ethics is the concrete reality of women and men are living as gendered and embodied selves. In comparison to feminist ethics, gender ethics considers women and men as responsible for changing the established gender order. This change includes the transformation of socio-economic and political gender barriers as well as the transformation of symbolical gender constructions. The ethical subjects are gendered and embodied selves. Body vulnerability serves as critical principle, gender and body issues are interrelated. Care, responsibility and justice for all embodied selves are the aim of gender responsibility in religious leadership. Religious leaders can count on God's presence and action through the Spirit and Christ.

NOTES

[1]  The majority of the people in Argentina say they are Catholics. Empirical statistics about Protestants (historical churches and Pentecostals) give a varying number of 5 % and 10 % (see Wynarzyck 2003, 31-33). Pentecostals are not as numerous in Argentina as in other Latin American countries, but they are still well represented, especially among poor people and indigenous communities. Protestant historical churches (Lutheran, Reformed, United, Methodist, Anglican tradition, etc.) are small in number and therefore rarely visible in public. Thus, their impact on politics and society is quite limited. The Jewish population represents about 2 % of the total population, and other religions, including Muslims, about 4 %. Argentina has engaged in interreligious dialogue in recent years. Two significant events took place in August 2005: Catholics, Jews and Muslims signed a declaration against terrorism and fundamentalism; and an interreligious conference (with Jews, Muslims, Catholics and Protestants) about the integration of differently abled persons was held in Buenos Aires.

2    About half of the population in Argentina is excluded from the current global economic system. Argentina, especially the capital Buenos Aires, seems to mirror the whole world 'in nucleon'. After the economical crisis in 2001, Argentina has become more 'Latin American', with about 47.8 % of the population (about 15.5 million people) living in poor homes and about 18.7 million people lacking daily food. Unemployment is an urgent problem and in many cases wages are so low that people need extra income resources. The gap between the richest and the poorest has increased between 1980 (with a ratio of 1 to 11.9) and 2002 (1 to 46.6). Communities of indigenous people are obviously the poorest of the poor.

3    In ecumenical discourses, emphasis has been put on a *theology of life*. See Raiser, Konrad, *For a Culture of Life. Transforming Globalization and Violence*, Geneva: WCC Publications, 2002; Robra, Martin, 'Theology of Life – Justice, Peace, Creation. An Ecumenical Study', in: *Ecumenical Review* Vol. 48, no.1, 1996, pp. 28-37.

4    See the recent publications about ethics of liberation and philosophy of liberation by Enrique Dussel, an Argentinian philosopher and theologian living in Mexico. For instance, see Dussel, Enrique, *Etica de la liberación*, Madrid: Trotta, 1998.

5    Thus, responsibility means to consider such consequences as success, failure, luck, or guilt. Responsibility is something coming in mind after having done an action, when one is called to account for her action. Secondly responsibility is also accompanying actions, especially when we feel responsible for something or someone. Thirdly responsibility is also at stake before having done something. If one agrees to do a work, one declares him as responsible. Responsibility normally is viewed as a positive thing, while people acting without responsibility are judged negatively because they harm other people, the community, the environment or cause danger. Consequently one should be conscious of her responsibility, because one is influencing other people either positively or negatively. Sometimes discourses about responsibility are hiding that one is aiming at getting power or conserving power for oneself.

6    'Other' written with a majuscule refers here to the alternate Other.

7    Pieper, Annemarie, *Gibt es eine feministische Ethik?*, München: Fink, 1998, pp. 22-23.

8    Benhabib, Seyla, 'Der verallgemeinerte und der konkrete Andere. Die Kohlberg/Gilligan-Kontroverse aus der Sicht der Moraltheorie', in: Seyla Benhabib, *Selbst im Kontext*, Frankfurt am Main: Suhrkamp, 1992, pp. 161-191. She asks: 'Can there be a feminist contribution to moral philosophy? That is to say, can those men and women who view the gender-sex system of our societies as oppressive, and who regard women's emancipation as essential to human liberation, criticise, analyse and when necessary replace the traditional categories of moral philosophy in order to contribute to women's emancipation and human liberation?' See Benhabib, Seyla, *Situating the Self. Gender, Community and Postmodernism in Contemporary Ethics*, Cambridge: Polity Press, 1992, p. 148.

9    Benhabib, Seyla, *Situating the Self. Gender, Community and Postmodernism Contemporary Ethics*, Cambridge: Polity Press, 1992, p. 168.

10   Benhabib, Seyla, 'Der verallgemeinerte und der konkrete Andere. Die Kohlberg/Gilligan-Kontroverse aus der Sicht der Moraltheorie', in: *op. cit.*, p. 183.

11   Gilligan, Carol, *In a Different Voice. Psychological Theory and Women's Development*, Cambridge, MA: Harvard University Press, 1982; Nunner-Winkler, Gertrud (ed.), *Weibliche Moral. Die Kontroverse um eine geschlechtsspezifische Ethik*, München: Deutscher Taschenbuchverlag, 1995.

12   Bonhoeffer, Dietrich, *Ethik*, ed. by Ilse Tödt *et al.*, Gütersloh: Chr. Kaiser Verlag, 1998 (1st edition: 1992).

13   Jonas, Hans, *Das Prinzip Verantwortung. Versuch einer Ethik für die technologische Zivilisation*. Frankfurt am Mainz: Insel, 1979.

14   Tödt, Heinz Eduard, *Perspektiven theologischer Ethik*, München: Chr. Kaiser, 1988; Schuhmacher, Wolfgang, *Theologische Ethik als Verantwortungsethik. Leben und Werk Heinz Eduard Tödts in ökumenischer Perspektive*, Öffentliche Theologie, Bd. 20, Gütersloh: Gütersloher Verlagshaus, 2006.

15   May, Roy A., *Discernimiento moral. Una introducción a la ética cristiana*, San José: 2004, p. 118 ff. Philosophers and theologians who worked on the topic include Franz Hinkelammert, Yung Mo Sung, Enrique Dussel and José Miguez Bonino.

16   See e.g. Praetorius, Ina, *Handeln aus der Fülle. Postpatriarchale Ethik in biblischer Tradition*, Gütersloh: Gütersloher Verlagshaus, 2005; Wendel, Saskia, *Feministische Ethik zur Einführung*, Hamburg: Junius, 2003; Schnabl, Christa, 'Feministische Ethik: Profil und Herausforderungen', in: *Salzburger Theologische Zeitschrift* 6, 2002, pp. 269-282, also on

http://www.sbg.ac.at/sathz/2002-2/sathz-2002-2-09_schnabl.pdf; Cahill, Lisa L., *Sex, Gender and Christian Ethics*, Cambridge: Cambridge University Press, 1996.

[17] See e.g. Mieth, Dietmar, 'Geschlechtertheorie als Subtext theologischer Ethik', in: *Theologische Quartalschrift* Vol. 184, no. 1, 2004, pp. 1-2; Wendel, Saskia, 'Hat das moralische Subjekt ein Geschlecht?', in: *Ibid.*, pp. 3-17.

[18] We can identify four main tendencies since the 1970s in European and US discourses on feminist ethics. Each tendency has contributed important aspects. Though these tendencies developed chronologically, all of them have been at stake up until now. Sometimes these main lines are put in competition and in conflict to each other. I combine basic ideas in order to elaborate gender ethics. See Kuhlmann, Helga, 'Ethik der Geschlechterdifferenz?', in: *Und drinnen waltet die züchtige Hausfrau. Zur Ethik der Geschlechterdifferenz*, Gütersloh: Gütersloher Verlagshaus, 1995, pp. 7-15.

[19] Some ethicians are suggesting an ethic of difference saying that a female morale of care is better than a male morale of justice, referring to the classical conflict between Carol Gilligan and Lawrence Kohlberg. Gillian's ethics of care inspired many feminist ethicians. Another example of combing the two aspects is found in: Schnabl, Christa, *Gerecht sorgen. Grundlagen einer sozialethischen Theorie der Fürsorge*, Freiburg im Brisgau: Herder, 2005.

[20] Connell, Robert W., *Der gemachte Mann. Konstruktion und Krise von Männlichkeiten*, Opladen: Leske + Budrich, 2000, pp. 97-102, here: p. 100 (Original in English: Connell, Robert W., *Masculinities*, Berkeley: University of California Press, 1995).

[21] *Op. cit.*, p. 102.

[22] Together with one women (Tania Oldenhage) and two men (Christoph Walser, Andreas Borter) we have built up a network on gender and theology for women and men including queer perspectives: Netzwerk geschlechterbewusster Theologie (NGT). So far we have begun networking with German speaking theologians and held a conference in Switzerland in January 2006.

[23] Butler, Judith, *Gender Trouble. Feminism and the Subversion of Identity. Thinking Gender*, New York & London: Routledge, 1990; Butler, Judith, *Bodies that Matter. On the Discursive Limits of 'Sex'*, New York & London: Routledge, 1993.

[24] Kriesel, Stefan, *Der Körper als Paradigma. Leibesdiskurse in Kultur, Volksreligiosität und Theologie Brasiliens*, Lucern: Exodus, 2001; see ecofeminist theologians like Ivone Gebara in: *Intuiciones ecofeministas: ensayo para repensar el conocimiento y la religión*, Montevideo: Doble Clic, 1998; 'Ecofeminism: a Latin American Perspective', in: *Cross Currents* 53, 2003, pp. 93-103; *Longing for Running Water. Ecofeminism and Liberation*, Minneapolis, MN: Fortress Press, 1999.

[25] In January 2005, Norwegian theologian Sturla Stålsett gave a speech about vulnerability ('Another world is here. Notes on religion and political power') at the World Forum on Liberation and Theology at Porto Alegre. His speech was highly appreciated by the Forum. See: http://www.pucrs.br/pastoral/fmtl/noticias/noticias24ing.htm (last accessed 15 August 2005).

[26] Proaño-Gómez, Lola, *Poética, política y ruptura, Argentina 1966-1973: Teatro e identidad*, Buenos Aires: ACTUEL, 2002.

[27] The Forum on Gender and Theology at the Instituto Superior Evangélico de Estudios Teológicos (ISEDET) had also been studying body discourses in the year 2005.

[28] Unfortunately I cannot develop the body concept here. One has to make the distinction between *Leib* and *Körper* as the *Leibphänomenologie* is doing it.

[29] In reference to this Trinitarian participation theology, see Johnson, Elizabeth A., *Friends of God and Prophets. A Feminist Theological Reading of the Communion of Saints*, New York: Continuum, 1998. This biblical verse is central for Johnson, see p. 2.

[30] In reference to the debate about gender deconstruction and feminist theology, church leadership with regard to body and gender discourses in ecclesiology, etc. see my doctoral thesis: Walz, Heike, *'Nicht mehr männlich und weiblich?' Ekklesiologie und Geschlecht in ökumenischem Horizont*, Frankfurt am Mainz (in print).

# 15

# THE EQUALITY OF WOMEN
# IN LEADING POSITIONS
# OF THE PROTESTANT CHURCHES.
# A GLOBAL PERSPECTIVE

*Hella Hoppe / Anne Walder, Switzerland*

## Introduction and Methodology

'Where there is power, there are no women. Whether in governments, in international organisations, in private economy or in NGOs, although women are on the advance and are increasingly assuming the most different tasks they only rarely make it to the top positions.' (Micheline Calmy-Rey, Federal Councillor of Foreign Affairs of the Swiss Confederation at the Open Forum Davos 2006)

'More Women in Top Positions!'[1] – this is a claim put forward by women – and occasionally also by men – not only to the address of politics and economy, but also to church institutions. In many countries, the reason for this demand is the gap between the political and legal rights of women to be equally represented in all areas of life and work, and the reality of women to be able to get to positions of power and even more rarely to get to top leadership positions.

The present paper intends to use selected examples to highlight the situation of women in senior positions of power in Protestant churches at the international level. As sources were weak, we proceeded to send out our questions to selected experts in various countries, and upon return of their answers we analysed the findings.[2] We collected the data of those countries that had information available. Yet, other countries provided us with more general assessments. At any rate, the feedback to our questionnaire sent out to all parts of the world clearly shows that in view of this question there is still an enormous need for research and even more for action.[3] At this point, it needs to be pointed out that the present analysis has an exclusive socio-scientific orientation.

## 1. Women in Church Leadership Positions in Various Regions of the World

### 1.1. Africa

The issue of women in church leadership positions in the Protestant churches of Africa is closely linked to the ecclesiastical legacy of each denomination. Hence, both the executive and the legislative leadership positions of many denominations in Africa and in other parts of the world are held by ordained clergy. The result is that the question of equality of women in church leadership positions is closely linked with the question of women's ordination (see also section 2 below).[4]

Another aspect that needs to be taken into account is that 'leadership' or 'guidance' in traditional churches in Africa is understood less in structural and hierarchical terms than in West European and North American churches.[5] Women's sphere of influence does therefore not exclusively depend on their presence in the upper hierarchies.[6]

According to our research, there are no established figures on women's equality in leadership positions in Africa. As in many other countries, this shows clearly how much research is needed as to the issue of women in leadership positions.

For further analysis it would make sense to differentiate between three types of churches, namely between the following:

a) churches exported from Europe and North-America via the modern missionary enterprise;

b) African Instituted Churches (AICs) which are in reaction against the above-mentioned missionary churches; and

c) charismatic and Pentecostal churches formed particularly in the 1980s and 1990s (and till this day) by younger African evangelists.

According to the director of the Programme for Ethics in Eastern Africa (PEEA) in Nairobi, there are almost no women in church leadership positions in category a) churches because of the patriarchal legacy and moral concepts of these denominations that originate from the North Atlantic region. This statement corresponds to the experiences for example in the Philippines where missionary churches have also exacerbated the existing inequalities (see section 1.2 below).

Churches in the category b), e.g. the Aladura churches in Nigeria, were partially founded by women and are often managed equally by women and men. Yet, it is contested whether women have more 'leadership' in the African Instituted Churches than in the churches from the West.[6]

It is interesting to note that category c) churches have comparatively many women on various decision-making levels. For example in Kenya, three of the most popular churches are founded and led by women – namely the churches of Akatsa, Wanjiru and Wairimu.

As to the question of how women theologians could increase their influence on church matters in African churches, the Programme Executive for Mission and Ecumenical Formation at the World Council of Churches (WCC) refers to the 'Circle of Concerned African Women Theologians'. This circle has as its goal to offer a platform for African women theologians to discuss, write, research, and publish their findings on theology. The communal character of this network and its results in the area of feminist theology create an important basis for African female theologians to exert greater influence in particular at the level of leadership positions: 'We in the Circle must hammer the fact that we cannot be effective, empowering, and responsible leaders without the right skills, tools, and resources.'[8]

## 1.2. Asia

Asia features selected comparative data and statistics. Hence, according to the indications of the Executive Secretary for Ecumenical Formation, Gender Justice and Youth Empowerment of the Christian Conference of Asia (CCA), out of the 50 CCA member churches in South East Asia, only one woman is on the list of full-time executive posts (see Table 1). She is the chairwoman of the Pasundan Christian Church in Bandung, Indonesia.

**Table 1: Number of women in top executive positions in CCA member churches**

| Country | Number of CCA member churches in South East Asia | Number of women in top executive position | Position | Name of church and woman in leadership position |
|---|---|---|---|---|
| 1. Indonesia | 30 | 1 | Ketua (full-time post) ('Chairman'/ Chairperson) | Pasundan Christian Church in Bandung Rev. Chita R. Bain |
| 2. Laos | 1 | – | – | – |
| 3. Malaysia | 3 | – | – | – |

| | | | | |
|---|---|---|---|---|
| 4. Myanmar | 7 | – | – | – |
| 5. Philippines | 7 | – | – | – |
| 6. Thailand | 1 | – | – | – |
| 7. Timor Leste | 1 | – | – | – |
| **Total** | **50** | **1** | | |

Source: CCA Directory 2006

With regard to the CCA National Church and member councils, the situation of women's equality in leadership positions is equally insufficient. Only one woman has the post of General Secretary out of the total of 15 member councils in South East Asia (see Table 2).

**Table 2: Number of women in the position of General Secretary in CCA Member Councils**

| Number of CCA member councils[9] | Number of member councils in South East Asia | Number of woman in top executive position | Position of country and woman | Name |
|---|---|---|---|---|
| 15 | 5 | 1 | General Secretary | Philippines Ms. Sharon Rose Joy Ruiz-Duremdes |

Source: CCA Directory 2006

Within the CCA organisational structure the number of women leaders is much higher: 10 out of 25 members of the General Committee and 5 out of the 11 members of the Executive Committee are women (see Table 3). Here, it stands out however that very often young women are elected into these bodies. This accumulation can possibly be explained by the fact that women are attributed with a double function, and that they cover both the factor 'age' and 'gender' in these bodies.

## Table 3: Women in the CCA organisational structure

| CCA structure | No. of members | No. of women | South East Asia women |
|---|---|---|---|
| General Committee* | 25 | 10 (5 young women) | 3 (1 young woman) |
| Executive Committee* | 11 | 5 (2 young women) | 1 |
| 3 Programme Area Committees* | 37 | 17 (4 young women) | 9 (4 young women) |
| Executive Staff | 8 | 3 | 2 |
| **Total** | **81** | **35** | **15** |

\* 2005-2010
Source: CCA Directory 2006

Remarks: CCA Constitution provides for policy on equal participation of women and men in CCA structures and programmes

To complete the picture, it is noteworthy to say that the Executive Director of the Association for Theological Education in South East Asia (ATESEA) is a woman.

There is a general assessment that women are still excluded from leadership positions in the churches of Asia and in particular of South East Asia, despite the Ecumenical Decade of 'Churches in Solidarity with Women'. Rather, there are numerous examples that show how women despite high qualification and proofs of commitment to the Church are denied ordination and/or leadership positions. In Myanmar for example, the Myanmar Baptist Convention refused to ordain a renowned feminist theologian and lecturer at the Myanmar Institute of Theology.

The CCA Secretariat mentions the following aspects as the main reasons for the lack of women in leadership positions of South East Asian church institutions:

- Patriarchal value concepts and gender-specific understanding of roles are essential elements of socialisation and culture in many regions of Asia, in particular in South East Asia. This is reflected in the church structures. Studies show that a patriarchal understanding of one's role in the family is very often directly transferred to structures related to society as a whole. [10]

- In the churches themselves, very often readings, sermons, liturgies, hymns with a patriarchal orientation dominate and strengthen existing value concepts. The same is true for the church structures that are marked by hierarchies dominated by men and that marginalise women. In addition, the responsibility to lead very often is executed by men according to patriarchal patterns of behaviour.

- There is lack of resources for the formation and further education of women especially in preparation for leadership positions.

- The increasing poverty and human insecurity in South East Asia caused by globalisation have had serious negative effects on women. Equality of these women is much more difficult to obtain due to these socio-economic developments.

Churches in Asia have launched several programmes and instruments to facilitate women's access to leadership positions. Many of these programmes focus on the struggle against violence.

The coordinator of the Women's Desk of the National Council of Churches in the *Philippines* estimates that violence against women is the biggest stumbling block to equality. Only when they can lead a safe and self-determined life and no patriarchal value concepts undermine a supposedly Christian theology will women have the opportunity to assume leadership positions in society and in the churches. To increase women's necessary empowerment and to promote their equality in all areas of life and work, the National Council of Churches in the Philippines has initiated a special ecumenical programme for women in churches. In substantiating this project it was stated that in the Philippines there is a long tradition of various societal discriminations against women and of their political, economic and social exclusion, but that the many colonial, respectively occupational, powers have clearly exacerbated this tradition.

According to the evaluation of the General Secretary of the National Council of Churches in the Philippines, a feminist leadership is specifically characterised by five basic elements: a spirit of integration caring about human relationships; a spirit of sharing and consensus-based decision-making; a spirit of mutuality not based on hierarchies; a spirit of subjectivity also allowing emotions and compassion; and a spirit of creativity constantly looking for new ways of doing and thinking.

In analogy to the CCA-Secretariat, the General Secretary also defines the deeply entrenched patriarchy in the Philippines to be the biggest barrier to women's equality in church leadership positions.

Even if there is a rather superficial comprehension of feminism, structures and contents have not changed much. Hence, in the name of feminism women are elected into bodies who do not represent the best choices available to strengthen the position of women. And, in her eyes the disunity between the secular and the church women's movement represents an additional obstacle in the Philippines.

The development of the Protestant churches in *South Korea* has to be assessed in close connection to the influence of colonial powers and missionary activities. The split into numerous denominations is the result of Western missionaries, in particular Presbyterians, Methodists and Baptists, who flocked into the country since 1884. The majority of these missionaries were characterised by their fundamentalist view of Christianity which, together with the widespread Confucianism – which has long been the national philosophy in Korea – caused women's oppression and discrimination to be rather reinforced. [11]

Despite their oppression women played a central role in early Christianity and in founding Protestant churches in Korea. In this regard, the devotion of Korean Christian women – the so-called 'Bible-Women' [12] – has been exemplary. At the same time, women's self-confidence and self-determination was strengthened through the Gospel and selected Bible readings.

However, in church structures women were still marginalised and men took on leadership positions. To this day, women have not reached equality in leadership positions, despite a general strengthening of women's organisations such as the large and influential National Organisation of the Korea Presbyterian Women. The theological faculties show a similar situation; only a few women can be found there and often these women do not represent feminist approaches. [13]

In South Korea as in other countries, the absence of women's ordination plays an essential role when it comes to women's equality in church institutions. [14] Only when feminist theologians come into play is it possible to break through patriarchal structures. Amongst others women have been ordained in the largest Presbyterian church since 1995 (Presbyterian Church of Korea, PCK, Tonghap), and this is also true for the Anglican church since 2001. The position of minister was already accessible to women in more progressive smaller Protestant churches and in the Methodist Church since 1955. And the Presbyterian Church in the Republic of Korea (PROK, Kijang) has ordained women for many decades. [15] As of May 2006, the Presbyterian Church of Korea lists 560 women ministers and 260 women elders, whereas the Presbyterian Church in the Republic of Korea numbers 169 women ministers and 252 women elders.

In *India*, women are sometimes very prominently represented. Out of the total of 28 states three are governed by women. However, if we compare India to international women's equality indicators, then the picture looks unfavourable for this country. [16] There exists for example still considerable discrimination against young women and their access to education. Seen from the overall societal perspective, there is hence a contradictory situation for women in India.

In the Protestant churches in India, [17] almost no women assume leadership positions. [18] If asked to give names of women in church leadership positions, people often mention two names: on the one hand it is the general secretary of the Synod of the Church of South India, Pauline Sathiamurthy, and on the other it is the (recently deceased) president of the National Council of Churches in India, Prasanna Kumari Samuel. Apart from these individual cases, the wives of bishops usually chair the different women's groups ('women's fellowships') in the dioceses and regional councils. But even here, exceptions are common, as the leadership of the women's group in the 'Mar Thoma' Church is assumed by a man.

### 1.3. Europe

Looking at the available statistics, the women's share in the Eglise réformée de France (ERF) can be called considerable. At the national level, 7 out of the 20 members of the national council *(conseil national)* are women, as are 54 out of the 150 members of the national synod ('synode national'). Women hold half the positions of national coordinators of the ERF *(coordinations nationales)*. The *Commission des ministères* is responsible for the high share of women as well as for raising the issue of women in leadership positions in general. This commission has indeed essential decision-making powers on the selection of future officers of the ERF. Here, 4 out of the 10 commission members are women. But out of the 8 chairpersons of the regional councils *(conseils régionaux)* in the ERF regions, only one is a woman. These *présidents des régions* exert a great influence on the staffing in parishes and regions.

On the regional level, two ERF regions are herewith presented as examples. The region Provence-Côte d'Azur-Corse is known for tourism, the settlement of new companies and research facilities as well as for its relatively high share of well-off and educated senior citizens. In the Reformed Church of the Region Provence-Côte d'Azur-Corse, 12 out of the 26 church parishes have women presidents *(associations culturelles)*. In addition, 146 out of a total of 275 chairpersons of the parish councils are women *(président-e* or *vice-président-e de conseils presbytéraux)*. The top body of the region, the *conseil régional*, numbers 14 people, out of which four are women.

The Reformed Church of the region Centre-Alpes-Rhône is the biggest ERF region and represents the overall situation in France in a nutshell. The region Centre-Alpes-Rhône includes both territories that are traditionally reformed and those where Protestants live in a minority, such as in the metropolitan agglomerations of Lyon and Grenoble. The president of the regional council *(conseil regional)* is a man and one of his deputies is a woman. Three out of the nine members of the regional council are women. Out of the 108 chairpersons of the parish councils – the presbyteries – 44 are women *(président-e* or *vice-président-e de conseils presbytéraux)*.[19]

To answer the question of women's equality in leadership positions of the *German* Protestant churches, we can resort to the May 2004 statistics of the Evangelical Church in Germany (EKD) referring to the years 2002 and 2003.[20] Here, three levels of church leadership positions are being differentiated: the synod; the bodies of the church councils of the particular territories (the *Länder*); and the governing bodies of church management.

As to the level of the *synods*, we need to identify that the proportion of women among the members of the synod of the national Protestant churches accounts to an average of 35 %, i.e. to a total of 885 out of the 2508 members of the synod. The differences are even bigger depending on the relevant member church of the EKD.[21] In the case of *church councils and spiritual offices* the average proportion of women is lower – amounting to 27 %. However, there has been an increase since 1993, when the share accounted for only 19 %. Also, the regional differences are rather important. Here, we need to mention that there are three female Lutheran bishops in Germany. Today, the Council of the EKD includes 15 members, out of which seven are women.[22] The proportion of women is most unfavourable in the *management of church administrations*. Although the proportion of women was raised from a low 8,3 % in the year 1993, it remained at a low level in 2003, with 19,5 %.[23]

Another important aspect that the statistics do not highlight is the distribution of the areas of responsibility within the church leadership. Here, women may be represented in the leadership, but very often 'powerful' responsibilities such as finances or the judiciary are assumed by men, whereas ecumenism, Christian social service or education are left to women. Even if a numerical equality can be achieved in the church leadership, it does not necessarily reflect women's equality on the level of decision-making competences.

Using the illustrative example of Germany, the relevance of women's equality within church associations can also be shown. Hence, diaconal institutions for example have traditionally served as large targets for criticism from the advocates of women's equality. It has been a long tradition that such church-based social service institutions are typically male-dominated in the upper hierarchies. This is manifested in the fact that approximately three-quarters of the full-time and of the voluntary staff working in the diaconal institutions are women. But these women are part of low wage groups and are almost non-existent in the leadership positions.[24] Yet, there are exceptions. For example, the executive director of the campaign of the church-based development cooperation Bread for the World and executive of the head office of the Social Service Agency of the Protestant Church in Germany is a woman.

Also in response to the Ecumenical Decade, Churches in Solidarity with Women, an agreement on the principles of equality was adopted in the head office of the Social Service Agency of the EKD in 1991. This increased commitment for women's issues was based on the understanding that women's equality will not automatically materialise but needs deliberate decision and planning strategies.

## 1.4. North America

Due to the waves of immigration during the 19th and 20th century, religious diversity is a distinct feature of the *United States of America* (USA). Religious pluralism has led to a few positive effects on women's equality in church institutions. In the USA, the first women were ordained as early as in the 19th century, amongst others Antoinette Brown in 1853. In the early 20th century, women then founded their first denominations, and the number of churches that implemented the ordination of women grew considerably after the Second World War. Afro-American churches formed the backbone of the civil rights movement in the 1920s, in which women also played an important role.

Without going into details of the religious complexity,[25] the USA serves as an appropriate example to discuss another central aspect of the issue of women in church leadership positions. Here, we talk about the connection of the categories of gender and race. In the United Methodist Church for example, the proportion of women in the group of active bishops is on the increase, but the proportion of women among the 'racial ethnic' bishops continues to be very low (see Table 4). In the South-East region of the United Methodist Church, three out of the 13 bishops are staffed with 'white' women and two with 'racial ethnic' men. 'Racial ethnic' women are not represented.

The programme The Black Women in Ministerial Leadership, for example, starts with the problem outlined above. This programme was formed by the Interdenominational Theological Centre in 2005, and because of a donation of the Lilly Endowment Foundation amounting to USD 1,4 million it could immediately start to be operational. Its goal is to facilitate Afro-American women's access to church leadership positions.[26]

## Table 4:  Proportion of women in the U.S. Colleges of Bishops of the United Methodist Church

2005-2008 Make-Up of the U.S. Colleges of Bishops
of the United Methodist Church

| Jurisdiction | Total active bishops | 'White' | | 'Racial ethnic' | | Total women |
|---|---|---|---|---|---|---|
| | | Men | Women | Men | Women | |
| North Central | 10 | 3 | 3 | 3 | 1 | 4 |
| North-Eastern | 11 | 3 | 2 | 5 | 1 | 3 |
| South Central | 11 | 6 | 2 | 3 | 0 | 2 |
| South-Eastern | 13 | 8 | 3 | 2 | 0 | 3 |
| Western | 6 | 1 | 1 | 2 | 2 | 3 |

2001-2004 Make-Up of the U.S. Colleges of Bishops
of the United Methodist Church

| Jurisdiction | Total active bishops | 'White' | | 'Racial ethnic' | | Total women |
|---|---|---|---|---|---|---|
| | | Men | Women | Men | Women | |
| North Central | 10 | 4 | 2 | 3 | 1 | 3 |
| North-Eastern | 11 | 3 | 2 | 5 | 1 | 3 |
| South Central | 11 | 6 | 2 | 3 | 0 | 2 |
| South-Eastern | 13 | 9 | 1 | 3 | 0 | 1 |
| Western | 6 | 2 | 1 | 2 | 1 | 2 |

Source: The General Commission on the Status and Role of Women (2006) Make-up of the U.S. Colleges of Bishops (http://www.gcsrw.org/research/COB.htm).

The Presbyterian Church in *Canada* has c. 125,000 members.[27] Its highest decision-making body is the Annual General Meeting, in which usually men and female Elders as well as ministers can participate. The percentage of women in the eldership amounts to about

40 % (as per 2006). On request of the committee 'Women in Ministry Committee,' the Presbyterian Church collected and published the proportion of women in the eldership of the individual congregations of the presbyteries in 2002. Hence, out of the 974 congregations, 872 did send back statistical data differentiating between man and women. These statistics show that overall in this category of 'eldership' 6181 men and 4178 women are represented. This corresponds to a proportion of women of c. 40 %.

## 1.5. Latin America

Even if there is no systematic overview on women's equality in Protestant churches and institutions in Latin America, it can be assumed that on the basis of the available material women's equality in church leadership positions suffers from great deficits in Latin America.[28] However, there are some positive examples, such as Nelida Ritchie, a Methodist bishop in Argentina, Gabriela Mulder, vice-president of the Reformed Church of Argentina and Gloria Rojas, president of the Evangelical-Lutheran Church in Chile. Also, a few Pentecostal churches are led by women in Latin America, amongst others the Iglesia Misión Apostólica Universal in Chile. Theological institutes are mostly governed by men, one of the rare exceptions being the president of the Comunidad Teológica Evangélica in Chile. Presently, two of the 16 Lutheran World Federation (LWF) member churches in Latin America and in the Caribbean are led by women.

Yet, the overall impression brings us back to reality again. In view of the existing deficits of women's equality in church leadership positions it is of special relevance that on the April 2006 Latin American Church Leader Conference (*Conferencia de Liderazgo – COL*) in Costa Rica it was decided that a working group on the issue of women in church leadership positions in Latin America should be established. Judith Van Osdol was nominated as the person in charge of the working group and became the coordinator of the Continental Programme for Women and Gender Issues of the Latin American Council of Churches (CLAI). She was to analyse a study that was submitted to the COL in April on 'Ministry and Power from a Gender-Perspective. Searching a Common Road,'[29] of which she intended to submit a revised version by September 2006. The working group's primary task is 'to elaborate further proposals for an intensive and broad dialogue as to the issue of women and gender questions on the bases of the revised document and of a dialogue that includes all the churches of the region.'[30] The goal of such consultations is to identify concrete recommendations to be discussed and adopted on the occasion of the COL 2007.

According to the estimation of the Area Secretary for Latin America and the Caribbean at the LWF, the COL document reminds us of the recommendation the LWF already adopted, which clearly states a need for action at the level of the Latin American LWF member churches. This is especially true for the recommendation to work out a Plan of Action emphasising the equality of men and women in church, and to work out concrete measures to pave the way for women to assume ordained ministries (in accordance with the 8th LWF Assembly in Curitiba, 1990). The indication in the COL document that there is a comprehensive need for action is an essential consensus and precondition for strengthening women's equality in church leadership positions. Furthermore, the document refers to the fact that some progress has been achieved in the church-related gender and women's issues, but that overall this progress needs to be analysed in more details. Similarly, the General Secretary of the National Council of Churches in the Philippines states that despite the regular use of a corresponding 'gender' terminology, there has been no sign of transformation of structures, contents and behaviour of the decision-making circles.

There are complex reasons for the lack of equality between men and women in church leadership positions in Latin America, and certainly both cultural aspects and also theological justifications play a role. With regard to the cultural barriers, patriarchal value and behaviour concepts, we need to state that they are still distinctive within society despite some improvements. Hence, the whole development must be questioned in as much as certain churches and theologies respond to these progressive transformation processes by tenaciously sticking to old traditions.

Apart from the COL process, let us mention a second example of positive developments: the activities of Con-Spirando, a women's collective that was created in Chile out of a common interest in spirituality, theology and ethics from a feminist perspective in 1991. The collective contributes a great deal to the feminist debate in Latin America by publishing, creating educational programmes, organising seminars and workshops, and in particular by celebrating seasonal and women-specific rituals. Within these activities, a panel discussion was staged in September 2005, putting nine women in leadership positions from churches, academy, politics and culture into the limelight. They were asked to talk about the barriers they had to overcome on their way to power, their experiences, and how to strengthen women's equality in leading positions. As it is, the patterns of experience that were shared at this panel looked similar to those of other countries. At different occasions, the burden of isolation felt by women in top positions of power was expressed by very different women such as Gloria Rojas, the president of the Evangelical-Lutheran Church in Chile, who stated that 'to be a leader means to live alone' ('un liderazgo es vivir sola') and Micheline Calmy-Rey, the Minister of Foreign Affairs of Switzerland, who said that 'Women taking over leadership positions are perceived as women who are leaving their innermost sphere and are forming a new, third category: [...] They remain strangers in the community of women and strangers in the community of men.'[31] Another controversial issue is the question whether women foster another style of leadership and to what extent is this leadership style marked by women-specific experiences and values. As to the question of which preconditions need to be fulfilled in order to have women assume leadership positions in a sustainable way, it was mentioned that for women it is especially important to have strong solidarity links and to be able to rely on a supportive network.

## 2. Women's Ordination

The World Alliance of Reformed Churches (WARC) conducted a survey on the issue of women's ordination for the years 1993 to 1999. The results showed that about 64 % of WARC member churches have approved of, and implemented, the ordination of women, whereas in 27 % of the member churches, no women were ordained. No figures have been indicated for about 8 % of the WARC member churches.

The WARC study was updated in 2003. Hence, 153 churches ordained women ministers (71 %), 48 did not allow women's ordination (22 %), and no information was available for 16 member churches (7 %).

However, these figures are only trends. Detailed statistics would for example be required to analyse the statements together with the number of members of the individual WARC member churches.[32]

In the many denominations where women are excluded from ordination, it is impossible for them to access leadership positions. Apart from patriarchal moral concepts that dominate the overall society (see section 1.2), the denial of women's ordination is one of the central obstacles for women to access church leadership positions. To combat this trend, WARC initiated in 1992 the Programme to Affirm, Challenge and Transform. Women and Men in Partnership in Church and Society (PACT). Among others, this programme conducted regional consultations, in particular on the issue of 'Women and Men in Church Leadership'.

The results of these consultations are quite similar despite different societal contexts. In Kenya, it was pointed out that there are considerable country-specific differences even within one region when it comes to women's ordination for example. In Edinburgh, it was pointed out that the comprehensive equality of women in the church, in particular in leadership positions, represented a *processus confessionis*. In India, women's equality in church leadership positions was discussed in the context of religious and cultural diversity. In the USA, the consultation showed that the opportunity to be ordained has not automatically led to women's equality in leadership positions. The consultation in the Netherlands questioned the extent to which the ordination of women had actually resulted in reforms in terms of content.[33]

## 3. Outlook

Women carry the Protestant churches of the world, men lead them – this theme seems to still be valid. However, not only the example of the church councillors of the Protestant churches in Switzerland but also the processes, programmes, initiatives and consultations on the way to women's equality in church leadership positions clearly show that there are some encouraging examples.

At the 9th Assembly of the World Council of Churches (WCC), the union of Orthodox churches, churches from the historic tradition of the Protestant reformation, as well as united and independent churches came together. In the new Central Committee, 42 % out of the 150 delegates are women. However, it has to be underlined that similarly to the Christian Conference of Asia, women delegates were often young women delegates and therefore cover two criteria. In addition, out of the eight WCC presidents three as well as one vice-moderator of the executive committee are women.

Despite many success stories there are also clear backlashes. As examples we refer to the Protestant churches of the Ukraine, the Lutherans in Poland and Latvia or even to the Old Reformed of the Netherlands. Hence, in the Ukraine, a decision taken by the synod ruled that the 'ordination of women to a spiritual ministry, their eligibility to become pastors of congregations and their authorisation to administer the sacraments' was repealed again in 2006. Among others, the protection of women from the hardships of difficult working conditions in unheated churches was mentioned to be a reason for the repeal.[34] We need to observe such steps backwards within the Protestant churches with great attention and to name all involved.

Furthermore, the incomplete analysis and open questions of the present article show that on the whole there is an enormous need for research on the question of discussing the lack of women in leadership positions in international and systematic terms. To do so, the church institutions would be required to undertake comprehensive efforts to collect differentiated statistics on the situation of women and men at the local, national, regional and international levels. In order to strengthen women for leadership positions such statistics must then be translated into political strategies to be implemented by the churches.

NOTES

1   This was the title of a panel discussion of the 2006 Open Forum in Davos, organised by the Federation of Swiss Protestant Churches and the World Economic Forum. The original motivation for writing this article resulted from the women presidents of Protestant church councils in Switzerland, who published a book on the extraordinary high number of women represented in the highest leadership positions of the Protestant cantonal churches. In mid-2006, 9 of the existing 26 cantonal churches are led by women! See Bandixen, Claudia/Worbs, Frank/Pfeiffer, Silvia (eds), *Wenn Frauen Kirchen leiten*, Zurich: TVZ, 2006.

2   The authors express their gratitude to Baffour Amoa, Evangeline Anderson, Nancy Carrasco Paredes, Meehyun Chung, Juliette Davaine, Josefina Hurtado, Sharon Rose Joy Ruiz-Duremdes, Martin Junge, Stephen Kendall, Liza Lamis, Jesse Mugambi, Setri Nyomi, Nyambura Njoroge, Patricia Sheerattan-Bisnauth, Cora Tabing-Reyes, Evelyn Tiercet, Heike Walz and numerous others for their deep and sound evaluations and feedback as to the issue of women's equality in leadership positions of Protestant churches in the prevailing contexts of their own country. It needs to be pointed out that the two authors assume the full responsibility for the present text.

3   The fundamental questions of how different religious traditions respond to women's claim for equality and how they deal with this claim are of central significance, but cannot be included at this point. Cf. to this the theme-journal 'La Religion: Frein à l'égalité hommes/femmes?', in: *Archives de Sciences Sociales des Religions* 41 (95), 1996, among other things with articles by Roland Campiche.

4   MacMaster, Llewellyn, 'Women and men in church leadership in Africa today', in: World Alliance of Reformed Churches (WARC) (ed.), *Partnership in God's mission in Africa today* (Studies from the WARC 28), Geneva: WARC, 1994, p. 50f.

5   'Traditional women leaders', as research project by Isabel Phiri and Lindiwi Mkasi on http://www.sorat.ukzn.ac.za/sinomlando/Women%20traditional%20leaders.htm (last accessed 21 July 2006).

6   See for example Phiri, Isabel/Govinden, Betty/Nadar, Sarojini (eds), *Her-stories. Hidden histories of Women of faith in Africa*, Pietermaritzburg: Cluster Publications, 2002.

7   Monohan, Bridget Marie, *Writing, Sharing, Doing. The Circle of Concerned African Women Theologians*, Boston: 2004, p. 43 on http://dissertations.bc.edu/cgi/viewcontent.cgi?article =1047&context=ashonors (last accessed 21 July 2006).

8   Njoroge, Nyambura J., 'A New Way of Facilitating Leadership: Lessons from African Women Theologians', in: *Missiology: An International Review* 33 (1), 2005, pp. 29-46.

9   These are the members: Conference of Churches in Aotearoa-New Zealand, Te Runanga Whakawhanaunga I Nga Hahi O Aotearoa, National Council of Churches in Australia, Bangladesh National Council of Churches, Hong Kong Christian Council, National Council of Churches in India, Communion of Churches in Indonesia, National Christian Council in Japan, Kampuchea Christian Council, National Council of Churches in Korea, Council of Churches of Malaysia, Myanmar Council of Churches, National Council of Churches of Nepal, National Council of Churches in Pakistan, National Council of Churches in the Philippines, National Christian Council of Sri Lanka, National Council of Churches of Taiwan.

10   Kim, Un Hey, *Family Leadership and Feminist Leadership as the Feminist Theological Alternative. From the Perspective of a Korean Christian Woman Salimist*, 2005, unpublished document; Camba, Erme R., 'Women and Men in Church Leadership', in: *Semper Reformanda* 31, 1996, p. 7.

11   Sa, Mija, 'Women in the Korean Church. A historical survey', in: *Reformed World* 45 (1 and 2), 1995, pp. 1-10; Chung, Meehyun, 'Introducing Korean Feminist Theology', in: Chung, Meehyun (ed.), *Breaking Silence – Theology from Asian Women*, India: ISPCK, 2006, pp. 77-89.

12   *Ibidem.*

13   *Ibid.*

14   Sa, Mija, *op. cit.*; Chung, Meehyun, *loc. cit.*

15   Information differs when it comes to the year of the first women's ordination: in 1974 or in 1977. As to a general assessment, also consult Beek, Huibert van, *A Handbook of Churches and Councils. Profiles of Ecumenical Relationships*, Geneva: WCC, 2006, pp. 286f.

16   See the different indicators of the United Nations Development Programme: Human Development Report 2005, New York.

[17]  In India, about three to six per cent of the population is Christian, out of which about 35 % are protestants (c. 19,565 mio individuals).

[18]  Anderson-Rajkumar, Evangeline, 'Engendering Leadership. A Christian Feminist Perspective from India', in: Stückelberger, Christoph/Mugambi, Jesse: *Responsible Leadership. Global Perspectives*, Nairobi: Acton Publishers, 2005, pp. 126-135. See also Chapter 2 in this volume.

[19]  *Mémento 2005-2006 Réveil, mensuel protestant réformé régional de l'Eglise réformée en Centre-Alpes-Rhône,* supplément au no 366 – septembre 2005, unpublished document.

[20]  EKD: Mitglieder der Kirchenleitungen in den Gliedkirchen und den Gliedkirchlichen Zusammenschlüssen in der EKD im Jahr 2003. Korrigiertes Ergebnis, Hannover: EKD, 2004, pp. 1-8.

[21]  *Ibid.,* pp. 2-3.

[22]  *Ibid.,* pp. 4-5.

[23]  *Ibid.,* pp. 6-7.

[24]  Trommer, Heide, *Gleichstellung in der Diakonie,* 2001, pp. 1f; Diakonisches Werk der EKD (ed.): *Schritte auf dem Weg zu mehr Gerechtigkeit für Frauen und Männer. Gender Mainstreaming als Handlungsstrategie der Hauptgeschäftsstelle des Diakonischen Werkes der EKD,* 2003, pp. 1-7; Diakonisches Werk der EKD (ed.): *Gender Mainstreaming in der Diakonie,* Fachtagung des Diakonischen Werkes der Evangelischen Kirche in Deutschland e.V. in Kooperation mit der Diakonischen Akademie Deutschland GmbH. 10-11 March 2005, Berlin, pp. 1-50.

[25]  Wessinger, Catherine (ed.), *Religious Institutions and Women's Leadership. New Roles Inside the Mainstream,* Columbia, SC: University of South Carolina Press, 1996; McKenzie, Vashti, *Not without a struggle. Leadership Development for African American Women in ministry,* Cleveland, OH: United Church Press, 1996.

[26]  See a short report in the press on http://www.gcsrw.org/newsarchives/2006/060316.htm (last accessed 21 July 2006).

[27]  Beek, Huibert van, *op. cit.,* p. 551.

[28]  See for instance Wagner, Juan Carlos, 'Women and men in church leadership in Latin America today', in: WARC (ed.), *Partnership in God's mission in the Caribbean and Latin America* (Studies from the WARC 37), 1998 on http://www.warc.ch/dp/bs37/04.html (last accessed: 21.7.2006); Estrada, Duque/Goulart, Leciane, 'A story from Brazil', in: *Reformed World* 49 (1-2), 1999 on http://www.warc.ch/dp/rw9912/02.html (last accessed 21 July 2006).

[29]  'Ministerio y poder desde género: buscar un camino común', 2006, unpublished COL document.

[30]  LWF News from 15.05.2006: 'Lateinamerika: KirchenleiterInnenkonferenz bestimmt Arbeitsaufgaben' on http://www.lutheranworld.org/News/LWI/DE/1929.DE.html (last accessed 21 July 2006).

[31]  Calmy-Rey, Micheline, *Platz da?! Frauen an die Spitzen der Macht* on http://www.calmy-rey.admin.ch/AttachmentView.aspx?AttachmentID = 412 (last accessed 9 October 2006).

[32]  Sheerattan-Bisnauth, Patricia, *Creating a vision for partnership of women and men. Evaluation report of regional workshops on gender awareness and leadership development,* Geneva: WARC, 1986; WARC (ed.), *Women in church leadership. Report of workshop held at the Ecumenical Institute,* 8-15 June 1986, Geneva: WARC, 1996; WARC (ed.), 'The ordination of women in WARC member churches', in: *Reformed World* 49 (1), 1999, pp. 1-18.

[33]  Sheerattan-Bisnauth, Patricia, *Creating a vision for partnership of women and men. Evaluation report of regional workshops on gender awareness and leadership development,* Geneva: WARC, 1999.

[34]  Luibl, Hans Jürgen, 'Ukrainische Reformierte: Frauen im Pfarrdienst abgelehnt', in: *Reformierte Presse* 18 (5 May 2006), p. 7.

# 16

# THEOLOGY AND PLURALISTIC ETHICS.
# AN INDONESIAN MUSLIM PERSPECTIVE

*Muhammad Machasin, Indonesia*

## Introduction

Religion has been coming to the fore in the debate of how Indonesia should be built so that each of its citizens give the best place to live. For Muslims it is really a problem of theology since they are told from time to time that there is no separation between what is religious and what is secular. For them the reality of a religiously pluralistic state is something new, about which they do not have any reference in their religious tradition. Islamic systems of government have been so far established on the basis of a single faith whereby no competitor was allowed to share the making. Thus, the Indonesian experience in which people of different religious backgrounds share the same rights and duties in front of the state challenges Muslims' religious attitude.

The success of the nationalistic view in making Pancasila the basis of the state – that means the failure of the Islamic model – does not mean the end of the struggle. Many Muslims take as their religious duty to implement the Shariah in the management of public life, although the acceptance of *Pancasila* (the five basic principles of Indonesia)[1] is still growing in the Islamic communities. There is nothing wrong with this attitude among Muslims, as long as its defenders take legal way in their efforts to make their dreams come true. In a democratic state, any group aspiration can be struggled for through constitutional ways. What is dangerous is that religion can be – and has been – misused to reach any objective, be it religious or not. It is, thus, the duty of religious leaders, especially theologians, to give religious perspectives to the believers in the struggle of fulfilling their obligations in the public domain. Religious leaders can do many things, especially provide theological leadership.

This paper will discuss some aspects of the debate, focusing on the religious struggle. It will deal with the following concerns: the very meaning of theological leadership as key concept, the theology of pluralism that has been condemned as un-Islamic by the Council of Indonesian Ulamas *(Majelis Ulama Indonesia)* together with secularism and liberalism, the concept of chosen people, *Pancasila* as frame for nurturing co-existence of people of different faiths and the emergence of less tolerant religious groups in the scene of present Indonesia.

## 1. The Concept of Theological Leadership

The Rev. Dr. Yahya Wijaya did not give a definition of this term, but an allusion to it as follows: 'Leadership in the context of Muslim-Christian encounters should take into account the need to reinterpret theological resources of both religions, since the early constructions of those resources contemplated a situation with a lesser degree of plurality than that of today.'[2] It seems from this quotation that the leadership of Muslims and Christians who are engaged in the encounters perceive no problem, while the reality is that there are many other kinds of 'leaders' who may engage in such encounters, such as political leaders, communal leaders and family/clan leaders. The gravity of this problem is even bigger at a time when many kinds of 'impersonal leaders' such as advertisements, campaigns and provocations take over the leadership.

The very term 'theological leadership' may pertain, at least, to two different things: (1) the function of leaders in a theological way; and (2) using theology to lead the people. To the second belong the leadership of religious groups where theology is very important, and in his paper the Rev. Dr. Wijaya deals primarily with matters relating to it. One important question is how we – people who are responsible for theology – disseminate the result of theological inquiries and innovations amidst congregations where leaders show exclusivist tendencies.

Concerning the first, it is very important to present theological messages of leadership to the leaders – the personal and the impersonal ones – in a language that can be understood easily as giving benefit to them, while giving room for the betterment of human life. The long history of the existence of religion has proved that religious advice can never have significant effect on leaders who fear losing or reducing their own authority by following the advice.

## 2. A Theology of Pluralism

Accepting the reality of plurality is not a problem, but it is by accepting and appreciating pluralism as a belief that peoples of various faiths can be saved by their own faith. The majority of Muslims in Indonesia – as indicated by the existence of strong reactions to the opposite opinion – are of the opinion that there is only one true religion of Allah, namely Islam, and that it is theirs. Accordingly, they will never accept the possibility of truth for any other religion, since otherwise they would compromise their own belief. In 2005, the Council of Indonesian Ulamas issued a *fatwa* condemning pluralism, liberalism and secularism. Their belief of single truth was the most important basis for claiming that pluralism may lead to relativism, liberalism and secularism. Under such influences one may question the essential principles of religion, while secularism will only push faith away from the life of humankind.

There is actually a strong need to speak of such concepts from within the tradition of religion. However, since some terms have provoked bitter reactions already from the Ulamas, other tactics should be created that will give understanding instead of creating pretexts for targeted attack.

## 3. The Concept of Chosen People

There are at least two terms in the Koran denoting the concept of chosen people for Muslims, i.e. *ummatan wasatan* (middle community),[3] and *khayr umma* (the best community).[4] However, when read carefully, the context of both passages will give the notion that these two attributes give Muslims more responsibility than privilege and emphasise more on obligation than on right. The first verse describes the challenge to be witness to all peoples as the proper mission for those who are in the middle, as has been done by the Prophet Muhammad who lived in the middle of the first Islamic community. The second verse gives as obligation for the best community to enjoin right conduct and to forbid indecency.

However, both verses can be understood as stating that 'being the best' is more an ideal state that must be pursued than a given fact for belonging to a certain congregation or religious group. It is only by shouldering the duty that you are called the best community or you are in good position that you can perform what you are obliged to do.

There is no monopoly of God's love. Those who cherish the claim of being the chosen people are like a child thinking that the mother's love to him/her is greater than it is for his/her brothers and sisters. Then, it turns to be the same for all and accordingly the idea is only true in the mind of the child and not in reality (internal faith). Such a claim is fruitful, to some extent, for nurturing one's own religious zeal. However, it may hinder the bearer from recognising the truth outside his faith enclosure. The failure to recognise and appreciate the truth is indeed a failure to know the encompassing love of God.

## 4. Acceptance of Pancasila

The acceptance of *Pancasila* is really a blessing for the pluralistic nation of Indonesia, by which the citizens with various backgrounds of cultures, religions and languages can live together as one nation. It was a fortune, too, that the New Order regime forced mass organisations to accept it as the sole basic philosophy since the 1980s. This top-down action means the weakening of resistance from Islamic groups to *Pancasila*. When the regime collapsed in 1998 and there was the possibility of basic philosophies other than *Pancasila*, some activists tried to bring Islam to the front. Nevertheless, the majority of the people did not accept this line of action. It is true that this reluctance to have another basic philosophy does not mean their total acceptance of *Pancasila*, but it gives an opportunity to elaborate this formally accepted philosophy of State in order to maintain the very existence of the nation. *Pancasila* is the best choice for this nation, since it gives everybody equal rights and duties before the state.

However, one should not forget the fragility of the acceptance of *Pancasila*. Many Muslims are reluctant to agree that it is 'the source of all sources' *(sumber dari segala sumber)* for all laws and regulations, since they have strong belief that it is the Shariah that is really so. They would not, and even could not, differentiate between the religious instances of life – comprising the personal and congregational – and the public ones.

One important cause for this reluctance is that there is no place for discussion of *Pancasila* and many other civic issues in theological education, at least in the Islamic institutions and systems. Some religious leaders even got their education outside Indonesia and accordingly sometimes do not have enough understanding of what should be done for the pluralistic nation of Indonesia.

There is also a lack of the cultivation of pluralism in religious education, leadership training in a pluralistic way. The plurality of the Indonesian nation has not yet created a commonly accepted awareness that in order to live together in a peaceful way the people should have a kind of pluralism that is not a substitute for religion, but a philosophy of handling diversities.

## 5. The Forthcoming of an Exclusive, Less Tolerant Islam

The peaceful living together of Indonesia people was disturbed in the 1990s by religion-coloured conflicts and since the fall of the Old Regime people have been witnessing anxiously the irruption of exclusive Muslim groups manifesting a less tolerant brand of Islam. There are some reasons usually mentioned to explain the situation. First, the longing for the lost majesty where Muslims were people of the most powerful class and the feeling that the loss of clout resulted from the unfairness of others, now considered as enemies. Second, the gravity of the hardliners' theology is so strong that teachings of peaceful co-existence seem to be indications of weakness. Third, Muslims' feeling of being treated unfairly, especially by foreign policies of the USA pertaining to Islamic countries. Fourth, the fact that some Muslims live in 'un-Islamic ways' and that there is much disobedience in public life without any significant action from the government to correct the trend.

The only cure – some say – is to strengthen Islamic identity and to take action by using force. A famous saying of the prophet Muhammad is usually quoted here: 'If any of you knows an atrocity, he should change it by his hand. If he cannot do that by his hand then by his mouth and if he cannot do by his mouth, then by his heart. Anyhow, this last is a sign of the weakest faith.' Some choose the first for it is really the best, sometimes without realising that their action may create other atrocities. Sometimes they do not also understand that to change an atrocity does not mean to beat or destroy the doer or the place.

## Conclusion

To conclude I suggest that there be interfaith encounters in the form of dialogues or through studying together different theologies in the framework of building a peaceful, pluralistic nation and humankind. Then, it is not only imperative to maintain the moderate theology by education but also to integrate civic values within the study of theologies. The pluralistic perspective is achieved and formed through cultivation. It is fragile, and risks being influenced by many kinds of insinuation. Accordingly, the supporters of moderate theology have to be patient and alert in maintaining, cultivating as well as spreading pluralistic ideas.

NOTES

[1]   This philosophy constitutes of: (1) believing in the sole God, (2) just and civilised humanity, (3) Indonesian unity, (4) democracy guided by wisdom in consensus and/or representation, and (5) social justice.

[2]   Wijaya, Yahya, 'Theological Leadership in Christian Muslim Encounters. An Indonesian Perspective', in: Stückelberger, Christoph/ Mugambi, J.N.K. (eds), *Responsible Leadership. Global Perspectives*, Nairobi: Acton Publishers, 2005, p. 83. See also Chapter 12 in this volume.

[3]   *The Koran*, Sura 2 (The Cow), verse 143.

[4]   *The Koran*, Sura 3 (The Family of 'Imrân), verse 110.

# 17

# CHURCH LEADERSHIP IS CHALLENGED. A PERSPECTIVE ON CHRISTIAN AND AFRICAN VALUES

*Samuel M. Kobia, Kenya/Switzerland*

## 1. Moral Crisis as a Challenge to the Church[1]

Moral leadership is by far the most critical area where the church is expected to play a specific role. My contention is that even more than the political and economic crises, the moral crisis represents the greatest challenge in Africa – and indeed in the world in general. There are serious ethical questions both at the African and world level that we must be prepared to give leadership in addressing.

The so-called new international economic order, which is being expressed through globalisation, is but a global economic apartheid. Basically, it is a moral question even before it becomes an economic and a social question. The moral leadership of churches should also be discerned in the area of debt and structural adjustment programs. These are fertile grounds for breeding corruption. Debt cancellation alone is not enough. Alongside with the campaign for debt cancellation, the church must raise ethical questions about borrowing, lending, and spending. How responsible have we been in those three areas? The church must unmistakably state that structural adjustment policies and programs as well as debt servicing and repaying are unethical as long as they result in massive suffering of the people.

The moral leadership of the church is critical in fighting corruption. As noted above, corruption and graft exist in all countries of the world. In some countries of Europe procedures get through as so-called commissions, in others they may be considered as corruption. So, we cannot say that corruption only exists in the South. However, a society in which corruption and graft are institutionalised and generally accepted as a standard behaviour will hardly progress in anything. In many African and non-African countries the churches have an enormous responsibility. This is even more so, as many of the countries heavily infected by corruption boast of very high percentages of Christianity. There is no doubt that a drastic change in the ethical and moral climate in Africa is necessary for the continent to be in a position to utilise and allocate its resources justly and efficiently. I insist on the role of the churches in fighting corruption not only because it is simply Christian to do so. It is also African. From the traditional African point of view to talk of a corrupt leader was a contradiction in terms. A leader was a person whose moral integrity was unquestionable. FECCIWA, the Fellowship of Christian Councils and Churches in Western Africa, which organised this consultation to overcome corruption, should pioneer in *promoting an ethical code of leadership in Western Africa*.

## 2. Traditional African Rulers Were Held Accountable

The second area in which FECCIWA should feel challenged to provide leadership is in *promoting a culture of dignity and integrity in public life*. How can FECCIWA help West Africans to truly become custodians of African heritage? Part of that heritage, as we have already demonstrated, is a continuous demand for impeccable integrity of the leaders. As Prof. George Avittey reminds us, 'traditional African rulers were held accountable at all times'.[2] He goes on to cite the example of Mantse Obli Taki who was dethroned in 1918. Obli Taki was accused of a number of offences but the most serious of all was 'the selling of Ga land in the name of the Ga people without consulting the owners of the land and pledging the stool throne itself as security on a loan'.[3]

Here, it is worth mentioning another example, one that happened in the last century. In 1883, the Asante people dethroned their king Mensa Bensu for excessively taxing the people and the failure to account for the taxes collected.

In more recent times, 'Chief Barima Adu-Baah Kyere of Ghana and his supporters fled following assassination attempts on them. The dispute concerned accountability regarding the village's revenue.'[4] Also, we should not forget that when Jerry Rawlings came into power in 1983, he had people executed that were found guilty of major acts of corruption.

Each community in Africa had its own traditional way of dealing with corrupt leaders. Almost without exception the punishment was severe. In Senegal, the king had to resign and this was signaled by a distinct drumbeat. Following an elaborate and exhaustive public trial a Yoruba king was required to go into the inner corner of his palace and commit suicide. This shows how serious the issue of corruption was taken in the African indigenous governance.

In conclusion, I suggest we ask ourselves crucial questions: 'Where are the sites in which Africans buried the truths that made it possible for the leaders to live such dignified lives? Where is the crucible of the spirit that enabled our people to name and deal ruthlessly with "the intolerable" in our community – thereby sustaining hope for all the people? Whatever happened to the generosity of the spirit that characterised the qualities of an African leader?' It is by answering such questions that we will begin to deal in earnest with the issue of spirituality as a foundation of society.

While it is possible to find cases of how to deal with corrupt leaders in all parts of Africa, few places (if any) would rival Ghana in documented instances of dethronement of chiefs/kings on accounts of corruption. It would therefore come as no surprise that I make a strong proposal that FECCIWA take the lead in exploring ways of ecumenical responses to corruption in this region and beyond. You have a lot to build on.

My emphasis would be to facilitate the rebirth of the African values that girded the ethical dimensions of leadership and governance. Those, coupled with Christian principles and values that genuinely promote justice and ethical conduct in public life could provide a solid basis and ecumenical agenda for building a culture of life in dignity and integrity in Africa.

NOTES

[1]   The text is an extract of a speech of Samuel Kobia (at that time Director for Africa and now General Secretary of the World Council of Churches): 'A Crisis of Conscience. The Roots and Route of Corruption in Africa'. FECCIWA-Sub-regional Conference on 'Corruption, Peace and Development', Accra/Ghana November 2000. Also published in: Stückelberger, Christoph, *Continue Fighting Corruption. Experiences and Tasks of Churches and Development Agencies*, Berne: 2003, p. 38-41.

[2]   Ayittey, George, *Africa in Chaos*, New York: St. Martin's Press, 1998, p. 199.

[3]   *Ibidem.*

[4]   *Ghana Drum*, June 1994, p. 12.

# 18

## CORRUPTION AND INTEGRITY.
## A CALL TO CHURCHES IN MALAYSIA

*Margaret Chen, Malaysia*

Ordinary people in the country find themselves unable to do business or other things in the ordinary ways. They are compelled to pay 'incentives' to get people to do the things they want. They are told extraordinary things about corruption in the high echelons of business and politics, especially where the two people meet. The thought of people being comfortable with the concept of being corrupt is frightening, especially since the systems – both in public service and on the free market – are actually workable. But more alarming than the corruption level is the acceptance level. More and more Malaysians are living with it as if it were a natural part of life. In the past and today, everyone is giving, everyone is taking, and that is how things move in this country.[1] Corruption has become an issue of national importance.

### 1. The Promotion of Ethical Values and Integrity

Ever since Malaysia elected its new Prime Minister, Dato Seri Abdullah Badawi, we have heard about war on corruption and inefficiency. Prime Minister Badawi has promoted good governance and ethical values, as well as the fight against corruption[2] as central pillars of the country and his administration. This promotion was based on: a) awareness and understanding of the current drives of global economic, political and social systems; and b) the desire of the Malaysian government that the cabinet be accountable to the parliament, and be trusted, reliable and with integrity.

The global economy needs to maintain a good system of governance in the public and private sectors, and a greater accountability and transparency to fight corruption. The government sees corruption as a practice which enables someone to obtain remuneration through illegitimate means, giving something to someone with power so that s/he abuses his/her power and acts in favour of the giver.[3] A country that offers a stable, efficient and cost-efficient business environment is able to attract more overseas investors to invest in the country. Acting against corruption helps increase confidence among investors.

If a country with high levels of corruption runs the risk to lose current and future investments, the harmful effects are especially severe on the poor, who are strongly hit by economic decline, most reliant on the provision of good economy to get jobs and a decent living, and least capable of paying the extra costs associated with bribery, fraud, and the misappropriation of economic privileges.[4] The desire to have a reliable and honest cabinet comes from the fact that money is wasted on unproductive projects whereas funds could have been channelled into healthcare, public transport, environmental protection, education, scientific research and development. The considerable resources at disposal could have been used to promote genuine human development, greater food security and a more independent economy.

Actually, a person's sense of right and wrong alone may not be sufficient to fight corruption. In order to eradicate corruption on a large scale, a system-wide approach has to be considered, especially in the area of good governance. Anti-corruption should not only be aimed at installing the right values and attitudes, but should go beyond that and strengthen processes and institutions as well as punitive measures. The Malaysian Integrity Institute has been launched to promote ethics and enhance integrity in the country, and to support anti-corruption measures. The police and other security forces will continue to be strengthened and upgraded to ensure peace and security in the country. Prime Minister Badawi's goal is to build a society of individuals showing high degrees of integrity, character and the fortitude to work towards a state of 'zero corruption'.

## 2. What Role Can Christians Play?

### 2.1. Religious Leaders With Unbending Integrity

What kind of religious leadership does help building strong Christian communities with integrity? Integrity is the most important attribute of a religious leader: 'The saying is sure: whoever aspires to the office of bishop desires a noble task. Now a bishop must be above reproach, married only once, temperate, sensible, respectable, hospitable, an apt teacher, not a drunkard, not violent but gentle, not quarrelsome, and not a lover of money. He must manage his own household well, keeping his children submissive and respectful in every way for if someone does not know how to manage his own household, how can he take care of God's church? [...] For those who serve well as deacons gain a good standing for themselves and great boldness in the faith that is in Christ Jesus.' (1 Tim 3:1-5:13)[5] Church leadership is a responsibility, not a right. It is extended to those who come under the authority of the church's teachings as expounded in the Bible and church traditions. It has always been a demanding calling. To live with integrity is captive to Christian conviction and biblical priorities. They are firmly convinced to the highest ethical standards in both personal and professional conduct.

Let me share an experience with you. It is common to bribe the policemen who catch you committing a traffic offence. I have been naughty, when stopped. My answer to the policeman was 'Sorry, I am wrong.' I was prepared to pay the fine (RM 100-300) instead of a smaller amount as bribe and asked for the ticket. Today, the gap between Christian and societal values makes this particularly challenging. As we serve Christ in leadership, we model what we really believe about our faith. Both our beliefs and our lifestyles are critical to the way we serve Christ and project Christian leadership.

Religious leaders teach others that they can hold firm to moral integrity without compromising themselves and without asking others to. Good religious leaders model the preservation of one's integrity for the rest of the believers in a way to encourage them to be honest and to refuse to give bribes to get what they want. God calls for men and women of heart, of mind, and of moral integrity, whom He can make the depositories of His truth, and who will correctly represent its sacred principles in their daily life. 'He [Christ] has given us his very great and precious promises, so that through them you may participate in the divine nature and escape the corruption in the world caused by evil desires.' (2 Pet 1:4)[6]

A religious leader, according to Christ's measurement, is one who will manifest unbending integrity. Deceitful weights and false balances, with which many seek the easy way, are dishonest in the sight of God. Yet many who profess to keep the commandments of God are dealing with false weights and false balances. When a man is indeed connected with God, and is keeping His word in truth, his life will mirror his inner condition; for all his actions will be in harmony with the teachings of Christ. He will not sell his honour for gain. His principles are built upon steady foundations, and his conduct in worldly matters is a transcript of his principles.

Building a church where one can worship is a right of the Christians in this country. Asking bribes against permission or approval to build a church is to force to bribe in order to deliver one's due. And unfortunately, the great majority of the government officials are corruptible. If a pastor/church leader is forced to pay unjustly to obtain what is due to him/her, s/he must continue to fight against corruption to get what is just.

## 2.2. Religious Leaders Are Committed to Serious Bible Study

The churches need to ask : 'How many of our "successful" Christians, both in church and on the market place, have been able to maintain a life of integrity that fully reflects the values of our faith in Jesus Christ?' Indeed, many Christians struggling with integrity find insufficient pastoral help from our churches to resist further corruption. The church needs to encourage the moral transformation of Christian communities through: a) living according to the right values and commit the right actions as Christians; and b) respond to the needs and challenges of the country as the duty of Christians towards moral transformation.

Therefore, religious leaders are committed to undertake serious Bible study and help church communities to educate themselves. They need to have a clear understanding of Christian moral principles, appropriately interpreted and applied to our context and situation. The Old Testament is very clear on the prohibition of the use of a bribe to pervert justice: 'Do not pervert justice or show partiality. Do not accept a bribe, for a bribe blinds the eyes of the wise and twists the words of the righteous.' (Deut 16:19)

But in the Asian culture, the line between a bribe and a gift is not always clear. What is the appropriate manner or action, then? If a gift is huge compared to what has been given (for example RM 20,000 for the approval of a church building plan), then it is unethical. What about giving a hamper of RM 200 to express one's appreciation? Is it unethical to oil somebody's palm to get a tender over another or others who deserve it more, thus causing injustice? It appears necessary to encourage serious Bible study to bring out in-depth theological reflection and to combine it with serious study on the Chinese or Indian cultures and customs. It will help Christians to gain the inner spiritual strength necessary to handle their work or business without having recourse to bribing.

### 2.3. *Christians' Role and Task*

As a full-time minister in the Malaysian Church (i.e. as a Deaconess and a lecturer in the Seminary), I see that the task faced by our Prime Minister is immense. We, the Christians in this country, should show our support with concrete actions and not mere lip service. What role must we play, as religious leaders and Malaysians, in our church and teachings? Here are a few responses:

- Live godly lives transformed by the daily work of the Holy Spirit.

- Practice what we teach.

- Hold fast with our integrity, and whatever the situation, give no bribe.

- Be keen to join hands and seek to collaborate with other Christian organisations or NGOs working towards a better Malaysian society.

- Encourage our members to live godly lives transformed by the daily work of the Holy Spirit, seek integration in every area of their lives, including in the area of their involvement in the marketplace and to take the mantle of exemplary leadership to be agents for change.

Changing the image of people by promoting a value-based society with a clear sense of morals will need the unfailing support of the Christian churches and religious leaders.

NOTES

1    Adapted from articles by Theresa Manavalan in *New Straits Times*, Kuala Lumpur Muslimedia, 1-15 May 1997.

2    Corruption represents a major leakage of funds in the country and will only aggravate the already significant budget deficit.

3    Speech given by the Prime Minister on the 'The World Ethics and Integrity Forum 2005' in Kuala Lumpur.

4    'Malaysia to Sign Anti-Corruption Convention,' see www.dailyexpress.com.my/print.cfm ?newsID = 23311.

5    See the Holy Bible : New Revised Standard Version.

6    *Ibid.*

# 19

# FIGHTING CORRUPTION IN AND BY CHURCHES. AN IMPORTANT TASK OF CHURCH LEADERS

*Christoph Stückelberger, Switzerland*

No, it is not because I was personally confronted with cases of corruption or because I have been tempted, and it is not because I have lost my job as a whistleblower (an informant who reports cases of corruption), that I have dealt with the issue of fighting corruption for the last twelve years. Economic and ethical analyses have much rather opened my eyes to the fact that corruption can enormously obstruct development and moral credibility. This insight inspired me to found in 1995 the Swiss chapter of Transparency International (TI), the worldwide known NGO against corruption that has chapters in 90 countries.[1] And, during my twelve years of church development cooperation as director of Bread for all, I heard many examples of corruption in churches and by church representatives on all levels. I have become a Wailing Wall for young professionals and church staff in developing countries who wanted to fight corruption but are not supported or are blocked by church leaders. It was them who showed me how much churches are also involved in these mechanisms. Churches are part of the problem, but also part of the solution. Together with church-related partners we therefore launched and supported projects in Africa and Asia for corruption-free schools and churches, described in various publications.[2]

*Responsible leadership must include transparent leadership.* Transparency is the opposite of corruption which conducts financial transactions in darkness, 'under the table' and not on the table. *To become corruption-free, churches have to ensure they have corruption-free church leaders.* The Mutirão (panel discussion) on 'How to become a corruption-free church?' at the 9th Assembly of the World Council of Churches (WCC) in Porto Alegre in February 2006 proposed as first step to elaborate a Code of Leadership which should be signed by church leaders as their personal commitment and underlining their credibility.

## 1. Not All Evils Are Based on Corruption

Today, the term 'corruption' is used excessively. Some are likely to apply this term to all the evils in the world. A few theologians refer to the Latin term *corruptio*, describing apart from corruption also bribery and generally including also the distance from God and the malice of the world from the Fall of Man to the New Testament. But in so doing, the term assumes such a broad meaning that it is no longer of any use and disguises the facts instead of making them transparent. Therefore, I plead for a restricted and simple definition, in the way it is widely used in political and economic contexts: *Corruption is the abuse of public or private power for personal interests.*

There are different kinds of corruption: the *corruption of poverty (petty corruption)* has its roots in poverty; the *corruption of power (grand corruption)* is rooted in the greed for more power, influence and wealth or in the safeguarding of the existing power and economic position; the *corruption of procurement* and the *corruption of acceleration* serve the purpose of obtaining goods and services that otherwise would not be available or delivered on time, or only with much greater administrative expenses; the *grey corruption* is the grey zone between corruption, nepotism, favouritism and collusion. This article refers to these limited and internationally acknowledged definitions and avoids calling all evils 'corruption'![3]

## 2. Many Forms of Corruption from Bribes to Sex

Corruption has diverse forms. In the private economic and state sector, many studies have been undertaken.[4] Here, we limit ourselves to the church sector. Two areas have to be distinguished: corruption within an institution and corruption in the interaction between the institution and society. In societies in which all sectors are affected by corruption (as in many developing countries), it is evident that – unfortunately – churches as part of society are also concerned. Here, we are talking about services ranging from paying kickbacks to obtain state services such as travel documents or legal papers such as land right titles or building permits to construct a church, up to influencing criminal law proceedings, ransoming drugs at customs for hospitals, etc.

More distressful is corruption within the churches themselves, because it could be avoided more easily than when it occurs in the interaction with other parts of society – at least, this is what one could assume. Examples of this kind of corruption are found or heard of in many countries, especially in Africa and Asia. They include signing over church property to private property (e.g. land or rectory), buying documents by means of bribes, buying electoral votes in cases of church leadership elections, allocating scholarship to one's own children according to non-transparent criteria or by circumventing the approved criteria, deviating ear-marked funds (e.g. from mission and development cooperation) for other purposes than those agreed upon (this action is often not tied to personal advantage, but simply shows that there is an overall lack of money or liquidity or that it is a consequence of inadequate management and planning of finances). Even admitting students into theological seminaries or church schools, or transferring project applications may here and there be corrupted by paying out bribes.

The sexual abuse of students as a condition to be admitted to a school or to pass an exam is a widespread practice in non-church schools – this has been clearly stated in the Program for Corruption-Free Schools in West Africa – but cannot be completely excluded in church-run schools. A study in East Africa estimated that it is even higher than in public schools. Sexual abuse is a direct form of corruption because it is an abuse of public power (e.g. as a teacher) for the benefit of personal interests.

Grey corruption in the form of clan nepotism or ethnical affiliation can be observed in particular when accessing church offices and positions. Yet, this occurs in another form not only in developing countries but also in industrialised countries. The necessity of larger church development organisations to have a substantial outflow of means with too scarce project staff or a cutback of job positions can foster corrupt practices, as too many funds always flow through the same channels and individuals. In the case of emergency aid, there are particular difficulties tied to it, namely, that one should be able to help as fast as possible and that one depends on material, permits or transport opportunities that are for example controlled by rebel groups that impose their own conditions.[5]

In the field of microcredits, the relevance of which has been rightfully promoted now,[6] corruption may arise for example in hidden and not easily recognisable forms of writing off credits. A credit officer grants a credit via two different detours to a relative who seemingly cannot pay the credit back, and the credit officer writes it off upon apparently comprehensive reasons (e.g. AIDS-incurred death of the first borrower). As president of ECLOF International (i.e. the Ecumenical Church Loan Fund), having its head office in Geneva, I was confronted with several such cases. They clearly lead to the dismissal of the involved staff members as such cases can not be tolerated.[7] The donors of church development agencies and missionary societies have a special co-responsibility not to support fallible partners but to openly call them to account. Here, I have identified – and it has been clearly confirmed at two conferences with German missionary societies – that often staff members of these agencies and societies are willing to apply the necessary standards including sanctions, but the church leadership of the Northern partner church recoils from it and protects the church leader from the South, because they are friends and he fears negative headlines. In contrast to that, it is my experience that donors react very positively when they learn that church agencies have courageously and outspokenly fought corruption, in particular among their own ranks.[8] So much can be heard and read about corruption, that it can only be beneficial to adopt a pro-active, forward-looking strategy. With such a communication strategy donations can even increase and must not be affected.

## 3. Carcinogenic Effects

As many studies show, corruption has disastrous effects on all sectors of society. These effects concern financial, political, ecological, cultural, moral and religious aspects: misdirection of development[9] (wrong allocation of resources); increased indebtedness; lack of tax and state income; tax evasion; reduction of quality in the provision of services, increased risks (safety, health, environment); negative economic effects[10] such as distortion of competition/market; economic inefficiency; obstruction to investments; increase of the gap of affluence and of non-transparency; extortion; loss of confidence in state and economy; weakening of the moral integrity of individuals and institutions; loss of democracy (corruption at elections); violation of human rights;[11] violation of the principle of gender justice; weakening of the law system; support of dictatorships and rebel groups (which partially finance themselves and their activities with money from corruption); risking the reputation of development cooperation and church credibility. It is particularly serious if the *four sectors* of society that should offer orientation are involved in corrupt practices: *courts of justice, religious communities, media* and *schools!*

In some countries, the corruption payments to and from state and private bodies amount to the country's overall indebtedness, as has been shown by several studies. Hence, its relevance as to the implications on development cooperation is huge. At the same time, development organisations and churches invest a surprisingly small amount of manpower and funds in the fight against corruption, compared to the important efforts for debt relief! It is also correct and important that the global fight against HIV/AIDS has received major support and that churches now run big programs against HIV/AIDS. AIDS kills, but if we consider the negative effects that were just enumerated, corruption also kills – directly and indirectly – hundred thousands of people annually. Corruption is to society what cancer or drug dependence is to a body: it infiltrates all segments and destroys from within the organs of life until the body (or a society) collapses. I will come back to this analogy below.

## 4. The Bible: in Unconditional Manner Against Corruption

Corruption not only has political and economic effects; it also undermines values that are vital for the coexistence within a society: injustice instead of justice; inequality instead of equal rights also for the poor; lies instead of the truth; extortion instead of freedom; theft instead of performance; unpredictability instead of rationality and efficiency; non-transparency instead of co-determination and partic-ipation; manipulation instead of human dignity; self-interest instead of general welfare; irresponsible use of power instead of power used with responsibility.

Corruption is almost as old as humanity, at least it is known to have ocurred since the beginnings of jurisdiction. When looking for ethical criteria to judge corruption, biblical insights may be illuminating. Var-ious comprehensive theological-ethical studies are dealing with it. [12]

The oldest reference to corruption in the *Old Testament* seems to be found in the book of Exodus, only three chapters after the Ten Commandments. 'Do not accept a bribe, for a bribe makes people blind to what is right and ruins the cause of those who are innocent.' (Ex 23:8) This prohibition of corruption dates back to the times before the kings and is not accidentally addressed to judges not to accept bribes. An unbiased jurisdiction is vital for every legal system. Also, in the environment of the Old Testament, in Egypt and Mesopotamia, the phenomenon of corruption was known, but here in the book of Exodus a law against corruption has already been drawn up! It is also important to note that the ethical justification used to prohibit corruption is truth and justice, in particular the legal protec-tion of the poor, as is shown in other verses. 'Ah, you who acquit the guilty for a bribe, and deprive the innocent of their rights!' (Isa 5:23) The goal of fighting corruption is to protect the poor and the weaker from the corrupt practices of the powerful. But at the same time cor-rupt practices of poor people are condemned and not justified. 'You shall not side with the majority so as to pervert justice; nor shall you be partial to the poor in a lawsuit' (Ex 23:3). One cannot justify cor-ruption because it is a result of poverty.

Even before the time of the kings the sons of Samuel are said to have accepted bribes for their own benefit (1 Sam 8:3). In the Book of Kings it becomes clear that corruption was also used in external affairs and in military matters: allies of the adversary were offered bribes to use military actions against him (1 Kings 15:19; 2 Kings 16:8).

The prophets are also very clear about the effects of corruption. Corruption kills. Corruption destroys life. 'In you, they take bribes to shed blood; you take both advance interest and accrued interest, and make gain of your neighbours by extortion.' (Ezek 22:12) Similar in Psalm 15:1 and 5: 'O Lord, who may abide in your tent? ... Those who do not lend money at interest and do not take a bribe against the innocent.' The prophet and the psalm mention in the same verse corruption and usury! The effect is the same: exploitation; reduction of life expectancy and violation of just distribution. Wealth must be rooted in good performance and not based on exploitation, therefore 'better is a little with righteousness than great revenues with injustice' (Prov 16:8).

The theological justification of refusing corruption becomes clear in particular with the prophets. God Yahweh is incorruptible, as he is the right and justice himself. This is why he is not trying to bribe King Kyros when he repatriates his people from exile to their land (as some individuals among the people may have proposed and hoped). Corruption destroys communities. Whoever uses the evil of bribery is called pagan and is thus called as being excluded from the community with God (Prov 17:23). Devout is he who does not take bribes (Ps 26:10).

Cases of bribery are also mentioned in the *New Testament*. And again, bribery is always condemned. In connection with the events around Passion and Easter, it is reported that Judas was bribed by high priests (Mark 14:10f). The elites of the Roman Empire under Pontius Pilate have been heavily corrupt. And Pilate in cooperation with the Jewish authorities (Synhedrium) killed Jesus. Corruption kills, in a double sense: it killed Jesus of Nazareth and Judas hanged himself (Matt 27:5) because he lost all self-respect through corruption. High priests and elders also bribed the soldiers to spread the lie that the body of Christ was not resurrected but stolen (whether these passages are historical is controversial). The Acts of the Apostles report on how judges were bribed, the governor Felix wanted some money from Paul, to sentence him less severely (Acts 24:26f). It is also documented that customs – controlled by the Romans – was corrupt at the time of Jesus; this fact is also shown by the story of chief tax collector Zacchaeus who illegally acquired goods and who later gave half of his belongings to the poor (Luke 19:1-10). The corruptibility of the spirit is probably the most dangerous form of corruption : Simon the magician offered money to the apostles Peter and John, thus trying to buy the power so that anyone he places his hands on would receive the Holy Spirit (Acts 8:8-24). To draw a moral from this story, it shows that what is an inalienable power of God cannot be acquired with underhand dealings.

The relevance of these biblical insights – mostly conveyed in narrative stories – for the ethics of fighting corruption lies in the fact that the stories reflect images of successful life and of a society that knows no corruption. There is no single verse in the Bible which justifies corruption! But many verses offer a very clear analysis of the effects of corruption and very clear values of a corruption-free society, which can be summarised as follows:

| | |
|---|---|
| • Corruption kills and destroys life | God wants life |
| • Corruption oppresses the rights of the poor | God wants justice |
| • Corruption hinders economic performance | God wants honest wealth |
| • Corruption destroys trust and confidence | God wants community |
| • Corruption strengthens violence and military forces | God wants peace |
| • Corruption destroys integrity and credibility | God wants dignity |

## 5. The Course of a Disease and the Healing Process

Let us take up the analogy of corruption as a disease like cancer or rather as an addiction, in order to describe six therapy stages towards overcoming corruption. How do we overcome an addiction?

*Stage 1: minimisation and justification.* Corruption is justified as a culture of giving presents. The language hushes up facts (in business: 'useful additional expenses' instead of 'bribes'), talks about corruption only in private.

*Stage 2: the problem starts exerting pressure.* The economic and political pressure on individuals and companies increases. The payments of bribes reach the limit of tolerability in economic terms.

*Stage 3: acknowledgement of the addiction.* 'Yes, I am sick, our institution or our society is sick. Measures are required.'

*Stage 4: decision of zero tolerance.* In the same way as an alcoholic recognises that he can only get away from his addiction if he completely renounces alcohol and not only a little; the zero tolerance decision as to corruption is taken. And subsequently, programs to combat corruption as well as codes of conduct are introduced, etc.

*Stage 5: accept support.* 'We need support as we are unable to get out of our addiction ourselves.' National laws and international conventions with inherent sanctions are important support mechanisms.

*Stage 6: healing. A corruption-free life is developing.* Yet, it is necessary to remain vigilant as corruption can come back at any time. Zero tolerance must be maintained even if corruption decreases.

## 6. Therapy Measures Undertaken by Churches

I witnessed and observed these stages of fighting corruption in particular as founder and president of the Swiss chapter of Transparency International in the years 1994-2004. Today, in the international debate and efforts we have reached stage 3-5 in the political and economic field. As to the churches, we have only reached stage 3 in many countries, sometimes even not this public acknowledgement. In order to move the healing process forward to stage 4-6 also in churches, we finally need concrete steps by implementing binding programs and agreements, initiated or at least led by the church leaders.

The beginning has been encouraging: in many places churches or parts of them start raising their voice against corruption, mostly against corruption within state and society, and increasingly against corruption within the churches. Public statements in Cameroon and Nigeria, codes of conduct connected to a plan of action in India, campaigns for corruption-free schools in Western Africa, publication in China, training courses for the church finance officers in Eastern Africa, self-commitment and anti-corruption clauses in agreements of missionary societies and aid agencies, publications about biblical reflections in Madagascar, a church campaign for corruption-free schools in Western Africa, a letter from the Argentinian churches from the South to the churches in the North on the connection of indebtedness and corruption, an anti-corruption plan of the All African Church Conference (AACC) in Nairobi – all these are just a few encouraging examples. [13]

Often these initiatives emerge from stress-induced suffering. Wherever it is about corruption in the state system, the church leadership publish relevant declarations. Yet, when we talk about corruption within the church structures, we often find courageous individuals in church-related special institutions or even staff members of church parishes who are very often called back or even sanctioned by their church leadership. When a church governing board has lost the trust of its members due to corruption, then the new church leadership feels often motivated and forced to introduce measures to fight corruption.

Women in churches have an important role to play in fighting corruption. Since they often are more affected by corrupt practices than men and since they often are still less involved in power structures of churches, they are more independent to speak and act against corruption. But women and men together have to undertake the efforts. Otherwise the addiction cannot be stopped. [14] The whistleblowers should not be punished but protected as it is more and more the case with anonymous call centres for whistleblowers in companies and governmental administration. [15] A doctor who tells a patient that he is sick should not be sanctioned, but taken seriously.

As examples of encouraging measures, I would like to mention two global church statements aimed at fighting corruption. The 8th General Assembly of the World Council of Churches in Harare in 1998 called its member churches – in the declaration 'The Debt Issue: A Jubilee Call to End the Stranglehold of Debt on Impoverished Peoples' – 'to work for an ethical governance in all countries and legislative action against all forms of corruption and misuse of loans.'[16]

The World Alliance of Reformed Churches (WARC) approved a plan of action for economic justice and environmental questions at its 24th General Assembly in Accra in August 2004. Upon the proposal of the author of this text it states in the 'Report of the Public Issues Committee' in the section on 'Economic and Environmental Justice' as recommendations to the churches that they should '…5. Commit themselves to eradicating corruption within the churches by implementing existing and new plans (e.g. AACC General Assembly and NCC India).'[17]

However, the encouraging measures taken by the churches so far are not enough. This is why the WARC proposal has now to be taken up and put into concrete steps.

## 7. 'Program to Overcome Corruption in Church and Society' (POC)

I hence propose an *ecumenical international 'Program to Overcome Corruption in Church and Society' (POC)*. In the same way as there was the famous WCC 'Program to Combat Raciscm' (PCR) and now there is the WCC 'Decade to Overcome Violence' (DOV), we now need extensive joint efforts to overcome the cancerous evil of corruption – undertaken within and by the churches. The program should set the following *two goals*:

- the WCC member churches are corruption-free churches – at the latest by the 10th General Assembly of the WCC; and

- the WCC member churches support the various sectors of their societies in order for them to abolish corruption.

The program can be implemented on local, regional, national, continental and international level. It should include *four activities*:

- biblical-theological reflections on corruption and its overcoming;

- analyses of mechanisms that foster corruption;

- exchange of information among member churches, regional ecumenical organisations and special services such as aid agencies and mission societies on existing and planned measures to fight corruption as a sign of hope; and

- development, implementation and regular evaluation of instruments such as plans of action, codes of conduct, administrative guidelines and sanctions.

The role of the WCC in these programs could be that of motivator, animator and networker. The WCC should motivate its member churches to increase, to interlink and to continuously implement their efforts. Yet, each of the member churches can also start with such a program on its own. The program could be turned into a part of the WCC Program to Overcome Violence – as corruption is an open form of violence against the weaker members of the church and society. It could also be turned into a part of programs for economic justice. How can churches fight for economic justice in society if they handle their own meagre resources in an unjust way? Either anti-corruption programs of governments, international organisations or Transparency International can support such programs for corruption-free churches.

As to the credibility of the churches in the future, the relevance of the program should not be underestimated, because the churches have not played a prophetic role so far. But, this is what they urgently have to comprehend, and do what others have already started to do – in order to credibly play their proclaiming and prophetic role of pastoral care within society.

NOTES

1   TI International: www.transparency.org; TI Switzerland: www.transparency.ch.

2   See Stückelberger, Christoph, 'Continue Fighting Corruption. Experiences and Tasks of Churches and Development Agencies', in: *Impulse* 2/03, Berne: Bread for all, 2003; and 'Fighting Corruption. An Urgent Task of Aid Agencies, Missionary Societies and Churches', in: *Impulse* 5/99, Berne: Bread for all, 1999. Can be found on www.christophstueckelberger.ch.

3   More on definitions in Stückelberger, Christoph, *op. cit.*, 1999, pp. 5 ff.; Pieth, Mark/Eigen, Peter (eds), *Korruption im internationalen Geschäftsverkehr*, Neuwied: Luchterhand, 1999.

4   As an example of two country studies see Friedrich Ebert Foundation/Gerddes Cameroon (eds), *Corruption in Cameroon,* Yaounde: 1999; Hajadj, Djillali, *Corruption et démocratie en Algérie*, Paris: La Dispute, 1999. Many country reports can be found on www.transparency.org.

5   Recent reports include: Ewins, Pete *et al., Mapping the Risks of Corruption in Humanitarian Action*, Transparency International, 2006; Transparency International, *Corruption in Humanitarian Aid. Working Paper 03/2006*. Both papers can be found in pdf format on http://www.transparency.org (last accessed 12 August 2006).

6   Especially during the International Year of Microcredit launched by the United Nations in 2005.

7   Examples from the field of development cooperation can also be found in Cremer, Georg, *Korruption begrenzen. Praxisfeld Entwicklungspolitik*, Freiburg im Brisgau: Lambertus, 2000, pp. 61-151. Cremer is the executive director of Caritas Germany.

8   See Gabriel, Lara *et al.* (eds), *The Role of Bilateral Donors in Fighting Corruption*, Washington, D.C.: World Bank Institute, 2001.

9    See Robinson, Mark (ed.), *Corruption and Development*, London: Frank Cass Publishers, 1998.

10   See Jain, Arvind K. (ed.), *Economics of Corruption*, Boston: Kluwer Academic Publishers, 1998; Elliott, Kimberly Ann (ed.), *Corruption and the Global Economy*, Washington, D.C.: Institute for International Economics, 1997.

11   See Borghi, M./Meyer-Bisch, P. (eds), *La corruption. L'envers des droits de l'homme*, Fribourg: Editions Universitaires, 1995.

12   E.g. Rennstich, Karl, *Korruption. Eine Herausforderung für Gesellschaft und Kirche*, Stuttgart: Quell, 1990, pp. 137-197; Kleiner, Paul, *Bestechung. Eine theologisch-ethische Untersuchung*, Berne: Peter Lang, 1992, pp. 83-160; Christian Council of Ghana, *Bribery and Corruption*, Christian Home Week 1999, Accra 1999; Cameroon Federation of Protestant Churches and Missions (FEMEC), *Jugulate Corruption. Anticorruption and Protransparency Code for Our Churches and the Entire Society.*

13   One can find an extensive description in Stückelberger, Christoph, 'Continue fighting Corruption. Experiences and Tasks of Churches and Development Agencies', in: *op. cit.*, pp. 8-29.

14   *Ibid*, pp. 42-50 on 'The Gender Dimension of Corruption'.

15   Leisinger, Klaus M., *Whistleblowing and Corporate Reputation Management*, München: Rainer Hampp, 2003.

16   Official Report of the Eighth General Assembly of the World Council of Churches Harare, Geneva: WCC Publications, 1998, especially the declaration on Debt issues, point 4.

17   Proceedings of the 24th General Council of the World Alliance of Reformed Churches in Accra, Ghana, 30 July-12 August 2004, Geneva: WARC, 2005, p. 200.

# 20

## CODE OF LEADERSHIP ADOPTED BY THE NATIONAL COUNCIL OF CHURCHES IN INDIA, 2004

### TRUTH AND PEACE THROUGH CORRUPTION-FREE CHURCHES: PLAN OF ACTION UNANIMOUSLY APPROVED BY THE NCCI QUADRENNIAL ASSEMBLY 9-13 FEBRUARY 2004

We, the delegates and fraternal delegates to the 25th Quadrennial Assembly, who participated in the Pre-Assembly Meeting on 'Life of the Church' that was held from 6-8 February 2004 at Tirunelveli (South India)

- strongly affirm that the Church embodies ethical and Christian values of truth, peace and justice that ensures equal opportunities to all, to enjoy the fullness of life;

- We also strongly affirm the heritage of eminent Church leaders and religious personalities who have been and are excellent stewards in the service of the Lord and society;

- However, we recognize that corruption which is rampant in society has penetrated the life of the Churches undermining truth, justice and peace, dividing the community and destroying the credibility of the institutions and of the life and mission of the Churches;

- We also recognize that the root cause of corruption lies in the misuse and abuse of power or privilege and therefore is an unethical act leading to moral crisis and conflicts.

Therefore, we recommend the following plan of action for approval by the NCCI Assembly.

**NCCI, the member Churches, Regional Christian Councils, Related Agencies, All India Christian Organizations:**

1. make anti-corruption a high priority in their mission and activities between now and the next assembly;

2. add anti-corruption clauses and mechanisms in the different regulations on Church-related free and fair elections of the respective bodies at all levels;

3. adopt and implement the 'Code of Leadership' (Appendix 1);

4. recommend that all candidates for elections of the respective bodies sign the code;

5. take immediate action to declare all church related institutions like schools, clinics, hospitals, offices etc. 'corruption-free zone' and conduct their business on transparent basis. The institutions should establish a mechanism of monitoring and control;

6. support efforts for sufficient and fair salaries for leaders of Churches and staff of Christian institutions in order to meet the basic needs and to overcome the temptation to increase income and allowances by corrupt practices;

7. promote an annual anti-corruption week including biblical reflection, practical action and publication;

8. encourage networking with Churches and NCC's in other countries and continents (e.g. All Africa Conference of Churches' program against corruption), other religious communities, civic society groups and governments committed to expose and end corruption;

9. improve mutual transparency and accountability between donors and the churches;

10. campaign effectively to eradicate corruption;

11. share annually with the NCCI information on their activities and action against corruption. NCCI secretariat will synthesize, coordinate and disseminate this information and provide an annual progress report to the members for their study and consideration.

## PROCESS OF IMPLEMENTATION

The Assembly requests the NCCI, the member Churches, Regional Christian Councils, Related Agencies, All India Christian Organizations to implement these recommendations in order to eradicate corruption.

## APPENDIX 1
## CODE OF LEADERSHIP FOR LEADERS OF CHURCHES, CHURCH-RELATED ORGANIZATIONS AND CHRISTIAN INSTITUTIONS IN INDIA

Realizing that responsible leadership is a central part of the strategy to fight corruption, we urge on the NCCI, the member Churches, Regional Christian Councils, Related Agencies and the All India Christian Organizations to impress on the leadership that the adoption of the following code will be a crucial contribution towards overcoming corruption:

1. to give precedence to public interest over personal interest;

2. to refuse to accept money or gifts which can be construed as bribes;

3. to maintain and update inventories that list out the properties of the institution and to ensure that properties are registered on behalf of the institution;

4. to avoid leasing and selling of Church properties (both movable and immovable) on the plea that current liabilities have to be met;

5. to declare the personal assets (movable or immovable) to the governing body while taking charge and relinquishing the office;

6. to decentralize powers and duties to allow proper control and management of responsibilities;

7. to refrain from engaging in long term litigations and pending cases and to establish an 'Ecumenical Adjudicating Authority' to arbitrate between conflicting parties;

8. to encourage and support people who are working against corruption as well as to protect the whistleblowers who expose corrupt practices;

9. to avoid attempts to close institutions which are reputed centres of education and empowerment;

10. to strictly utilize the finance that is earmarked for specific programs and purposes without mismanagement;

11. to adhere to minimum labour standards with fair appointments and selection procedures, issuing of employment contract letters, medical and pension benefits to church employees and their families;

12. to avoid involvement of family members in the decision making as well as administrative bodies of the respective institution.


This code was designed and approved by the 25th Quadrennial Assembly of the National Council of Churches of India 9-13th February 2004.

The organ that plays the role of governing body, represented by its president, shall ratify this code.

# 21

# AFRICAN CHURCH LEADERSHIP.
# BETWEEN CHRIST,
# CULTURES AND CONFLICTS

*J. N. K. Mugambi, Kenya*

## 1. Christianity and Culture

The question of the relationship between Christianity and culture is a perennial problem that has endured since the beginning of Christianity. It is a challenge for all churches and a specific challenge for church leadership in Africa.

In his book *Christ and Culture*, H. Richard Niebuhr[1] suggests at least five different ways in which this relationship might be expressed. Niebuhr's analysis is helpful for anyone interested in discerning how Christianity has been appropriated for social change in the contemporary world, especially in Africa. It is worthwhile to summarise that analysis.

### 1.1. Christ Against Culture

When Christianity is presented as an alternative superior to the existing culture, the prospective convert is placed in a dilemma, to follow Christ or remain in 'paganism'. This particular relationship has been presupposed by most missionaries from the North Atlantic to Africa. By 'Christ' they have meant their own cultural and religious heritage, which is supposedly 'Christian'. Since Christianity cannot exist in a cultural vacuum, any claim to preach 'pure gospel' becomes pretentious. A Christian, no matter how puritanical, is a product of his culture. When he goes out to win converts, he does so from his own cultural background, using the cultural tools which he has accumulated through the process of socialisation and education. The portrayal of Christ as being against culture, in practice becomes a declaration of conflict between the culture of the missionary and that of the prospective converts. This produces a serious social crisis. The proliferation of independent churches in Africa is a manifestation of that crisis. Ngugi wa Thiong'o in his novel *The River Between*[2] portrays this crisis in the conflict between Joshua, the staunch Christian, and Muthoni, his daughter, who seeks wholeness in the traditional African way of life. Okot p'Bitek also portrays the same crisis in his two long poems, *Song of Lawino* and *Song of Ocol*.[3] Kosuke Koyama[4] described a similar crisis in Thailand, where local people could identify themselves with Christ, while the missionaries portrayed Christianity as a movement against the Buddhist tradition.

## 1.2. The Christ of Culture

On the opposite end of the spectrum, some Christians consider Christ to be the 'Son of God' and 'Son of Man' who comes to affirm the cultural and religious heritage of peoples. The Gospel is then viewed as the fulfilment of culture, not a threat to it. The Sermon on the Mount (Matt 5-7) is interpreted as an endorsement of this perspective. Christ is then portrayed as the 'Man for All Cultures', who helps people to discern and live according to God's will in the context of their respective cultural and religious traditions. Under this perspective, Christianity cannot be culturally uniform. The churches of the apostolic period presupposed this perspective of the relationship between Christ and culture. Though they were in communion with each other, they retained each its uniqueness and cultural particularity.

## 1.3. Christ Above Culture

Between these two extremes of affirmation and negation of culture, some Christians evade conflict by presenting a Christ who is 'above' culture. Under this perspective, Christianity becomes transcendentalist, concentrating on 'salvation' in heaven and in future. In practice, such religiosity becomes irrelevant to the needs and demands of the present.

## 1.4. Christ and Culture in Paradox

Other Christians avoid the conflict by suggesting a paradox, in which Christ is at the same time identified with culture and contrasted with it. The Church is in the world, though it is not of the world. The problem of this perspective is the lack of clarity with regard to the circumstances under which Christ is portrayed in support of culture and those when culture is negated. Who has the authority to decide on such questions? In the context of the modern Christian missionary enterprise, this authority has been vested in missionaries, who in general have been biased in favour of their own cultures and against the cultures where they are guests.

## 1.5. Christ the Transformer of Culture

The fifth perspective portrays Christ as the transformer of culture, who makes all things new (Rev 21:5). Conversion is viewed as a challenge for the convert to change his ways and become a new being. St. Paul's conversion is often cited as an example. He was transformed from a 'persecutor' of Christians to a 'perfector' of Christianity. The notion of transformation, however, presupposes that the earlier way of life is not abandoned; it is transformed through adoption of new insights and commitments. If the ingredients of transformation are taken from the invading culture, the resulting change becomes comparable with any other process of acculturation. In Africa, most cultural change under colonial rule and missionary tutelage has been of this kind. It is for this reason that many of the African elites have blamed the modern Christian missionary enterprise for the cultural alienation which Africans have suffered under the pretext of modernisation.

These five perspectives on the relationship between Christianity and culture have all been applicable in Africa. In one African country, and in one particular denomination, all the perspectives might be present, causing tensions and confusions and factions. Part of the cultural crisis in the continent arises from the lack of consensus amongst Christians and churches, on the most relevant and constructive approach *to reconcile Christianity and culture.*

## 2. Piety and Politics

A second severe challenge for African church leaders is the instrumentalisation of religion in politics. Alan Geyer, in his book *Piety and Politics,*[5] outlines six approaches through which religion can be used in political mobilisation. In each of those approaches, religion becomes a means to an end – as a source of loyalty, a sanction for loyalty, a sanction for conflict, a source of conflict, a sanctuary from conflict, and a reconciler of conflict. This section explores each of these appropriations of religion, with particular reference to contemporary Africa.

### 2.1. Religion as a Source of Loyalty

When religion is used as a source of loyalty, the leaders try to wrench social cohesion by appealing to a common faith. The Old Testament and the Koran have often been interpreted as scriptures which portray religion as a source of loyalty. This approach is used both by regimes in power and by groups struggling for liberation. In Africa, the apartheid regime used the Dutch Reformed Church as a source of loyalty among the Afrikaners, until apartheid was declared a heresy by the World Alliance of Reformed Churches (WARC) in 1983. Islam is sometimes used as a source of loyalty. Such is the case in the countries of the Arabian Peninsula. Secular states avoid this approach to religion by constitutionally detaching religious affiliation from citizenship. National cohesion is impossible to achieve when religious affiliation becomes entangled with citizenship. Former Yugoslavia, which seemed united during the cold war, disintegrated when various nationalities claimed their sovereignty on the basis of cultural, religious and historical identity. The civil strife in Sudan revolves around the question of religious, cultural, racial and ideological identity.

## 2.2. Religion as a Sanction for Loyalty

Geyer illustrates this approach by describing the influence of Calvinism on the development of national consciousness in the USA. He shows that the separation of powers between church and state, which has become a dominant feature in that country, produced not a secularist nation, but one in which both civil religion and national patriotism flourished. Citing a book published by Lord Bryce in 1889 under the title *American Commonwealth*, Geyer highlights the features which have characterised American identity: [6]

- Christianity is, in fact if not in name, the national religion;
- the world view of average Americans is shaped by the Bible and Christian theology;
- Americans attribute progress and prosperity to Divine favour;
- political thought is deeply influenced by such Puritan emphases as the doctrine of original sin;
- American constitutional government is peculiarly legalistic;
- American religion is marked by emotional fervour; and
- the social activities of American religion are singularly developed.

In contemporary Africa, the use of religion as a sanction for loyalty can be illustrated in such countries as Ethiopia under Haile Selassie, and in Zaire under Mobutu. In the former, the Ethiopian Orthodox Church was the symbol of Ethiopian sovereignty, even though there are adherents to other religions. In Zaire, an attempt was made to bring all Protestant churches under one umbrella organisation, as a means of control. This attempt did not succeed, particularly because the denominational missionary links with Europe and North America could not be severed.

## 2.3. Religion as a Sanction for Conflict

Throughout history religion has been used to justify conflict and war, especially in the context of imperial expansion. From the 8th century onwards, Islam was used to justify Arab expansion across North Africa and into Europe. Europeans used the Crusades to justify invasion and plunder of foreign peoples. The missionary enterprise was fuelled by a similar crusading spirit, in which non Christians were considered enemies of Christ if they resisted conversion to Christianity. Geyer cites Psalm 18:34, 39-40, as an example of Christian-Judaic scriptural references which portray religion as a sanction for conflict:

> He trains my hands for war,
> So that my arms can bend a bow of bronze.
> For thou didst gird me with strength for the battle;
> Thou didst make my assailants sink under me.
> Thou didst make my enemies turn their backs to me,
> And those who hated me I destroyed.

In contemporary Africa, many civil conflicts are often portrayed in such adversarial terms. It is in Sudan, perhaps more than in any other part of the continent, that religion is portrayed as sanction for conflict. The civil war in Sudan, which has been raging since 1956, is generally portrayed by the mass media as a conflict between 'the "Arabised" and "Islamised" North against the "Christianised" and "Animist" South'. This adversarial caricature of a very complex problem, tends to oversimplify the dynamics of the conflict, which has historical, political, economic, ideological and cultural dimensions. The media image of the conflict overlooks the fact that there are Muslims and Christians on both sides of the conflict.

## 2.4. Religion as a Source of Conflict

The religious conflicts in Palestine-Israel, India (Punjab and Kashmir), and Sri Lanka are examples where religion is a source of conflict. In Africa, the declaration of Shariah in Northern Nigeria is another example. The civil strife in Algeria can also be cited in this context. One important question is whether in the 21st century it will make political sense to organise nations and states on the basis of religious identity. While religion is important as a pillar of culture, it ought not to divide peoples whose survival can be sustained only through interdependence.

## 2.5. Religion as a Sanctuary from Conflict

This approach to religion can have at least two meanings. First, it can mean the retreat of religious leadership and laity from involvement in social controversies, on the ground that religious commitment does not permit social engagement. Second, it can mean that in times of conflict the victims caught in crossfire will find refuge and sanctuary in places of worship. With regard to the first meaning, there is a long tradition in Euro-American Protestantism, in which Christianity is used as a justification for withdrawal from social action. The Puritan emigration from Europe to the Americas was thus justified. Those who refused to conform to the norms of the political establishment took sanctuary in their religion, and fled to the Americas where they established their own social system based on the separation of church and state. Within the same country, religious individuals and communities can withdraw from engagement in social affairs and retreat into individualistic pursuits. William Lee Miller observed such a tendency in North American Protestantism. Such withdrawal and retreat leads to political alienation. Geyer explains the withdrawal and retreat as follows: in part, he suggests, the Protestant withdrawal from politics is a function of the Protestant withdrawal from the city. That withdrawal reinforces the Puritan image of the city politics as corrupt, machine-ridden and Catholic-controlled. The retreat into suburbia leads to the following liabilities:

- the escape from the invasion of racial and religious minorities removes Protestant leadership from the stage of those domestic conflicts for which there is now a worldwide audience, while actually intensifying those conflicts within American society;

- the abandoning of urban centres weakens Protestant identification with those unsolved economic and welfare problems which threaten the country with domestic stagnation;

- Protestants become more vulnerable to the artificial compartmentalisation between domestic and international issues, leaving them increasingly with the paradoxical combination of a sentimental internationalism and a socioeconomic conservatism;

- the retreat from the city is a retreat from exposure to the cosmopolitan and intercultural influences of the city; and

- Protestant participation is increasingly withdrawn from such national and international centres of foreign policy discussion as New York, Boston, Baltimore, and Chicago.

Geyer's analysis of North American Protestant withdrawal and retreat from politics is helpful in explaining the social aloofness of African Christianity. The withdrawal and retreat from public life has been exported to Africa through the modern missionary enterprise, with all the liabilities highlighted above, especially in the post-colonial period. In view of the fact that the African elite has been trained mainly in institutions owned or sponsored by missionary agencies where these principles of withdrawal and aloofness have been inculcated, it is understandable that campaigns for political transition in Africa have been lukewarm, if not dormant. Where political activism has been vigorous, the activists will either have been trained out of such missionary establishments, or rebels alumni critical of those principles.

## 2.6. Religion as a Reconciler of Conflict

It is ironic that although peace on earth and goodwill amongst humankind are key principles in the doctrines of most religions which claim universal appeal, in practice all the promoters of these religions have generated conflict whenever they have come into contact with peoples of other cultures and religions. Part of the reason for this tragedy is that universalistic religions have almost always become tools for use by expansionist principalities and powers. In response to this paradox, the World Council of Churches (WCC) in 1954 formulated nine guidelines[7] to facilitate peaceful coexistence between and amongst nations. Considering that these guidelines were formulated at the beginning of the cold war, they were quite progressive. If they had been followed, many international conflicts could have been avoided:

1. All power carries responsibility and all nations are trustees of power which should be used for the common good.
2. All nations are subject to moral law, and should strive to abide by the accepted principles of international law to develop this law and to enforce it through common actions.
3. All nations should honour their pledged word and international agreements into which they have entered.
4. No nation in an international dispute has the right to be sole judge in its own cause or to resort to war in order to advance its policies, but should seek to settle disputes by direct negotiation or by submitting them to reconciliation, arbitration, or judicial settlement.
5. All nations have an obligation to insure universal security and to this end should support measures designed to deny victory to a declared aggressor.
6. All nations should recognise and safeguard the inherent dignity, worth and essential rights of the human person, without distinction as to race, sex, language or religion.
7. Each nation should recognise the rights of every other nation, which observes such standards, to live by and proclaim its own political and social beliefs, provided that it does not seek by coercion, threat, infiltration or deception to impose these on other nations.
8. All nations should recognise an obligation to share their scientific and technical skills with peoples in less developed regions, and to help the victims of disaster in other lands.

9. All nations should strive to develop cordial relations with their neighbours, encourage friendly cultural and commercial dealings, and join in creative international efforts for human welfare.

The United Nations system was designed to promote peaceful coexistence. However, it appears that the powerful nations can always impose their will and power on the weaker ones, even when the former are in the wrong. We can only hope that the future will give birth to a New Order in which the strong nations will restrain themselves and protect the weak rather than dominate and exploit them, while the weak in their turn will have the courage to assert themselves in order to share their intellectual and cultural resources for the good of posterity and all humanity.

## 3. The Future of Religion in Africa

During the 1980s and 1990s many books were published in Europe and North America on the present features and future prospects of religion in Africa. Some sociologists of religion have predicted that Africa will become increasingly 'Christianised'. As evidence of this trend, they have alluded to the dynamism of African Christianity, especially in tropical Africa. Most of these predictions were made by foreign observers using macro-statistical indicators and variables. African scholars have been much more cautious in their predictions, taking into consideration their acquaintance with actual situations and contexts. For example, they have expressed concern that the numerical growth of Christianity in tropical Africa is not matched with corresponding theological growth and institutional development. There is too little African theological literature written by Africans for consumption by Africans. How could a religion grow without its own theologians? Portuguese priests baptised thousands of African Christians in Angola during the 16th and 17th centuries. They must have boasted the number of converts that they had made. However, that early Angolan Christianity did not last, because it lacked internalisation and theological originality. How long will this dynamic African Christianity last?

Roland Oliver warned in 1950[8] that Christianity in Africa risks expanding at the circumference while disintegrating at the centre. He was referring to the rapid numerical growth which was not matched by a corresponding growth in theological and institutional development. Half a century later, this caution is still valid. African Islam faces the same risk. The construction of mosques in African cities and rural areas does not necessarily suggest numerical expansion of Islam. In the end, both these religions will survive in Africa, in the long term, only if they produce African theologians who can appropriate the African cultural and religious heritage in such a way as to make African Christianity and African Islam at home amongst Africa's peoples.

If both succeed, African Christianity and African Islam will have two things in common: the African cultural and religious foundations on the one hand, and the Abrahamic tradition on the other. The challenges of urbanisation, industrialisation and secularisation will take their toll on religious propaganda, unless the promoters of religions in Africa will communicate in terms with which the African youth and students can identify. Liberal capitalism has brought advertising to the doorstep of even the remotest homestead in Africa. Religious clerics and laity can hardly match that record. This is the challenge that expansionist religions have to face in coming decades and centuries in Africa.

It is clear that religion is given a very high public profile in Africa. Religious leaders are invited in conflicts between political factions. Religious agencies have become dispensers of relief goods and services, including food, clothes and medicines. Social services such as schooling and medical care are provided largely by religious agencies. Under these circumstances, is it possible to envisage the secularisation of religion in Africa? If Asia and the Arab zone are instructive, we may expect that Africa will not follow the North Atlantic model. Rather, religion will continue to have a central role for many decades, perhaps for centuries to come.

NOTES

[1]   Niebuhr, H. Richard, *Christ and Culture*, New York: Harper Torchbooks, 1975.

[2]   wa Thiong'o, Ngugi, *The River Between*, London: Heinemann African Writers Series, 1967.

[3]   p'Bitek, Okot, *Song of Lawino and Song of Ocol*, Nairobi: East African Publishing House, 1971.

[4]   Koyama, Kosuke, *Waterbuffalo Theology*, London: SCM Press, 1974.

[5]   Geyer, Alan F., *Piety and Politics*, Richmond, VA: John Knox Press, 1963.

[6]   *Ibidem*, pp. 39-40.

[7]   *Ibid.*, pp. 126ff.

[8]   Oliver, Roland, *The Missionary Factor in East Africa*, London: Longman, 1970 (1st edition: 1952).

# 22

# RELIGIOUS STATISTICS IN RUSSIA. A CHALLENGE FOR RELIGIOUS LEADERSHIP

*Roman Silantyev, Russia*

## 1. Conflicting Interests for Counting Religious Groups in Russia

The first national census to be conducted since 1989 took place in October 2002. Unfortunately, it was not compulsory and provoked a great deal of scandals; still it allowed for the production of a body of officially recognised data that, if processed, can give answers to many questions concerning the nature of Russian society today. One important question however has remained unanswered. As early as the initial stages in preparations for the census, many authoritative scientists insisted that the census questionnaire should include a question about the religious affiliation of respondents and proposed to omit instead the questions about their living conditions as such data are easily obtained from housing and communal services. They heard in response that this replacement was difficult to make technically and that, generally, religious leaders strongly disapproved of such questions, allegedly afraid to face the truth when they saw how low in fact the numbers of their followers were. To be sure, it was just a lame excuse because major religious organisations in Russia were concerned in the first place with obtaining such data and never objected to having the questionnaires corrected accordingly. As a result, the request of scientists was rejected, thus depriving them of an opportunity to handle official statistics as to the religious convictions of Russian citizens for at least ten more years, while engaged specialists retained the *carte blanche* to continue speculating on the subject. Followers of scientific atheism will thus continue arguing that it is they who make up the majority of the population, while supporters of the interests of religious minorities will continue insisting on having as many as 35 million Russian Muslims, 5 million Protestants and 1.5 million Catholics. It is much easier to refute such claims than to substantiate them. However, a natural question arises here: 'What is it in fact that the Russians believe in?' In order to answer, let us undertake an analysis of the four principal sources of information concerning the religious composition of the Russian population.

## 2. First Source: The 2002 National Census

The latest census remains the main official source of information about the ethnic make-up of the Russian population. At first glance, the ethnic make-up has no direct correlation with the religious preferences of the population. However it helps identify the upper limit in the number of followers of some religious traditions, such as Orthodox Christianity, Islam, Judaism, Buddhism, Catholicism, Lutheranism, Mennonism and Heathenism. To this end the assumption is made that, for instance, all the Poles, Lithuanians, Czechs, Slovaks, French, one third of the Germans and one twentieth of the Ukrainians confess Catholicism, while the number of Catholics among the Russians and other peoples is negligible. Then the total number of the so-called 'ethnic Catholics' is calculated and the figure thus obtained is considered to be the upper limit of the number of Catholics in Russia. Certainly, any qualified scholar of religions or ethnographer will raise an objection that there are considerably fewer real Catholics among the Russian Germans than one third, just as many Poles and Lithuanians actually confess Orthodox Christianity. The procedure described above however does not claim at all any high accuracy, but it makes it possible to show vividly that the number of Catholics living in our country is no more than 460 thousand, that is, 0.3 % of the population. Out of the 145 million Russians covered by the census, 1.5 million did not indicate their ethnic origin, or rather considered themselves among some exotic peoples, with the Elves, Hobbits and Goblins occupying an honorary place among them. There is every reason to believe that the general ratio of major ethnicities in Russia can apply to this group just as well, though this hypothesis needs to be proved. Therefore, the upper limits of the strength of major religious groups in our country appear as follows:

| | | |
|---|---|---|
| *Orthodox Christians* | *86.5 %* | *(app. 126 million)* |
| *Muslims* | *10 %* | *(app. 14.5 million)* |
| *Armenian Gregorians* | *0.8 %* | *(app. 1.1 million)* |
| *Heathens* | *0.5 %* | *(app. 670 thousand)* |
| *Catholics* | *0.35 %* | *(app. 480 thousand)* |
| *Lutherans and Mennonites* | *0.3 %* | *(app. 430 thousand)* |
| *Buddhists* | *0.25 %* | *(app. 380 thousand)* |
| *Judaists* | *0.15 %* | *(230 thousand)* |
| *No mention of ethnic origin* | *1.15 %* | *(app. 1.5 million)* |

It is necessary to make some additional clarifications at this point. All those who claimed to be Jews are considered to be Judaists. Half the Buryats, half the Tuvins, two thirds of the Kalmyks and all the

Mongols are assumed to be Buddhists; all the Armenians, Armenian Gregorians; half the Finns and Latvians, Lutherans; two thirds of the Germans, Lutherans and all the German Mennonites, Mennonites proper; one fourth of the Buryats, the Mary and the Altaians, half the Tuvins and up to 20 % of the minor peoples of the North, Heathens. The proportion of Muslims among the Ossetians is assumed to be 25 %, while the Tatars are all Muslims except for 26 thousand Orthodox Kryashens. The Estonians are considered to be Orthodox, while the Kurdian Jesides are followers of Jesidism rather than Islam.

All these calculations can be challenged, but they look most plausible in the author's view.

## 3. Second Source: Polls and Field Ethnic and Confessional Studies

The very rough 'upper limit' procedure can be corrected by two other methods, namely polls and appropriate field studies. As the most authoritative polls sample today from 2000 to 2500 people and are fairly accurate in establishing the rating of politicians and in predicting returns, they can be used to clarify the religious picture. In this case, it is sufficient to include into a questionnaire only one additional question: 'What religious tradition do you belong to (believe to belong to)?' A more detailed questionnaire designed to unveil also whether believers are aware of the basic doctrines of their religious tradition and how far they are religiously active is certainly helpful, but it cannot give grounds for alleging that there are only 2 or 3 % of genuine believers in our country, because in most religions the actual strength of one's faith is defined only by one's life after death – in paradise or hell. Notably, nobody anywhere would test non-believers or atheists for the strength of their non-belief. Otherwise it would turn out indeed that there are few classical representatives of this kind of people in our country, while Heathens and occultists are far too many. The correct polls have produced on average the following religious picture of Russia today:

| | |
|---|---|
| *Orthodox Christians* | *60-70 %* |
| | *(baptised in Orthodoxy: 75 %)* |
| *Non-believers and atheists* | *10-15 %* |
| *Muslims* | *4-5 %* |
| *Protestants & followers of new religious movements (NRMs)* | *1-2 %* |
| *Buddhists* | *< 1 %* |

*The rest of the religious groups falling under the limits of admissible errors.*

Thus, the polls have made it possible to identify a new group of believers who do not belong either to the Lutherans or Mennonite Protestants or NRMs and who are greater in number than the followers of many traditional religions. The principal shortcoming of all these polls is that their sample is rather small and not quite representative, covering mainly the population of large cities. This peculiarity leads to an underestimation of the proportion of the Orthodox, Muslims and Heathens and to an overestimation of the number of Buddhists (at the expense of non-traditional Buddhists), Protestants, NRMs and non-believers. Because they are contradictory and not quite reliable, these polls have on the whole been seldom used as a principal source of information about the religious picture, and are called mainly to illustrate the tendencies of religious processes. Ethnic and religious field studies are aimed predominantly at identifying small religious groups, such as Old Believers, Catacomb Church members, traditional Heathens, covert NRM groups, who do not come into the field of vision when other methods are used, but can help solve other important problems. It was only a field study that could establish that Tatarstan is a predominantly Orthodox republic, that in Tuva, shamanism has crowded out Buddhism, while Burhanism, which used to be so popular in the Mountainous Altai, has become almost extinct.

## 4. Third Source: Statistics of the Russian Federation Ministry of Justice

Nearly 75 % of the religious groups and organisations active in Russia now enjoy the status of 'legal identity' and are registered with the Ministry of Justice. The Ministry of Justice register represents one of the most important resources for mapping the religious picture. Its only shortcoming is its failure to give the size of each particular community, and this prevents it from becoming universal. A simple analysis shows that even within the same religious organisation, communities may differ in size by dozens or even hundreds times, and in order to realise it, it is sufficient to compare an Orthodox parish in a 'sleeping' district in Moscow with a parish in a largely depopulated village. If this important point is neglected, the Ministry of Justice register can become seriously misleading, since, if judged by the number of communities registered in it, the Protestants leave the Muslims far behind, while the Judaists outnumber the Buddhists. Besides, it should be taken into account that in some religious organisations the number of registered communities exceeds by far that of truly active ones, such as most of the NRMs and some alternative Orthodox and Muslim organisations, while in other religious organisations, such as traditional Heathens and some trends of the Old Belief, the status of legal identity is enjoyed by fewer than half the communities. In total, 21,664 religious organisations were registered as of the beginning of 2002. They break down as follows:

| | | |
|---|---:|---|
| *Russian Orthodox* | *11,525* | *(53.2 %)* |
| *Protestants* | *4097* | *(19 %)* |
| *Muslims* | *3537* | *(16.3 %)* |
| *New religious movements (NRMs)* | *1040* | *(4.8 %)* |
| *Old Believers* | *284* | *(1.3 %)* |
| *Judaists* | *267* | *(1.3 %)* |
| *Roman Catholics* | *253* | *(1.2 %)* |
| *Buddhists (including non-traditional)* | *192* | *(0.9 %)* |
| *Non-canonical Orthodox jurisdictions* | *137* | *(0.6 %)* |
| *Heathens* | *25* | *(0.1 %)* |
| *Others* | *274* | *(1.3 %)* |

## 5. Fourth Source: Assessments by Religious Leaders

This source is actually only good for defining the strength of small religious groups whose leaders can count their parishioners precisely. Certainly, in larger religious organisations, the leaders of some communities do have an idea of how many people come every day or holiday to pray in their church, mosque or synagogue, but it is technically difficult to compile these data even for a hundred places. As a result, the religious leaders of large organisations, in assessing the number of their followers, have to use only the data produced by the first three sources. At the same time, one should bear in mind that representatives of religious minorities often tend to overstate their strength, while the proportion of Orthodox Christians can be overstated by 10 % at the most, otherwise it will exceed 100 %, indeed. A researcher can also be confused by an apparent dissension of opinions within the same religious tradition. Thus, in a poll conducted by a Jewish newspaper among representatives of the Judaist establishment the number of Jews in Russia varied from 250 thousand to 10 million.

A special place in this review should be given to the question of how many Muslims there are in Russia. This subject has long been a stumbling stone for Muslim leaders as well as state officials and researchers, whose assessments sometimes radically differ. As was already mentioned, the 2002 census reported the total number of ethnic Muslims in Russia as being at least 14.5 million. Most of the Muslim leaders would insist on the figure of 20 million, which was voiced by the Russian president in August 2003. More politicised muftis give numbers as high as 25 to 50 million, while many Islamic studies scholars argue that the actual number of real followers of Islam do not exceed 8 to 10 million. In assessing the views cited above, one can observe that the author of each is right in his own way. Those who bring the number of Muslims into proportion with the total strength of Muslim peoples are right. Those who proceed from sociological polls and establish the number of Muslims somewhere between 8 and 10 millions are also right. Moreover, the authority of the Russian president does not allow any doubt as to his assessment, but at the same time the figure of 35 to 50 million Muslims is manifestly overstated. The only way to smooth away the existing contradictions is to propose a figure between 17 and 19 million people (the round-off figure will be 20 million) staying in Russia at a time. In spite of the State Statistics Committee leaders' assurances of otherwise, the census could not really embrace all these people, as many of them are evidently not Russian citizens, but those who came in search of a job from Central Asia and the Transcaucasus.

In assessing the strength of the Russian Muslim community, one should bear in mind that there is a great number of non-believers and followers of other religions among these ethnic Muslims. Thus, the recent census in Estonia, which included a question about one's religious affiliation, has shown that nearly one fourth of the ethnic Tatar believers there actually confess various forms of Christianity. Similar figures were produced when processing the data of the census conducted in Lithuania. Therefore, it can be presumed that up to 10 to15 % of the ethnic Muslims in Russia really confess not Islam, but Christianity. This figure is indirectly confirmed by the data of sociological polls and the sampling of the ethnic make-up of Orthodox and Protestant communities. Muslim leaders themselves do not deny either that thousands of Tatars, Bashkirs, Kazakhs, Adygs and Kabardinians have embraced Christianity, while the total number of the newly-converted Muslims does not exceed 3,000. The Christianisation of ethnic Muslims is not so much due to some purposeful missionary work conducted among them only by Protestants as it is to the influence of Russian culture in the expression of Christian roots. The assimilation of ethnic and religious minorities is an inevitable process in any society, and in Russia it goes even faster because of the negative image of Islam created by the mass media. The percentage of non-believers among the ethnic Muslims is definitely lower then among peoples belonging to the Christian culture due to the deeply religious nature of the peoples in the Caucasus and Central Asia, but here too it can hardly be lower than 10 %. In total, between 20 and 30 percent of the people of Muslim culture do not really consider themselves as Muslims – and this is the figure to be reckoned with in assessing the strength of the Islamic community in Russia.

## 6. Basic Tendencies in Russia's Religious Life Today

a) The proportion of believers in the Russian population is gradually increasing, while that of people indifferent to belief and of non-believers is, accordingly, decreasing. An increasing number of people are returning to the fold of traditional religions, on one hand, and the number of materialists is decreasing due to the intensive propaganda of esotericism and mysticism, on the other. The number of committed atheists, with the most active of them united in sect-like associations, is negligibly small today.

b) The high birth rate among the North Caucasian Muslims and the intensive immigration of Muslims from Central Asia and the Transcaucasus is offset in many ways by the 'russification' and Christianisation of most children born in mixed marriages, and also by mass conversion of Tatars, Bashkirs, Kazakhs, Adygs and many other people to Christianity. Therefore, any considerable increase in the proportion of genuine Muslims can hardly be expected in the nearest future, though the proportion of ethnic Muslims will surely grow.

c) Compared to what it was in 1989, the number of Catholics, Lutherans and Mennonites has decreased and continue to decrease due to, first of all, intensive emigration of Germans and continued russification of Poles and Lithuanians. The mission of Russian Catholics proselytes, called as it is to preserve their position if only partly, has not been met with a noticeable success, and the community of 'Russian Catholics' can hardly amount to more than 10 thousand now.

d) The growth in the number of Baptists, Adventists, Evangelical Christians and other non-charismatic Protestants has stopped. The outflow of their parishioners to charismatic groups has become ever more visible; many Protestants are returning to the fold of the Russian Orthodox Church. The Mormons, Moonies, scientologists and most of the other new religious groups have almost exhausted their reserves for growth, their target groups being worked out, their missionary methods being out of date, their ill fame preventing them from using effectively the riches they have accumulated. Only Jehovah's Witnesses and neo-charismatics have maintained a relatively rapid rate of growth, but their ranks have been replenished mostly by non-believers and Baptists and Adventists.

e) The proportion of the Judaists and traditional Buddhists is declining. A radical decrease in the number of Judaists is accounted for, in the first place, by the continued emigration and assimilation of the Jews, while peoples of Buddhist culture are experiencing intensive Christianisation (mostly through the efforts of marginal Protestants) and expansion of shamanism.

f) The proportion of traditional Heathens is slowly growing, while the Old Believers, the True Orthodox Christians and adherents of the non-canonical Orthodox jurisdictions are gradually losing their positions.

# PART III
# RESPONSIBLE BUSINESS LEADERSHIP

# 23

# BUSINESS LEADERSHIP AND SUSTAINABLE DEVELOPMENT. A PERSPECTIVE OF CORPORATE SOCIAL RESPONSIBILITY

*Jeffrey D. Sachs, USA*

## Introduction

Why are we talking at all about corporate social responsibility?[1] The topic has been around for decades, but there is something, if not new, at least pertinent for us to be talking about. Not only are we in the aftermath of the biggest financial bubble collapse in modern times, but corporate corruption has been rampant in the United States and in other countries. We know that many major corporations engage in abusive behaviour, writing several trillion dollars of wealth off the balance sheets. Business ethics are being held up to scrutiny, especially by the anti-globalisation movement, which is notably really an anti-corporate movement. Whether or not it is completely misdirected or, as I believe, mainly misdirected, it is nevertheless directed at the business sector.

'Corporate ethics' refers to the set of rules we would like to see the business community adhere to that would have some good sense and good performance for our societies more generally; not only for the individual business, not only for the individual manager in the short term, but for the long-term functioning of our societies. There is basically a market theory that says: 'Don't worry too much about this.' It says: 'Let business maximise its profits; it will worry about that. Others can worry about ethics, business will worry about business.' And, in the end, as Adam Smith told us 227 years ago at the *Wealth of Nations*, 'things will more or less work out alright.' If you ask what lies behind that theory, there are two elements that are crucial. One is that managers of businesses maximise shareholder value, that is what they do for a living. Second, shareholder value maximisation leads to social value maximisation – the Milton Freedman view. In summary, managers maximise market value, and market value maximises social value, and so let managers be managers.

## 1. When Managers Steal

I have to say there is a lot of truth in that, but unfortunately it is not completely true. There is a lot of slippage in both parts of the proposition, and it is in that slippage where we find most of the meat of the subject that we are talking about today. One part of the slippage is that there is a big difference between what managers do and maximising shareholder value. Why? Well, one good reason is that managers sometimes steal from shareholders and therefore do not necessarily operate in the interest of shareholders. They commit outright fraud frequently, as has become quite apparent. Some of the largest businesses in the United States (Enron, most famously) went down in a flame of fraud because the managers were wildly stealing from the shareholders by misrepresenting the balance sheets.

Managerial governance, in general, is very hard to align with the interest of the shareholders. For example, maximising shareholder value does not necessarily mean maximising the value of minority shareholder rights, which brings us to another kind of abuse: managers steal from minorities to give to majorities. There are all sorts of factional interests within companies and protecting minority shareholder rights is not an automatic proposition. We know that maximising shareholder rights does not mean maximising short-run profits to grab every moment of opportunity; reputation matters, the long-term good will of the community matters, and the brand name matters. Here is where individual ethics might directly translate into better shareholder value, but unfortunately managers also have all sorts of incentives to go after the short-term offer and not consider the long-term. These problems create a gap between what the manager does and what shareholders get that often results in scandalous headlines.

## 2. When Managers Buy Politicians

There is a second distinction that is even more important than the first: the gap between the shareholder value and the social value. Nobody with even the remotest knowledge of a modern economy could any longer believe that profits, per se, are signals of social value. However, that is the whole theory of capitalist free-market organisation: prices send the right signals, and a high price or high return dictate where capital should go. In reality, there are huge gaps between the private signals and the social values, and some are absolutely obvious. Among the most well-known is pollution like the emission of carbon dioxide into the atmosphere, which leads to climate change, including perhaps a drying of northern Italy's climate. These so-called 'externalities' – gaps between private value and social value – are not captured in the private market values of companies. There are innumerable social goods that do not have a private market value, the most important of which is the production of knowledge of various kinds, especially scientific knowledge. If we left science purely to the marketplace, we would be nowhere. Fortunately, governments figured out hundreds of years ago to serve as patrons of science because private market returns could not do this. So, closing that second gap is also absolutely essential.

Now where do corporate ethics come into this? It is true that if we could narrow the gaps between private and social value, we would be doing a much better job for our societies. Self-regulation is a delusion. We need rigorous law and we need business people going to jail when they engage in corporate abuse. We need to close the gap between managerial responsibility and shareholder values more effectively than we do.

Public policy, not private action, must lead the effort to close the gaps between social and private value. Free-market ideology will fail unless, for example, it acknowledges that carbon emissions must be taxed in order to stabilise the climate in a sensible way, since private business has no reason to voluntarily cut back its emissions. There must be regulation one way or another, through taxes or quantity limits on emissions of toxins. If we could do all those things, we would surely have a much better functioning society, closing the managerial abuses and closing the gaps of private and shareholder value.

So why do we not regulate well? Part of the reason is that we keep finding new risks needing regulation. Nobody knew about carbon dioxide twenty years ago, it is a relatively new scientific insight, which is why policy is trying to catch up. In the financial arena, transactions are more and more complicated to monitor. Derivatives and off-balance sheet transactions have become more complex and are therefore new instruments of evasion. But I do think that there is another risk: abusive corporate power can translate into political power, which is then used to create more corporate power. The political economy of capitalism depends on the private sector maximising shareholder value subject to proper regulation provided by the public sector. But what happens when the private sector takes over the public sector? It can create, as we have in the United States now, an abusive system in which corporate power is translated into massive campaign donations, which elects governments to enact laws to improve corporate profits and not social value, further increasing corporate power and potentially putting us on an explosive spiral. The United States might really be on that spiral right now.

The United States has never had larger inequalities in recent history and has never had the political system attended to the rich as it does today. Despite massive budget deficits, the present administration chooses to vote new tax relief for the super rich. The real losers are the social programs of the United States, like social security and Medicare. What the public does not understand is that this administration's policies will starve those programs to death. What happens in the United States is that the poor are told, 'Well, it's true that the rich are going to get a hundred thousand dollars in tax relief, but you're still going to get fifty dollars,' and the poor happily accept the fifty dollars without realising that the hundred thousand dollars was going to pay for their health insurance in five years. Massive corporate power is wielding too much political influence and controlling the media with increasing concentration. This is, I think, the biggest risk of corporate irresponsibility: campaign finance from the corporate sector, media monopolisation, lobbying and conflict of interest, cronyism, perhaps even outright bribery. Halliburton, Vice President Cheney's business, has received five hundred million dollars of contracts in the last two years in Afghanistan and Iraq for post-war reconstruction. That is not healthy for American politics.

## 3.  When Managers Distort the Truth

A third distortion is when business lacks transparency and distorts the truth (for example, when the tobacco industry claimed for years that its products pose no risks to the American people). Beyond stopping internal abuse and closing the gap between private and social value, a third requirement for corporate responsibility is having business leadership keep its hands off public policy. Lobbying and cronyism are turning the public sector into a vehicle for private sector maximisation, which drives the gaps between the public and private vastly wider than they would be otherwise. Restraint of the powerful business sector in the political arena is absolutely essential, and if it is not self-restraint, then there must be mechanisms of restraint, such as campaign financing laws. Other elements of corporate responsibility in addition to not stealing from the shareholders, honesty in reporting, recognising social value and responsibility in the political sphere include the following six aspects.

## 4.  When Managers Promote Poverty Reduction, Justice and Philanthropy

First, government policing can never work alone in enforcing the laws, so industry groups need to have self-policing mechanisms alongside like industry associations that are committed to ostracising, publicising, heaping scorn on those who commit corporate abuse.

Second is the special set of responsibilities for multinational companies that operate in poor countries. In general, foreign direct investment is one of the ways that poor countries can hope to get a little less poor, so the anti-globalisers are completely wrong to say we should stop foreign direct investment. However, when a business goes to a poor country, it is almost certainly going to a weak government as well, one that will probably ask for bribes and will almost certainly be susceptible to them. The government will perhaps not care to regulate, but will almost surely not know how to regulate. When businesses go to a poor country, they cannot ethically pollute or dump toxics simply because there is no law there. When you are dealing with the poorest countries, governance is very fragile and therefore self-restraint in business becomes more important.

A third area is when businesses have monopoly privilege or monopoly position, then the Milton Freedman theory cannot apply and managing appropriately becomes imperative. One important example is when companies operate under patent law and receive a government grant of a twenty-year monopoly; that patent law system works reasonably well to produce a lot of incentives for research and development. However, at the same time it is keeping vital medicines out of the hands of the poorest people in the world, who are dying because they cannot afford to pay the patent-protected prices. The pharmaceutical industry in the United States and Europe has not been socially responsible in finding ways to combine the incentive structure with the need to get medicines to poor countries. It is indeed a lack of corporate social responsibility to continue caring only about making temporary monopoly profits without recognising the deaths that come inadvertently from that system. People are being killed inadvertently by an industry failing to face up to new and effective solutions to this problem in a timely fashion. Some companies have done more than others, but the industry as a whole has not done enough.

A fourth area is private philanthropy. One of the great things about giant American business in the last century is that some of the biggest business leaders became great private philanthropists that made a big difference in the world. The Rockefeller Foundation, which John D. Rockefeller established in 1913, was truly one of the most important, positive forces for scientific and social change in the 20th century. They discovered the vaccine for yellow fever, they helped rid Brazil of malaria, and they helped introduce the 'green' revolution to Asia, all through one foundation. These days Bill and Melinda Gates donated 25 billion dollars of their own money to the Bill and Melinda Gates Foundation, which is now the leading force in global public health in the world, often spending much more than the United States government or even the G8, which is both a shame on the G8, but also a great tribute to Bill and Melinda Gates. As part of corporate social responsibility, albeit private social responsibility, is that billionaires should give a significant amount towards social purposes.

A fifth area involves responsibility when government rules of the game are complete. Milton Freedman is completely wrong, for example, in the situation of a business that figures out that all the animals in the lake where it produces are dying due to a compound that, in our country, the Environmental Protection Agency does not know exists. You are not breaking the law necessarily. Is there a social responsibility to address that? Absolutely. It must be that when a business executive sees a huge gap between private and social value and a lack of regulation, then transparency and ethics and concern for long-term value of the company dictate a response to the social values and make the concerns known. The tobacco industry did exactly the opposite. A large part of the asbestos industry did exactly the opposite. Business must help close the private value and social value gap, because it will never be closed on time by governance alone. Companies must stop claiming innocence in the face of insufficient legal restraints.

The sixth area is corporate philanthropy. Corporate philanthropy is by definition limited in comparison to private philanthropy because companies are not philanthropies and we should not remake them as philanthropies. However, every company needs to have some limited, well-defined philanthropic arm. It will improve its value in the short term by improving reputation and relations with the community it works in. In addition, it also is appropriate because it fills the inevitable gaps between its performance and its social contributions.

Finally, corporate responsibility involves public leadership by the business community. It is not good enough only to not cheat on the books, and it is not good enough to abstain from lobbying for abusive privileges. It would actually be wonderfully helpful if leading business executives who are icons in the world, are featured on covers of magazines and who are on radio and television, also talked about social values, talked about the needs to attend to the poor, talked about the risks of globalisation, and talked about the needs to close the gap between public and private values. The business community has lots of credibility; when Bill Gates speaks about public health (besides spending money on it), you would be amazed how many others listen because if Bill Gates is talking about children dying of malaria in Burkina Faso, he probably is onto something. So the business community has to be a leader, also, in promoting values. Social values are created by society – besides business leaders, we need baseball players, artists and rock stars and others to be talking about social values also.

## 5. The Business Community Can Show the Way

Let me conclude with a couple of words about globalisation. There are a billion people on the planet that are so poor that they can die any day of their poverty. Even though we live with greater riches and splendor than at any time in human history, the amount of desperate poverty in the world is somehow considered normal. Three million children will die this year of malaria, while it only requires USD 0.2 to 0.5 a dose to cure a bout of malaria. Three million children will die because they do not have the necessary medicines. The communities are too impoverished; the households cannot buy them; the governments are too poor to buy the medicines. Three million people will die of AIDS. The treatment is more expensive, but it is only a dollar a day. We are letting millions of people die and millions of children become orphans because of a lack of a dollar a day. These people know that people in our countries are living with the disease, and they wonder why they will die without getting any help at all. People will die of lack of food and inadequate nutrition. The point is not to say: 'How sad…' The point is to ask what we are doing.

At a minimum, ethics requires us to ask, 'Is this necessary? Is that the way of the world? Are the poor always with us?' Or maybe, 'Is there something that can be done?' When you look at it in this case, there are actually solutions to these problems and they are not very expensive. For much less than 1 % of the income of the rich countries, people would not have to die of poverty in the world. They will still die and they will still be poor, but they will not be dying because they cannot get a dose of quinine or because they cannot get treated for their AIDS or they do not have enough food to eat.

So for less than 1 % of the income of the rich world, we could end the scourge of poverty that is so extreme that it kills millions of people every year. That is where I would like to see the business community also stand up. It is not just the business community that is going to spend the money. They cannot do it. It has to be all of us. But the business community is working in these countries, seeing people dying and taking it for granted and not coming back to tell us, 'We've got to do more.' If we do more, by the way, for the poor in those countries, maybe we will also be led to do more for the poor in our midst. And maybe we will also be led to do more for our own good performance and good behaviour. In other words, it will strengthen our hearts while strengthening the world and keeping people alive. That indeed would be a good thing.

NOTES

[1]   This text was delivered as a speech at the Accenture Foundation, Palazzo Clerici in Milan, Italy, on 12 June 2003.

# 24

# CAN BUSINESS ETHICS BE INTERRELIGIOUS? AN INDONESIAN PERSPECTIVE

*Yahya Wijaya, Indonesia*

Max Weber's provocative thesis regarding the influence of religion on work ethic has stimulated further investigations by theologians as well as sociologists and other social scientists searching for more roles played by religion in economic life. Peter W. F. Davies, an expert in management, admits that Christian perspectives have made a significant contribution to the development of the Western business philosophy. [1] Princeton theologian Max Stackhouse even believes that 'Protestant thought nurtured the growth of the corporation in the first place' and that referring to it for ethical works in the new global business context still is worthwhile. [2] Similarly, David Krueger sees Christian faith as a resource for 'a transformative ethic of responsibility' needed in making business corporations contribute to the development of a good society. [3]

## 1. The Influence of Religious Traditions on Business

Dennis McCann observes how Asian religious traditions, including Hinduism and Confucianism, have a significant influence on the economic performance of people in several Asian countries. He thus argues with Stackhouse that 'real progress toward economic and social justice in the twenty-first century depends upon a constructive religious engagement with capitalism, its institutions, their histories, and the transformative praxis of business management'. [4] The role of Islam in the global economy is also worth observing. Robert Hefner, who studies Indonesian Islam, points to stories in the Koran and the Hadith tradition that depict trade and commerce as respectable activities. He thus concludes that 'Islam is not only compatible with capitalism, but positively supportive of it'. [5] Indeed Islam offers not merely philosophical references for a moral economic life, but also a practical economic system operated alongside the existing (Western) capitalism. The Shariah banking and stock exchange play an increasingly significant role in the economy of countries like Malaysia and Indonesia. [6] Although the relation between business and religion on the philosophical level is quite obvious, it is not always so on the practical level, apart from what would be attempted by Islam with the Shariah system. The development of modern economy tends to go in a direction where religion is considered to be irrelevant. In terms of Western economy, there is what Richard Higginson calls 'the marginalisation of Christianity by business,' which ends the 'several centuries of positive interaction between business and Christianity.'[7] This marginalisation, according to Higginson, is the result of a series of factors, including the rise of the discipline of economics which is utilitarian in nature, and the influence of Marxism strongly suspicious of the impact of Christianity on economic life.[8] In fact, from the side of religion, particularly Christianity, there is a reciprocal affinity. Borrowing H.R. Niebuhr's typology, Krueger mentions two theological positions, which tend to alienate business from constructive theological reflection. The first is the 'prophetic/perfectionist' position, which radically opposes capitalism and its institutions. The second is the 'accommodative' position, which either confuses Christian ethical norms with norms practised in the existing economic life, or recognises no connection between the two.[9] In many poor countries like Indonesia, the prophetic/perfectionist position tends to be popular among theologians working in academic institutions and non-governmental organisations. Their voice is most often referred to in traditional Protestant churches' documents and statements concerning economic life, although it does not automatically reflect the aspiration of ordinary members of the churches. The accommodative position is normally taken by fundamentalist groups and by communities that refer to a theology of prosperity, which record a dramatic growth resulted from both 'fresh' conversion and exodus from traditional churches.

## 2. The Challenge of a Single Religious Approach

The challenge for religion in relation to business ethics is first of all to reclaim its appropriate role in economic life. This means to construct approaches which would be effective in helping business to work ethically as well as economically and inspiring for those involved in day-to-day business life. As Hans Küng argues, it is not enough to 'appear to be economically naïve enthusiasts who in a religious way gloss over poverty and sweepingly discredit riches.'[10] Krueger, who relegates the 'perfectionist' and 'accommodative' positions, considers three other positions prospective, namely those of 'incarnational/synthetist', 'dualist/paradoxal', and 'transformative/ conversionist'. Whilst the synthetist position is represented by the modern Roman Catholic social teaching, and the paradoxal position is demonstrated by many Evangelical groups, the transformative position is close to the characteristics of the Reformed tradition. These three positions obviously differ in their degree of optimism, but they share an appreciative yet critical attitude toward the market economy and business life.[11]

Krueger offers an interesting outlook. Yet, he seems to assume that an approach based on a single religion would be adequate. A single religious approach may be effective as long as it addresses that religion's own adherents. However, the marketplace and the internal bodies of most modern corporations have the characteristics of a religiously plural community. In such a context, a single religious approach works more likely on an individual-pastoral level, such as in the forms of individual character building and counselling assistance. In many cases, that kind of approach is obviously useful. Yet it offers little help when the virtues it promotes bring the individuals into a confrontation against the values operated in the workplace. Massive unemployment and tight competition, which mark the situation in poor countries, make the workplace strong enough to force the individuals give up their moral preference. An individual-pastoral approach, hence, is not enough to respond to the corporate moral challenge.

A single religious approach may also play an institutional-political role, such as the role of a chaplain to the business community. Such a role, however, is only realistic if that religion, or an organisation of it, has a strong political or cultural position, such as the Orthodox Church in Russia, as Pavel Shashkin depicts.[12] In the case of Indonesia, despite its majority position, Islam has a limited opportunity to play a chaplaincy role to the business community, since a significant number of business people precisely belong to minority religions.

## 3. The Challenge of an Interreligious Approach

In the context of a religiously plural society, a religious approach to business ethics should be developed with a perspective on interreligious encounters. In constructing an interreligious approach to business ethics, it may be helpful to learn from the experience of Indonesian Christian-Muslim encounters, which shows that an interreligious project requires theological reinterpretation, political consensus and practical cooperation.[13] Theological reinterpretation does not necessarily mean to leave behind each religion's unique ethical resources. On the contrary, it includes an attempt to broaden the effectiveness of religious messages transcending the border of a particular religious community. Theological reinterpretation thus is intended to make resources of a particular religion accountable in different religious communities. A political consensus is needed to focus the ethical project on particular economic or business issues, and to ensure that the aim of the project is to contribute to the common good of the people, so as to avoid a sectarian interest. Theological reinterpretation and political consensus would provide a strong foundation for religious bodies to develop interreligious moral actions which would be worth considering in both political and business contexts.

## 4. Bank Interest and Corruption as Examples

One theological topic worth reinterpreting concerns the issue of bank interest. Opposition to usury is found in both Judeo-Christian and Islamic scriptures. The Shariah banking system is a form of literal faithfulness to that anti-usury theology. Yet, such an interpretation is controversial within the Islamic community itself. In fact, more Muslims are consciously involved in ordinary, interest-applying financial systems than others who strictly confine themselves to the Shariah banking system. Christianity does not accommodate the anti-usury theology in the form of a particular financial system. Christians tend to take the interest-applying financial system for granted. Few Christian theologians refer to the biblical account on usury in constructing a contemporary economic theology. There is a notion in Christian theological discourses that the anti-usury theology is totally irrelevant in the context of modern economy. However, the problems related to that theology are still prevalent or even more crucial today than in biblical times. For instance, the repayment of foreign debt and its interest is a real problem affecting multi-dimensional areas of life in poor countries. Such a problem cannot be faced only with economic consideration. An ethical contemplation is needed, and for this purpose the anti-usury narratives would be useful. If the literal interpretation on those narratives is no longer relevant, then a reinterpretation is needed. Since several religions share the anti-usury narratives and have attempted to apply them in different ways, an interreligious reinterpretation would benefit not only each religious community, but also the whole society.

There are big issues in business ethics, which need a political response from religious communities. In Indonesia, one of such issues is corruption. Indonesia is always ranked among the most corrupt countries in the world. The problem of corruption in Indonesia is related to the political realm where democracy does not work well. Large-scale corruption normally includes collusion involving government officials and business people. The collusion is basically a patron-client relationship, in which business people have to buy the political protection from the government officials. In Indonesia, this comes from the business community's weak political position; most Indonesian business people belong indeed to an ethnic minority group that has been the victim of discriminatory policies since the colonial times. [14] One root-cause of corruption, hence, is political, namely the non-democratic policy of minority-majority relationships. Many believe that a strong structure of civil society would be powerful enough to challenge such a non-democratic practice. A strong civil society would counterbalance both the power of the state and that of the business community, so as to prevent them from forming a collusion, which endangers the common good. Yet the idea of civil society in countries like Indonesia would not be realistic without including religious communities as a vital element. Therefore, a political consensus of different religious communities to play a role of civil society would be a real contribution to the anti-corruption movement. The two largest Islamic organisations in Indonesia, Nadhlatul Ulama and Muhammadiyah, have come to such a consensus. To make their attempt more effective, the consensus should include other religious groups, particularly those whose adherents make up a significant portion of the business community.

NOTES

[1]   Davies, Peter W. F., 'Business Philosophy. Searching for an Authentic Role', in: Davies, Peter W. F. (ed.), *Current Issues in Business Ethics*, London: Routledge, 1997, pp. 16-17.

[2]   Stackhouse, Max L., 'Christian Social Ethics in a Global Era. Reforming Protestant Views', in: Stackhouse, Max L. *et al.* (eds), *Christian Social Ethics in a Global Era*, Nashville, TN: Abingdon, 1995, p. 32.

[3]   Krueger, David A., 'The Business Corporation and Productive Justice in the Global Economy', in: Krueger, David A. *et al.* (eds), *The Business Corporation and Productive Justice*, Nashville, TN: Abingdon, 1997, p. 18.

[4]   McCann, Dennis P., 'Reforming Wisdom from the East', in: Stackhouse, Max L. *et al.* (eds), *op. cit.*, p. 97.

[5]   Hefner, Robert, 'Islam and the Spirit of Capitalism', in: Stackhouse, Max L. *et al.* (eds): *On Moral Business. Classical and Contemporary Resources for Ethics in Economic Life*, Grand Rapids, MI: Eerdmans, 1995, pp. 363-367.

[6]   In Indonesia, even international banks, including HSBC and Standard Chartered, have opened their Shariah units.

[7]   Higginson, Richard, *Questions of Business Life. Exploring Workplace Issues from a Christian Perspective*, Carlisle: Authentic Lifestyle, 2002, p. 1.

[8]   *Ibidem*, pp. 9-14.

[9]   Krueger, David A., *op. cit.*, pp. 30-31.

[10]   Küng, Hans, *A Global Ethic for Global Politics and Economics*, London: SCM Press, 1997, p. 236.

[11]   Krueger, David A., *op. cit.*, p. 31.

[12]   Shashkin, Pavel, 'Business Leadership and Social Responsibility in a Transition Country. A Russian Orthodox Perspective', in: Stückelberger, Christoph/Mugambi, J. N. K. (eds), *Responsible Leadership. Global Perspectives*, Nairobi: Acton Publishers, 2005, pp. 111-117. See also Chapter 26 in this volume.

[13]   See Wijaya, Yahya, 'Theological Leadership in Christian-Muslim Encounters. An Indonesian Perspective', in: *Ibid.*, pp. 71-84. See also Chapter 12 in this volume.

[14]   For a historical review concerning the discrimination against the Chinese-Indonesian community, see Wijaya, Yahya, *Business, Family and Religion. A Public Theology in the Context of the Chinese-Indonesian Business Community*, Oxford, etc.: Peter Lang, 2002, chapter 2.

# 25

# BUSINESS RESPONSIBILITY.
# AN AMERICAN CHRISTIAN PERSPECTIVE

*Heidi Hadsell, USA*

One widely shared approach in North America to business ethics in recent decades has often envisioned some combination of a three-fold responsibility that corporations have in society: the responsibility to the shareholders, to the consumer, and to the wider society. It is generally assumed for those who use this rough notion of corporate responsibility, that when big business manages to balance its responsibility to these three stakeholders and thus to negotiate their separate and often competing interests, business is acting in an ethically responsible way.

According to this common logic, when a given business engaging in economic activity of some kind, thinks not only of the profits that go to the owners or shareholders of the business, but also about the consumer, and therefore about things like the reliability of the object or service being provided, about honesty in advertising, about quality and durability, and when a business thinks not only of profits and customers or consumers, but also about the wider society, and thus about the role of the business in the community, and more largely about the use of the resources of the community, and the people in the community not directly connected to the business – then business may be said to be acting in a responsible manner.

## 1. Primary Responsibility: Profits

On the whole, I think that this recognition of the various 'stakeholders', and the need to create some kind of balance among them, is a formula that in a capitalist economy can be used to promote and to assess business responsibility. But there are of course problems with this formula. Who is to define the interests of each of these stakeholders for example? More importantly, what about the many times when the interests of the stakeholders collide? What of the many actual or potential moments for example, in which business responsibility to the stockholder which is centrally to maximise profit, competes with the often very nebulous (and difficult to define) responsibility to the consumer or to the wider society?

Although business ethics is not my area of expertise in ethics, it seems that in recent years, the various problems of this formula for business responsibility – perhaps especially the potential brake on the drive for maximising profits that it represents – have led many in the business community to abandon it, and to retreat to the notion that business's only primary responsibility is to its stockholders or owners. In other words, although it is still widely recognised that at least these three categories of primary stakeholders are related in a variety of ways to business ethics, there is something of a consensus, at least in the United States, that the primary stakeholder – the owners – will (and should) receive primary attention. This is to say that the notion of business being about 'the bottom line' is not widely questioned, and it is presumed that attending to the 'bottom line' is the way in which business contributes to customers and to the wider society.[1]

In this way the drive for profits remains the major, and practically the sole, responsibility that businesses recognise as theirs. Everything else – all moral responsibilities, beyond the very narrow rules of business ethics, and also concerns like the quality of the products, the way the work force is treated, wages, etc. – is sacrificed to this goal. And of course, top managers are theoretically remunerated accordingly, although many studies show that at least in the United States currently, salaries of top management have actually little to do with performance.[2]

This unbridled drive for profit clearly leads many businesses into ways of thinking and acting that are less than morally responsible, even though they very well may be run by people who are highly morally responsible in their individual lives. While many in the corporate world focus on the primary responsibility for business, which as they define it is making profits, there are those in the business world who continue to insist that business ethics is far more complex than this, especially in an age where corporations are primary global actors, where destruction of the environment is accelerating, where the gap between rich and poor within and between countries is growing, and so forth.

## 2. The Price of the Environment

In the last several decades, environmentalists and some economists have carried out empirical and theoretical studies on the many questions posed by the intersection of big businesses and the natural world. Together they point at what often seems to be fundamental problems in the way business is taught to think about the natural world, in relation to the economics of making a product and running a business.

One primary problem is that economics does not traditionally include in its calculations of economic behaviour the elements of the natural world that inevitably go into making products of almost any kind, or go into providing services. The air, the water, the land used in the production process have traditionally been left out of the economic calculus, as have the many costs that go into cleaning up air and water and other parts of nature, once they have been fouled in the process of making products. These natural elements used in the production process are called 'externalities'. As the name indicates, traditionally they have been considered as external to the production process, and therefore presented little interest to the discipline of economics, which for some time did not known how to think about them and how to attribute costs to them.[3]

For example a logging company may establish itself on a river and use that river for energy, for transportation, and also as a way to dispose of the toxic by-products of the production processes, such as those created in the making of paper. The river in traditional capitalist economics is not part of the economic calculus, and business is not taught to think about it, in terms of trying to price it, either as an element of production – transportation, energy etc – or as an economic loss, in terms of the many costs of spoiling the river in the short and long term. It is hardly surprising that as a consequence, business does not think about its responsibility to maintain the quality of the water in the river, or about the costs associated with doing so, and, when it is finished with the river, often the business simply moves or closes, and never takes economic or moral responsibility for the effect of poisoning the river.

Natural elements that go into the production process are also more or less plentiful and more or less likely to be exhaustible or finite. Since economics has not really known how to think about natural resources, it does not know either how to think about finite natural resources and about larger issues such as sustainability.[4] Thus for example, oil is a finite resource. Automobile companies continue to make cars which rely on oil, and they have little economic incentive to think about alternative forms of automobiles which are not dependent on this finite resource. Recently they have begun to look for alternatives, since the price of oil is high, and the outside pressure is mounting both because of prices and because of the pollution oil produces. Public pressure and finite resources are blunt instruments for change in the automobile industry, and come late in the day. Greater attention to the wider society and to the consumer would have motivated change much earlier, and perhaps the creation of a greater range of options as well. While perhaps unintentionally so, this ignorance (and egoism) induced by the sole drive for profit, ends up creating behaviour that is morally irresponsible in relation to the natural environment.

This irresponsibility is compounded by the inability of the economic calculus to think in the long term.[5] Since profits are measured in the short term, businesses which think little about anything but profits, have little incentive to think beyond the short term. This short term thinking adds of course to the moral irresponsibility of much of the business community around the world, who in planning and evaluating success and failure think little about a foreseeable future, and much less about the next generation or the ones to come. In the long run, future generations will tragically be confronted with toxic waste, ruined water supplies, air pollution, vanishing animal species and the like. This is a prime example of inter-generational inequity and irresponsibility.

### 3. 'Savage' Capitalism

Most of us have heard the expression 'savage capitalism'. Part of what 'savage' capitalism denotes is capitalist activity that roams the world looking for quick profits, in the form of cheap labour and natural resources, or investment opportunities, along with few government laws and regulations, and is not tied to, or controlled by, local or national communities and loyalties. 'Savage capitalism' sees itself as having few or no civic responsibilities. It is in a given place only to make profits and leave. One of the things that makes this economic behaviour 'savage' is that it is the opposite of truly human behaviour, which takes place in, and through, responsible relationships.

I can see these global dynamics at work in Hartford, Connecticut where I live. Until the last decade or two, our city was at the centre of the United States' insurance industry. As that industry has been transformed by global capitalism, thus making Hartford just one part of global insurance strategies, the local insurance companies have become, as long-time citizens of Hartford observe, much less engaged in the community, much less interested in Hartford itself, and thus much less helpful to the wider community. Since the decisions are made elsewhere, and since time lines are so short, there is little incentive for the insurance companies to be responsive to, or care about, the local community.

This situation is of course multiplied many times over in places in the world where people are economically more vulnerable, and have little or no political power to exert. It is clear that businesses in general will not self-regulate. The only thing likely to change this situation and encourage responsible business behaviour is political pressure as well as national and international regulation. Popular movements like labour movements and environmental movements can also help by adding to political awareness and pressure.[6]

## 4. The Role of Religious Groups

Religious groups from many religions can be advocates for regulations that motivate, and if necessary force, businesses into responsible behaviour. They can use their abilities to convey alternative economic values through life in religious congregations and through reading and reflection on sacred scripture. They can also use their resources towards investments in businesses that are socially and environmentally responsible. Socially responsible investment (SRI) sends a market-oriented message to businesses that religious groups care about values besides the profit motive, and that they are willing to put those values into operation in the market place. Many church related initiatives and organisations are now working for SRI. One of the first such initiatives was the Interfaith Center on Corporate Responsibility (ICCR) in New York, a 'coalition of faith-based institutional investors' founded in 1970.[7] Churches and church-related organisations in Europe developed a platform for SRI[8] and the International Association of Investors in the Social Economy (INAISE) was created.[9]

The movement to divest church stock portfolios of stock in South Africa as a protest against apartheid, was for example an excellent teaching tool for members of those denominations who were involved, and it was also a way to send a powerful message to the companies involved, and to show public and concrete solidarity with black South Africans. Although perhaps more controversial, the movement to divest stock in those companies involved in the violence against Palestinians similarly raises the visibility of the issue and sends a strong message.[10] In each of these cases, one of the messages being communicated is that human beings, including religious groups, but including many others, care for much more than for their own economic self-interest.

Christians and those from other religions will and should debate these questions among themselves and with others. For many religions one of the biggest obstacles to overcome is the tendency to separate faith from economic activity, and thus to assume that faith has little or nothing to say to the powerful economic actors or about the dominant issues in the world. In fact, faith is economically relevant and Christian scripture, like that of other religions, is full of moral reflection on issues that are essentially economic. The question of business responsibility is also a question of faith.

NOTES

[1]  In a 1981 statement the Business Roundtable of the CEOs of the 150 largest public corporations in the USA said: 'The shareholder must receive a good return but the legitimate concerns of other constituencies (customers, employees, communities, suppliers, and society at large) also must have the appropriate attention ... (Corporate leaders) believe that by giving enlightened

consideration to balancing the legitimate claims of all of its constituents, a corporation will best serve the interests of its shareholders.' In 1997 they changed this statement to: 'The notion that the Board must somehow balance the interests of stockholders against the interest of other stakeholders fundamentally misconstrues the role of directors. It is, moreover, an unworkable notion because it would leave the Board with no criteria for resolving conflicts between the interests of stockholders and of other stakeholders.'

[2]   This issue is currently much discussed in the USA, since there seems to be little if any correlation between a company's performance and the remuneration of its top executives.

[3]   See for example the work of Herman Daly, a former Senior Economist of the World Bank, which critiques this economic logic.

[4]   See for examples: Daly, Herman E., *Steady-State Economics*, Washington, D.C.: Island Press, 1991 (2nd edition); and Daly, Herman E., *Beyond Growth: The Economics of Sustainable Development*, Boston, MA: Beacon Press, 1996.

[5]   White, Allen, 'The Grasshoppers and the Ants. Why CSR Needs Patient Capital', in: *Business for Social Responsibility*, Summer 2006.

[6]   The 2000 international Jubilee campaign is an example where religious people, many in the business community, NGOs and other international organisations came together to work to alleviate Third World debt.

[7]   www.iccr.org.

[8]   *Transparency in Investments* and *Socially Responsible Investing*, Amersfoort 2005. The text can be ordered at www.oikocredit.org

[9]   www.inaise.org.

[10]   The Presbyterian Church in the United States for example as well as some other denominations around the world, has voted in the last several years for, and then reconsidered, divestment in companies making products used by the Israelis to harm the Palestinians.

# 26

# BUSINESS LEADERSHIP
# AND SOCIAL RESPONSIBILITY
# IN A TRANSITION COUNTRY.
# A RUSSIAN ORTHODOX PERSPECTIVE

*Pavel Shashkin, Russia*

## 1. From Socialism to Consumerism

Nowadays the moral evaluation of economic processes and the fair distribution of material welfare have become enormously actual topics in Russia. The Russian Orthodox Church has always testified about two religiously justifiable labour motivations. The first of them is to work for creating adequate living conditions for oneself and one's family. The second is the labour for the benefit of the needy.

Unfortunately, the contemporary system of economic values, making people do their best to increase consumption to the detriment of spiritual development, is considered to be sinful by the Russian Orthodox Church. The Church reminds the business society that any economic activity can be morally justifiable only if a person works not only for himself but also to help the needy. This labour motivation can be called a moral dimension of economy. Its sense is that any employee, and particularly any employer, must work so effectively to make as much profit as possible from his/her activity to be able to transfer the surplus to those who cannot earn their crust or to those who do not produce material values by profession. The effectiveness and fairness are the principal requirements of the orthodox ethics to economy.

Only such an economy can be viable as its aim is not to satisfy egoistic interests of an individual corrupted by sins, but the interests and needs of the whole society and nation. Such a model might seem illusive. According to the position of the Russian Orthodox Church it is not. And it is quite well proved by the experience of orthodox business that existed in the Russian Empire at the beginning of the twentieth century. It is a mistake to believe that the only possible stimulus for the development of economy is the desire to get more material goods. The successful merchants were not only the promoters of business activity in pre-Revolutionary Russia, but also pedantically followed the norms of traditions and customs, sincerely and actively participating in the life of the Orthodox Church. Such a moral attitude to welfare is a convincing alternative to the principles of the consumption society. The businessmen who are willing to work productively are supported by the Orthodox Church, as long as the results of such work are used for social initiatives, for the maintenance of social peace and stability.

Unfortunately, the old socialist economic system used to create a gap between a person and the results of his/her work. Therefore, employees were not personally interested in making more profit. Labour was not beneficial and any business activity constituted a crime under the criminal law. Such a system could not exist for a long time. The lingering crisis of both Soviet and Russian economy was caused by the absence of personal interest in the results of the work.

However the economic and political reforms of the 1990s did not have the desired effect. The collapsed state-planned economy was replaced by an even more awful idol – the cult of consumption, greed and unfair distribution of public income. Finally, the vast majority of Russians were deprived of the opportunity to earn enough money for an adequate level of life. Many highly-qualified and professional specialists were among them as their knowledge and skills were no longer needed under the new circumstances. In the new conditions of 'wild capitalism' some high-tech branches of industry were destroyed (the decrease in some branches was up to 40-50 % compared with 1990). Meanwhile, the raw material and trade sectors, which were flourishing, left people in the position of slave-like servants of the new owners of the principal capital goods. The profit from such an industry was and is distributed among 2 percent of the population, whereas 98 percent are deprived of the opportunity to provide a normal level of life for themselves and their families in a legal way. As a result, Russian society is in the situation of permanent instability and social mistrust. How can the current situation be changed?

## 2. Orthodox Labour Ethics, Charity and Justice

It is up to the state to change the unfair system of distribution of public income. Not interfering in governmental functions, the Orthodox Church supports the idea to create a socially responsible economic regime. The first step here is to draw the attention of the Russian business society to the fact that only moral understanding of economy by the business leaders of the country can create conditions for economic growth, secure a stable position for different social groups and can provide a respectful attitude to labour and property. The most important element of the process is the creation of a moral attitude to the participants in public life. The propaganda of the ideals of orthodox labour ethics is also very helpful.

What are the real mechanisms for social responsibility of the business sector in modern Russia? Charity plays an important role in the redistribution of surplus material means. History shows the importance of charity in the country's social life. However we should keep in mind that charity cannot be the only means of fair public income distribution for the benefit of the needy, conduction of social initiatives, payments to those who create spiritual and intellectual goods. The state has to play the main role. It must be the state that is responsible for the fair public distribution of income, i.e. for the spiritual dimension of the economy. The instruments of the state are reasonable tax and budget policies aimed at fair profits of the few and its redistribution for the benefit of the whole society, including for the help of the needy and for the support of necessary institutions such as armed forces, scientific and educational organisations, medical centers, governmental structures, etc. Unfortunately, modern Russian legislation predominantly based on neo-liberal values in the economy, is incapable of solving this task. Moreover, today's legislation is often to blame for the bankruptcy of small business entities as it creates various preferences for the big business such as monopolies in the raw material and banking sectors. To abide all prohibitions, to pay all taxes and duties together with corruption, means to put your small or medium business in danger.

In this situation, the Orthodox Church urges the state to work out an effective and fair legislation that is not only an economic but a moral and even a religious task. Society realises step by step that morality is a means of survival of the Russian people and a warranty of stable and secure development in the 21st century. However the process is only at a primal stage. The current situation does not stimulate the formation of business ethics and economic ethics. The problems of tax evasion, outflow of capital and corruption are still unsolved.

## 3. New Beginning of Business Ethics

The following should be done to change the situation. First, to work out legal mechanisms that will strengthen the system of collection and distribution of means. And, second, to give the business sector an opportunity to work for the benefit of society. History proves that involuntary welfare redistribution never leads to the creation of a fair society. It is possible to build an effective and fair economy without revolutions and coups, by means of permanent and reasonable dialogue between the state, business, trade unions and employees. Only in such a way will it be possible to deal with the social strain in Russia. All the organisations of the civil society must participate in the creation of the fundament for a fair and socially responsible economy. Among them are organisations of businessmen, trade unions and, certainly, religious organisations.

At the moment the Russian Orthodox Church, fully realising its mission in the post-soviet space, develops and supports many social activities. The core of this activity is to strengthen dynamic and effective business based on moral traditions and business ethics. In their numerous statements, orthodox hierarchs (among whom His Holiness Patriarch of Moscow and all Russia Alexy II and His Eminence Metropolitan of Smolensk and Kaliningrad Kirill) stressed that the problems of economy and social fairness, of taking care of the poor and the oppressed are important elements of the mission of the Church. This is particularly important in today's transition period of Russia. The consciousness of the Orthodox Church has never escaped from economic problems. The ideas of economic regress and stagnation are alien to it. The Orthodox Church is ready to be a moral arbiter and pastor of the Russian businessmen.

It is pleasant to note that recently some positive tendencies are visible in the area of business ethics. Many documents, stating the principals of internal corporative responsibility of business are adopted. An example is The Charter of Corporative and Business Ethics adopted by the Russian Union of Manufacturers and Businessmen. The Chamber of Industry and Commerce of the Russian Federation actively realises a 'Russian business culture' program. Within the scope of the program the principals of the business code of conduct and a program to introduce business ethics in organisations are worked out. Some big Russian companies such as SUAL-holding, Norilsk nikel, Ruskij aluminij showed interest in working out the principals of business ethics.

The rebirth of the business culture of contemporary Russian businessmen is based on the traditions of tsarist Russia. There existed a well organised system of the merchant's guilds with its code of honour, rules of work and rank system. In 1912 Russian merchants worked out seven principals of business in Russia, which are actual, even today. The content of them is below.

## 4. Seven Principals of Business in Russia

1. Have respect for the authorities. The authorities are a necessary condition for effective business. Keep order everywhere. In this context demonstrate your respect to the officials who are in power.

2. Be honest and truthful. Honesty and truth are the fundament for business, prerequisite for normal income and harmonic business

relations. A Russian businessman must be a stainless example of the virtues of honesty and truth.

3. Have respect for property. Free business is a key to the welfare of state. A Russian businessman must work for the benefit of his Fatherland and give all his best. Such efforts are only possible on the basis of property.

4. Have love and respect for each person. Such love and respect for a worker from the side of a businessman, stimulates love and respect in response. Harmony of interests appears in such circumstances. In such an atmosphere, people develop different talents and express themselves in the best way.

5. Keep your word. A businessman must keep his word: 'If you tell a lie once, who will trust you?' Success in business depends on the extent of trust others have for you.

6. Live in accordance with your income. Do not show off. Choose such a business you can cope with. Act in accordance with your means.

7. Be purposeful. Always have a determined aim. A businessman needs an aim as air. Do not be distracted with other aims. It is unnatural to work for two masters. On the way to the desired aim, do not break moral rules. No aim can be above moral values.

The adoption of the law on 'Self-governed Organisation' by the Russian Federal Assembly, in 2004, is considered to be an important event. The law prescribes imperative abidance of rules and standards of business and professional activity, of business ethics and trade usages by all non-governmental structures. But the Russian community, including the Russian Orthodox Church, emphasised that the implementation of the standards must be done in a transparent way, only in accordance with the law. That must not be turned into a strict state control over business. The business ethics of the business sector and its social responsibility can be initiated only by businessmen, and not imposed from somewhere.

The Russian Orthodox Church realises that contemporary Russian businessmen bear a great responsibility. As businessmen are the most active and prosperous part of the population, they are obliged to cooperate with the state in taking care of the needy. The state and the unions of businessmen in Russia come to the conclusion that social responsibility is the only way to decrease social strain and to support the authority of the state power and business.

At the same time, there is an ideological and spiritual vacuum in the Russian business society. The old socialist economy collapsed but the new economy is built on principles which are far from Christian. In this situation the Russian Orthodox Church, the most important and influential structure of Russian civil society, puts forward an initiative to organise a dialogue between society and the state on the aims and principals of economic development of the country.

The Church suggested to evaluate modern economic realities from religious points of view (in a broad sense, not only from the point of view of Christian values) and working out basic moral principles and business rules that can be used by private businessmen, trade unions, employees and state entities in their everyday work. Society should be united to build a fair and competitive economy. The result of the work is the 'Code of Moral Principles and Rules of Economic Activity' (see below Chapter 28).

The World Russian People's Council, an influential forum of different Russian and foreign non-governmental organisations united by Orthodoxy, initiated to work out the Code. In December 2002 the Council, devoted to the topic 'Faith and labour. Spiritual and Cultural traditions and economic future of Russia' decided to work out the document. The final version of the draft was adopted on the 4th of February 2004 by the VIII World Russian People's Council. The representatives of all traditional religions of Russia, including Islamic, Buddhists and Jewish leaders, participated in the work of the Council and support the Code.

The document, prepared by a working group which included well-known Russian economists, gives a clear moral evaluation of objective economic realities of today's Russia and simultaneously helps the representatives of power, business and employees to undertake effective economic activities not only for the benefit of oneself and one's family, but also for the benefit of society as a whole.

The draft of the Code was discussed by all main representatives of business and trade unions, leaders of the Chamber of Industry and Commerce of the Russian Federation, the Russian Union of Manufacturers and Businessmen, organisations of small and medium business 'Support of Russia' and the Federation of Independent Trade Unions. All of them supported the Code without reservations, what can be considered to be a first step in opening a reasonable dialogue between all social groups about the role of moral values in economy.

The appeal of the Russian Orthodox Church to businessmen to follow the ancient Orthodox business traditions voluntarily was heard. So, during the Economic Forum held in May 2004 in Tver, a contract giving a binding force to the Code was ceremonially signed. The Tver Union of Manufacturers and Businessmen, the Administration of the Tver region and the Tverskaja and Kashinskaja diocese of the Moscow Patriarchate consented the Code to be bound in their relations.

The Code reflects the values which are common to all traditional Russian religions: effective and fair economy, free and responsible business, protection of the weak and poor, respect to the state-power, fair labour. We hope that comprehensive discussion of the Code and its use in everyday life will help the Russian business society to see its place in the future of the country in a more responsible way.

# 27

# THE RUSSIAN ORTHODOX CHURCH AND ECONOMIC ETHICS. EFFORTS AT THE TURN OF THE MILLENNIUM

*Pavel Shashkin, Russia*

In the 1990s and 2000s, the state of the economy and the social sphere in the post-Soviet states have become objects of close attention by the Russian Orthodox Church in the persons of her Supreme Authority, clergy and laity, including those united in church public organisations. It is small wonder, considering the stormy economic and social changes that have affected literally every citizen in Russia and in other countries of the Commonwealth of the Independent States in the post-totalitarian period. Called to be concerned with the spiritual and material welfare of every person, the Church has responded to these developments by seeking to answer numerous questions asked by her spiritual children. While in the early 1990s the Church's response in the economic and social sphere focused primarily on particular pressing problems, by the end of this decade and especially in the beginning of the 21st century, the Orthodox socio-economic thought has addressed the profound ethical issues involved in this field.

## 1. The Shock of the Early 1990s. Economic Transformations and Moral Crisis

The collapse of the Soviet economy at the end of the 1980s, followed by the disintegration of the political system, forced the state authority and society to undertake the difficult task of reforming the economy of this vast superpower as it was focused on heavy industry, mainly armaments. This task had no precedent in world history. Most of the Orthodox Christians were enthusiastic about the end of the Soviet political regime not only because of the state atheism it implanted but also because of the extremely ideologically-oriented economic policy that had been imposed on society against its will and that had destroyed by force of repression the Russian traditional order of economic life. At the beginning of the 20th century's last decade, the post-Soviet societies came to a consensus that the unsustainable Soviet economy should be reformed according to the market patterns adopted in other countries.

Such were the patterns adopted as the basis of the radical changes introduced at the beginning of the 1990s: the Soviet economic control structures were abolished; market mechanisms were activated; the state property was privatised *en masse*. The reformers sincerely believed in the power and truth of Western neoliberal economic doctrines. Their favourite term was 'shock therapy,' that was to bring Russia to prosperity in a matter of a few years. They relied on 'the invisible hand of the market' (Adam Smith).

The Russian liberal reformers are comparable to their chronological predecessors (the communists) in that they view economy as determining the entire life of a society, including its spirituality, morality and policy. Both accorded little value to non-economic factors in the life of a country or a state. As a result, the reliance on market as 'putting everything in order' led to a disastrous crisis of public morality both in politics and in the economy. In the first half of the 1990s, the slogan of enrichment by all means prevailed in Russia and other post-Soviet states. The vast opportunities opened up for private initiative were not seized first of all by honest workers, who found it difficult to adjust in no time to the rapidly and repeatedly changing 'rules of the game,' but by people not overburdened with conscience or any principles whatsoever. The privatisation carried out by dubious methods enriched those who were only recently the Soviet economic bureaucrats as well as apt manipulators and criminals. Multi-million fortunes were built thanks to one's closeness to high state leaders or to the illegal use of force. The 'rules' adopted in the criminal world sometimes proved to be the only regulators of local economic relations.

The economic transformations were accompanied by a tremendous social tragedy. While a handful achieved a rapid and blatant enrichment, dozens of millions were slipping into poverty. Most people's pensions and salaries were only enough to buy food and even these means were paid out casually or not at all. The savings accumulated under the Soviet rule depreciated completely. Those who worked at gigantic defence plants became legally or practically jobless. The system of free education and medical care began to weaken and rapidly disintegrated.

The rapid departure from a stable social state, to which the people of the Soviet Union were accustomed, generated mass disillusionment in the reform policy and utter demoralisation of society. It cannot be denied that the architects of the economic reforms have managed to accomplish the impossible as the radical reconstruction they carried out has laid a legal and political foundation for market economy in a country that lacked the proper adjustments. In doing so, they managed to avoid a disintegration of the country, civil war and mass social outbreak. The changes however proved to be not as easy as the liberal politicians of the early 1990s imagined them to be.

However, it is the moral decay of society that appears to be the most negative result of the early post-perestroika decade. The ruin of the social justice ideal, personal tragedies of most citizens, spite and social apathy, helplessness in face of tycoons and criminals – all this, like a heavy burden, lay on the people's conscience and therefore could not but trouble the Church.

## 2. A Russian 'Code of Moral Principles'

A certain tension between the ideal of 'poverty in Christ' as radical contempt for earthly blessings, on the one hand, and desire for Christian influence upon the pragmatic order of the earthly world, on the other, continues and will probably continue to prevail in the Russian-speaking Orthodox discussion on socio-economic themes. This tension, which appeared in the Russian Orthodox thinking as far back as the dispute between 'the Non-Seekers' and 'the Josephites' in the 16th century, needed and still needs to be harmonised.

The 7th World Russian People's Council, a public forum chaired by His Holiness Patriarch Alexy II, head of the Russian Orthodox Church, and uniting clergy, politicians, leaders of public organisations, representatives of the scientific community and world of arts, took place in December 2002 in Moscow. This time the Council was devoted to the theme 'Faith and Labour: Religious and Cultural Traditions and Russia's Economic Future.'

Among the speakers at the Council were representatives of various political forces and adherents to various views on the ways in which Russian economy should develop. Among them were also representatives of the economic committees of the Russian Federal Assembly and leaders of major trade unions and business associations.

The Council's Word, the final document of the forum, stated in particular, 'Today the governmental authorities, scientists, businessmen, public organisations are seeking for ways to overcome the negative developments in the economy. This search cannot be limited only to the field of figures and market laws. National economic problems cannot be solved without taking notice of the moral and spiritual state of society. Indeed, many reasons for the present difficulties are concealed in the human hearts and minds. Scientific recipes and governmental decisions will not make people happy unless the moral foundation of human activity is restored and the rules of behaviour for the businessman, worker, public servant and any other participant in economic processes are established and really observed.

'We have to learn to resolutely reject criminal amorality in economy and refuse to cooperate with dishonest and unscrupulous people. Those who do not pay wages in good time, humiliate the worker and stifle business through red tape deserve persistent and staunch public condemnation. ... Economy should be not only effective, but also equitable and merciful, addressed to the human being, not only money and goods. We should realize that the goal of economic activity is first of all the welfare of people, young and old, strong and weak, those living now and those who will come to replace them...

'The determination of the fate of national economy however should not become an 'apanage' of officials, businessmen and economists. We all, the people, state, Church, trade unions, business associations, scientific community and civil society should see in Russia's economy a field for our care and creative efforts. The country needs an open and comprehensive dialogue on economic and social problems that will influence important decision-making.'[1]

The Council decided to develop a code of economic activity. The document with the title a 'Code of Moral Principles and Rules in Economic Activity'[2] was published in 2004. It deals with a diversity of aspects of economic and social life. It was formulated on the basis of the ten commandments of the Mosaic Law (the structure of the Code represents a kind of Decalogue) and the experience of their assimilation by Christianity and other religions traditionally confessed in Russia.

### 3. Prospects for Orthodox Moral Influence on Economic Ethics

It can be hoped that economic thought only begins to develop in the Russian Orthodox Church and will flourish in a way unprecedented in the history of our Church even in the pre-revolutionary time, particularly, during 'the Solver Age' of Russian religious philosophy in the late 19th and early 20th centuries. This development is expected to go in several directions.

Firstly, the voice of church hierarchy will continue to be heard both on the level of the Church's profound documents reflecting her world outlook and on the level of responses to various developments in economic and social life. Thus, the 2005 and 2006 actions in Russia in protest against replacing social benefits with monetary payments have prompted His Holiness Patriarch Alexy II to make the following statement: 'The Church does not intend to point out to the state what economic mechanisms it should use in pursuing its social policy. What is important for us is that this policy should be fair and effective and understandable to the people. The recent developments have shown that these principles have not been realised in proper measure... Changes by no means should deprive people of a real opportunity to use transportation and communication, to keep their housing, to have access to medical aid and medicines. Otherwise a tragedy will become inevitable for millions of our fellow-citizens – those who worked for the good of the Motherland all their lives and today need care and protection.'[3]

This statement was widely covered in the mass media, arousing a largely positive reaction, though some politicians and journalists hastened to appeal against the participation of the Church in the discussion on urgent economic and social problems. Vladimir Zhirinovsky's fellow-fighter, State Duma deputy Alexey Mitrofanov, who said that 'the Church's interference in real politics is a dangerous process,' made the most conspicuous statement.[4] Not only representatives of the Church and some journalists, but also Mr. Mitrofanov's colleagues in the Russian Parliament, challenged this attitude. The State Duma Vice-Speaker Sergey Baburin stated during the same session: 'I would like only to welcome the fact that church ministers identify with their parishioners, with the people, and it is immoral and anti-state to prohibit them from stating their own point of view.'[5]

Secondly, various church research centres and Orthodox lay public organisations will continue producing scientific works and public statements concerning socio-economic issues. New studies, papers, analytical reviews and proposals devoted to the Orthodox economic ethics and analysis of economic problems from the Orthodox perspective are expected to appear. Orthodox public lay organisations will apparently give special attention to the economic globalisation and international economic relations in general. Already now these themes are actively discussed at religious public conferences, where participants call for a greater justice in the world economic order and protest against the growing control of the 'gold billion' countries and their financial elites over the global market and the economic order in other countries. Criticism levelled against international economic organisations will certainly have an effect on the attitude of Orthodox public organisations towards the economic policy pursued by governments in Russia and other post-Soviet countries. This criticism has not always been and will not always be competent and professional. It has been dominated by protective emotions. However, it cannot be disregarded by either church hierarchy or the state.

The thinking on economic subjects will develop in other religious communities as well. For instance, the leaders of Protestant churches, the Old Believers and the Jews have expressed their views on economy. In case of the Protestants and Muslims, conceptual documents are also being discussed now to be addressed to public at large.

Thirdly and finally, the state of the economy will be influenced by the gradual growth in faith of a considerable number of businessmen and workers. If in the early 1990s the outburst of religion as a fashion was still accompanied with crying religious ignorance, and old women made up an overwhelming majority in churches of all religions and confessions, at the turn of the century the situation has radically changed. Most parishioners now, at least in cities, are families with children and middle-aged individuals. Many of them are well versed in doctrine, take an active part in church life and observe religious rites practically forgotten in the Soviet period even by many believers. Thus, various sociological polls showed that about 20 % of the Russians observed Lent in the early 2000s.[6]

A fasting menu has become a usual diet in the canteens of state institutions and large corporations. There are more and more icons in offices of businessmen and at working places of ordinary workers. Finally, many companies give considerable aid to the Church, declaring Christian morality as their motivation for charity. A considerable number of enterprises have based their entire corporate culture on Orthodoxy. It should be noted that there are also companies in Russia who observe Protestant and Muslim ethics.

In short, the influence of Orthodoxy and religion in general on the economic and political life of post-Soviet countries is growing, contrary to allegations by Communists and liberals about 'a near end of the religious renaissance.' We hope that this tendency will continue, helping those patriots who are still experiencing a moral crisis to fulfil moral values and standards and to build a free, fair and effective economy aimed at people's welfare – something unthinkable without a solid moral foundation.

NOTES

[1]   http://www.russian-orthodox-church.org.ru/nr212173.htm. English version: http://www.russian-orthodox-church.org.ru/ne212173.htm. The text is also published in Stückelberger, Christoph/Mugambi, J.N.K. (eds), *Responsible Leadership. Global Perspectives*, Nairobi: Acton Publishers, 2005, pp. 141-153. See also Chapter 28 in this volume.

[2]   http://www.mospat.ru/text/news/id/6353.html;
      English version: http://www.mospat.ru/text/e_messages/id/6682.html.

[3]   http://www.mospat.ru/text/news/id/8397.html.

[4]   http://www.religare.ru/news13579.htm.

[5]   http://www.religare.ru/news13579.htm.

[6]   According to ROMIR Monitoring, they made up 22 % in 2004; see the Blagovest-Info report of 11 March, 2004.

# 28

# CODE OF MORAL PRINCIPLES AND RULES OF ECONOMIC ACTIVITY ADOPTED BY THE 8TH WORLD RUSSIAN PEOPLE'S COUNCIL IN MOSCOW, 2004

*The World Russian People's Council, an influential forum of different Russian and foreign nongovernmental organisations united by Ortho-doxy, initiated to work out the Code. In December 2002 the Council, devoted to the topic 'Faith and labour. Spiritual and cultural traditions and economic future of Russia' decided to work out the document. The final version of the draft was adopted on 4 February 2004 by the 8th World Russian People's Council. The representatives of all traditional religions of Russia, including Islamic, Buddhists and Jewish leaders, par-ticipated in the work of the Council and support the Code.[1]*

Moscow, 4 February 2004

This Code of Moral Principles and Rules is offered for voluntary reception by leaders of enterprises and commercial structures, busi-nessmen and their communities, workers, trade unions and all other participants in the economic processes including state bodies and public associations involved in economic activity.

This document does not repeat legal provisions. Nor does it touch upon any conventional specificity of economic relations regulated by decrees of state and professional communities.

The ethical principles and rules formulated below are based on the Ten Commandments given by God and on the experience of their implementation by Christianity and other religions confessed tradi-tionally in Russia. These principles and rules should not be taken however for a literal interpretation of the Biblical text. They are rather provisions stemming from God's commandments in their broad sense and from the age-old religious and moral heritage, includ-ing that of Russia. The Code of Moral Principles and Rules describes an ideal model of economic activity, which does not exist today but the implementation of which can and must be sought every day. Per-haps, reality will not conform to this document for yet longer time. However, one cannot say beforehand that the aim of observing it is unattainable, for a person seeking good faith and life in dignity can cover, with God's help, the hardest possible ways even in such complex area of human life as economy.

I.  *Without forgetting about one's daily bread, one should keep in mind the spiritual meaning of life. Without forgetting about one's own good, one should show concern for the good of one's neighbour, the good of society and the Fatherland.*

In the history of Russia, there have been various approaches to the issue of what takes priority – the material over the spiritual, or private over public interests. Many times the spiritual ideal has been sacrificed to utilitarian interests and vice versa. In some periods, things public were preferred to private things, while in other periods, the opposite was the case.

This problem became a subject of discussions between 'Josephites' and 'Non-seekers', Westernisers and Slavophils, and among public leaders in the post-Soviet period. However, the very fact of such discussions shows that the individual and the common good, the spiritual and the material are equally integral parts of the human existence.

That is why neither the spiritual ideal, nor the search for the material benefit, nor one's vital interests, nor the good of one's neighbour and society can be neglected.

Historically, the Russian spiritual and moral tradition has been inclined predominantly to give priority to the spiritual over the material, the ideal of personal selflessness for the sake of the good of the people. However, the extremes of this option would lead to terrible tragedies.

Remembering this, we should establish such an economic order as to help realise in a harmonious way both spiritual aspirations and the material interests of both the individual and society. This harmonisation, as the historical experience has shown, is promoted by rules based on biblical principles.

II.  *Wealth is not an aim in itself. It should serve the building of a worthy life for the person and the people*

The worship of wealth and morality are incompatible in the human being. The attitude to wealth as idol will inevitably destroy the economic and legal culture, generate injustice in distributing the fruits of labour and cause a social war 'of all against all'.

The accumulation of wealth for the sake of wealth will lead the individual and his business and the national economy to an impasse.

Wealth in itself is neither a blessing nor a punishment.

For a moral person, property is not only a means of profit, but also a means of service for the ideals of good and justice.

Property brings return only if it is used effectively, while the fruits of its use are distributed equitably and responsibly and invested in social stability. Those who produce material goods exclusively for themselves, for their own families or social groups, while ignoring the interests of others, violate the moral law and loose much economically.

The greater one's property is, the more powerful one is over others. Therefore, the use of property in an economy should not be of narrow egoistic nature and should not contradict the common interest.

Honest economic activity excludes any enrichment at the expense of society. The welfare of conscientious businessmen and workers should correspond to their working contribution and result from their diligence in creating, utilising and augmenting universally beneficial goods.

It is a duty of a wealthy person to do good to people without expecting public recognition. Both the businessman and the state should proceed from the principle of justice in making economic decisions.

The level of consumption and the living standards should be reasonable and moderate and should take into account the state of the environment.

Money is only a means of achieving a stated goal. It should always be in movement and turnover. It is a business, real and engrossing, that is a businessman's richness. Rejection of the cult of money emancipates a person, making him internally free.

One's poverty or richness in themselves does not speak of one's morality or immorality. A poor person who wastes his abilities or uses them only for selfish purposes is no less immoral than a rich one who refuses to donate some of his income to public needs.

Poverty, just as richness, is a test. A poor person is obliged to behave in a dignified way, to seek to make his work effective, to raise his professional skills so that he may come out of his misery. State, society and business should help him in this endeavor.

*III. The culture of business relations and fidelity to given promises help both the individual and economy to become better.*

Business relations should be built on respect for the rights and legitimate interests of their participants. In an economy, the principles of justice and affectivity should be combined.

Having power over material resources and people, the employer including the state should be responsible for his economic decisions, for the actions of his employees and for the consequences of these actions.

Honesty and professionalism in one's relations with customers and business partners would win confidence and strengthen the economic condition of one's enterprise, while unfair play would doom one to inevitable collapse.

Observance of verbal and written agreements is a foundation of harmonious relations in an economy, whereas the failure to meet one's engagements will undermine the authority of both the business community and that of the country as a whole.

Such conduct should be put to public censure. The forms of this censure are manifold, including denial of personal contacts, public boycott, expulsion from professional communities, etc.

The same rules are applicable to unscrupulous workers who fail to fulfil the labour contract. An enterprise can be successful only if internal obligations are mutually fulfilled.

The state is called to adopt laws which support and develop the culture of fulfilling obligations. At the same time, the state itself gives an example of such culture, especially in the fields of economy and administration and in fulfilling political promises. The most important function of the state is to ensure effective control over the fulfilment of obligations.

Such vices as foul language, sexual harassment, assault and battery, debauchery, familiarities are inadmissible at work and in business relations.

The good name of one's company cannot be used for private purposes and private profit at the expense of the common cause.

Commercial fraud and service fraud lead to the loss of confidence and often to bankruptcy. Bourishness, laziness, negligence, untidiness of a worker dealing with a customer – all this antagonises him and does damage to the business.

Moral participation in economic activity is expressed, among other things, in politeness and propriety, self-control in critical situations, respect for others' opinion even if it is considered wrong.

It was not accidental that the principal motto of the Russian merchants was this: 'Profit is above all, but honour is above profit'. One's fair business reputation is one's long-term asset. It takes a long time to build up, but it is easy to lose.

IV.   *A human being is not a 'perpetual machine'. A person needs time for rest, spiritual life and creative development.*

Continued monotonous work, even if intellectual, depletes the personality, leading to its degradation. Nothing can justify the renunciation of one's legitimate time for rest, days off and wholesome holidays. In addition, one should have an opportunity for changing one's sphere and type of work.

It is necessary that businessmen, authorities and society should be concerned about the intellectual, spiritual and physical development of every person. The material and financial capital can be neither built up nor held today without the intellectual capital – the voluntary use of individual capabilities, skills and knowledge. The individual must have access to the knowledge and the depository of culture and an opportunity for self-fulfilment through education and scientific and creative work. A part of one's working time spent on this will be repaid a hundredfold. A far-sighted employer will take care of the self-improving leisure of his employees.

Indeed, the individual whose potential and talents are fully unfolded will be of maximum benefit to society as a whole and to a particular business.

V.   *State, society and business should be together concerned for a dignified life for workers, especially those who cannot earn their living. Economic activity is a socially responsible type of work.*

A national economy will destroy itself if it does not take effective measures to offer social protection. A worker who has no prospects for earning an appropriate pension and is deprived of access to education, healthcare and social security will never work with joy and satisfaction. The lack of social support forces a person to look for additional opportunities for earnings on the side, which affect his or her professional level. The aim of such a worker is social survival, rather than conscientious, constructive and purposeful endeavour. Disability for such a person is tantamount to the loss of everything.

On the contrary, a person's confidence in the future creates a necessary condition for professional growth and makes it possible to draw up a long-term strategy for the development of an enterprise.

The employees of an enterprise should have opportunities for responsible participation in its management in accordance with their professional level and education, so that they could feel themselves partners and co-participants in a common cause.

An employer, including the state, should bear public responsibility for their participation in social and retirement insurance programs.

The state bears responsibility for the protection of the life, health and human dignity of old people, the disabled and destitute children. It should not only support the disabled, but also create conditions for developing works of charity undertaken by enterprises, religious and public organisations and individuals.

The degree of society's welfare depends directly on its attitude to the disabled and the old. Allocation of a part of income for the support of the old and the sick, the disabled and deprived children should become a norm for any profitable enterprise as well as any well-off working person, including an employee.

An enterprise is called to give special attention to the retired and the disabled who contributed their own labour to its welfare. An employer who acknowledges the past and present working services of his or her employees reconciles the past and the future and increases the strength of his or her business.

## VI. *Work should not kill or cripple a person*

Creating adequate work conditions and observing safety measures at work is an area in which an employer including the state bears a heightened responsibility.

However, an employee should take seriously the safety requirements by excluding carelessness or drunkenness, especially in operating dangerous machinery. An employee should remember that his or her irresponsible attitude may threaten the life and health of other people.

Work for an employee is the principal bread-winner. Therefore, ungrounded dismissal, low salary, delayed or partial wage payment put him or her on the verge of survival, while an employer's careful attitude to the work, health of life of his neighbour is beneficial for both him and his employees.

Enterprisers should reject the unlawful methods of doing business with the use of force or threat of force.

A desire of success by all means and disregard for the life and health of others is a crime and a vice.

VII. *Political power and economic power should be separated. The participation of business in politics and its impact on public opinion should be open and transparent.*

The entire financial support given by business to political parties, public organisations and the mass media should be made public and verifiable. Any secret support is to be condemned publicly as immoral. Private mass media should declare openly the sources, amounts and use of their funds.

Production and entrepreneurial structures, which belong to the state fully or partly, should not show any political preferences.

In the economy, there is no place for corruption and other crimes.

It is inadmissible for the state authorities to be involved in any competitive activity and in settling economic disputes. The assertion of its interests by a business before the authorities should be lawful and open for public control.

Individuals and structures guilty of grievous crimes, especially those involved in corruption, should be unacceptable as business partners or participants in the business community.

A morally responsible business cannot have anything in common with such things as traffic of people, prostitution, pornography, medical and spiritual charlatanism, illegitimate trade in arms and drugs, and political and religious extremism.

VIII. *Appropriating others' property, neglecting a common property, refusing to reward a worker for his labour, deceiving a partner, a person violates the moral law and does damage to both society and himself.*

The state, an entrepreneur, an employee and any citizen should treat common and any other property with care. The habit of stealing from the state, a neighbour or a work collective and of damaging their property should be condemned and driven away from our life. Those who take what does not belong to them from the common or other people's pocket are to be held up to public shame.

Stealing from a business partner and depriving him of his nego-
tiated part of the common profit should become generally
known and should necessarily lead to sanctions from the business community.

One of the forms of misappropriation is inequitable distribution
of the fruits of labour among partners and employees. Society
should not be divided into the super-rich and the super-poor.

Production and all other forms of economic activity should not
do irreparable harm to nature which is the property of not only
those who live on the Earth today but also the future generations. The natural resources, which are necessary to people
today but which cannot be restored tomorrow, should be used
counting on many centuries ahead and be replaced, if possible,
by renewable resources. The ecological aspect of the activity of
all economic subjects should be transparent for society and open
for control by it. Participation in projects aimed to protect the
environment and the introduction of resource-saving and zero-
discharge technologies is an essential task for the business
community.

A businessman should remember that the failure to pay taxes
prescribed by the law is a theft from orphans, the elderly, the disabled and other unprotected people. The transfer of some of
one's income in the form of tax for the needs of society should
become not a painful obligation discharged involuntarily and
sometimes not discharged at all, but an honorary cause deserv-
ing the gratitude of society.

Concealing profits and carrying them off to other countries are
tantamount to the robbery of one's own compatriots.

Robbing their employees are also those who do not pay them adequate salaries, dooming them to poverty and bitterness and
depriving them of the joy of labour. In determining the amount
of payment for labour and the share of income to be paid out in
salaries, an employer should be guided by the principle of justice,
not looking back at the standards of the hard past or at the examples of the poorest countries. The despair of those who agree to
a low salary just to earn their daily bread must not be abused.

The remuneration of labour cannot be below the subsistence
wage. It should allow an employee not only to eat well, but also
to buy goods necessary for everyday life, for raising children and
securing accommodation.

Those who fail to pay salaries, who delay them systematically and allow them to stay below the subsistence wage are to be censured by society.

The state existing on public funds should assess its share in the common wealth proportionally. Unburdensome taxes are one of the foundations of effective and moral economic activity in which citizens can cover public expenses without unreasonable burdens.

IX. *In competitive struggle, one must not lie or insult, nor exploit vices or instincts.*

Competition is one of the motors of economy. Monopolism is tantamount to mothballing and backwardness.

Results of conscientious competition serve the interests of society; competition puts its members in equal conditions and gives them the right to choose.

Competition is appropriate and morally justified if it does not destroy business relations.

The most reliable partner in concluding a bargain is he who is confident of the decency of his colleague. The more credible your business is, the faster it grows in profitableness. Honesty is an investment in the future.

In competitive struggle, morally abject methods must not be used. Thus, a businessman should not hurl public insults at his competitors or spread wittingly any false or unverified information about his business partners.

Advertisements containing blunt deception, exploiting the sexual instinct, encouraging people to drinking and smoking, using the spiritual immaturity of children and teenagers should be viewed as immoral and should not be supported by the business community. Advertising must not insult people's religious and ethnic sentiments.

X. *The institution of ownership and the right to own and dispose of property must be respected. It is immoral to envy the welfare of a neighbour and to encroach on his property.*

Ungrounded requisition of property undermines economic stability and ruins people's faith in justice.

The nationalisation of private property is morally justified only if the way it is used obviously contradicts the security and life of people. In any case, property may be requisited strictly by law and with an appropriate compensation.

This equally applies to the alienation of state and public property. Its usurpation is almost always accompanied with the destruction of the national economy and the suffering of millions of people.

Privatisation is not an aim in itself. Legal transfer of public property to private hands is morally justified. This should result in a real improvement of goods and services, lower prices, stronger economy and the building of a dynamic and harmoniously developing society with justice.

Any unlawful re-distribution of property is always a crime against society and a violation of the moral law. A private person who has come into possession of a property through deceit has neither moral nor legal right to be called its owner. In such a case, the state is called to restore justice, observing the law and the moral duty.

The state of an economy stands in direct dependence on the spiritual and moral condition of the personality. Only a person with a good heart and lucid mind, spiritually mature, industrious and responsible, can support himself, while being of benefit to his neighbours and his people. May it be so in Russia as she has entered the 21st century.

NOTES
[1]  See more above in the article by Pavel Shashkin, Chapter 27.

# 29

# STRENGTHENING THE COMMON GOOD. THE RESPONSIBILITY OF STATES, INVESTORS AND INTERNATIONAL ORGANISATIONS

*Richard Ondji'i Toung, Cameroon*

## Introduction

The international trend to liberalisation and privatisation seems to favour individual and private interests about the Common Good. The growing gap between the poor and the rich increases social tensions and conflicts in many societies. Business ethics with its emphasis on Corporate Social Responsibility (CSR) looks for ways to reconcile private interests with the responsibility for the interests of the different stakeholders and therefore the Common Good. What is the responsibility of states, the private sector, especially the finance sector, and international organisations to strengthen and to protect the Common Good? This is the question of this article.

From the reading of Pavel Shashkin's article on 'Business Leadership and Social Responsibility in a Transition Country' in Russia, [1] and from the article of Jeffrey D. Sachs on 'Business Leadership and Sustainable Development', [2] both in this volume, it appears that – as in contemporary Cameroon [3] and in international economic relations [4] – the main concept they tackle in their studies is the Common Good as a challenge, a stake or an objective to achieve. Shashkin, for instance, asserts that the fair distribution of material welfare is an actual topic in Russia and that 'a socially responsible economic regime' [5] is to be created, while Sachs speaks about the necessity of 'managerial governance', about the 'need of rigorous law' and about the 'business community'.

Both authors speak about the social responsibility [6] of states, governments or corporations, and both worry about the solidarity in society. They understand solidarity as an historical, social and anthropological link between people based in a unifying experience or tradition.

## 1. The Common Good as an Ethical Principle

What I call the theory of the Common Good in this essay is the combination, the compilation and the organisation of ideas around the notion of the Common Good. The Common Good is a principle of political and social ethics. [7] As a general principle of decision in the area of the realisation of justice, the Common Good must help indirectly to satisfy the aspirations of individuals and society. According to Plato and Aristotle, the public order is considered as reasonable when the private and the collective material needs, and the individual pursuit of happiness, are reasonably held together. Thus, all ethical prescriptions on both the individual and social levels derive from the concept of the Common Good which is to be seen as the supreme good of the community (or, in Aquinas' terms, the *bonum commune*), to which these ethical precepts are subordinated, as they are subordinated – in a teleological account – to the higher finality of the action. The Common Good is justified in various ways as a rational superior or divine interest.

As an ethical imperative of politics, the Common Good requires both the distinction between private and general interests and their mediation. The general interest is not the sum of the particular interests (as Vilfredo Pareto thinks [8]), but the juridical and political equilibrium between the interests of the individuals and the social groups. Such an equilibrium in states' decisions ensures, I argue, just and stable social conditions.

The Common Good is therefore perceived as a general criterion for the equilibrium of public interests, but it does not define its concrete contents: the equilibrium of public interests must be reasonably legitimated as creating conditions which advance the quality of human life. In sum, the Common Good presents the advantage of representing a general socio-political and ethical criterion from which we can search the legitimacy of the equilibrium of public interests, which in turn warrants a good human life. Therefore, the Common Good must be the object of a social, political and economic consensus.

In the financial perspective, and according to the quarterly *Finance & The Common Good*, the notion of Common Good 'embraces two separate concerns: the social concern where the question is what the financial sector brings to the community; and the personal concern where the question is how finance contributes to the growth and self-realisation of each and every member of society'. [9]

To examine the relationship between the present financial system and the Common Good, the authors of this quarterly propose four main avenues of research, which can provide a basic structure for assessing how finance contributes to the Common Good:

The *first* concerns the changing relationship between politics and finance and its impact on the Common Good. The *second* concerns the way theorists approach finance and the role of the financial sector. The *third* examines how finance, spurred on by theory, is endeavouring to create a risk-free society. The *fourth* concerns the contribution of finance to other economic activities and its impact on the Common Good.

The ways in which decisions are made and in which individuals and institutions approach and assume their responsibilities, are the common thread in the above four avenues of research. Hence *Finance & Common Good* analyses the relationship between finance and common good in the perspective of responsibility.

## 2. The Responsibility of States, Investors and International Organisations

According to Claude Rochet,[10] economic performance and social cohesion can only be reconciled if society is thought and construed from the overall aim of enhancing the Common Good. In my sense, thinking and governing society is the shared responsibility of states, investors or managers, international organisations (therefore the individuals in these institutions) at certain levels.

### 3.1. States

In general, one of the main socio-economic responsibilities of the state is to promote and defend social justice. In particular, at the national and the international level, states have the responsibility of regulating the market. For Philippe Quéau of UNESCO, the market cannot regulate all. Issues like education, health, or social peace belong to the political domain.[11]

### 3.2. Investors

In the second section of the above-mentioned issue of the quarterly *Finance & The Common Good*,[12] entitled 'Using Investment and Capital Remuneration as Instruments to Serve the Common Good', Luca Pattaroni wrote an article on the topic of 'Responsabilités des investisseurs: Fondements, limites et formes'.[13] As most authors, Pattaroni mentions that responsibility includes legal and moral aspects. From this double reference he deducts two ways to conceptualise responsibility in the fields of investment: first what he calls 'negative screening', which is a rather limited way of assuming responsibility, in which being responsible means refraining from committing illegal or strikingly immoral acts, and second, responsibility based on concern for the vulnerable, through which it is acknowledged that the consequences of one's power require more sustained forms of commitment. This conception of responsibility presupposes constant supervision and vigilance, and it attempts to influence businesses' strategies and is based on a genuine concern for the weaker rather than on the mere quest for compromise between the motive of enhancing profit and the wish not to break the rules.

### 3.3. International Organisations

The international society as such is a virtual reality, nevertheless one cannot analyse national phenomena without taking into account the international environment and its actors. In the case of international financial institutions such as the IMF, Jacques Généreux rightly points out that, in order to foster international financial stability, coercive intervention with regard to the distribution of losses resulting from financial crises (e.g. measures to ensure that national governments comply with the rules) will only be possible if the international financial institutions enjoy a high degree of authority and political legitimacy.[14] For him, the international financial institutions will only enjoy political legitimacy if they have political executives who guide and supervise their technical executives. Correspondingly, Généreux's political argument can also be applied to other international organisations in their respective competencies (such as trade or labour organisations). What we can underline here is the importance of the political role and the responsibility of international organisations with regard to the realisation of the Common Good. In our opinion, NGOs bear the same responsibility, though they do not have the same power as intergovernmental organisations.

## 3. Value-Based Business for the Common Good

The Common Good is both a socio-political and an economic objective. In order to achieve this objective, business must be based on values. Progress should be measured not by 'whether we add more to the abundance of those who have much [but by] whether we provide enough for those who have too little.'[15] In the present mixed economy, moving towards this vision 'requires hard-headed examination of *values* and a careful assessment of the way in which processes such as supply and demand are actually working'. Values such as transparency, cooperative efforts, sustainability, freedom and equality can help to lead to a greater Common Good.

According to the values mentioned above, Herman E. Daly,[16] through his book *For the Common Good*, gives some fundaments on which these values are rooted and toward which economy has to be redirected. The challenge is to put together these values which seem to be sometimes contradictory or at least in tension with each other. The fact that the current epoch is characterised by 'opened economies'

(Claude Rochet) and the development of technologies, notably communication, raises hopes that it is possible to achieve a 'reconciled performance', i.e. a reconciliation between economic performance and
social cohesion. [17] Such a conception corresponds to an account of
social ethics that favours an ethics of mediation. The private and the
public interests, the personal and the common good has to be reconciled for a life in dignity and the survival of the planet. In the Fang culture, my own culture in Cameroon, the concept of *anyôs* [18] is a concept
of mediation which reconciles conflicts and community life. It has its
roots in family life, especially the resolution of conflicts among children of the same family. The question is how to make this concept
fruitful for economic and political relations in society, beyond families.
The society as the family can be considered as a body like the body of
a human being (as Paul, the Apostle, did it in the New Testament for
the Christian parish). The body is only healthy if it integrates the plurality of the different parts of the body to a harmonious unity. This is
the meaning of the Common Good as the benchmark for individuals,
states, the private sector and the international community.

NOTES

[1]   Shashkin, Pavel: 'Business Leadership and Social Responsibility in a Transition Country. A
     Russian Orthodox Perspective', in: Stückelberger, Christoph/Mugambi, J.N.K (eds), *Responsible
     Leadership. Global Perspectives*, Nairobi: Acton Publishers, 2005, pp. 111-117. See also Chapter 26
     in this volume.

[2]   Sachs, Jeffrey D., 'Business Leadership and Sustainable Development. A Perspective of Corpo-
     rate Social Responsibility', in: *op. cit.*, pp. 118-125. See also Chapter 23 in this volume.

[3]   In Cameroon today and according to the debt reduction conditions for economic boosting and
     social justice, the government and the International Financial Organisation together have
     responsibility for planning the governance of the states' enterprises, see Touna, Richard, 'Pour
     sauver le point d'achèvement. Le plan fétiche de Abah Abah', in: *Le Messager*, 11 August 2005.

[4]   See for example Stückelberger, Christoph, *Global Trade Ethics*, Geneva: WCC Publications,
     2002, esp. 6.8: Fair Trade, 6.18: Trade and human rights; Noll, Bernd, *Wirtschafts- und
     Unternehmensethik in der Marktwirtschaft*, Stuttgart: Kohlhammer, 2002.

[5]   Shashkin, Pavel, *op. cit.*, p. 113.

[6]   Concerning the question of the state's social responsibility, Amartya Sen, for instance, thinks
     that individual freedom is the main point of reference for the social responsibility of states. And
     Claude Rochet refers to the common good as the condition of individual freedom, therefore, one
     may conclude, the common good is part of the social responsibility of states.

[7]   For more details on this notion, see for example Höffe, Otfried, Art. 'Bien commun', in: *Petit
     Dictionnaire d'Ethique*, Paris: Cerf, 1993, 25f.

[8]   Before Pareto, Adam Smith thought that the general equilibrium as Common Good is a result
     of the invisible hand that conducts the economy.

[9]   See the 'Opening Editorial Statement', in: *Finance & Common Good* 6/7, 2001.

[10]  Rochet, Claude, *Gouverner par le bien commun*, Paris: Editions François-Xavier de Guibert, 2001.

[11]  Quéau, Philippe, 'Du Bien Commun mondial à l'âge de l'information', http://2100.org/
     conf_queau1.html (last accessed 2 August 2006), in particular the section on 'Le marché et l'in-
     térêt général: un besoin de régulation' (The market and the general interest: a need of
     regulation).

[12]  See note 9 above.

[13]  Engl.: Responsibilities of the Investors: Fundaments, limits and forms.

14   Généreux, Jacques, 'Principes politiques d'un système financier international au service du bien commun – quelques pistes de réflexion', in: *Finance and Common Good* 6/7, 2001.

15   Borsch, Frederick H., 'The Common Good and the Invisible Hand: Faith-Based Economy', in: *The Anglican Theological Review,* Winter 2005, www.anglicantheologicalreview.org/read/article_view.php?id = 352 (last accessed 2 August 2006). Frederick H. Borsch quotes Franklin Roosevelt who speaks about an *oikonomia* or economy of living together.

16   Daly, Herman E., *For the Common Good. Redirecting the Economy toward Community, the Environment, and a Sustainable Future,* Boston: Beacon Press, 1989.

17   Rochet, Claude, *Actualité du bien commun,* http://perso.orange.fr/claude.rochet/bc/Actu BC.PDF (last accessed 2 August 2006), p. 1.

18   See also Ondji'i Toung, Richard, 'Responsible Family Leadership. Traditional and Christian Approaches in Cameroon', in: Stückelberger, Christoph/Mugambi, J.N.K. (eds), *op. cit.,* pp. 46-58. See also Chapter 4 in this volume.

# PART IV
# RESPONSIBLE POLITICAL LEADERSHIP

# 30

# RESPONSIBLE POLITICAL LEADERSHIP

*Jephthah K. Gathaka, Kenya*

## Introduction

In this paper we intend to look at what constitutes responsible political leadership. We first explore the definitions so that we may be able to clearly state our conceptual perspective and reduce misunderstanding, considering that words mean different things and connote different ideas in different times and different contexts. What do we understand to be the meaning of politics, leadership and responsibility? It is my intention, after looking at the definitions, to discuss what I consider to be the essential *virtues* and *values* in political leadership for it to be regarded as responsible. It should be noted from the beginning that this is an issue of ethics, in which a diversity of perspectives and opinions is possible. In applied ethics, what some people may consider to be moral may not be accepted as such by others.

## 1. What is Politics?

According to Max Weber, 'politics is striving for a share of power or for influence on the distribution of power, whether it be between states or between the groups of people contained within a single state.'[1] Thus politics has to do with interests in the distribution, preservation or transfer of power as the decisive role in determining the decision defining the sphere of activity; anyone engaged in politics is striving for power, either power as means to attain other goals (which may be ideal or selfish), or power for its own sake, which is to say, in order to enjoy the feeling of prestige by power.'

In this discussion therefore, we will explore how leaders are expected to behave to demonstrate that they are responsibly striving not only in the distribution of power among the citizens and other leaders, but also in distributing resources equitably among the electorate.

## 2. What is Leadership?

In his book *Kenya African Nationalism*, Daniel Arap Moi (the former president of the Republic of Kenya), writes:

> ... leadership is the dynamic and catalytic ability of an individual or a group to liberate, engage and direct the constructive endeavours of a people for the betterment of individuals and/or whole communities, for their material prosperity and for their socio-cultural uplift, spiritual peace and mental productivity.[2]

He however warns that leadership can either be bought or sold, and emphasises that 'Responsive leadership must evolve from the people, by the people and for the people.'[3] Weber also warns rightly that leadership could be attained violently. For this reason we directly plunge to our subject and suggest that responsible leadership must live for the concern and the welfare of those being led. Leadership which is not mindful of the welfare of others is fake and mercenary. We will come back to this point later. At this juncture I wish to add a less complicated definition as we use it in civic education.

> Leadership refers to being in a position of responsibility. Leadership plays roles in terms of advice and decision making. It is about torch-bearing. Leadership involves being at the forefront and taking charge of events and issues arising from and touching on the leaders' area of jurisdiction. Most fundamentally, leadership is about service to the people. Leaders worth their salt consider themselves to be servants of the people they lead. Many leaders fail to realize this crucial fact. This failure has resulted in dictatorial leadership, with all its attendant misrule. The need for leadership arises from the fact that we need to be organised both as groups or societies for smooth interaction. Viewed within this context, leadership presupposes the existence of formal and informal rules which govern our interactions. In this case, leadership acts as the custodian of these rules as well as of common property. Leadership becomes the custodian of public good.[4]

## 3. What Do We Mean by 'Responsible'?

The *Oxford Advanced Learners' Dictionary* defines 'responsible' as:

> ... having the job or duty of doing something or taking care of somebody or something so that you may be blamed if something goes wrong... being able to be blamed for something... being the cause of something ... have to report to somebody/something with authority in a higher position and explain to them what you have done... (usually before noun) needing somebody who can be trusted and relied on involving important duties.

We shall therefore discuss along these lines as far as political leadership is concerned. However I have found another philosophical defiition which we cannot afford to dismiss. In a discussion paper entitled 'Existential Responsibility' – The Civic Virtue', Helmut Danner makes a distinction between 'juridical' 'and 'existential' responsibility. Though he is discussing this in the realm of education, he concludes: 'Depending on which kind of society we are referring to, responsibility will serve society best as "juridical responsibility" when it is a "closed society" and as "existential responsibility" when it is an "open, democratic society".'[5] In juridical responsibility, he argues, there is somebody who is judged by somebody else as having done right or wrong. Such a person is expected to act in a certain way. In this case Danner observes: 'A rule, a law, is the measure for judgement. Accordingly, the judgement will be: He/she fulfilled his/her responsibility or he/she failed.' He also calls this kind of responsibility 'accountability.' In what he calls 'existential responsibility' Danner explains that 'imputation does not function in the same way as in juridical responsibility' because it does not follow a certain pattern and one has to dig deeper to place the blame (or praise).

## 4. What Responsible Political Leadership Entails

Having dealt with the definitions we may now proceed to explain what responsible political leadership entails. Since norms and values may differ from place to place we will limit ourselves to what is commonly agreed and current in Kenya today.

a) Legitimacy: Any politically responsible leadership must be drawing its legitimacy from the people. Leadership that has come in power through violence for example, through a *coup d'etat*, will not bother to be responsible to anyone except itself while serving its own interests. An elected leadership is expected to be accountable and responsible to the electorate. Such leadership will always look at the promises it made to the voters during its election campaign and strive to fulfil those promises. This is because such leadership knows that after the set period, in our case after every five years, there will be another election and the leaders may be re-elected or rejected. It suffices to say that responsible political leadership can only succeed in a democratic environment. Since politics is about distribution of power and resources, responsible leadership will strive to ensure that this distribution is done equitably. The leadership which derives its legitimacy from the people, is organised through political parties. Unfortunately, as Professor Jesse Mugambi suggests, political parties have stolen leadership from the people. In many countries, he observes, democracy has evolved as government of political parties, for political parties and by political parties.[6] Thus political party leaders have organised their parties not as mass movements but as clubs controlled by the elite, without the mandate and legitimacy from the people they claim to represent.

b) Justice: The expectation of the Kenyan people as enshrined in the National Anthem is that 'Justice be our Shield and Defender'. This is what St. Paul had in mind when he was writing those verses in Romans chapter 13, which have been used to support oppressors when they invoke biblical authority. This passage, Romans 13:1-7, should be titled 'responsibilities of leaders and citizens in a state'. Verses 3 and 4 suggest that the responsibility of the rulers is to punish those who commit crime and to praise those who do good. This is what is called 'justice'. The quest for justice is what made St. Augustine retort:

> Remove justice, and what are kingdoms but gangs of criminals on a large scale? What are criminal gangs but petty kingdoms? A gang is a group of men under the command of a leader, bound by compact of association, in which the plunder is divided according to an agreed convention. [7]

I have quoted St. Augustine so that we can link his advice to what we have observed above in regard to political parties as far as equitable distribution of resources is concerned. The just distribution of resources is what we may call 'economic justice'. If the leadership will not exercise justice, then it has no business in being in power, and should be removed during the next elections. We do not have the time and space to explain fully what we would want the leadership to do in order to demonstrate that it has provided justice. However when the people see that those who are involved in corruption are not punished, they wonder what has happened with their rulers. When they witness leaders amassing wealth while the gap between the rich and the poor is widening, they cannot be convinced that there is justice.

c) Integrity: The *Oxford Advanced Learners' Dictionary* defines 'integrity' as 'the quality of being honest and having strong moral principles'. Former president Moi insists that 'Leaders will never win the confidence and co-operation of the masses, unless they live an upright life and unless the people see them to be leading that upright life'. [8] In this case, although this is not what many Kenyans would believe, he argues to have striven persistently and relentlessly to cleanse the country of corruption, moral turpitude, intellectual delinquency and cultural decay'. [9] He terms these as '… accurate symptoms of loveless greed and avarice'. He describes leaders who practise them as no more than hypocritical exhibitionists'. [10]

We fully agree with this statement, despite the manifest outcomes of his leadership of this country for 24 years when he was president. Leaders without integrity would not act responsibly and cannot lead any country to prosperity, as they will always be concerned about themselves.

d) Visionary Insight: Visionary leaders will be able to foresee the needs of the people they lead. They will then plan and mobilise resources in order to meet those needs. The Sessional Paper No.10 of 1965 on *African Socialism and its Application to Planning in Kenya* articulated a very clear vision for this country. The leaders spelt out what they envisaged for the Republic of Kenya, especially in the fight to eradicate the three problems facing this country up to now — poverty, disease and ignorance. After more than forty years of national sovereignty, the country is still plagued by those problems. The main reason is that we have never had visionary leaders. Such leaders would be like Nehemiah, that leader in the Old Testament who had a vision for reconstruction of the walls of Jerusalem. Professor Jesse Mugambi graphically summarises Nehemiah's visionary action thus: 'Nehemiah's approach is useful to the extent that he helps us to appreciate the relationship between prayer and planning; between work and worship; between despair and hope; between the elite and the ordinary people; between the priesthood and the laity'. [11] Leaders who are visionary will in no doubt be as responsible just as Nehemiah was.

e) Role Models: Responsible leaders would wish to be role models not only for the adults they are leading but also for the youth who are soon to take over from them. They must therefore set good examples. The responsibility of being role models goes hand in hand with moral probity. The conduct of leaders will greatly influence the behaviour of their followers and their youth. Since this is a matter of ethics we have to formulate the moral code that will guide us. Max Weber extensively discusses this point and outlines the core values that may be found in religion – whether it be Christianity or other religions of the world – which he calls, 'Ethics of Conviction'. [12] He further describes the 'Ethics of Responsibility,' which theologians could argue is provided for in 'general revelation'. Weber rightly concludes: '... the ethics of conviction and the ethics of responsibility are not absolute opposites. They are complementary to one another, and only in combination do they produce the true human being'. [13] It is important for us to appreciate the fact that in practice, we shall be guided by the virtues presupposed in our cultural and religious traditions and in the teachings of the missionary religions that we adhere to.

The values in these religions and in our cultural traditions do not differ much as far as political responsibility is concerned. For example, we know well that according to our traditions, our lives revolve around living as a community and therefore most of the resources should be distributed among and within the community. Though traditionally there were rich and poor people, the survival burden was shouldered by the community as a whole. The abnormal gap between the rich and the poor came with colonial domination and imperial rule. The insatiable greed among the leaders can never be a model to be followed. The conduct of some leaders in public has been far below the expectations of ordinary people. Some leaders are not ashamed to be captured by television cameras while quarrelling and fighting.

f) Stewardship: Responsible political leaders are expected to exercise proper stewardship or good management of resources. In this case we are concerned in matters of the environment. Responsible leaders should be in the forefront of protecting the forests and the wetlands of this country. Such a focus would be an indication that they are thinking about the future of the country. There seems not to be a policy on water harvesting. When the rains come all the waters flow to the lakes and the Indian Ocean. Yet later on we cry that there is no water. Stewardship and being visionary go hand in hand. Industries and infrastructure in this country are dilapidated because of bad management and lack of responsible political leadership, which could provide proper supervision in preservation and conservation of resources. Politics of patronage and nepotism have destroyed work ethics. The policy of merit and competence is no longer respected. Jobs and promotions tend to be given through patronage rather than on professional merit and competence. There are many qualified young people who cannot get employment because of tribalism, nepotism and corruption.

g) Succession: Political leadership that is responsible will train other leaders who will take over on expiry of mandatory and contractual terms. Moses prepared people like Joshua and Caleb. He involved them in leadership roles to prepare them for future responsibilities. It is only visionary leadership that would undertake such preparatory training. The youth of this country have been taken for granted for long. This is not consistent with our cultural and religious traditions, which always provided for succession in leadership.

h) Rewards and Awards: It is important to recognise those who are achievers in the country (heroes and heroines). However that has not been the case. We have many Kenyans who have excelled in various fields, in athletics and sports as well as in business. There are also those who fought for the national independence of the country. There are also those who struggled for political liberalisation. During the presidential awards and Head of State Commendations one finds that the high achievers are hardly ever recognised, while many are decorated whose integrity is doubted by ordinary citizens. Loyalty seems to be rated as more important than integrity, diligence and procuctivity.

i) Human Rights and Human Dignity: The protection, respect and promotion of human rights is an important responsibility for any political leadership that has been democratically elected. A country will be peaceful and prosperous whenever and wherever there is no discrimination. When the citizens are aware that their rights are respected they will also exercise their responsibilities such as paying taxes and obeying the just laws. It is therefore very important to inculcate an ethos of human rights among the people at all social levels. Institutions to enforce human rights should be developed and allowed to do their duties without any hindrance. The citizens should also be encouraged to form groups that will ensure that human rights are not violated. With commitment to human dignity, institutions of correction and remand should be subjected to strict scrutiny on how they treat the inmates. Where political leadership respects human rights there should be no discrimination of any kind. The rights of the minorities should be respected in order for democracy to thrive. Peace is guaranteed when all people consider each other as equal partners in national endeavours. Ethnicity that has destroyed the unity of our country will not have room where human rights are respected. Responsible leadership should respect the international conventions and protocols on human rights. In these ways political leaders can win the confidence of the electorate to whom they are accountable.

## 5. The Future of Responsible Political Leadership

Here we need to discuss how to guarantee responsible political leadership in Kenya. What are those things that we need to do as citizens and as leaders? First, we need to advocate for discussions in various fora where people thrush out what they expect from their leaders. Second, we also advocate for seminars for leaders of all cadres. When people have been elected to various positions it is important to have seminars to discuss their role in the positions to which they have been elected. Many councillors, for example, do not understand their work. Many are semi-illiterate. Third, there should be programs to train the youth for leadership. Responsibilities should be delegated to them. The current constitution has contributed to the election of irresponsible leadership in this country. Wherever the constitution makes provision for elective leadership, it demands qualifications and not qualities. It is gratifying to note that the proposed Draft Constitution has provided two chapters on responsibility, one for the citizens (chapter 4 section 23), and the for leaders (chapter 9). In these sections there are provisions for what are considered to be responsibilities for citizens and leaders.

*The responsibilities of a citizen include:*

'23(1) In order to fulfil the national values, principles and goals, all citizens have the responsibility to:

a) acquire basic understanding of the provisions of this constitution and promote its ideas and objectives

b) uphold and defend this constitution and the law

c) vote and become involved in other forms of political participation

d) engage in work, including home making, for the support and welfare of themselves and their families, for the common good and to contribute to national development

e) develop the ability to the greatest possible extent through acquisition of knowledge, continuous learning and the development of skills

f) contribute to the welfare and advancement of the community where they live

g) contribute to the welfare and advancement of the nation by paying all taxes lawfully due

h) strive to foster national unity and live in harmony with others

i) promote democracy, good governance and the rule of law

j) promote family life and act responsibly in the context of the family

k) protect and safeguard public property from waste and misuse

l) protect the environment and conserve natural resources

m) co-operate with law enforcement agencies for the maintenance of law and order

n) desist from acts of corruption and

o) understand and enhance the Republic's place in the international community'

*Responsibilities of leadership include:*

'94(1) Any sovereign authority of the people assigned to a State office –

a) is a public trust to be exercised in a manner that –

    i. is consistent with the purpose and objects of this Constitution;

    ii. demonstrates respect for the people;

    iii. brings honour to the nation and dignity to the office; and

    iv. promotes public confidence in the integrity of the office; and

b)   vests in that State officer the responsibility to serve the people, rather than the power to rule them.'

*The guiding principles of leadership and integrity include:*

a)   selection on the basis of integrity, competence and suitability, or election in free and fair elections

b)   objectivity and impartiality in decision making and in ensuring that decisions are not influenced by nepotism, favouritism or other improper motives

c)   selfless service based solely on the public interest, demonstrated by –

    i. honesty in the execution of public duties; and

    ii. the declaration of personal interest that may conflict with public duties

d)   accountability to the public for decisions and actions

e)   discipline and commitment in service to the people'

It can therefore be seen that despite other contentious provisions of the Draft Constitution, Kenyans already have expressed how they can conduct themselves responsibly and what they expect from their leaders with regard to responsibility and accountability.

## Conclusion

In the foregoing discussion we have established that responsible political leadership should be a concern not only of the leaders, but of all citizens — both the leaders and the led. It is from the led that the leadership gets their legitimacy and to whom they are accountable. Responsible leadership can only be practised and checked only in a democratic environment. It is therefore of paramount importance to have a vibrant citizenry able to monitor the performance of their leaders. The citizens should strive to zealously exercise, demand and protect their rights. At the same time, political leaders should endeavour to know what their citizens expect from them. They should always consider the welfare of citizens as their priority while in elective positions. We have also observed that responsibility is a moral issue and therefore we should revisit the question of what we consider to be our core values. These values are to be found in our cultural traditions and religious beliefs. National laws may not successfully inculcate a discipline, unless they are consistent with, and reinforced by cultural and religious values. As statutes, laws can only be punitive and correctional.

NOTES

1    Weber, Max, *Political Writings*, edited by Peter Lassman and Ronald Speirs, Cambridge: Cambridge University Press, 1994, p. 311.

2    Moi, D.T., *Kenya African Nationalism: Nyayo Phyilosophy and Principles*, Nairobi: Macmillan Publishers, 1986, p. 97.

3    *Ibidem.*

4    Center for Law and Research International (CLARION), *We Are the Government*, Constitutional debate no. 3, Nairobi: Claripress, 1996, p. 90.

5    Danner, Helmut, 'Existential Responsibility – The Civic Virtue', in: *Studies in Philosophy and Education* 17, December 1998, Dordrecht: Kluwer Academic Publishers, p. 261.

6    Mugambi, J.N.K., *Christian Theology and Social Reconstruction*, Nairobi: Acton Publishers, 2003, p. 42.

7    Bettenson, Henri (transl.), *St. Augustine: Concerning The City of God Against the Pagans*, London: Penguin, 1984, p. 139.

8    Moi, D.T., *op. cit.*, p. 25.

9    *Ibidem.*

10   *Ibid.*

11   Mugambi, J.N.K., *op. cit.*, p. 76.

12   Weber, Max, *op. cit.*, p. 361.

13   *Ibidem*, p. 368.

# 31

## POLITICS OF RESPONSIBILITY
## AND RESPONSIBILITY OF POLITICS.
## A PERSPECTIVE OF POLITICAL ETHICS
## ON PRESIDENTIAL ELECTION IN THE USA

*Heidi Hadsell, USA*

### Introduction

The evident influence of moral values on political decision making, made moral values the big winners in the 2004 American presidential election. Based both on the different styles of the two campaigns, and on the election polls the day of the election, in which many voters indicated that they had voted for George Bush because of his 'moral values', values have rapidly become a dominant political theme. Many political pundits are convinced that George Bush won the election at least in part because he openly declared his own religious beliefs and the moral values he connected to them, while Kerry was more hesitant to do so, and when he did, he did so with more subtlety and nuance. Conservative Christians across the country are ready to cash in on the political influence of conservative Christian values, and thus on the power of conservative Christian leaders, and to translate them into political power to help shape public policy.

So prevalent is the theme of moral values in this post election analysis, it tends to eclipse the fact that whether they be self-interested or altruistic, foolish or wise, straight forward or hidden, values have always been at the heart of the political process. Similarly eclipsed is the fact that not just conservative Christians voted their values, but so too did Jews, Muslims, atheists, people of other religions, and more liberal Christians. Once one recognises that everyone votes his or her values in one way or another, one can see that this election among many other things, demonstrates a genuine divide within the Christian community. There is in fact, a struggle about the meaning of Christianity going on inside Christianity. It is a struggle which often finds political liberals and Christian liberals on one side and political conservatives and Christian conservatives on the other. It is a dynamic that can be seen not simply in public life, but inside many Christian denominations, in the United States and around the world.

## 1. Ethics of Conviction against Ethics of Responsibility

A lot can be and had been said about this struggle. Both sides view themselves as authentic carriers and interpreters of the core of Christianity, and both can point to scripture and tradition to legitimate their moral positions. My purpose here in not to explore this question. Rather I intend to explore another division within Christianity, and indeed within many religions, which has already been, and promises to continue to be at least as decisive and important in the formation of American public policy and foreign policy as that between conservative and liberal Christians. This is a division that was also in evidence in this presidential campaign, and which also divided votes. To put it in the words of the 19th century sociologist Max Weber, this is the division between an ethics of conviction *(Gesinnungsethik)* and an ethics of responsibility *(Verantwortungsethik)*. Julian Freund described Weber's two ethical types in a helpful summary:

> Let us take the famous distinction which Weber made between the ethic of conviction and the ethic of responsibility. One who acts according to the former wants the absolute victory of a cause, without concern for the circumstances and the situation or for the consequences. This is the case of one who applies rigorously the receipts of the Sermon on the Mount, who offers the left cheek when struck on the right one, and who, consequently, refuses to resist even that which he considers evil. Inversely, one who acts according to the ethic of responsibility evaluates the available means, takes the situation into account, makes calculations with inevitable human failings, and considers the possible consequences. Thus, he assumes responsibility for the means, the shortcomings, and the foreseeable consequences, baneful or not. [1]

The ethics of conviction is often greatly admired. Groups, nations, peoples, celebrate especially those of their heroes who take a stand according to their moral convictions. Heroes who, acting regardless of the circumstances and regardless of the consequences, are often greatly revered and remembered, as attested to through song, poetry, holidays and the like, perhaps especially when their convictions lead them to pay the ultimate price. In contrast, an ethic of responsibility, with its awareness of and its careful calculation not just of the moral principles at stake, but of the consequences their application may or may not have in the world, is less immediately or easily viewed as admirable. Indeed an ethics of responsibility often fails to ignite the moral imagination, since it often seems too mushy, too shaded with gray, too morally ambiguous.

Those voters who identified moral values as the primary motivation for the way they voted in the presidential elections, are people who are attempting to do the right moral thing, often according to an ethic of conviction. Who can blame them – we live in an age in which moral certainty is a welcome relief from constant change, fear, conflict and war, and a helpful guide to people who genuinely seek to do the right thing. These voters who follow or advocate for an ethic of conviction do so not spontaneously or accidentally, but because they have learned to do so. They listen to and learn from the articulation of such an ethic of conviction put forth by religious leaders who persuade them that this ethic is the morally correct path to follow. Inevitably, political leaders, who share their moral values, draw upon and appeal to a shared ethic. In doing so the political leaders implicitly or explicitly promise to lead according to this ethic of conviction once they are elected. They promise, in other words, to make political and policy decisions not just on the moral values shared, but also according to an ethics which as described above, gives little thought to consequences or to the complexities of the political world.

## 2.  Dangerous, Simplistic, Inadequate

However admirable such an ethic of conviction may seem, and however psychologically satisfying it may feel, an ethic of conviction – regardless of who articulates it (left or right) and what its content is – is unsuited to the political leadership of nations, particularly the most powerful nation on earth. It is unsuited for political decision making because it is quite literally irresponsible – it does not take the consequences of its acts into consideration, or as part of its calculation.

The nature of contemporary life and politics demonstrates why an ethics of conviction is inappropriate and even dangerous for political leadership. Complexity and plurality characterise societies like the United States. An ethic of conviction, whether it be centered on opposition to abortion, stem cell research, or gay marriage to name several moral issues that generate considerable heat, is simply not adequate to deal with these issues as they are played out in a very complex and plural society.

An ethics of conviction, again however satisfying it may feel to its adherents, is woefully inadequate to a world grown ever more interdependent. In this world leadership such as that held by the United States by virtue of its vast military and economic power, requires the political ability to do something more than simply declare and follow an ethic of conviction, letting the chips fall where they may. Leadership requires the ability to listen, to compromise, to adjust competing interests, to think through and understand the many consequences of possible actions. One cannot assert effective and fair leadership by simple conviction, leading others to pick up the pieces, in areas such as international trade, environmental questions, economic development, immigration, terrorism, nuclear proliferation, and the like. All such issues require multi-lateral cooperation and decision making. The lopsided power held by the United States today makes leadership according to an ethic of responsibility an urgent necessity. This is of course what European allies and others have sought to make the United States understand in recent years.

Perhaps the most disturbing and dangerous, and also one of the most attractive attributes that accompanies an ethic of conviction in public life is the certainty that moral conviction imparts. At a dinner table such conviction may simply be unpleasant company. At a negotiating table it may do lasting and serious damage. If one is simply sure that one is right, one need not think about consequences, complexity or the position of others. Worse yet, one need not question whether or not one's own convictions are morally correct or practically tenable. An ethic of conviction is therefore especially vulnerable to hypocrisy, since the strength of one's convictions leads one towards blindness regarding the possible equivocation of one's own position, while at the same time encouraging one to attribute all error and evil to one's adversaries. This dynamic is all too familiar in the post 9/11 world in which each side demands an ethic of responsibility from its enemy while it itself embodies an irresponsible and dangerous ethic of conviction.

The Christian theological ethicist Reinhold Niebuhr was a careful observer of the political world. His moral and political analysis gave him a healthy respect for the power of hypocrisy in politics. He therefore viewed political ethics as necessarily quite distinct from personal ethics, just as Weber viewed an ethics of conviction as distinct from an ethics of responsibility. Because of the difference between the personal and the political arenas, and because of the propensity of groups to fool themselves as to the nobility of their cause through self-serving hypocrisy, Niebuhr strongly criticised what he viewed as the idealistic attempt to transport personal ethics into the political arena: 'What is lacking among all these moralists, whether religious or rational, is an understanding of the brutal character of the behaviour of all human collectives, and the power of self-interest and collective egoism in all intergroup relations'.[2]

## 3. Moral Obligations of Citizens

It is not surprising but disturbing that a party and a president imbued with the fire and the power of their own ethic of conviction, find and build on the echoes and the energy of such an ethic in the American population. It is disturbing because what the American citizen requires from its political leadership, Republican or Democrat, left, right, or center, is not the uncritical confirmation of an ethic of conviction applied in the political arena, but rather careful explanation, education, and debate, which encourage citizens to see the fundamental differences between a private ethic of conviction and a public ethic of responsibility; which enable citizens to comprehend and to evaluate an ethic intended for the political arena, adequate both to the political questions internal to the United States, and to its position of leadership in the world. An ethic of responsibility requires not that our politicians confirm and amplify our prejudices and private moral convictions, but that they challenge us to think and act beyond them.

The absence of this kind of challenge to the voters, and the absence of the exercise of this kind of pedagogical role in relation to the voters, on the part of many contemporary American politicians amounts to the abdication of one of the most important roles of responsible political leadership. One result is a relatively passive, self-satisfied, and often ignorant population which allows its leaders to engage the country internally and externally in actions which have grave consequences no one has thought carefully about and for which, when disaster and tragedy is evident, no one takes responsibility.

In this context one helpful role of Christian religious leadership would be, along the lines of Reinhold Niebuhr, the education of Christian individuals and congregations regarding the complexities and ambiguities of morality in the political arena. The effort should be not to confirm certainties nor to scare people away from the public arena, but rather to soberly educate as to the global as well as national responsibilities of the United States, and thus the moral obligation of citizens to engage the issues, to think about the consequences of any position and to demand from political leadership that it do likewise.

NOTES

[1]   Freund, Julien, 'German Sociology in the Time of Max Weber', in: Bottomore, Tom/Nisbet, Robert (eds), *A History of Sociological Analysis*, New York: Basic Books, Inc., 1978, p. 181.

[2]   Niebuhr, Reinhold, *Moral Man and Immoral Society. A Study in Ethics and Politics*, New York: Charles Scribner's Sons, 1932, *passim*.

# 32

# POLITICAL LEADERSHIP IN LATIN AMERICA.
# A CHRISTIAN PERSPECTIVE

*Paulo Fernando Carneiro de Andrade, Brazil*

## 1. Faith and Politics [1]

Throughout history men and women have built different societies by means of a broad range of actions, collective and individual, public and private, with a specific intentionality or not. Among these actions is political action, which is the group of human acts that have a public dimension and that relate to society's power structures. It must be observed, however, that political actions are not all the same. Militancy in syndical and neighbourhood movements as well as movements of citizenship action, voting or taking part in a political party and running for elective offices are all political actions. In this last case, there is party politics, which is a specific kind of political action in which people and social groups, articulated in political parties, create and try to implement projects for administrating the State and organising society, and also offer to represent the interests of various social sectors and classes, running for elective legislative and executive functions. [2]

Today the political-party dimension of political action is, in Western democratic societies, indispensable, although it has clearly defined limits. The strengthening of other dimensions of political action also becomes necessary to express the needs of the various social groups and to allow these groups to intervene in the administration of public matter, without having either a global project for the organisation of the State, or even the direct responsibility for its administration. In this sense, so-called popular movements, non-governmental organisations, non-party citizenship movements and campaigns are of great importance. However, these other dimensions of political action cannot, in the present model of State and society, replace party political action. Even though we can criticise the limitations of political parties' representation and underline the defects of contemporary party politics, present democracies have as their basis party political action, such that its suppression would imply today, inevitably, the imposition of authoritarianism or totalitarianism.

Nevertheless, it must be observed that we cannot exclude the possibility of, in the future, perfecting the democratic processes leading to other kinds of State constitution, in which party politics as we know it today is overcome *(Aufhebung).*[3]

Although it may seem strange, it was only recently in the history of Christianity, that is, just less than a hundred years ago, that the legitimacy of the articulation between faith and politics was questioned. For centuries it seemed so natural for Christians that their faith had a social and political dimension that nobody questioned the pertinence of this relationship, but only the way in which this articulation should take place. It was rationalism and liberalism that decreed the radical separation of the two spheres, reducing religion to the private sphere and disarticulating what should always be articulated. Thus, this created either a faith without efficacy, restricted to the level of private practices, or an ingenuous faith, used so many times for political purposes and subordinated to them. This same way, a politics disconnected from the Transcendent and from ethical values was also created, many times making power only something to be conquered and to be used in one's own benefit or in the benefit of a small group and not for the common good. It must be observed that in a politics detached from ethical values the very notion of Common Good becomes ambiguous. If we affirm, in the one hand, the legitimacy of the articulation between faith and politics, on the other hand we must recognise that in the last decades, however, a new and alarming phenomenon has taken place in the relationship between faith and politics. That phenomenon is the relationship between a specific way of experiencing faith, which has been referred to as religious fundamentalism, and the politics which has taken place not only among Christians, but also among Muslims and Jews, crossing different nations and continents, has also been referred to as religious fundamentalism.[4]

## 2. Fundamentalism and Perversion in Politics

Here it becomes necessary to make an interpretive analysis of the contemporary fundamentalism phenomenon. In order to do that, we will use some concepts from Lacanian analysis applied to culture as approached by Slavoj Žižek.[5] We try to understand fundamentalism from the point of view of the different structural positions that the subject can occupy *in* the Symbolic Order and *in face of* it. The first position, called hysterical,[6] is characterised by the question the subject asks the Big Other (the Symbolic Order): 'What am I in the eyes of the Other? What does the Other want from me?' The subject structurally takes the position of a question; there is a distance and a displacement, a background uncertainty that asks the Other the following question over and over again: *'Che Vuoi?'* This question never finds a definitive answer and allows the subject to become, in his autonomy and his otherness, an incomplete and craving subject, always searching for something that is missing; a being made not of certainty, but of doubt.[7] The second position, called psychotic, can be characterised by the vanishing of the question: an answer appears where the question is not even made. The subject is subsumed, invaded by the Big Other. The Other speaks in him, the distance disappears, as does the distinction between him and the Other, and consequently the subject looses his autonomy. The Big Other acquires a consistency and a density that inscribes him in the sphere of the Real. In this case, the symbolic efficiency gives place to the material and direct efficiency of the word.[8] The third structural position is the one that corresponds to perversion. In it, the question is displaced to the Other. The subject has the answer to the question he imposes on the Other. He does not recognise himself as being summoned by the Symbolic Order, nor summons it with a question, but with an answer that creates the question in the Other. The subject puts himself ambivalently in two places: in the position of being an instrument for the enjoyment *(jouissance)* of the Other, that is, he recognises the Symbolic Law, putting himself in an instrumental position in face of it, and simultaneously refuses to recognise the Symbolic Law, denying its symbolic efficiency and putting himself in the position of the Law.[9]

In the religious sphere, when the subject puts himself structurally in face of the Sacred in one of the two last positions, we have what we call fundamentalism. The second position, called psychotic, gives place to a kind of fundamentalism usually labelled, in an accusatory and disqualifying tone, as fanaticism. In it, the subject looses distance from the Sacred and is absorbed by it. The Word makes him a prisoner, he is the Word itself; message and messenger become one. Maybe we can say that this position was more common in Pre-Modernity. In the third position, called perverse, and maybe the one that best qualifies what has been called today as fundamentalism, the subject puts himself simultaneously as the one who should give the Other what he knows that the Other needs and as the founder of the very Sacred. In F. Dostoevsky's *The Brothers Karamazov* the parable of the Grand Inquisitor, the story within the story, exemplifies this type of fundamentalism.[10] The scene takes place in sixteenth-century Seville. In the morning following a spectacular public religious ceremony in which a hundred heretics were burnt alive, a smooth walking man appears without making himself noticed, until he is suddenly recognised by everyone. He silently blesses the crowd that surrounds him. When asked, he cures a blind man, resuscitates a child. In that moment, the Grand Inquisitor passes by, observes what is happening, and demands the soldiers to arrest that man who was, in that moment, the centre of attention. At night the old inquisitor visits the prisoner in jail. He summons and censors him: 'Is it Thou? Thou?' but receiving no answer, he adds at once. 'Don't answer, be silent. What canst Thou say, indeed? I know too well what Thou wouldst say. And Thou hast no right to add anything to what Thou hadst said of old. Why, then, art Thou come to hinder us? For Thou hast come to hinder us, and Thou knowest that. But dost thou know what will be to-morrow? I know not who Thou art and care not to know whether it is Thou or only a semblance of Him, but to-morrow I shall condemn Thee and burn Thee at the stake as the worst of heretics. And the very people who have to-day kissed Thy feet, to-morrow at the faintest sign from me will rush to heap up the embers of Thy fire…'[11] In face of the prisoner's silence he prides himself on making men happy taking away their freedom. He condemns the prisoner for, during the temptation in the desert, to not deprive men and women of their freedom, having refused to give humanity what it truly longs for: the bread, the safeness of material wealth, and the governing from someone who decides for his subjects, freeing them from the burden of choice. Men are 'weak and vile'. What they need and long for is not freedom. Thus, he argues: 'We have corrected Thy work and have founded it upon miracle, mystery and authority. And men rejoiced that they were again led like sheep, and that the terrible gift that had brought them such suffering, was, at last, lifted from their hearts. Were we right teaching them this? Speak! Did we not love mankind, so meekly acknowledging their feebleness, lovingly lightening their burden, and permitting their weak nature even sin with our sanction? Why hast Thou come now to hinder us?'[12]

Osama Bin Laden's Al-Qaeda offers a contemporary Islamic version of this fundamentalist position. Its terrorist acts apparently do not have a purpose nor demand anything. The same way, its interpretation of Islam does not follow explicitly any of the great schools or traditional spiritual masters. Bin Laden is moved by a superegoic categorical imperative: he must give the Other what the Other searches but does not have, and will not be able to have, except by means of this one subject who has, and only he has, the power to satisfy him. Death, pain and terror inflicted to the Other are, even more than punishment, an answer to what the subject in this structural position 'knows' that the Other desires, needs, craves. The answer is what raises the question.

We can perceive this same structural position in some neo-pentecostalist manifestations and in certain Christian groups that give political support to the Republican Party in the United States.[13] The claim made by Tom DeLay, former Republican majority leader in the American House of Representatives, being himself considered a fundamentalist in North America, expresses this position: 'Only Christianity offers a lifestyle that relates to the realities we find in the world – only

Christianity!'[14] In this speech there is no place for any kind of difference, nor for dialogue, nor for the recognition of the Other in a perspective of otherness. Only Christianity, as interpreted by the one who gives the speech, can respond to the needs of the Other. It is an answer given before the question. The subject knows something about the Other, even if the Other does know it yet, and this subject must give something to the Other, for his own happiness. When this kind of fundamentalist faith is related to politics, this last one becomes a mere instrument for the imposition of the truth about the Other on the Other, this truth being carried by the fundamentalist subject.

In a secular manner, we have the same kind of structure when a political party, even without any religious inspiration, judges itself the only interpreter of the people or of popular aspirations. Or yet, when political leaders put themselves in the position of being the only carriers of a knowledge and of a competence that makes them the only ones capable of deciding wisely and justly the matters of public interest. No critiques can be made, no dissonant voices can arise or, even worse, be accepted. The only sentence, repeated as a mantra, is: 'Trust me'.

In contrast to these two structural positions that represent two possible forms of fundamentalism, there is the first one, in which the subject recognises the Symbolic Order without being neither subsumed by it nor becoming an instrument. In religious terms it is this position that allows us to keep creatural distance, maintaining, may it be the absolute and totally Other character of the Sacred, or human autonomy founded in the free and gratuitous gift of freedom. This position unfolds in a spirituality which we recognise as being authentically Christian, and which includes a continuous search to perceive the will of the Creator in each moment of history. The question about what God wants from us *(Che Vuoi?)* in this given moment, a question which we always pose and to which we return unceasingly, always demands from us a double look: one on the Revelation and one on the reality in which we want to perceive the answer to be given to God's questioning.

If we want to articulate faith and political action it becomes necessary, in this perspective, to maintain this double look. On the one hand the theological look on the Scriptures and on Tradition, in which and through which the Word of the Living God is passed on to us. On the other hand, the look from Social and Human Sciences, which allow us to understand the world more deeply.

## 3. Political Leadership in a Christian Perspective

Thus, in a non-fundamentalist Christian perspective, an appropriate Christian formation for political action should not only look at

the Scriptures and Tradition, but also at the sociological, historical, and philosophical studies as well as the political and juridical
sciences that allow a more profound approach to the reality in which
one acts.

As for the theological aspects, throughout its history Christianity
established a long social teaching tradition, through which it tried to
perceive the Gospel's values and principles that have social occurrence.
The central nucleus of Christian Social Ethics lies in the evangelical
preference for the poor. This is the basic criterion from which the
other criteria and values present in the great Christian social tradition
shall be ordained. Far from being discriminatory in relation to other
social groups, it makes us see Christ in the poor and clamours us all to
take on the cause of the poor as if it was our own, making it real in the
promotion of justice (Matt 25:31-46; Luke 10:29-37; Luke 12:33-34).

God's preferential love for the poor does not base itself upon a
merit of the poor, but it obeys the logic of gratuity and necessity.
According to the Scriptures, God loves them preferentially because
they are needy (Luke 15:1-24). In the 1960s various ecclesiastical sectors, especially religious men and women, created a movement for
coming closer to the poor all over Latin America. Many times, this
movement demanded that they shared the same living and working
conditions of the poor, leading them to search for theoretical instruments that could explain the causes of poverty in our continent. The
contact experience with the real poor, experiencing their real living
conditions, coming close to them, as did the Samaritan who came
close to the man who had been a victim of outlaws on the road and
was injured and exhausted (Luke 10:29-37), made the more traditional explanations about the cause of poverty (backwardness, ignorance, indolence) become unreasonable.

In contrast, the critical interpretations of Latin American poverty,
proposed either by the Dependency theories or by Marxist sociology,
started to be more accepted as being more plausible in face of what
was experienced. The poor began to be understood as marginalised
and, above all, exploited and oppressed. Theology and pastoral practice now have as their central matter how to spread and live the
Gospel in a continent where men and women are exploited and
despoiled. When we reject the traditional explanations about the
cause of poverty we also change our relation with the poor, who are
not understood as ignorant or indolent anymore and go from being
the object of social action to being the subject of political transformation. In this context it became clear that economic oppression maintained by political domination was the causer of poverty, which
demanded solidarity and engagement in liberation practices. The
effort for development was not enough; it was necessary to overcome
the unjust structures that oppress the poor.

If on the one hand we can claim that the preference for the poor is a constant in Christian tradition,[15] on the other hand we should underline how peculiarly this preference was updated in Latin America. The new point was, as we have already stressed, the change in perspective that transforms the poor into the subject of the story and proposes another look: to see the world with the eyes of the poor. It should be observed that, in a first moment, in the Latin American pastoral context the poor were identified originally with low income rural and urban workers. This concept was enriched over the years, either by a more complex analysis of the oppression mechanisms, or by the recognition of other forms of domination, such as the sexist and the ethnic-racial, causers of other realities in need of liberation.

A new sensibility in relation to the so-called 'marginalised' was also created. This originates a broader concept of 'poor', which includes various groups with their different necessities and demands. Because of that, it becomes more complex to think of an alternative to the present society, making simplified images of an ideal society fall flat. In part, this need for making the matter more complex, together with the crisis of the real socialism, provoked a rupture in utopian thinking, leading many agents to enter profound subjectivity crises. The reconstruction of the utopian horizon presents itself as a great challenge: is it still plausible to think of a global alternative society project? In what terms? In this new society, what would be the role of market and property? How will this change from our society to an alternative one take place? Today we have fewer answers to all these questions than we did yesterday, which does not mean, however, that the past fights have been pointless nor that we are still not convinced that it is possible to organise a society in a more just and fraternal way.

We must understand the Christian social tradition from this fundamental hermeneutic-theological point of view, characterised by the evangelical preference for the poor. In this social tradition we must identify dynamic aspects and a nucleus of constant, irradiating teachings. Among the more constant teachings we can underline the following ones:

- the dignity of the human being;
- human rights;
- the relationship person-society, in which society is seen as something that exists only in socially united people and for their service;
- the Common Good;
- solidarity and subsidising as regulating principles of social life;
- conceiving social life as organic;
- the right and the obligation of responsible participation in social life;

- the right to freedom; and
- universal destination for the goods of the earth.

The permanent values present in this Tradition are: *truth, freedom, justice, solidarity, peace, and charity or Christian love.* We must observe that this nucleus of principles and values is considered permanent, especially because of its greater centrality in Christian Social Teaching. However, it also presents a not-always linear historic development. We can analogically apply to this nucleus the same hermeneutic method proposed by J. Alfaro, in a Catholic scope, for the interpretation of dogma.[16] According to the model proposed by J. Alfaro,[17] we should try to understand this central nucleus in a *retrospective* perspective – to search for the signification and the delimitation of the proclaimed truths since their pre-history –, in an *introspective* one – insertion of the affirmations, criteria and values presented in the hierarchy of the revealed truths bearing in mind the salvation of men and women and of all the Creation – and in a *prospective* one – an always renewed comprehension of this content, so that it can be vitally and constantly assimilated in a given moment and in a given culture.

In political and social grounds, the task of perceiving the correct Christian action in a precise historical context (prospective perspective) can only be achieved if the double look is maintained: one on the Scriptures and Tradition, and one on reality. Revealed texts give us a set of criteria and values that, however, can only be historically efficient as long as they highlight concrete options and practices among the possible ones in a given historical context. Thus, the political formation of Christian militants must include theological aspects but also technical ones, which allow the political agents to recognise the possible options and practices in their context, as well as the presumable consequences of their actions. In this way only can we make real political action that, being Christian, is a true contribution to the construction of a more fraternal world, in accordance with God's love for His creation.

A political pastoral formation must count on a wide variety of actions and instruments. It must be locally organised but regionally and internationally articulated. The creation of local schools of political formation can prove to be an important experience that permits the formation of a specialised group that can produce documents and processes of permanent formation and instruments of pastoral action for the strong moments of electoral times. The capillarity of the communities allows us to think of a process of permanent formation that having the poor as a subject is not a formation for the other, but a formation with the other. Latin American Christian churches' decades of experience in popular education originated many methods and a vast capital of knowledge of how to proceed to a formational process that permits the person to be the subject of his own formation and that the formational process takes place in strong articulation with the subject's practice.

If on the one hand we can underline the need for permanent and systematic formation aimed at everyone, it is not less important, at these schools, to think about the formation of a body of popular pastoral agents who can assume leadership positions in the political formation process and in political action itself. However, together with political formation, it is necessary to create an Assistance Pastoral for the ones who are engaged in the party political process. In not a few cases Christian militants complain that they feel abandoned by their communities and their pastors.

Permanent political formation is, by means of an appropriate ecclesial action that includes assistance to militants directly engaged in the political process, the best contribution that the Christian churches can give, be it for the overcoming of neo-fundamentalism, which can cause so much damage to society, be it to contribute for the construction of a more just society that is more in accordance with evangelical values, which are not exclusive of the Christian, but are values that correspond to what is most central and intimate in the human being and in all Creation.

NOTES

[1]  See Andrade, P., *A participação política dos cristãos. Critérios teológico-pastorais* in REB 54 (215), pp. 629-642. This first article was later incorporated in: *Texto Base da Campanha da Fraternidade da Conferência Nacional dos Bispos do Brasil (CNBB) de 1996: Justiça e Paz se Abraçarão*.

[2]  See Bobbio, N., *Teoria geral da política. A Filosofia Política e as lições dos Clássicos* (M. Bovero (ed.)), Rio de Janeiro: Campus, 2000.

[3]  Bobbio, N., *Il Futuro della democrazia*, Turin: Einaudi, 1984; Bauman, Z., *Em busca da Política*, Rio de Janeiro: Jorge Zahar Editor, 1999.

[4]  Safran, W. (ed.), *The Secular and the Sacred. Nation, Religion and Politics*, London: Frank Cass Publishers, 2003; Jelen, T./Wilcox, C. (eds), *Religion and Politics in Comparative Perspective. The One, the Few, and the Many*, Cambridge: Cambridge University Press, 2002; Brasil Carvalho da Fonseca, A., 'Enfrentando o Mal aqui fora. A Igreja Universal do Reino de Deus e sua prática política', in: Caminhos 1 (2), 2003, pp. 11-32; Silveira Campos, L., 'O Bem e o Mal nas representações de Novos Pentecostais Brasileiros quanto à economia, in: *Caminhos* 1 (2), 2003, pp. 33-68.

[5]  Of the vast work of Slavoj Žižek we make reference here especially to the books: *The Metastases of Enjoyment. Six Essays on Woman and Causality*, New York: Verso, 1994; *The Ticklist Subject. The Absent Centre of Political Ontology*, New York: Verso, 1999; *Il Grande Altro. Nazionalismo, godimento, cultura di massa* (M. Senaldi (ed.)), Milan: Feltrinelli, 1999; *The Fragile Absolute. Or, Why is the Christian Legacy Worth Fighting For?*, New York: Verso, 2000; *Il godimento como fattore político*, Milan: Raffaello Cortina Editore, 2001; *On belief*, New York: Routledge, 2001; *Tredice volte Lenin. Per sovvertire il fallimento del presente*, Milan: Feltrinelli, 2003. *Bem vindo ao Deserto do Real*, São Paulo: Boitempo, 2003.

[6]  It is important here to distinguish between the structural position of the subject in face of the Symbolic Order and the 'personality' of concrete individuals. This distinction must be understood in a way similar to the widely known distinction between *person* and *individual* in the Social Anthropology field (see Mauss, M., 'Uma categoria do Espírito Humano: a noção de pessoa e a de "eu"', in: Mauss, M., *Sociologia e Antropologia*, São Paulo: Cosac & Naify, 2003,

pp. 369-397). What is claimed in these pages about the possible structural positions of the subject in face of the Symbolic Order and the discourses and practices that are created when one occupies such positions does not allow us, without any more information, to characterise the concrete individuals who, in a given moment and in a certain situation, make use of these discourses and practices, as pathological personalities, accusing them of being hysterical, perverse or psychotic, and making a kind of false pseudo-psychologic diagnosis which may be condemned in all aspects. See Dejours, C., *A banalização da injustiça social*, Rio de Janeiro: Fundação Getúlio Vargas Editora, 1999, pp. 77-81, especially note 12 in pp. 78-79.

7   Žižek, S., *The Metastases of Enjoyment, op. cit.*, p. 83.

8   Žižek, S., *The Ticklist Subject, op. cit.*, pp. 322-323.

9   *Ibidem*, pp. 322-334; Lacan, J., 'Kant com Sade', in: *Escritos*, Rio de Janeiro: Campo Freudiano Brasileiro /Jorge Zahar Editor, 1998, pp. 776-803; Julien, P., *Psicose, perversão, neurose. A leitura de Jacques Lacan*, Rio de Janeiro: Companhia de Freud, 2004.

10   Dostoievski, F., *Os irmãos Karamázovi*, Rio de Janeiro: Abril Cultural, 1970, pp. 184-194.

11   *Ibidem*, p. 187. Our highlighting.

12   *Ibid.*, pp. 187-192.

13   Green, J./Rozell, M./Wilcox, C. (eds), *The Christian Right in American Politics. Marching to the Millennium*, Washington, DC: Georgetown University Press, 2003.

14   See Della Cava, R., 'A direita cristã e o Partido Republicano', in: *Religião e Sociedade* 23 (1), 2003, p. 10.

15   See the doctrine of the church's priests about the poor in Bravo, R.S., *Doctrina Social y Econômica de los Padres de la Iglesia*, Madrid: Compi, 1967, and the issue of the poor in the Middle Ages in Molat, M., *Les pauvres au Moyen Age*, Paris: Hachette, 1978.

16   See Alfaro, J., 'La Teologia di fronte al Magistério', in: Latourrelle R./O'Collins, G. (eds), *Problemi e prospettive di teologia fondamentale*, Brescia: Queriniana, 1980, pp. 413-432, especially pp. 425-432.

17   *Ibidem*, pp. 425-432.

# 33

# REAFFIRMING LIFE.
# POLITICAL LEADERSHIP
# IN DEFENCE OF HUMANITY

*Wim Dierckxsens, The Netherlands/Costa Rica*

## 1. Towards Political Leadership in Defence of Humanity

The economic policy of neoliberalism is fundamentalist and leads to the methodic exclusion and threatens elimination of 'other' nations, cultures and religions. The neoliberal policies of the G7, through the International Monetary Fund, the World Bank, and the World Trade Organisation (WTO) have condemned to death by starvation, in a methodic and systematic way, great majorities in periphery nations with 'other' cultures and religions. Such methodic strangulation policies of whole cultures can be considered as silent genocides and constitute a crime against all humanity. As the policies of world market acquire a military expression of 'our' nation, culture, race or religion against 'other' nations, culture, race or religion, this silent genocide is transformed into state terrorism. As political leaders committed to humanity, we use religion as a force to solve conflicts, not create them. As a social movement committed to 'another possible world', ecumenism facilitates struggles for a world where many 'worlds' can co-exist, and against the use of culture or religion to save 'our' culture or religion, at the expense of the 'others' that are a menace to 'ours'. Leaders committed to a fairer 'alternative world' will combat any ideological argumentation insisting that 'our civilisation, religion, culture, or gender' is superior to that of any of the 'others' and claiming any exclusive right to be on this world at the expense of 'others'.

Neoliberal fundamentalism that sustains the infallibility of markets supports itself in the religious fundamentalism regarding the infallibility of the Bible. With the crisis of the myth regarding infinite growth, capitalism has ended being a utopia, and starts the battle over the distribution of the world, supported by the theology of prosperity that legitimises the concentration of wealth in the hands of the 'rightful' at the expense of the 'wrongful.'[1] Occidental fundamentalism leads thus to official terrorism. This tendency foments other fundamentalist responses, which tend to escalate a spiral of terrorism.

The terrorist attacks in New York on September 11, 2001, may be considered as an answer to exclusion and scorn. It is a terrorist response against official terrorism. Official terrorism thus foments terrorism by those excluded, in this way sowing more and more terror and death in their own centres of power, as was demonstrated in Madrid and London.

The spiral of terrorism reaffirms a world of exclusion where fewer and fewer will be saved. The 'chosen' culture, religion or nation legitimises killing ever more enemies and progressively isolates itself behind an ever more militarised wall. When the world drowns this way, the lecture of occidental fundamentalism is that Christ will come. It is God's will.[2] In this 'each for its own', however, ever larger majorities will take conscience that nobody will be saved unless we show solidarity with 'other' cultures, religions, or nations. The political leaders who believe in 'another possible world' have to move forward in their solidarity ethic as an indispensable condition to achieve the Common Good of all humanity.

While the great powers insist on keeping nuclear weapons, arguing that they need them for their national security, they cannot possibly hope to prevent other nations, and even terrorist groups, to acquire them. The double morality of nuclear weapons being good for 'us' but bad for the 'others' shows the logic of the bullies. Those that call themselves 'realists' erroneously believe that they can survive even the use of nuclear weapons. However, in reality they push the 'others' into using those weapons. It is time for political leaders, and first amongst them those in the nuclear club to commit their nations to total nuclear disarmament. Political leaders have to fight for an open world where all nuclear weapons are verifiably destroyed. The political leaders that believe that 'another world is possible' have to promote the idea that nobody will be safe with the nuclear arms policies for 'us' to defend 'ourselves' from the 'others'. The only doubt is if this conscience is achieved before or after official terrorism makes use of nuclear weapons and causes a holocaust.

The intolerance and horror of this downward spiral of terrorism demands a strong *alternative social movement and leadership in defence of humanity*. Faced with this real threat of a spiral of terror, it is necessary to foster the conscience that nobody on this planet will be safe. Political leaders committed to the defence of humanity need to work to obtain the political will that will allow us to mutually save ourselves. Solidarity with the 'others' is the necessary condition for 'my' salvation. To promote this type of conscience is precisely the role of those social movements and political leaders committed to another possible world where there would be a place for many other 'worlds'. Solidarity ethics allow the creation of a place for the 'others', without regard to race, culture, gender or religion.

## 2. Towards Political Leadership with Solidarity Ethics

The neoliberal market economy is based on totalising mercantile relations. Since the 1970s, neoliberalism introduces a new accumulation of capital, based not on economic growth as a whole, but through the distribution of existing markets in favour of the transnational corporations and the financial capital linked to them. At the end of the 1990s the division of the existing world markets was tilted in favour of transnationals based in the industrialised countries at the expense of the rest of the world. The accumulation of capital, through the division of the world, however, is finite. Once the division of space is exhausted through agreement amongst the major powers at the WTO, the division of the world acquires a more bellicose character. This was announced after September 11, 2001 with the invasion of Afghanistan and Iraq. The battle for markets in favour of a 'chosen' culture or nation, and without regard to cost, inevitably leads sooner or later to a world recession without precedent.

Amidst the pain from the methodic exclusion and elimination, global resistance is generated, which not only delegitimises the system as such, but also gives fertile ground for a solidarity ethic where the great majorities will realise that 'we' have no salvation unless we do not try to save the 'others'. The solidarity ethic that 'we' cannot live unless the 'others' (other people, other races, other genders, other nations, other cultures) also can live is produced amidst the pain from the 'each for its own'. The Common Good, consequently, is presented firstly as a resistance. The ethics of the Common Good rises in a conflictive relation with the current system. The Common Good is the solidarity ethic that recognises that there will be no life for 'us' if the 'others' cannot live. Political leadership requires anticipating this solidarity ethic in the quest of the Common Good.

## 3. Towards Political Leadership that Cares for Natural and Future Human Life

Solidarity-based leadership places the economy in function of *life* itself, and does not sacrifice life in the function of the market economy. From the point of view of the market, as a totalising system, the demands of human life are perceived as distortions. Human and natural life are perceived as mere resources or as means of accumulation. If accumulation does not include majorities, these constitute a distortion for capital. From the point of view of those affected humans, however, the totalisation of the market economy appears as a grave distortion for all human life. As the exclusion advances, we experience this vulnerability in a more acute and generalised way. While 20 % of the world population is included in the market economy that consumes 80 % of resources, this contrasts with the remaining 80 % of the world population which is ever more excluded, and even considered as superfluous for the system. The screams from the excluded collective subject are claims for an alternative economy with a right to live without exclusion. Alternative social movements and political leaders committed to another possible world demand the guarantee of a Basic Citizenship Income at a world level, a basic income that guarantees all persons to live as citizens without dependence on the markets.[3]

A responsibly led economy cares for *life*. Care, not accumulation, is the purpose. Nature is seen as wealth and source of all life. The natural wealth as a conserved use value will surround us for a longer time. Therefore, preserving the current natural wealth is increasing the wealth stock in the present and in the future. For an ever more accelerating totalised market economy, sacrificing ever more resources constitutes the source of accumulation. From here derives disparagement of nature, for the conservation of natural wealth. The same occurs with the produced wealth. The shorter the life of the produced goods, the bigger the profits will be. Conservation of the natural or produced wealth increases present wealth and therefore human welfare, but not wealth as expressed in currencies. When we discard ever more produced wealth, nature is exploited again with an ever increasing speed. In this way genuine wellbeing is eroded, but capital prospers.

In the measure that natural life is reproduced at a slower rate than capital reproduces, the collapse of nature is a question of time. With this risk, all human life is at stake. If one starts from the permanent accumulation of capital, which requires permanent growth, it is impossible to talk about sustainable economies. The accumulation of capital sacrifices ever more natural, material and human life as a function of accumulation. As the destruction of nature puts human life at stake, resistance is developed, and the preservation of the environment as a common good or patrimony of humanity is glimpsed. Responsible leadership stands for sustainable economy based on an ethic of solidarity. Solidarity will be not only with nature, but also with future generations. The loss of natural life is a decrease in wealth not only for current generations, but also for future generations, and thus constitutes an economy without any solidarity. This loss of nature is not accounted for in a market economy, nor can it be accounted for in numbers. The loss of non-renewable resources means an incalculable loss. Responsible leaders have to 'take care'.

Responsible leaders in an alternative economy will take care that extraction of resources will not be greater than the rate in which nature can replace them in the long run. In a care economy, the speed of reproduction of materials in the economy has to decrease to adjust itself to the speed of reproduction of nature itself. The consumption of natural renewable resources, in other words, cannot go faster than what nature is able to replace. The consumption of non-renewable resources imposes more strict limits. Biodiversity has to be placed at the heart of an economy oriented towards regulation of the natural life in harmony with human life. The starting point for a sustainable economy is the conservation and care for human, material and natural life span through time. Responsible leadership towards an economy in function of life implies a revalorisation of all life around us, including air, water and the environment in general. The natural and produced wealth, with care will lower contamination and so increase the genuine wellbeing, placing less emphasis on monetary accumulation and enhancing the prolongation of all life around us.

## 4. Towards Political Leadership that Cares for All

Responsible leadership stands for an economy that aims towards a society of equal and free human beings who as subjects construct their future. It is not a mere illusion but a mobilising project from the needs and particularities of life. The success of this mobilising project presupposes the exhaustion of the capitalist rationale. The limit for the capitalist rationale is found in the fact that capitalism has shortened the average life of even its own means of production. Since the Second World War, the average life of the used technology in companies has been relentlessly shortened. With this, the cost of technological innovation has risen in a geometrical rate. The incorporation of new technologies allowed the reduction of labour costs, but at a slower rate. Since the 1970s the cost of the labour force has fallen at a lesser rate than the cost of technological innovation. The result was a reduction in the rate of return. Due to this fact, capital investors had to look for cheaper labour costs in the periphery, and principally in China. Consequently, investment abandoned the productive sector in the West. Investment in the West has centred more on the division of the world as a means of accumulation of great capital at the expense of productive investments. With this tendency, the rate of growth of the global economy as a whole has fallen.

As the rate of economic growth falls, accumulation increasingly depends on the distribution of the world markets and resources. As the division becomes more aggressive, its economic cost tends to rise above any benefit. The final result is the prolonged crisis of capital we are going through nowadays. To save capital today, there is a tendency to mortgage the future. As we use up more and more credit as citizens, companies or states, demand and current consumption are reduced, with corresponding impact on the market economy for a while. The whole system, however, is mortgaged. As any subject of credit, there is a limit to credit even for the most powerful nations. This limit is being reached nowadays. Testimony of this is the rise in the interest rates. As interest rates rise, the debt becomes unpayable and the systemic crisis of capitalism will become apparent as it cannot solve its own self-contradiction. The return to productive investment will become both a necessity and impossibility under the current rationality. As the average life of technology decreases, it lowers the profit rate, but as it is lengthened it will also decrease, as fewer products will be sold.

Faced with the global crisis, responsible leadership will inevitably have to be integrated in companies to lengthen the average life of a product as a function of the quality of those products. Capital will try to save profits through intellectual property rights. This artificial monopoly on knowledge gives an unproductive rent. Responsible leadership will stand for intellectual property as a patrimony of humanity. Responsible leadership will stand for longer average life of all products in the world. If its life span doubles, the most consumptive quintile in the world will need half the resources and products that nowadays are generated to keep their genuine level of welfare. It could keep on living without a loss in welfare, with half the work and half the money. On this basis, responsible leadership will stand for a global redistribution of income from the core to the periphery to boost production, employment, and income.

## 5. Towards a Responsible, Horizontal, Political Leadership

As the average life of everything produced is extended at the core, the quicker national product can grow in the periphery, the faster the income levels are evened around the world. Responsible leadership will stand for a combination of the 'economy of the necessary' and the 'economy of the sufficient'. This combination between the necessary in the South and the sufficient in the North will only be achieved with a radically participative democracy. In this context, as well, it is obvious that nature can only be saved if the rhythm of growth at the periphery is less than the rhythm of liberation of resources in the centre. Responsible leadership will stand for life in all its dimensions and thus try to achieve the Common Good as a joint project of all humanity. Responsible leadership stands for a utopia in a world where there is place for all 'worlds' in the highest possible equality and in harmony with nature. Responsible leadership stands for a post-capitalist society with a participative democracy and the inclusion of everybody in the political decisions. Responsible leadership stands for a more horizontal inclusive relationship.

NOTES

[1]   Franz Hinkelammer, 'La transformación del Estado de derecho bajo el impacto de la globalización', in: *PASOS* 117, February 2005, pp. 9-10.

[2]   *Ibidem.*

[3]   María Julia Bertomeu *et al.*, 'La propuesta de la renta básica de ciudadanía', in: *El Dipló (Le Monde Diplomatique, Argentinian edition)* 73, July 2005, p. 8.

# 34

# CONGOLESE LEADERS FACE GENETICALLY MODIFIED ORGANISMS

*Afumba Wandja, Democratic Republic of Congo*

## Introduction

In regard to the global food situation, hunger is considered an injustice and a challenge to humanity. Despite progress accomplished these last years in terms of economic growth and increase in world food production, hunger figures are more and more worrying: more than 842 million people are underfed, of whom 798 million live in underdeveloped countries, 34 million in transition countries and 11 million in developed countries. Worst, according to specialist predictions, the world population will reach 9 billion in 2050. One obvious question faced by humanity is how to cope with future food needs, as there are no answers now.

Fighting against hunger implies fighting fiercely against the deep causes. Many causes are pointed to, in particular the productivity of production factors (work, soil, seeds, etc.), low accessibility to food, and population growth. In fighting against hunger, politicians and scientists try to suggest radical and lasting solutions. Biotechnologies, precisely applied in agricultural and food domains, stand amongst the proposed and used solutions. Biotechnologies have produced new techniques such as the artificial transfer of genes into what we are now referring to as 'Genetically Modified Organisms' (GMOs).

Many biotechnologies, especially GMOs, are being discussed in some circles. On the one hand, some people consider them as the mainstay for the fight against hunger that will improve not only the food quality and quantity, but also the quality of the environment. On the other hand, some think that they impede food independence, biodiversity protection, and sustainable development.

Beyond agronomical, food, and economic considerations, another opinion questions this issue from an ethical point of view. This is because GMOs question certain values and principles that have always guided humanity. In fact, at the creation, God blessed man (male and female) by saying: 'Be fruitful and increase in number; fill the earth and subdue it. Rule over the fish of the sea and the birds of the air and over every living creature that moves on the ground.' (Gen 1:28) Through this blessing, God provides human beings with what may be called a 'charter of privileges', which is the basis of any material and scientific progress realised by humankind since s/he was created as 'Imago Dei' (in the image of God). God has given humankind the privilege of subduing the universe so as to acquire the mastery and knowledge of his/her environment. *This is to serve the human race and safeguard the whole creation for the good of humankind and for the glory of God.* As a consequence, *man is called to be responsible towards not only God but also the humanity* by bearing in mind this ethical question: 'What should I do well in the search for the good of humankind and God's glory?' The ethical question related to GMOs, and to any other issue, is linked to 'legitimising' and humankind's responsibility towards any innovation.

## 1. Genetically Modified Organisms (GMOs): What Are They?

The evolution of molecular biology, genetic engineering, [1] and computer science has allowed greater access to the genetic heritage of living beings through the development of new sciences such as biotechnology. The latter has brought about sophisticated tools that allow modification or improvement of the genetic heritage of living beings. The expression 'Genetically Modified Organisms' defines organisms, the genetic characteristics [2] of which have been modified by a technique excluding multiplication or natural combination. In other words, GMOs are living organisms, animals or plants, the genetic material of which has been modified by incorporating one or more genes [3] from another living organism. [4]

The development of GMOs in the food processing industry network present advantages, as well as risks of various kinds. This article deals with GMOs in two respects: economic advantages and real and/or potential risks.

## 2. Advantages of GMOs

According to their advocates, GMOs offer the following economic and agricultural advantages: [5]

a) *Economy of inputs:* the use of GMOs resisting to certain diseases or insects permits to avoid or reduce the contribution of pesticides and, hence, limits the consumption of such products in agriculture.

b) *Economy of time and technical itinerary simplification:* the use of GMOs helps save time and simplifies technical itineraries. In fact, GMOs possess characteristics that allow, for instance, the agricultural exploitation to drop or reduce the number of plant health treatment per year.

c) *Possibility of launching new products for new prospects:* a transgenic plant is a plant in which one or more new characteristics have been transferred. With the transfer of genes, new products can be developed that would better respond to farms' and consumers' needs. This is the case where gene grafts were integrated in rice and wheat plants to increase their nutritious value, or where genes producing a precursor of vitamin A were injected in rice plants to create 'golden rice'. As rice feeds more than fifty percent of the world population, GMOs could help reduce the deficiency in vitamin A in underdeveloped countries.

d) *Potential sources of considerable agricultural progress:* the yield loss is without doubt one of the greatest problems faced by agriculture. In spite of plant health treatments, it still remains a major problem all over the world. According to statistics issued by the National Institute of Agricultural Research, 38 % of the production of main cultures (rice, wheat, barley, potato, corn, cotton, coffee and soya) is lost for the world of agriculture. Transgenic plants seem to be a potential source of considerable agricultural progress.[6]

## 3. Risks Associated with GMOs

Not only advantages are associated with GMOs – there are also risks:

a) *Dependence risk relating to sector prior to agriculture:* where it has been introduced, the cultivation of GMOs has disrupted farmers' behaviours. These changes generate a risk of dependence in the following areas:[7] *Economic:* for their treatment, a majority of transgenic plants need plant health products elaborated by the very company that markets the said transgenic seed. This situation is quite restricting for farmers as they are forced to buy costly 'complete kit' constituted of plant health seeds. *Legal:* the cultivation of GMOs generally goes together with relationships under contract with partners. In fact, some suppliers of transgenic seeds impose contracts on farmers obliging the latter to supply exclusively to them during a relatively long period. Others forbid farmers to use part of the harvest as seeds. *Biological:* biotechnological industries have identified genes that make some harvest unproductive. This is the case of the sterilisation gene known as 'Late Embryogenesis Abundant' by Delta & Pine (subsidiary of Monsanto). This gene sterilises seeds emerging from the previous harvest. This situation obliges the farmer to renew his/her seed stocks every year, which is very costly.

*b)* *Prior integration risk:* since their appearance, GMOs have segmented the market. This segmenting presents the farmer with two difficulties, namely, guaranteeing prospect markets that are more and more difficult, and respecting closely rigorous specifications. As a consequence, this may almost lead to a unique network. The farmer will then be obliged to multiply his/her production and delivery contracts for many years, running the risk of disappearing from the market.[8] It is worth noticing that demands connected to GMO exploitation will no doubt lead to more specialisation and technicality in the production and agricultural transformation sectors.

*c)* *Appropriation risk and management of genes of interest:* a growing number of international texts recognise the right to issue patents over living beings.[9] Private firms that lead the production of GMOs fear the appropriation of genes used in their production work. The latter will become unavoidable for seeds firms and farmers.

*d)* *Agricultural risks:* agricultural risks associated with GMOs are not objects of great debates; yet they should not be neglected. These risks include, among others, the appearance of problematic weeds because of *cross-breeding* of a GMO with a related wild plant, the growing again of plants *resisting* to one or more *herbicides* – which might considerably hinder the weak killing of the following cultivation, *unexpected resistances* developed by devastators exposed permanently to toxic substances produced by GMOs.

*e)* *Human health risks:* the problem of human health is still on the table. If some people find that GMOs present a potential danger to human health, others see in them no real danger. They think that the risk evaluation of consuming GMOs by human beings is still theoretical as there is not any evidence about their recent consumption. It is worth reminding scientists that the zero risk is nearly nonexistent. In terms of potential risks, the following can be cited. *Toxic risks:* the integration of a new gene into a living organism may provoke the expression of one or more ineffective genes at the normal state. This expression caused by the transgene may both lead to the production of new toxins, or increase the production of toxins that were produced naturally in insignificant quantity. Some toxins exist at a natural state and are produced in non-toxic quantity. These include potato's solanine, tomato's tomatine, or colza's erucique acid. Though the risk is minimal, it may prove real and no one knows its consequences, at least up to now. *Risk of allergy:* cross-reactions may threaten people who are allergic to certain food. In fact, a person eating a potato in which a tomato gene has been introduced may develop an allergy to that gene and not being able to link his/her allergy to the tomato. We have to recognise that these risks of allergy already exist apart from GMOs.

At this level, it is important to notice yet unidentified secondary risks that food from transgenic cultivation may have on consumers' health.

### 4. GMOs in the Democratic Republic of Congo. Political Leaders' Responsibility

Africa is probably the continent most affected by hunger and malnutrition. Following the example of developing countries, African countries face a high demographic growth and a low agricultural productivity due, in most cases, to natural disasters, armed conflicts, bad governance, etc.

As GMOs are advancing globally, they appear as an excellent remedy proposed by science to Africa to fill the gap between its demographic pressure and agricultural productivity. They provide great prospects for the growth of productivity and fight against insects and rodents that decimate harvest, desertification and dryness, epizooties and other plant sicknesses. It is worth noticing that most African countries are very late in the domain of transgenic plants and have very little access to the appropriate technology, except Senegal, Egypt and South Africa. [10]

The Democratic Republic of Congo (DRC) has no concrete implication in the domain of transgenic cultivation. To begin with, there is a serious lack of information on several levels. [11] Moreover, there is no legal framework to handle this question. The lack of official position by the government puts Congolese consumers, as well as state services, in an uncomfortable and irresponsible position.

What are the responsibilities of Congolese political leaders facing this situation?

*a) Information:* emphasis needs to be put on the enormous lack of information regarding GMOs in the DRC. Without an informed population and international community, any attempt carried on in this field will be affect. For instance, there are no valid and possible surveys to identify the impact of GMOs on consumers and on agricultural and rural development in the country.

*b) Agricultural policy:* for rural farmers in developing countries as in the DRC, what is needed is not really this high and new technology, but simply a good policy that permit an easy accessibility and a fair distribution of the country's wealth in order to allow them to sell their products very well, transport them easily to centres of great consumption, supply rapidly and easily necessity products, and have education facilities. So, political leaders have to:

- establish a national agricultural policy that takes into account real farmers' needs and that guarantees their independence;

- call for people to go back to the land and work so as to be independent in order to put an end to a kind of generalised idleness;
- take legal positions and regulations towards GMOs; and
- provide researchers with sufficient financial means for considerable specialisation.

*c) Food policy:* it is possible to find products on the market emerging from this new agricultural technology, particularly as food aid from the USA, Japan, Italy, and other countries. Hunger results from the normal functioning of the market economy where food goes to those who can afford it, a theory supported by the economist Nobel prize Amartya Sen. GMOs and technologies of rich countries may on the contrary reinforce the food dependency of poorest countries and not reduce hunger in the world. That is why effort should be turned towards understanding the real aspirations of people, and searching for positive answers through sustainable, GMO-free food policy, instead of reinforcing structures that worsen hunger by a total foreign dependence. Leaders should therefore:

- inform the population, particularly on possible consumption testing of these products, and already evaluate effects;
- take into consideration supposed or real fears formulated by specialists;
- take bravely any measure, possibly including the refusal of certain doubtful food aid as allowed by the food aid guidelines issued by the Food and Agricultural Organisation;[12]
- avoid the trap of consuming only from abroad because it is better; and
- reinforce and encourage teachings that fight malnutrition and promise a balanced diet.

### Conclusion

The present survey is not designed to terrify the opinion by totally discrediting new agricultural technologies and GMOs as products that science proposes to the humanity. Now is the time to draw people's attention, bring governments to define a 'proactive' policy, and become more responsible towards the realities that make up our modern world. This is the modest call that this article wants to launch, so that leaders (politicians, scientists and others) be more conscious of their own responsibilities in view of the lasting development towards GMOs and dangers for the agricultural independence and the food sovereignty of the DRC.

BIBLIOGRAPHY

Anderson, Per, 'Agriculture, Food and Responsible Biotechnology', in: Bloomquist, Karen (ed.), *Lutheran Ethics at the Intersections of God's One World*, Lutheran World Federation Studies 02/2005, Geneva: Lutheran World Federation, 2005, pp. 169-192.

Madeley, John, *Food for All. The Need for a New Agriculture*, London/New York: Zed Books, 2002.

Pretty, Jules/Hine, Rachel, *Reducing Food Poverty with Sustainable Agriculture. A Summary of New Evidence*, Final Report from the SAFE-World Research Project, Colchester, UK: University of Essex, 2001.

Stückelberger, Christoph, *Global Trade Ethics. An Illustrated Overview*, Geneva: WCC Publications, 2002.

Swiss Ethics Committee on Non-Human Gene Technology, *Gene Technology and Developing Countries. A Contribution to the Discussion From an Ethical Perspective*, Berne, 2004. (For the French and German version, see www.ekah.ch)

Internet resources: www.cafe-geo.net; www.ogm.org; www.fnsea.fr; www.local.attac.org; www.fao.org; www.legrandsoir.info; www.ekah.ch.

NOTES

[1]   The science of changing the characteristics of a living thing by altering or manipulating its genes.

[2]   Set of hereditary characteristics of an individual or a group of individuals.

[3]   A chromosome's segment that contains the information responsible for hereditary characteristics.

[4]   Berlureau, C., cited in Muyengo, Mulombe, *Ethique et génie génétique*, Kinshasa: Presse Universitaire Sud, 2004, p. 270. To read more about the creation or construction of a transgenic plant, i.e. the transgenesis, one can refer to 2002 publications by the Institut français de l'environnement.

[5]   FNSEA, *Les OGM en agriculture*. Report of the Economic Committee, Paris: FNSEA, 1998, pp. 9-14.

[6]   INRA, cited in FNSEA, *op. cit.*, pp. 10-11.

[7]   *Ibidem*, p. 12.

[8]   *Ibid.*, pp. 13-14.

[9]   Recognition of an intellectual property right upon living matter on the benefit of the person who made the discovery.

[10]   Comité permanent inter-Etats de lutte contre la sécheresse dans le Sahel, *Etat des lieux de la réglementation, de l'autorisation et de la circulation des OGM dans le Sahel*, Bamako: Institut du Sahel, 2004, p. 4.

[11]   This is serious, for God himself through his prophet purposely deplores the lack of knowledge of his people: 'My people are destroyed from lack of knowledge.' (Hos 4:64)

[12]   FAO, *The Right to Food. Voluntary Guidelines to Support the Progressive Realization of the Right to Adequate Food in the Context of National Food Security*, adopted by the 127th Session of the FAO Council November 2004, Rome: FAO, 2005, Guideline 15: International Food Aid.

# 35

# RESPONSIBLE POLITICS IN AFRICA AND SOUTH AFRICA. A FEMINIST PERSPECTIVE

*Puleng LenkaBula, South Africa*

## Introduction

This essay sets out to discuss politics and responsible political leadership. It situates the discussion in the context of Africa in general and South Africa in particular. The essay does not purport to paint a comprehensive and broad representation of politics and political leadership but employs an African feminist pragmatic critical methodology in discussing responsible politics and political leadership. This approach uses contextual case studies, stories and experiences to elucidate political, ethical, and epistemological concepts and discourses.

Feminist pragmatic critical approaches are generally premised on the understanding that theological and ethical reflection ought to be grounded on the commitment to justice and 'the fullness of life' (John 10:10) for all humanity, especially for those members of society who are marginalised, excluded or undermined by politics and/or by political leaders. As aptly put by Chopp, the general norm for pragmatic critical approaches is 'emancipatory transformation'.[1] This approach recognises that theological and ethical reflections are historically, individually, and socially contextual. It does not purport to promote universal arguments that are valid for all people, all places and all times. It affirms that all reflections evolve out of specific situations.

Due to their commitment to emancipatory transformation and commitment to justice, African feminist pragmatic critical approaches are relevant to the constructive development of responsible ethical leadership in specific contexts. They are also generally counter-cultural to the dominant political epistemological conceptions of political leadership, which to a large extent tend to emphasise distance and objectivity in theological and ethical reflections. The present paper comprises a contextual case study and social, political and gender analysis of political leadership in South Africa. The analysis will explore the use and abuse of political power and gender justice in politics and political leadership. This will be followed by identification of African feminist ethical strategies that can inform responsible, life-affirming, political leadership doing justice to gender in Africa.

## 1. Contemporary Political Leadership Questions in South Africa. A Case Study

In June 2005, South African President Thabo Mbeki announced before the Parliament the dismissal of South Africa Deputy President Jacob Zuma. The former claimed that the decision was informed by a number of considerations, including that: a) it was his constitutional prerogative to do so as the leader of the country; b) although Zuma had not been found guilty in a court of law, the decision was in part influenced by the information contained in Judge Hillary Squires judgement in the fraud and corruption case of the Durban business-man, Schabier Shaik (in this judgement, Judge Squires had concluded that there was a 'generally corrupt relationship' between the deputy president Zuma and the businessman who was his financial advisor); and c) the decision and the sacking of Zuma was a practical demon-stration and commitment by the South African government and the African National Congress (ANC) leadership to deal with corruption in government and society, and to consolidate democratic leadership. [2]

A week after the dismissal of Jacob Zuma, Mbeki appointed Phu-mizile Mlambo-Ncquka, the first ever woman in the history of South Africa to be appointed to the office of deputy president. Before her appointment, she had held positions as the minister of minerals and energy. She had led a non-governmental organisation in Cape Town during the apartheid era. She was also a member of parliament rep-resenting the ANC party.

The sacking of Zuma and the appointment of Mlambo-Ncquka as the deputy president of South Africa were met with divergent politi-cal reactions. Opposition parties commended Mbeki for doing the morally right thing. Patricia de Lille, a party political leader and founder of the Independent democrats, called it 'a proud day for South Africa'. Bantu Holomisa of the United Democratic Movement (UDM) said that 'the president's decision, which although difficult, was made in the interest of the country'. The Pan African Congress party leader Motsoko Pheko said that this was a good pronouncement and will pro-tect the image of the nation. (However, he also pointed out that the former president should be given the opportunity to clear his name, stating that the trial of Zuma by the media was 'unfair', and that this had created confusion and uncertainty in the country. [3]) The chamber of business stated that this was the right thing to do, and so did the South African Council of Churches. Transparency International com-mended the President's commitment to uprooting corruption, affirm-ing gender justice and the capability of women's political leadership. [4]

Others, however, such as the biggest trade union in South Africa (COSATU) and the South African communist party (which are in a tripartite alliance with the African National Congress party) as well as the ANC youth league contended the decision. They claimed that Zuma's sacking was not solely based on his association with Shaik, but was also due to his popularity amongst the ordinary, the poor and majority members of the ANC and South African society, who were weary of the dominance of pro-capital leaders promoting neoliberal economic agenda instead of being pro-poor. Others even went on to suggest that Zuma had been sacked because he had expressed his apprehension with the South African government/Mbeki's trend to fast-tracking hyper-capitalist policies through the macro-economic policy of Growth Employment and Redistribution, which was similar in mode to the former structural adjustments programmes imposed to Africa by the International Monetary Fund and the World Bank through processes such as privatisation of public assets and services. Newspapers such as *Business Day* carried out news articles that highlighted the contradictions and ethical discrepancies in appointing Mlambo-Ncquka as the deputy president of South Africa. According to Mde, the contradictions were that the incoming deputy president was also indirectly embroiled in a corruption case involving a South African petro-chemical company, which her brother benefited from during a term when she sat on the board as the minister of energy and minerals.[5] Three months after the appointment of the new deputy president, who had been well received by the public in some quarters and booed in others in September 2005, the leader of the ACDP party Kenneth Meshoe enquired about the policy measures that were put in place to accord proper respect she deserved. This was after calls had been made in the gatherings of COSATU and ANC youth league for Zuma to be reinstated, as well as the booing of Mlambo-Ncquka in public gatherings. The president is recorded to have said she was 'a very grown-up girl' and did not need any protective measures to ensure she was respected.[6]

Before the analysis of this case study, it is important to point out that corruption by political leaders has been caricatured as inextricably bound to politics and political leadership in Africa through literature on international corruption, such as the corruption indexes of Transparency International and others. While these caricatures are important in enabling countries to gauge the levels of corruption in their regions, they have tended to be flawed in the sense that they never discuss or even dismiss the activities of the bribers, whom in many instances come from corporate sectors based in countries of the North. This is true in the corruption scandals in the Lesotho Highlands Water project where, for example, French companies bribed the senior leaders in the project. It is also true in the South African Defence scandal where Tony Yengeni received a high discount from Daimler Chrysler leaders who had in turn benefited from the arms' deal. The overemphasis or association of corruption with Africa as the popular political scandal of African politics is tantamount to stereotyping because corruption is not only found in Africa. It would be presumptuous therefore to assume that corruption represents the full range of ethical challenges which African states or African political leaders are confronted to.

There are a number of issues that the case study above reveals about the conception of politics and political leadership: gender justice and equality of women and men in political leadership; external and coercive international control; the desire by some African leaders to be seen to be dealing with corruption by the world and the images and tensions that these create in local politics as well as issues of authority, representation versus participation in liberal democratic politics.

## 2. Politics and Political Leadership. Clarification of Concepts

My attempt in this section is to analyse the conceptions of politics and political leadership that are in part observable in the case study, but also in the literature or discourses on politics and political leadership. Mainstream definitions of politics and African political leadership tend to focus on male-stream public leadership. Politics is defined as 'striving for the share of power or for influence on the distribution of power, whether it be between states or between groups of people contained within a single state.'[7] In agreement to this definition the Kenyan theologian Gathaka thus suggests that 'anyone engaged in politics is striving for power, either power as a means to attain other goals (which may be ideal or selfish), or power for its own sake, which is to say, in order to enjoy the feeling of prestige by power.'[8]

Nürnberger presents a somewhat similar explanation of politics.[9] He sees politics as the attempt of a society to make collective life possible and prosperous through the establishment and maintenance of a social order that binds all its members. He puts forward 10 elements that he asserts characterise politics. These are:

- maintenance of security, prosperity and dignity for a small group, a larger section of the population, or all members of the population;

- political power which he refers to as 'the capacity to influence one's social environment. In economic life the means is wealth and in social life, it is status, in political life it is power;'[10]

- the third element is that 'the use of power must be legitimate in the eyes of society concerned;'[11]

- the fourth idea is that politics is pervasive. It affects all parts of our common life;

- the political dimensions of life are inescapable. Human life needs to be structured whether we like it or not. There are sections of population that are deliberately excluded from the normal channels of political activities. These include the young, women and certain racial groups;

- political life is always concerned with politics as well as with institutions which determine policies and which shape institutions such as state, economic order and organisation of social relations and smaller institutions;

- the presence of stable political institutions, which are however, not immutable. He further asserts that 'the political order is man-made, under the control of man and meant to serve the interest of man' [12] (note the exclusive language);

- the existence of competition of views. An example he uses to demonstrate this is that 'the political process involves people of all persuasions, clashes of opinions cannot be avoided... opinions differ at 3 levels... basic convictions, interests of competing groups in society (self-interest) and the ideological justifications of the differing groups;' [13]

- clashes of opinion become politically potent through the use of power with different groups struggling with each other for greater influence; and

- there are always two extremes of political power: a stronger and a weaker group. The stronger group coerces the weaker group into submission. The stronger group also expects the whole population to subscribe to its particular sets of convictions.

These descriptions of political power tend to portray power as something that politics is about. They also tend to portray competition as normative for politics. In order to conceive of notions of responsible political leadership, it is important to examine discourses on political leadership in Africa and to explore whether they merge or differ with the definitions of politics above. In his article 'Pan-Africanism, Democracy and Leadership in Africa: The Continuing Legacy for the New Millennium,' the famous African social scientist, Ali Mazrui, identifies at least eight types of leadership which he observes in African politics. These are: charismatic leadership based on drawing large support from society (e.g. Ghanaian leader Kwame Nkrumah); mobilisation leader (e.g. Julius Nyerere); reconciliation leader, in which a leader seeks compromise and consensus among disparate points of views (e.g. General Abdulsalami Abubaker); housekeeping political leader-style, in which the leader uses political power in the minimalist sense of purposely governing without leading – it is more maintenance without movement (e.g. Kenyan political elite since 1980); disciplinarian leader who is an austere no-nonsense figure (e.g. Murtala Mohammad of Nigeria); patriarchal leader, who is perceived as a father figure and therefore has the right to lead (e.g. Jomo Kenyatta); elder and patriarch, who because of his age and gender is perceived as a leader for all (e.g. Nelson Mandela) and finally technocratic political leaders, who advance and shape development (e.g. Thabo Mbeki).[14]

It would seem to me that mainstream and male-stream discourses on politics and political leadership tend to associate leadership with men. They are also inclined to emphasising contest and competition of power by differing and rival and/or hostile groups. They limit politics to activities taking place in the public sphere, forgetting or discounting those taking place in what is called the 'domestic' sphere as constituting the realm of politics. In the entire typology of political leaders provided by Mazrui, the association is made to men. This in my view is a distortion and promotes the myth that leadership models are synonymous with men. Association of political leadership with men as though they are synonymous erroneously promotes the perception that women's leadership is a gift to women. It also 'reminds us of how embarrassingly sexist the field [of politics and political leadership] has been... with distinctively 'masculine' virtues as opposed to women whose feminine features are almost inevitably include some for sentimentality.'[15] They also explain in part why politics has become dispassionate to the plight of the downtrodden, the poor, and the excluded in contemporary political discourse.

African feminist conceptions of politics are different. Politics and political leadership are not understood merely as matters of interest groups competing for power within the state. They are understood as the constant and ongoing personal and collective 'negotiation of all aspects of organisation, public activities and social and cultural practices.'[16] They are under girded by the view that 'power is inherent in all these activities and institutions, all are open to the possibility of political critique and action.'[17] They are also grounded on the understanding that politics ought to include women and those marginalised by party politics or institutional politics. Burdezeij expresses this view beautifully when he says that the notions of political spheres 'possess much broader meaning: they embrace social spheres that cannot be reduced to their temporary and institutional forms.'[18]

Politics and political leadership for African feminist ethicists therefore encompass the mutual and respectful cooperation of various individuals, communities, groups, and individuals in their different locations, motivated by their own beliefs and acting toward some common good (such as the fullness of life for all people, men and women and the earth as politics). This view to some extent critiques the liberal distinction and/or polarisation between the public and private. It points to the fact that such a polarisation reduces the scope, dynamism as well as the complexity of politics and political leadership. Such polarisations are distortions. This is because both the private and public are not static; they inform and transform each other.

African feminist conceptions of politics and political leadership also embrace the realm and activities of those outside formal political institutions such as political parties and others. Politics are also understood as collective and cooperative attempts to further common interests or goals outside established state institutions. This implies that political activities and leadership are characterised by collective/individual organising, deliberate work on specific political/thematic issues, for example, gender justice and equality or advocacy, and not necessarily by competition and hierarchical domination of others as suggested by mainstream conceptions of politics. Feminist politics and leadership, whilst collective or communal, can be differentiated from other collective behaviour such as those of gangsters, crowds, mobs and so on.

## 3. Contradictions and Ambiguities. Experiences of Feminist/ Women in Public Political Leadership

Women in general, and feminist political leaders in particular, face several issues, challenges, obstacles and sometimes, ambiguous experiences. These include patriarchy[19] and the notion of female political leaders as helpers/helpmates and liberal political notions of politics that polarises public/private spheres as well as external indifference to local challenges. South Africa for example, is rated as a country that promote women's political leadership. This is noticeable in laws, policies and institutions of government. However, the ambiguity is that whilst legislation is progressive and some political parties endorse women's political leadership, there are policies that still disadvantage women, as it is the case in the economy. There is also sometimes a huge gap between legislation and implementation of these laws.

Byanyima suggests that there is a subtle but obvious assumption that women ought to participate as helpmates in political leadership. This assumption manifests itself through what she calls the 'deputy factor'. Byanyima says the 'deputy factor' became a norm in Uganda's political life. In almost all levels of local government there was a male chairperson and a female deputy. Most ministries had male heads, and women were appointed junior minister. Parliament had a male speaker and a female deputy speaker. Committees, independent commissions and other state institutions tended to follow a similar pattern. 'Researchers found that in local governments women deputies hardly ever chaired sessions as the substantive chairs always made sure meetings took place when he was present.'[20] The post of deputy for Byanyima is sometimes presented as a 'glorified ghetto for women, a token and nothing to demonstrate their capacities and have moved on to more powerful posts.'[21]

Women politicians in Africa struggle to be heard and to be taken seriously by African governments on gender, social and economic justice in the conduct and policies of states. But at the same time they have come to realise that their government has little influence on macro-economic policies. Byanyima poignantly states this reality when she says that 'National agendas are not entirely shaped by national leaders. Increasingly feminists have to engage with powerful decision-makers at various levels, local, national, regional and international to have an impact. Neoliberal economies are driven externally. We must understand the decisions of politicians in this context and endeavour to influence what is decided beyond our borders.'[22]

International multilateral institutions and financial institutions externally shape many African governmental policies. Technical advisors from international multilateral institutions such as the World Bank and the International Monetary Fund, who work on economic and political concerns such as the Poverty Reduction Strategy Papers of the World Bank, the Medium Term Expenditure Framework, agriculture health, education, transport and other sectors, 'are even less sensitive to the questions of gender justice than our own government officials.'[23] These experiences therefore require political leadership that promotes participation and includes the voices of the poor and marginalised.

Despite comprehensive advocacy for women leadership in politics in Africa and South Africa, there is subtle, broad resistance in society against women in public politics or offices. In the case study presented above, those who believed that she ought not to be the deputy president can observe this in the booing of Mlambo-Ncguka. On the one hand, there are those who promote solidarity with women and assert women leadership. In such contexts, one of the ethically responsible things to do is to promote and create political spaces, institutions, policies and processes that enable women and men to challenge patriarchal politics.

## 4. How to Advance the Feminist Agenda and Political Leadership in Africa?

In several ways feminist political leadership holistically promotes the welfare of all including of those who are marginalised by contemporary mainstream conceptions of power, politics and leadership.

These obstacles, in the words of Byanyima, can be overcome through inculcating some of the strategies she suggests below:

> Being a feminist in African politics requires having a vision of an alternative world, a realist doable agenda of issues, a clear plan of how they can be achieved and a good sense of the political environment. It requires forging many alliances some of them temporary and others more enduring. It is important to understand that extent to which a party in power is ready to prioritise gender issues and not to underestimate the patriarchal attitudes of individual leaders but which can be camouflaged by politically correct feminist rhetoric. The work of an African feminist politician consists of... taking some steps forward and painfully holding back one's fire, as some gains are rolled back sometimes by allies. It involves refusing to compromise on a matter of principle and risking being abandoned on the floor of parliament and suffering public humiliation. It is about winning the trust of poor women and men and other marginalised people... A feminist politician has to be ready to pay a high price for being a voice of conscience especially when operating in an environment where politics of defending the status quo are dominant. But a lone voice or a few voices if honest, realistic, clear and consistent can be powerful and can drive change. [24]

Feminist political leadership can also be drawn from women and men political leaders who espouse those values or norms that promote life. African leaders such as former South African President Nelson Mandela, Chief Manthatisi of the Batlokwa in Lesotho who promoted the exercise of just relationship between the led and the leaders and between communities that had before not lived peacefully with each other, are also moral leaders whose views can be tapped to promote responsible leadership. Advocacy regarding responsible leadership can also be encouraged through public insistence on ethical values such as integrity, honesty, commitment to the poor and those marginalised because of their social location (class), gender, sexuality, ethnicity/race, and which also 'deal with the sensitive issue of use, misuse and abuse of power.' [25]

Furthermore, feminist political leadership ought to be focused on the vision beyond intra-party or state politics as defined by the notions of power and politics in liberal discourse. They ought to always be the voice of conscience and the glue that promotes critical solidarity with those whose lives and voices are made invisible. They also ought to continue challenging liberal conception of power, politics and leadership which are preoccupied with party politics, control, dominance and processes of democracy whilst undermining the content or the implications of politics on humanity and the earth. They ought to persuade African political leaders to liberate themselves from the captivity of seeing politics as an avenue of domination, competition, and hyper-insensitive masculinity in public and private spheres.

## Conclusion

This essay sought to demonstrate the ambiguities of political responsibility in African politics. It has pointed out the distortion in mainstream and liberal conceptions of politics and political leadership, particularly in relation to the ideas that the content of politics is not only political power and contest, public activity and or state activities. The paper has demonstrated that the scope of politics and political leadership encompasses the public and private, men and women and both individuals and collectives. In addition, the essay highlighted that responsible political leadership in Africa also consists of models that embrace and affirm the capability, capacity and participation of women in politics. The view that the essay promotes is that responsible political leadership ought to engender gender, social and economic justice. Responsible leadership in Africa will thrive when respect, integrity and full participation by all are encouraged. This will require constant advocacy by women and men in church and in society.

NOTES

1    Chopp, Rebecca, 'Methodologies', in: Russell, L. M./Clarkson, J. S. (eds), *Dictionary of Feminist Theologies*, Louisville, KY: Westminster John Knox Press, 1996, p. 180.

2    Thabo Mbeki's speeches: see South African government home page on http://www.sagov.org

3    'Zuma's Axing a Proud Day for SA' on http://www.iafrica.com (last accessed 14 June 2005).

4    'Corruption Body Hails Zuma's Sacking' on http://iafrica.com/news/sa/950387.htm (last accessed September 2005).

5    Mde, V., 'Scandal in Air as New Deputy Steps Up', in: *Business Day*, 9 September 2005.

6    *The Mercury*, 9 September 2005.

7    Lassman, Peter (ed.)/Speirs, Ronald (transl.), *Weber. Political Writings*, Cambridge: Cambridge University Press, 1994, p. 311, quoted in Gathaka, J. K., 'Responsible Political Leadership', in: Stückelberger, Christoph/Mugambi J.N.K. (eds), *Responsible Leadership. Global Perspectives*, Nairobi: Acton Publishers, 2005, p. 85. See also Chapter 30 in this volume.

8    *Op. cit.*, p. 85.

9    See Nürnberger, Klaus, *Ethics of Political and Economic Life* (Study Guide for TEA 304f), Pretoria: University of South Africa Press, 1996.

10   *Ibidem*, p. 2.

11   *Ibid.*

12   *Ibid.*, p. 4.

13   *Ibid.*

14   For a typology of African political leadership, refer to Mazrui, Ali, *Pan-Africanism, Democracy and Leadership in Africa. The Continuing Legacy for the New Millennium*, accessed on http://igcs.binghamton.edu.

15   Solomon, Robert. C., *Ethical Leadership, Emotions and Trust. Beyond Charisma*, Kellogg Leadership Studies Project, Center for Political Leadership and Participation, College Park, MD: University of Maryland, 1996, pp. 69-90, and on http://www.academy.umd.edu/publications/klspdocs/rsolo_p1.htm.

16   Bounds, E. M., 'Politics', in: Russell, L. M/Clarkson, J. S. (eds), *op. cit.*, p. 212.

17   *Ibid.*

[18]  Burdzeij, Stanslaw, 'Religion and Politics. Religious Values in the Polish Public Square since 1989', in Walters, P. (ed.), *The Keston Journal of Religion, State and Society*, Vol. 33 (2), Abingdon: Routledge Taylor and Francis, June 2005, p. 165.

[19]  The word patriarchal-kyriachy was coined by Elisabeth Schussler-Fiorenza. It refers to the lordship of men over women in the sense of a master/servant relationship. It is thus an impediment to the full life of women and disables their possibilities to contributing fully as political leaders in their churches and society.

[20]  Byanyima, Winnie, *Perils and Promises: Living Feminist Politics in Uganda*. A panel presentation at the African Gender Institute Panel discussion at the International Women's Day on 8 March 2004.

[21]  *Ibid.*

[22]  *Ibid.*

[23]  *Ibid.*

[24]  *Ibid.*

[25]  Kobia, Samuel, *Ecumenical and Ethical imperatives in Theological Responses to Contemporary Challenges in Africa*. An address at St. Paul's United Theological College, Limuru, Kenya, 13 October 2001, p. 23. See http://www.wcc.coe.org/wcc/wht/education/mf96.pdf.

# 36

## LEADERSHIP, MORAL VALUES, AND DEMOCRACY. A GLIMPSE FROM LATIN AMERICA

*Guillermo Hansen, Argentina*

### 1. Convictions, Responsibility and Ideology. Max Weber Revisited

Some ethical analysis of the contemporary U.S. political scenario bring into the fore Max Weber's categories. The ethicist Heidi Hadsell, for example, has underscored how political rhetoric – both liberal and conservative – is mostly framed within the paradigm of an *ethics of conviction* that short-circuits the necessary and responsible consideration of means and ends. Voluntarism, or just acting on the basis of one's moral convictions in the midst of the complexity and plurality of today's globalised world, leads to political and moral consequences which are dangerous and simplistic. The solution is to encourage an *ethics of responsibility* implemented through a careful explanation, education and debate which will allow citizens to perceive the fundamental differences between (public) responsible ethics and a (private) ethic of conviction. The underlying belief is that in a democratic and electoral regime, a change in the citizens' perception would have the leaders following suit.[1]

Is this use of Weber's categories fair? Can they be applied to understand a radically different scenario? It should be remembered that Weber's arguments were forged during the tumultuous years of the post-war Weimar Republic. It was a time of deep polarisations where right-wing forces were savvy enough to master the necessary *means* to abort democratic, liberal and popular programmes. For him the ineffective response by left-wing parties, populists, pacifists and trade unions were examples of inspired ethics applied in wrong circumstances. Often their convictions reflected an 'idealistic ethics' derived from the Sermon of the Mount, unsuitable for instrumentalising the necessary means in the pursuit of rightful and just ends. In Weber's view, conservatives seem well aware of the mechanisms of a *Verantwortungsethik*, while progressives (and Christians) seemed bogged down in the moral maze of a *Gesinnungsethik*. Weber's main point, however, is not moral, but *anthropological*: those who act according to an ethics of responsibility take into account the '*normal flaws of people*,' and therefore do not assume that human beings are of a good and perfect nature.[2] Politics, which always presents the best case for its own ends, requires often dubious means – including violence.

What does happen, *mutatis mutandis*, when Weber's categories are applied to U.S. electoral politics dominated not by the idealism of the Sermon of the Mount, but by a *neo-conservative cultural élan*? Are these voters and their leaders simply moved by an ethics of conviction in Weber's sense? Perhaps it would not surprise him to see how neo-conservative shrewd confinement of Christian maxims into a 'moral agenda' effectively establishes a new hierarchical political order that disciplines 'deviants' at home while calling for military intervention against 'rogues' abroad. But Weber would certainly be dismayed if we were to call this a *Gesinnungsethik*! For *neocons* – and their voters – seem to be quite aware of the *means* required in order to achieve a particular *world moral order*. As stated in the (in)famous ideological blueprint of Bush's administration, *Project for the New American Century* (1997), military strength and even territorial control are key in the larger project of spreading appropriate codes of conduct upon the rest of the world.[3] Violence in the pursuit of 'security' combines ends and means which are typical of conservative visions.[4]

Therefore while we could certainly agree with statements such as 'everyone votes his or her values in one way or another',[5] this can hardly be what defines an ethics of conviction. For neo-conservative hearts – churchly or otherwise – ends and means seem to be obvious terms in the political equation. All too aware of the 'perils and evils' of the world, the 'normal flaws of people', they thereby legitimise the needed disciplinary (violent) means to spread accumulation by dispossession through *imperial order and hierarchy*. Acting 'responsibly', or giving thought to 'the consequences or the complexities of the political world', is precisely what right-wing politics is all about. *If the notions of responsibility and complexity are not thoroughly deconstructed, any political argument will just circle around the cogs of the neo-conservative ideological machine.*

In brief, that people vote on the basis of convictions and values is a *truism*. The fact that people *feel* strongly about certain moral issues (where 'moral' is usually associated with sexuality and 'cardinal' virtues, never with economics and politics!) is not enough for calling it an ethics of conviction. Even voting on more pragmatic reasons such as security and one's own wellbeing involve certain types of moral convictions and values, both conscious and unconscious. A critical vision, however, *should address the type of (explicit) values and (implicit) interests which guide those decisions.* Just seeking to explain the victory of *neo-conservative values* from the purview of Weber's ethics of conviction acquits the U.S. electorate from political accountability. We thus end up focusing the problem on the fact that the

(Christian) electorate has not been *taught* correctly the difference between a *Gesinnungs* and a *Verantwortungsethik*![6]

The problem thus framed betrays the assumption of an idealistic anthropology: people are good, subject to reform, reasonable and well disposed once facts and information are distributed and made public. This being the case, blame must lay upon the *leaders* – religious and political – who deceive people into believing that there is a straight line stemming from convictions to policy, from the private to the public. But what about the *core values* and *interests* which people themselves embrace? Values cannot be equated with 'neutral' convictions; they are *ideological nodes* which undergird the power configuration of a society. The dominant neo-conservative outlook that holds sway within vast segments of the U.S. population and churches is not just a naïve crystallisation of a sound moral core, but a purposeful embrace of values perceived to be effective in tackling today's 'evils' through the appropriate 'strong' means. Violence, war, territorial occupation, undercutting of social programs, healthcare for the fittest, restrictions in education, increasing power distances, patriarchalisation of the family, are not political and social fallouts of sound moral values, but the enactment of conservative *myths and metaphors* constellating discipline, authority, order, boundaries, homogeneity and power.

Weber's categories certainly illuminate some of the problems of moral and political deliberation within Christian communities. How ethics become politics is also an acute dilemma in many countries of Latin America where 'popular' political leadership stemming from Christian circles had to face thorny issues – from *revolutionary violence* in the time of the Sandinistas to the debates in Brazil around allegations of *corruption* in Lula's government. But a straightforward application of Weber's distinction misreads a political scenario crisscrossed by *more serious contradictions* – even when limited to the Christian community. One cannot transplant Weber's analysis in order to understand political motivation affecting electoral politics, for he is mostly talking about those who are actively involved in the power struggle of (democratic) politics – not about those who delegate power through electoral mechanisms. For this reason his ethic of conviction could easily be misunderstood as a signifier of any electoral exercise that involves 'moral' convictions. Do we have, then, other categories for better understanding what goes on at the complex level of moral formation? Perhaps the notion of pre-cognitive constructions of societal models around *root metaphors* – as suggested by George Lakoff – may be of greater help. The *strict father* or *nurturing parent* family paradigms, for example, seems to be much more useful for grasping the complex basis of political motivations, as well as the values and interests that guide these constructions.

Any ethical-political debate is not merely a matter of being aware of the required means for implementing moral goals, or streamlining our values through a better grasp of ethical models. It is a matter of a *larger vision* able to go beyond the possible relations between *ends and means* by pondering the horizon that gives direction to a political program. In this vision an important role is played by the *theoretical tool* employed in the analytical appraisal of our present socio-historical trajectories. The *intellectual gauging* of the situation, making a *choice* as to where we want the world to go, and seeking and negotiating the *means* in order to approach these goals *is simultaneously an intellectual, moral and political task.*[7] We cannot discuss ethics, or *responsible* political leadership, without a consideration of larger political goals. This implies a full appraisal of the perverse logic of Empire, neoliberal globalisation, and the problem of power distance in social and political formations.

## 2. A Case of Cultural and Social Shift. Power Distance and Democracy in Post-2001 Argentina

Get rid of them all! *(¡Qué se vayan todos!)*. This was the slogan chanted by thousands, if not millions of Argentineans during the political and economic collapse of December 2001. While enraged middle class citizens smashed bank windows and doors attempting to rescue their frozen life savings, the jobless and excluded gathered on roads, thoroughfares, highways and bridges demanding jobs and the end of neo-liberal policies. *Cacerolazos*, the banging of pots and pans symbolising hunger and destitution, took place within neighbourhood assemblies and the smoke of burning tyres of the *piqueteros* barricades. Despite their class differences they had something in common: *a rejection of politics as usual.* 'Get rid of them all' was a slogan aimed mostly at the political leadership of the country. While the chorus gathered momentum several presidents were tumbled, the economy plummeted, popular mobilisations were quelled with bloodshed, and the whole country seemed to slip through the uncaring and oblivious meshes of the Empire.

Nothing will be the same in Argentina after December 2001. For some it was another case of the recurrent fits of an unstable Latin-American republic. But for others it signified a bold stand against the current neo-liberal regime and its enforcing global network. Social analysts such as Naomi Klein, Immanuel Wallerstein, Michael Hardt and Antonio Negri saw in these events the spearhead of a *cycle of protest* spreading across the very web spawn by the Empire itself, perhaps heralding a bifurcation toward a new social order. What caught their eye was the mushrooming of autonomous organisations and popular assemblies that instead of calling for *law and order* (a euphemism for 'military coup') sought to deepen an invaluable political and cultural tool: *democracy*. Hardt and Negri put it thus:

> The response of the Argentinean population was immediate and creative: industrial workers refused to let their factories close and took over managing the factories themselves, networks of neighbourhood and city assemblies were formed to manage political debates and decisions, new forms of money were invented to allow for autonomous exchange, and the *piqueteros*, the movement of the unemployed... experimented with new forms of protest in their conflicts with police and other authorities. [8]

What happened in this country so used to authoritarian outcomes, relationships of subordination rooted in *clientelage* and political leadership based upon charisma rather than law? Has an alleged cynical anti-political mood taken the country's imagination captive, as some observers fathom?[9] There is no doubt that something radical has happened; but this mood has nothing to do with a cynical hang-over. The situation has to be appraised from a cultural-anthropological angle capable of identifying and underscoring an ongoing *cultural and social shift*. Not only have people learnt to impose social sanctions on political leaders and financial institutions, but they have moved into something deeper, namely, a radical challenge of the *power distance* separating citizens and the political and economic establishment. Here we are facing a remarkable cultural shift. As Geert Hofstede has shown, power distance – a negotiation of equality and inequality – is a key dimension structuring any society and culture. Its patterns, however, do not fall from above but are *constructed* through dynamics learnt in family, school and workplace. [10] Therefore when an economic and political crisis catalyses new forms of association and affection, it indicates that something important is happening 'below' at the level of the 'microphysics of power' (Foucault). Deprivation and poverty may breed anger, indignation and antagonism, but revolt arises only on the basis of 'wealth' – a *surplus* of intelligence, vision, experience, knowledge and desire that is generated by a shift in social practices and cultural patterns. [11]

Among the different expressions of power distancing, that of *political representation* has been identified as one of the main causes leading to the revolts sweeping Argentina and other Latin American countries. The sociologist Guillermo O'Donnell has coined the notion of 'delegating democracy' to indicate an institutionalised mechanism which widens the power distance between citizens and political leadership. [12] Sooner or later this form of political arrangement erupts in extra-parliamentary strategies of political action and deliberation. However, as in any form of representation, two sides are always involved; electoral rituals which confirm the concentration of power upon a person or political cadre can only function through the *connivance* of the citizenry. *Uncertainty avoidance* is traded by formal democratic power through delegating it to a 'strong leadership.' While Latin American countries experienced important political shifts during the 19th and 20th centuries, a basic *patriarchal, caudillista and cliental* mode has prevailed since the time of Spanish colonisation. It goes without saying that this *caudillo* relationship was perceived as bringing long lasting 'benefits' – real or imagined – to the population. We are speaking, therefore, of a *shared political culture* which tolerated power distance in exchange for some benefits.

The gauge of power distance is what Max Weber employed as a criterion for his typology of political representation.[13] He defined the strongest separation as *appropriated representation*, where political representatives are neither elected, nor appointed or controlled by the represented; they just interpret their will. This mostly patriarchal form of representation is not a mere feudal remnant, but the way in which dictatorships and many supranational institutions still operate today. The *free representation* form stands in the middle – analogous to O'Donnell's 'delegating democracy'. Typical of presidential and parliamentary systems, the represented have some connection with the political leadership, but their control is severely constrained or limited between electoral cycles. Finally when the represented constantly control the representatives we are facing a third form, *binding representation*. Frequent elections, shorter terms, revocability of delegates, and specific ways to control mandates tend to shorten power distances between the citizenry and political leadership.

One could say that in Argentina the crisis of free representation or 'delegating democracy', the expansion of the horizontal voice, and the strengthening of the social capital, are signalling together the *passage* from the second to a third form of political representation, discarding once and for all the *appropriated*-dictatorial form. Of course, reality is always messy and hybrid, shunning ideal types. It would also be wishful thinking to go along all the way with Hardt and Negri's view that true and radical democracy abolishes any and every form of representation in favour of 'the rule of everyone by everyone.'[14] For anthropological, psychological and sociological reasons I believe this to be impossible. But I do believe that a *binding form* of representation set in tension with a *free* or delegating form of representation can hybridise and catalyse democratic policies.

For example in Argentina many popular organisations of *piqueteros*, neighbourhood assemblies and autonomous local parties are now key players in the centre-left national-popular government presently in power. A traditional cliental and *caudillista* party as the *Peronist*, through a 'strong' and free representational type of leadership as President Néstor Kirchner's, has built power by waving *simi-*

*lar claims and banners* as those of the popular movements. Thanks to these radical experiences of democratic demand and participation the neo-liberal model was debilitated, allowing in turn for populist parties such as the Peronist to take power. But as it builds power to legitimate the new *neo-keynesian* role of the State, it also co-opts and divides the movements along with their most capable leaders.[15] The political equation is simple: active and mobilised movements, added to the constant demand for a more binding and democratic representation, relentlessly *erodes and undermines* a 'delegating' regime's capacity to govern. The political conundrum is that refraining from doing so may allow stronger powers like the International Monetary Fund, the World Bank, foreign governments and multinational corporations – jointly with their local kingpins – to regain clout and power. To use a Lutheran metaphor, the government acts as a dike against the extreme forms of evil and injustice, but does not bring in the 'kingdom'. On the other hand, the only guarantee for a more radical form of democracy is precisely the independence of popular movements from traditional political organisations. Until the whole system definitely bifurcates – something impossible to predict – a radical democratic political leadership may have to learn to live within the shadow cone cast by the old form of politics, paradoxically nourished by the anti-systemic thrust of grass-roots movements.

## Conclusion. Towards an Ethics of Democratic Conviction *and* Responsibility

In sum, what underlines the upheaval that took over Argentina goes beyond a mere disgust for political representatives or for the moral virtues of business and political leaders. Rather it was and still is a galvanisation of anti-neoliberal *doléances* which simultaneously challenges an impaired form of representation, undermines the erstwhile political leadership, and expresses a political culture seeking to reduce power distance at all levels in society – family, work places, schools, etc. The multiplication of the 'horizontal voice' and a new self-esteem through the exercise of the power of citizenship materialise within the contradictory web or circuits that the Empire itself has generated, propitiating *decentralised democratic action* as an effective means in a very asymmetrical confrontation.

In a way perhaps unthinkable to Weber himself the distinction between an ethics of conviction and an ethics of responsibility can now be applied constructively in today's multi-faceted political scenario. A radical democracy, a *binding* representational form of political organisation, requires the constant *utopia* of grass roots groups and associations which, as it confronts the State and the economic power of the Empire, negotiates a *teletopia*, namely, measurable goals advancing quality of life in different spheres. In this type of democracy 'politics' is not tied to the State, its power, or its mechanisms, but is built upon the autonomous free play of convictions and proposals seeking to subvert the lame and miserly handouts given by a system based on accumulation through dispossession. As the Zapatista revolt exemplifies, the goal of these new movements is not to take control of the mechanisms of State but to relentlessly proclaim their 'gospel': another world is possible. For this a staunch *ethic of democratic conviction* is needed, a constant critique of arms, power and violence analogous to the *'usus politicus evangelii'* whose weapon is love. This conforms the binding of those singularities (neighbourhood organisations, churches, *piqueteros*, popular assemblies, NGOs, etc.) who discover their common *doléance*, their common desire to live rather than fear death. To the extent that this is done, an *ethics of democratic responsibility* is exacted from state and supranational organisations that must heed to the differentiated demands of a multitude of desires for life. This ethic of responsibility is therefore something *gained* through the sheer *creative struggle* by means of the weapons of peace and affection. It is the result of what Hardt and Negri call *biopolitics*.[16]

What is the meaning of responsible political leadership in this context? For one, the acknowledgment that we are indeed citizens of 'two kingdoms,' belonging to both/and rather than either/or dimensions. Democracy is the only political system where both conviction and responsibility can find expression. As Niebuhr once asserted, human capability for justice makes of democracy something possible – *conviction*. But its inclination to injustice makes of democracy something necessary – *responsibility*. Therefore responsible leadership will be measured both by the capability to voice grievances pertaining to a singular group as well as by the ability to *connect* different forms of grievance: representation, poverty, human rights, education, ecology and health. These grievances give countenance to a multitude through whom the future of democracy is at stake. It is not a mere transformational type of leadership, but a biopolitical one which bridges ideas, hopes and affections allowing a moving yet rational identification with a network of differentiated democratic power. Here a capacity to separate oneself from the immediate situation and tirelessly construct mediations, envisioning different tactical games in the continuity of a strategy, inviting us to live an ethics of conviction that always needs the dimension of self-critique proper to the ethics of responsibility.

BIBLIOGRAPHY

Auyero, Javier, 'Fuego y barricadas: retrato de la beligerancia popular en la Argentina democrática', in: *Nueva Sociedad* 179, 2002, pp. 144-162.

Burbach, Roger, 'Throw Them All Out. Argentina's Grassroots Rebellion', in: *NACLA. Report on the Americas*, July-August 2002, pp. 38-40.

Gaudin, Andrés, 'Thirteen Days that Shook Argentina. And Now What?', in: *NACLA. Report on the Americas*, March-April 2002, pp. 6-9.

Hardt, Michael/Negri, Antonio, *Empire*, Cambridge, MA: Harvard University Press, 2000.

Lakoff, George, *Moral Politics. How Liberals and Conservatives Think*, Chicago, IL: University of Chicago Press, 2002.

Oliveres, Toni Comín, '¿Cuáles son las condiciones ético-políticas para un liderazgo planetario legítimo?', in: *Sal Terrae* 92/5, 2004, pp. 401-412.

NOTES

[1]   Hadsell, Heidi, 'Politics of Responsibility and Responsibility of Politics. A Perspective of Political Ethics on Presidential Election in the USA', in: Stückelberger, C./Mugambi, J.N.K.(eds), *Responsible Leadership. Global Perspectives*, Nairobi: Acton Publishers, 2005, p. 109. See also Chapter 31 in this volume.

[2]   Weber, Max, *Política y ciencia*, Buenos Aires: Leviatán, 1989, pp. 83 ff.

[3]   Harvey, David, *The New Imperialism*, Oxford: Oxford University Press, 2003, pp. 184 ff.

[4]   'Statement of Principles', 3 June 1997, www.newamericancentury.org.

[5]   Hadsell, *op. cit.*, p. 105.

[6]   'These voters who follow or advocate for an ethic of conviction do so not spontaneously or accidentally, but because they have learned to do so.' *Ibidem*, p. 107

[7]   Wallerstein, Immanuel, *Un mundo incierto*, Buenos Aires: Libros del Zorzal, 2002, p. 83.

[8]   Hardt, Michael/Negri, Antonio, *Multitude. War and Democracy in the Age of Empire*, New York: Penguin Press, 2004, p. 216.

[9]   Dirmoser, Dietmar, 'Democracia sin demócratas' in: *Nueva Sociedad* 197, 2005, pp. 28-40, here p. 38.

[10]   Hofstede, Geert, *Cultures and Organizations. Software of the Mind*, New York: McGraw-Hill, 1997, p. 23 ff.

[11]   Hardt/Negri, *op. cit.*, p. 212.

[12]   Echegaray, Fabián, 'Razones para un optimismo politológico' in: *Nueva Sociedad* 179, 2002, pp. 130-143, here p. 136.

[13]   Weber, Max, *Economía y Sociedad,* vol. 1, Mexico: FCE, 1944, 307 f.

[14]   Hardt/Negri, *op. cit.*, p. 247.

[15]   Zibechi, Raúl, 'New Challenges for Radical Social Movements' in: *NACLA. Report on the Americas*, March-April 2005, p. 15.

[16]   Hardt/Negri, *op. cit.*, p. 249.

# 37

# POPULAR LEADERSHIP IN A CONTEXT OF OPPRESSION. A LATIN AMERICAN LIBERATION PERSPECTIVE

*Paulo Fernando Carneiro de Andrade, Brazil*

### Introduction *

Growing social and political tensions at the beginning of the 1960s divided the Catholic clergy. Although most bishops identified with the agrarian oligarchies, which were against social transformations, many were developmentalists or held even more deeply-rooted transformative beliefs. Faced with the threat of communism in Brazil – actually more an issue in the imagination of then-President João Goulart than a real threat – in the end, the Catholic clergy supported the 1964 military coup, which installed a dictatorship in Brazil. We should note that, in spite of support for the coup, some sectors of the clergy expressed concern with the military government. They had been working toward social reforms during the administration of the deposed government, and believed that the continuation of these reforms were indispensable for the future of Brazil. They also believed that democracy should be restored within a short period of time. [1]

## 1. The Catholic Church in Brazil and the Military Dictatorship

The period of the military coup coincided with that of the Vatican Council II and with increases in awareness on social justice and human rights. For this reason, wide sectors of the Catholic Church rapidly distanced themselves from the military government. In Rio de Janeiro in 1968, many priests and religious followers participated in the 'March of 100,000', a massive demonstration to end the military government. At the end of the same year, the government responded by hardening its authoritarian line. It declared *The Institutional Act No. 5*, which modified the Brazilian Constitution to expand its dictatorial powers. The military shut down the congress and set off an even greater wave of repression, widely and systematically employing practices, such as torture, that go against the most basic legal norms.

Because arbitrary imprisonment and torture affected members of the clergy, many felt they should intervene against the government and position themselves in defence of the rule of law. These included laymen linked to the hierarchy, family members of some bishops, and wide sectors of the Church hierarchy itself, even those who held moderate and often conservative positions. The Episcopal Conference of Bishops of Brazil *(Conferência Episcopal dos Bispos do Brasil, CNBB)* came to assume a central role in the struggle for human rights and became a permanent focus of democratic resistance. Tensions between the military government and the Catholic hierarchy grew to the point of near rupture. Even some members of the highest hierarchy in the Church that had initially supported the military coup because it was anti-communist, became hostile to the military. They opposed the government's most authoritarian acts, as with D. Agnelo Rossi, at the time the Cardinal Archbishop of São Paulo. [2]

Many Catholic bishops, such as D. Waldir Calheiros from Volta Redonda and D. Helder Câmara from Recife, were faced with embarrassing situations. High-ranking members of the military gave speeches and made statements accusing the Church hierarchy and the CNBB of being at the service of international communism. Priests were imprisoned and often tortured; some were condemned in military tribunals and others, because they were foreign, were forced to leave Brazil. In April 1969, an extreme-right military commander assassinated Father Antônio Henrique Pereira Neto, assistant to D. Helder Câmara for youth in the Diocese of Recife. [3] In 1970, D. Aloísio Lorscheider, at that time Secretary General of the CNBB, was detained for nearly four hours at the entity's headquarters and impeded from meeting with the Justice Minister. [4]

The Vatican supported Brazilian bishops' actions against human rights violations. The Vatican Radio and *L'Osservatore Romano* (the official organ of the Holy See) denounced abuses committed by the military government and published an article by the CNBB. Pope Paul VI himself publicly supported Brazilian bishops and condemned torture. [5] In spite of the growing tension there was never a total rupture between the military and the Church. Some channels of communication were left open, such as the so-called Bipartisan Commission, created in November 1970 in Rio de Janeiro, where the CNBB was housed at the time. The Commission was extra-official and membership was divided between the Church and the military.

On one side, the Commission was composed of the CNBB leadership, the Núncio Apostólico, the Cardinals from São Paulo (D. Paulo Evaristo Arns) and Rio de Janeiro (D. Eugenio Salles), and the advisor of the CNBB, Prof. Candido Mendes; on the other side were General Antonio Muricy, Ten. Cel. Roberto Pacífico, Maj. Leone da Silveira Lee and Prof. Tarcisio Padilha. Although a recent study by the

K. Serbin has given great prominence to the role of this commission,[6] it is important to understand the context in which it operated as well. It was important because of the pressure on the government, rather than because of a respect by the military for the Church or for members of the Catholic hierarchy. The CNBB and important members of the hierarchy made public denouncements – both nationally and internationally – that had the support of the Vatican. An example is the case of D. Paulo Cardenal Arns, whose solidarity with, and unconditional support to political prisoners, human rights and the rule of law were inestimable. The commission was interesting to the government, mainly to its more radical sectors, as an instrument to decrease tensions and improve Brazil's image in the rest of the world. In this sense, its limited effectiveness was strongly dependent on the action of Catholic leaders who played a key role in denouncing torture and defending civil rights and liberties internationally.

During the most repressive years of the military dictatorship, some documents promulgated by the hierarchy of Brazilian Catholicism were fundamentally important. These included dozens of collective and individual briefings, homilies read in Sunday masses in all the parishes of a Diocese, articles published and protests carried out by the national clergy. Particularly noteworthy was D. Cândido Padin's hallmark study, which critically analysed the Doctrine of National Security in light of the Social Doctrine of the Church and was presented to the CNBB Assembly in 1968. In addition, the following documents should be highlighted: 'I Heard the Clamoring of My People' *(Eu ouvi os Clamores do Meu Povo)* by bishops from the Northeast, in May 1973; 'Pastoral Communication to the People of God' *(Comunicação Pastoral ao Povo de Deus)* by the Representative Commission of the CNBB in 1976; and 'Christian Demands of the Public Order' *(Exigências Cristãs de uma Ordem Política)* in 1997. These documents – elaborated in different moments and different contexts – were rare examples of how the Church was able to break the censorship imposed by the military regime, which tried to silence any voice critical of its actions and ideology.

## 2. Grassroots Ecclesiastical Communities

The strong positioning of the Catholic hierarchy in support of human rights and the rule of law, then, was evident in documents and actions, and was as much personal as collective during the military rule. At the same time, an intense pastoral movement organised the so called Specific Pastorals *(Pastorais Específicas)*, such as the Workers Pastoral of the Land *(Pastoral dos Trabalhadores, da Terra)* with the Pastoral Land Commission *(Comissão Pastoral da Terra, CPT)*, the

Indigenous Peoples Pastorals, with the Indigenous Missionary Council *(Conselho Indigenista Missionário, CIMI)*. It also created Grassroots Ecclesiastical Communities, beginning in the mid-1960s in some dioceses, and soon spreading over all of Brazil.[7] *Grassroots Ecclesiastical Communities* (GECs) are small groups of neighbouring families, mainly residents of rural zones and peripheral areas of cities, that meet regularly to discuss the teachings of the Bible and reflect on their lives in light of a biblical text. Their faith led them to become involved in transformational struggles, at local as well as national levels. GECs were in general directed by laypeople from within the groups, and co-ordinated by the diocese or parish. We should observe here that, at least at the beginning, the Church thought GECs might take over traditional parishes. With the passing of time, however, we see that the Grassroots Ecclesiastical Communities did not bring about the end of parishes but actually revitalised them. The two structures are not mutually exclusive and can be combined.[8]

In order to better understand the pastoral experience of the GECs and the popular leadership that emerged from them, we should consider that this is a consequence of the work of *aggiornamento* brought to term by the Vatican Council II (1962-1965). One of the most fundamental points of this Council was the emphasis on a logic that valued the local Church and plurality, as well as diversity of ministries and vocations. This view re-situated the role of the laypeople and their responsibilities, not only in the world but also inside the Church. A strong outcome of the Council was a growing commitment to the poor, assumed above all by a group of bishops who wanted to identify with the dispossessed. In the years that followed the Council, numerous religious followers left comfortable and traditional homes and schools to work with communities in the popular context. In the same way, many secular priests sought to live and work amongst the poor, trading the parish houses for modest homes in the peripheries and in rural areas.

## 3. Contextual Theology of Liberation

With these changes, pastoral practice began to be based on analyses of local problems, and was no longer imported from other latitudes and longitudes. This led to the creation of a more independent theology that reflected on local questions. This brotherhood with the poor, together with political repression by the military dictatorship beginning in Brazil in 1964, placed as a central question for theology the very significance of being Christian in a continent of poor people. This same question presupposes a certain interpretation of the causes of poverty in Latin America. The experience of increased contact with the poor, of sharing in their real-life situation, found a parallel in the biblical passage of the good Samaritan. In this passage, the Samaritan helps a man who is attacked and left on the road, wounded and prostrate (Luke 10:29-37).

This ideology made traditional explanations about the causes of poverty (backwardness, ignorance, indolence) seem unreasonable. On the other hand, interpretations of Latin American poverty, as articulated in key critical reflections by development theorists or by Marxists sociologists, were accepted as more plausible in light of this real life experience. The poor came to be understood as a marginalised and, above all, exploited group. The central question for theology and for pastoral practice became how to live a Christian life in a continent of men and women who have been exploited and plundered.

In rejecting traditional explanations to the causes of poverty, the relationship with the poor also changed. The poor – no longer seen as ignorant and indolent – came to be seen as objects of social action and subjects of political transformation. The new pastoral that emerged in Latin America, then, was based on the so-called *option for the poor*. This was not exclusive to the Catholic Church, as it was also incorporated by other historical churches. In concrete terms, the option for the poor means to try to see the world through their eyes and allow them to transform themselves into ecclesiastical or politico-social subjects.

In 1994 the Centre for Religious Statistics and Social Research *(Centro de Estatísticas Religiosas e Investigações Sociais, CERIS)* and the Institute for Religious Studies *(Instituto de Estudos da Religião, ISER)*, both in Brazil, conducted a study that estimated that there were around 100,000 communities in the country at that time.[9] Later, research carried out by Inter-ecclesiastical Meetings of GECs concluded that although they were less visible in the media, these communities continued to grow and maintain ecclesiastical and social vitality.[10] Another study by ISER over a ten-year period (1984-1995) aimed to evaluate pastorals in ten dioceses in different parts of the country. The research observed how, through Grassroots Ecclesiastical Communities, Catholics pertaining to popular groups, from the socio-economic point of view, took part in different social struggles and even entered into political participation, mainly in parties more linked to social transformations, such as the Workers Party *(Partido dos Trabalhadores, PT)*.[11]

We should also point out here that during the most repressive years of the military government, in which for a long period nearly all the channels of democratic participation were blocked, the GECs constituted a space of participatory learning. Within these groups, participants developed democratic practices, reached decisions following exhaustive debate, and exercised their right to engage in social criticisms. [12] In this sense one can say that the GECs had an important role in the democratic resistance to the military government and in the democratic restructuring that happened in the country after 1996. They provided an excellent popular framework for the social, labour and political party movements. [13]

Data gathered from the 2,395 delegates/participants in the 10th Inter-ecclesiastical Meeting of GECs in Ilhéus, Bahia in 2000 indicated that at least 84 % of the 1,439 delegates/participants who returned the questionnaire had been involved in some social struggle. Another 76 % of them had participated in some civil society organisation, and at least 58 % had suffered some type of persecution, such as threats or even prison or physical violence as part of their involvement in social struggles. [14] Leaders that emerged from the GECs were fundamental in many regions to retake the labour movement in the city and countryside, as well as to organise the popular movement, both during the military dictatorship and in the time of reconstruction of democracy.

## 4. Participatory Political Leadership

In terms of political-partisan participation, we observe the same small sample of growth in the number of those affiliated with political parties (56 % had party affiliations, versus 30 % of the delegates/participants who responded to a similar questionnaire in 1981). Of those who are affiliated, 75 % are with the PT and just 8 % are with the parties that made up the base that sustained the Fernando Henrique Cardoso government (PSDB, PMDB, PFL). [15] The electoral force of GECs has been interpreted in different ways. Some authors attribute the clear victory of PT candidates in traditionally conservative regions such as Acre and Amazonas to the activities of these groups. [16]

We should mention here that at the time of the reconstruction of Brazilian democracy, when reforms undermined the bipartisanism imposed by the military government, some even discussed the possibility of founding a Catholic party, following the example of the Italian Christian Democracy. The Catholic-Brazilian hierarchy was mainly against this perspective, encouraging the centres to act in accordance with the values of plurality and supra-partisan politics for the Catholics. GECs do not constitute a centralised movement and do not recommend political candidates. However, many different candidates have come out of them, and many GECs do support specific candidates – most frequently candidates of the PT.

## 5. Characteristics of Popular Leaders

The main characteristics of the leaders working with GECs are the following:

a) *Popular social origin.* The leadership originates from less favoured social classes including workers, labourers, and home-makers who have become politically active through political parties, labour unions, or in organised social movements.

b) *Commitment to progressive social causes.* Within their parties, the leadership defend social change and lead movements to support social causes within political parties.

c) *Formation in action.* In general, these leaders are not well educated in the formal sense. Their education comes from action, through meetings, popular courses, seminars, and exchanging experiences.

d) *Spirituality.* These leaders have created a strong link between action and spirituality. They read the Bible and pray together in community gatherings, linking these with the practice of social justice. This feeds their faith and gives sense to their actions.

e) *Organic links with popular and community sectors.* These leaders maintain their link with the faith community and with popular sectors from which they originate. They seek to share experiences of action and take decisions on their collective actions with *companheiros* or companions from their community, and with popular sectors to which they are linked.

f) *Respect for autonomy of the socio-political reality.* Although these leaders are Christians and understand that their social or political commitments come about as a result of their faith, the underlying drive for their work is a desire to promote justice and fundamental ethical values – they do not impose their religions on others.

These are the characteristics that mark the emergence of a new political and ecclesiastical movement, capable of transforming society through actions that are at once ethical and effective.

NOTES

\*    Translation from the Portuguese by Jessica Galeria (jessica@vivario.org.br).

1    Bernal, Sergio, *CNBB. Da Igreja da Cristandade à Igreja dos pobres*, São Paulo: Loyola, 1989, especially pp. 48-56.

2    Azzi, Riolando, 'Presença da Igreja Católica na Sociedade Brasileira', in: *Cadernos do ISER* 13 (1981), pp. 90-91.

3    *Ibidem*, p. 93.

4    *Ibid.*, p. 98.

5    *Ibid.*

6    Serbin, Kenneth, *Diálogos na Sombra. Bispos e Militares, Tortura e Justiça Social na Ditadura*, São Paulo: Companhia das Letras, 2001.

7    Caramuru de Barros, Raimundo, *Comunidade Eclesial de Base, uma opção Pastoral decisiva*, Petrópolis: Vozes, 1967.

8    Lesbaupin, Ivo (ed.), *Igreja. Comunidade e massa*, São Paulo: Paulinas, 1996.

9    Valle, Rogério/Pitta, Marcello, *Comunidades eclesiais católicas: resultados estatísticos no Brasil*, Petrópolis: Vozes/CERIS, 1994.

10    Oliveira, Pedro A. Ribeiro de, *Perfil social e político das lideranças das CEBs no Brasil*, in: REB 245 (2002), pp. 172-184.

11    Lesbaupin, Ivo *et al.*, *As Comunidades de Base em Questão*, São Paulo: Paulinas, 1997.

12    Wanderley, Luiz Eduardo V., *Comunidades de Base e educação popular*, in: REB 164 (1981), pp. 686-707.

13    Of the communities studied by ISER, more than 60 % said they had participated in protest struggles, covering a wide range of issues from struggle for land, labour unions, neighborhood associations, etc. See Lesbaupin, Ivo, 'As Comunidades de Base e a Transformação Social', in: Lesbaupin, Ivo *et al., op. cit.*, 1997, pp. 47-74.

14    Oliveira, Pedro A. Ribeiro de, *op. cit.*, pp. 179-182.

15    *Ibidem*, p. 183.

16    Iulianelli, J., 'Eleições e algumas lições, em, Eleições 98: encaixam-se as peças', in: *Tempo e Presença* 302 (1998), pp. 17-19.

# 38

# LEADERSHIP IN SOCIAL MOVEMENTS IN ASIA

*Josef P. Widyatmadja, Indonesia/Hong Kong*

A movement often emerges through the dreams of a vision of particular pioneers. They entertain a vision of the future, facilitated by a radical analysis of how to change the present and their experience of working with the people. A majority of movements were born and grew in the enthusiasm and vision of such leaders. Even in the absence of conditions adequate to the birth of a movement, the great spirit they possessed enabled them to do a difficult task. We cannot deny that some of the leaders were authoritarian, charismatic and that they emphasised results more than relations. This is understandable given the situation of the past; nevertheless, they are not examples to be followed.

## 1. Charismatic Pioneer Leaders

There are some benefits as well as major pitfalls in having a charismatic leader even in contexts where a visionary has been leading continuously the movement for a long time. Of course the continuity in leadership provides continuity in the goals, perspectives and approaches, yet it creates a culture similar to that of authoritarian and oligarchic rulers. It also denies the opportunities for the emergence of new leadership. Each new generation brings the need for a leader that suits the specific challenges of the era. A charismatic leader often has a great vision, commitment, dedication and a sense of sacrifice, and most of the time it is hard to find a replacement. The task of the Social Movement is not to find a charismatic leader with the same ability as his predecessors', but to create circumstances where everybody can develop his/her gifts and talents to improve the life of the poor and the marginalised. A charismatic and visionary leadership is not to be copied or repeated.

Some social movements, church organisations and community service institutions face difficulties in replacing their pioneers. The older the organisation gets, the older its leaders and staff, and still older the programmatic devices of the movement; it tends to be harder for renewal and replacement. If the old paradigms and slogans are not modified, they become artificial, rhetoric and dogmatic.

In many occasions there are crises of spirituality and vision struggling for many years to realise their dream and vision. The spiritual crises these movements face have the potential to destroy and completely root out their ability to provide any meaningful service to people. In some cases, if the pioneers do not want to leave the organisation, their leadership may become a curse more than a blessing.

Working in local social movements for more than twenty-five years has given me a valuable lesson on social movements leadership. I learned much from the experiences of many seniors and ecumenical leaders from various countries, and also from the wisdom contained in books written in various national contexts about the qualities needed by a leader, and the challenges he may face.

## 2. Requirements for Social Movements Leaders

Based on my experience and observation for this long period, social movement leaders should at least meet the following four (main) requirements:

- *Heart:* they should have an open and humble heart. Spiritual devotion, dedication and commitment are imperative qualities as well as a means to strengthen a pure heart. An ability to see all human beings as equal irrespective of the religious class, or other differences is an expression of a spiritual heart. Every leader must have commitment to the vision of the movement;

- *Organising ability/brain:* it includes the intellectual ability to comprehend the complex realities of the world as well as a systematic knowledge allowing him/her to organise his/her work;

- *Mouth:* being eloquent in communicating with others, developing an articulated style to capture the imagination of the listeners are important qualities; and

- *Organs:* the leader must possess a healthy body and strong muscles to do the difficult task. Leaders must have good health.

Those four words, if abbreviated, become HOMO. Without HOMO, it is hard to become a leader of integrity in the church and social movements.

## 3. A Challenge to the Future of Leadership

In entering the 21st century, a leader must be able to keep up with the developments and fast changes in science and technology, as well as the changes in socio-economic, political, and cultural contexts. A leader is expected to be a good shepherd and to work productively and efficiently. S/he must be able to lead the organisation in comprehending the changing context and shall show an ability to redefine the programmes and strategies corresponding to such changes.

Some of the requirements to be met are the following:

1.  a leader must seek opportunities and identify the right moment for action. These opportunities often do not come twice. Therefore, a leader must train his/her intuition to apply properly;

2.  a leader must generate new ideas and initiate programmes to translate those ideas into reality. It is the responsibility of a leader to make dreams come true, thus, to create change. A good quality change is often the expression of the creative mind of a good leadership. Changes in strategy and work system are crucial in facing the changes around the movement. This means that a leader must listen and read without any limits, and be able to filter and get the best yield of all information creatively;

3.  a leader must find ways of working more productively and efficiently. 'To kill seven flies in a clap of hands; to drink while diving', as the Indonesian proverbs say;

4.  a leader must strengthen his/her organisation and be a good shepherd to his/her sheep;

5.  a leader must be able to predict changes, anticipate those changes and give appropriate responses;

6.  a leader must eliminate racist practices, gender injustice, injustice and discrimination based on religious differences. A person who is fanatic and fundamentalist cannot be accepted as a leader;

7.  a leader will spur and motivate his/her staff, and should be open to the creative suggestions of the colleagues;

8.  a leader does not dwell in her/his past successes, but continues to create new successes.

To be a leader is not merely a matter of having a ruling position, but of being a good shepherd and a good steward. A good shepherd and steward is expected to inspire others, build self-confidence, fight hopelessness and anxiety among people, overcome fear, initiate productive and life oriented actions, provide new light, define goals and provide a foundation for the future.

## 4. Born or Made?

Is a leader born or made? This is a perennial debate. Not everyone who is educated and trained has the ability or opportunity to become a leader. On the other hand, there is no leader who does not have to go through training. If a person has a natural ability for leadership, then what is the use of leadership capacity building? Moreover, leadership capacity building does not guarantee anybody to be a good leader. Some people will become leaders; others will not. Some people will become 'Peter' and some others 'Thomas', and still others will become 'Judas' in their own history. In reality, there is a fusion of both these factors, being born and being made a leader.

## 5. Many Leaders but No Leadership

The present-day reality is one of many leaders but no relevant leadership. A leadership that builds and sustains the capacity of a group so that its members mutually support each other instead of letting themselves being fragmented with complex interpersonal differences is far more important than the leader himself/herself. Leadership is a matter of calling, devotion and process. It is not merely a matter of money, position and authority. A good leadership is an art that a person and movement cultivate and blossom in changing a dream into reality; and transcends the perversions of today to a future with full of hope. What we require is not very smart and highly educated leaders, but competent leaders. It does not mean that the quality of education is unimportant, but that education does not guarantee successful leadership. Education, experience, talents and character become factors that cohesively create leaders. Certain types of education and skills can support a person's resolve as a bureaucrat and a technocrat, but it may not help him/her to become a competent leader. Competency is the important aspect of any future leadership.

In the new century, the church and social movements are at a crossroad. Sincere and committed effort should be made to avoid the old pattern of leadership fertilised by power and authority in our resolve to vivify and develop a leadership based on servant-hood spirituality. Many people fight for leadership positions in the church even though they do not have servant-hood spirituality or a life-sharing leadership character. In order to be a true leader, a person should make himself/herself humble and allow the others, especially the poor and the marginalised, to acknowledge and taste his/her fruits of wisdom and commitment.

# 39

## RESPONSIBLE LEADERSHIP IN DISASTER REDUCTION. A GLOBAL PERSPECTIVE

*Peter Walker / Ben Wisner, USA*

We would like to propose the following twelve 'big questions' as a filter and run the events, statements and outcomes of the World Conference on Disaster Reduction (Kobe, Japan, 18-22 January 2005) through them. As far as we can see the formal output from Kobe will do precious little to address good governance, the collateral damage of globalisations, violence, climate change or urbanisation.[1] It will also not materially affect the obstacles that face innovative civil society groups and local governments. The draft Program of Action also does not link the Kobe outcomes to poverty eradication as laid out in the Millennium Development Goals,[2] to date the only truly global consensus framework humanity has for sustainable development. The approach of the Kobe meeting with respect to knowledge and communication is likely to be one-sided, privileging the hard ware and top down transmission of warnings without providing resources for increased public hazard awareness 'from the bottom up'.[3] Certainly it seems there will be no targets set for UN member nations to reach. There will be lots of rhetoric but not much to be held accountable to. That was indefensible before Christmas, but now coming directly after the tsunami, it is nearly immoral.

We know that over the last two decades, disaster deaths/year have gone down by around 30 %, whereas the number of people affected by disaster has gone up by 59 %. It is largely the technical fix of warning systems better communication and cyclone shelters that has reduced the death toll, taken the extreme worst off disasters, but it is the lack of human rights, political, global process fixes that is allowing the numbers affected to raise so. Fewer are killed but many more living their lives in abject poverty and on the brink of survival. They are vulnerable to the extreme events to follow as the 21st Century rolls along.

The call for a tsunami warning system in the Indian ocean is all very well, it has been made before, but as the successful Bangladesh cyclone warning system shows, the technology is not effective if it cannot connect with the people and both get the warning to those who are vulnerable (on mud flats, in small villages, in shanty towns, in the rebel held areas) and, give them a viable option as to what to do (get to the cyclone shelters in Bangladesh's case). Once again technical fix is not enough. It is a human rights and governance issue. Therefore we encourage participants in, and observers of the Kobe conference to ask what light is shed and what concrete resources are provided by each public and scientific session and each pronouncement as regards these twelve critical clusters of questions.

1. *Governance and respect for people's rights.* Good governance leads to concern for the right to life with dignity. Is it not the basis of all disaster mitigation? Just look at Haiti for an example of what appalling governance can do to disaster vulnerability. With no government in place, Somalis are highly vulnerable to drought and, in fact, many thousands of coastal Somalis were affected by the tsunami. In neighboring Kenya and Tanzania the government was able to warn most coastal dwellers.

2. *Globalisation & disasters.* Economic globalisation, at least with the corporate model, seeks to externalise risk (external from the corporation that is). It is not that corporations act immorally, they act amorally, but in the process people are attracted into low wage jobs and crowded in shanty towns and in coastal cities. Can economic globalisation be re-thought and 'tamed' so that people do not suffer increased disaster risk in the process? (See the report of the World Commission on Social Dimension of Globalization, chaired by the Presidents of Tanzania and Finland: http://www.ilo.org/public/english/fairglobalization).

3. *War & disasters.* Where there is war there is little chance of building against disaster using our normal models. In Aceh, Indonesia and Sri Lanka and other places, war or at least violence and unrest has been the norm for many people today. Internally displaced people fleeing war in Colombia, Congo, Sudan, and elsewhere live in conditions that make them vulnerable to disaster. You cannot wait for it to end before mitigating against disaster, so where are the models and approaches to deal with this? Does a 'window of opportunity' open up after a disaster that might allow conflict such as those in Aceh and Sri Lanka to be finally resolved? (See Disaster Diplomacy http://www.arct.cam.ac.uk/disaster diplomacy).

4. *Climate change.* Rising sea levels and more extreme events such as cyclones and other storms mean more disasters: no way round it. The Netherlands is going flat out to adapt to this reality, but where else is adaptation to climate change taking place fast enough?[5]

5. *Urbanisation.* Most population growth today is in urban areas, mostly in shanty towns, and most large cities are on coasts where sea level rise effects them, and where they are exposed to storms and possibly tsunamis. How can urbanisation be guided so that vulnerability to such hazards is minimised? Mega city urbanisation also puts a very large number of people at risk to earthquakes. How can the risk be reduced rapidly in Tehran, Istanbul, Mexico City, Addis Ababa, Manila, and other large cities facing earthquake hazard?

Concerning possible ways forward, we think it is necessary to ask:

6. *Local initiatives and innovations.* What are the obstacles that face civil society and local government in expanding important successes in 'bottom up' disaster risk management? Where can the necessary financial and other resources needed come from? How can initiatives 'from below' negotiate sub-national and national bureaucracies?

7. *Meaningful and effective local participation.* How can local initiatives and citizen participation in planning escape capture and control by dominant political elites that have been quick to appropriate the language of 'participation' and 'people centred' planning while giving up no control or resources to civil society?

8. *Knowledge and communication.* What is the role of knowledge, early warning and communication in risk reduction? What are the obstacles to implementing what science already tells us? Jeanne Johnson, director of the Tsunami Museum in Hilo, Hawaii, did a Master of Arts thesis in risk communication at the University of Hawaii. She found that without communications in place 96 people died in Hilo's 1946 tsunami. 61 still died in 1960, in another large tsunami, despite the existence by then of warnings via radio, television, sirens, and the police. Clearly public awareness and other social issues are also important – not just the information and communication technologies (ICT).

9. *Merging risk reduction and development.* How can the Millennium Development Goals (formulated in 2000, reaffirmed in 2002 at the WCSD in Johannesburg and monitored in September 2005 at the UN M + 5) be implemented in a way that simultaneously addresses risk reduction? In fact, is it possible to achieve the MDGs without attention to risk reduction? What are the *precise* links between opportunities for risk reduction and the manner in which the MDGs are currently being implemented? (One example: some 100 million children of school age are to be absorbed

into the school system. However, who is looking at the hazardousness of the school locations and schools themselves where these new students will find themselves?).

10. *Global alliances of disaster concerned and disaster affected peoples.* There is great power in the sharing of suffering and outrage. For example, tsunami victims from 10 countries or earthquake victims in Turkey, Japan and California coming together to lobby for better and more people-focused governance. Can the World Social Forum and other new people-focused institutions be made to see this as a priority?

11. *Women's crucial role in disaster reduction.* How can the potential of women as proactive agents of disaster reduction be acknowledged and fully utilised? Women and children may suffer more in disasters, but women should not be stereotyped as 'victims'. Women have a large contribution to bring to disaster risk reduction and local resilience. They have knowledge, skills, and relevant capacities and experiences. This has been very well documented, but women's contribution is often ignored.

12. *Full national accountability and transparency.* Given that the final documents produced by the WCDR did not include targets, timetable, or indicators of success in implementing the 'framework' for disaster risk reduction, what steps can be taken to ensure that nations actually take the Hyogo Programme of Action seriously and move concretely to implement it?

NOTES

[1]   In fact, in the end, the Hyogo Declaration as well as the Hyogo Programme of Action did mention climate change several times – a small step in the right direction.

[2]   The MDGs, were, in fact, mentioned explicitly in the final documents issued from the World Conference on Disaster Reduction (WCDR). However, none of the specific eight MDGs were linked to the framework for disaster risks reduction developed and agreed by international consensus. At the moment considerable effort is going into programmes worldwide to reduce poverty, increase child survival, expand access to clean water, etc. Without identifying specific links between disaster risks reduction and the manner in which these MDGs are being pursued, a key opportunity for concrete implementation is going to be missed.

[3]   In announcing an International Early Warning System at the WCDR, Jan Egland called it 'people centred.' A major challenge for civil society is to take up this challenge and give content to this phrase.

[4]   The Small Island Developing States (SIDS) were very active at the WCDR, and a paragraph on their particular vulnerability to the hazards of climate change was included in the Hyogo Programme of Action.

# PART V
# COMMON PERSPECTIVES

# 40

## GLOBETHICS.NET ELEMENTS FOR RESPONSIBLE LEADERSHIP

*A result of the Globethics.net International Conference*
*Bangkok, Thailand, 22-26 September 2005*

*In today's globalised and interconnected world, most societies are challenged by a fast transition of structures and values. Therefore, former models, guidelines and practices of leadership are changing. The call for ethical orientation for responsible leadership is widespread.*

*'Responsible Leadership – Global and Contextual Ethical Challenges' was the topic addressed at the International Globethics.net Conference, 22-26 September 2005 in Bangkok, Thailand. The participants explored elements of principles for responsible leadership in five areas, namely family, education, religion, business and politics. The principles outlined in this paper represent the outcome of the Bangkok conference.*

*The participants, mostly ethicists, came from 22 countries in five continents in the South and North. They shared concerns and issues of crisis in leadership in various fields and different social, political, economic and religious contexts. Five keynote speeches and 25 papers were discussed in workshops and showed common concerns such as poverty and wealth, war and violence, lopsided development, the speed of transformation and its effects on family, education, religion, media in the light of the impact of globalisation on all spheres of life. Most of the contributors of Globethics.net came from a Christian background; however, the inclusion of interreligious perspectives is now increasing.*

*The elements of principles for responsible leadership outlined below do not form a closed list but rather a suggestion for ongoing debate both among participants of the conference and a wider public interested in the topic.*

### 1. Responsible Family Leadership

*The overall criterion in family leadership is love understood as action.*

Responsible family leadership means:
- to respect the dignity, integrity and uniqueness of each person;
- to establish mutual trust [that upholds and affirms the other];
- to empower others;

- to promote autonomy in the context of mutual dependence;
- to nurture, care and give life, seeking the wholeness of each member in their spiritual, intellectual, physical and emotional dimensions;
- to give space for differences and be open for mutual critique;
- to be mutually available for the other and willing to serve and sacrifice;
- to seek justice, peace and the common good;
- to promote participatory family management.


## 2. Responsible Educational Leadership

*The impact of globalisation and the current trends in development show how dominant knowledge systems and paradigms have prolifer- ated, in many cases resulting in alienating the poor from their traditional and culturally shaped educational resources. Whereas 'education' needs to be understood as a cultural process through which individuals are socialised to become responsible adults within the community and soci- ety, the dominant school systems often represent a type of 'schooling', which can lead to cultural alienation. Holistic education is a tool to lib- erate and transform people to be better human beings.*

Responsible educational leadership means:
- first and above all; to warrant access to education;
- to focus on learning and teaching values that help people to mutu- ally affirm their own and other cultures, religions and traditions and also respect the whole of creation;
- to develop a critical way of thinking among ordinary people, edu- cators and ethicists about the implications of being schooled in the dominant institution and value systems;
- to search for alternative paradigms and patterns of education;
- to prevent the market from considering education as a business tool;
- to raise awareness about the inter-linkages between the oppressive socio-political-economic structures in society and the existing par- adigms of education;
- to ensure that education is structured within the national cultural and religious framework;
- to lobby and to network as ethicists and educationists with people's organisations and movements to design and implement a holistic pattern of education.

### 3. Responsible Religious Leadership

*Responsible religious leadership should take into account the particular contexts such as minority/majority situations of religions and currents within religions, the relation between religions and the State, the history of religions, the democratisation process of religious communities, the demographic reality (variety of membership, manipulation of statistics for political or other reasons), the relationship between ideology and theology in a pluralistic context, and the gender sensitivity.*

*The following paragraph looks at the issue mainly related to Christian churches.*

Responsible religious leadership means:

*within the church*

- to be committed and faithful to the spiritual tasks of a religious leader;
- to promote mutual respect of believers of other religions and other churches;
- to sensitise against the abuse of religion for ideological and other interests;
- to ensure the full and active participation of women, men and young people in all aspects of church and life;
- to give priority to the most vulnerable individuals and communities under their care;
- to ensure that, in the training of personnel, the focus lie on looking after the most vulnerable and the weakest;
- to fight all forms of corruption in religious institutions and society;
- to fight all forms of discrimination based on race and ethnicity in religion and society;
- to be open to continuing theological re-interpretation and hermeneutics in order to avoid ideological abuse of the respective scriptures;
- the openness to build bridges between religions;
- transparency and accountability in the leading bodies;

*in relation with the state and with the society*

- to support legislation protecting religious rights within the state;
- to ensure mutual respect of religious and secular values;
- to support legislation against manipulation of society by quasi-religious cults;

- to encourage the state to recognise the particular contexts of religious histories;
- to promote participation of citizens in the political and social life of the nation;
- to encourage constructive involvement in civil society;
- to avoid the temptation to exploit the demographic status of their respective religions and denominations for political interests.

## 4. Responsible Business Leadership

*The agents of business leadership are understood as the members of the management on different levels and the shareholders represented by board members (explore and enlarge). In the broader sense they include the politicians, consumers, economic associations, etc. In general, the following paragraph speaks about the need to respect the core values of sustainability, justice, peace, participation, and human rights.*

Responsible business leadership means:
*in general*
- to equally weigh the needs and interests of the different stakeholders such as employees, shareholders, the state, consumers, and nature, and being accountable to them;
- to enter into competition in a transparent, fair and honest way;

*economically*
- to work for financial stability and at least maintain the value of the borrowed and invested capital;
- to actively resist all kind of corruption while respecting the national laws and international anti-corruption conventions;
- to look at a fair distribution and redistribution of income within the company, but also of the added national value;
- to anticipate early enough and in a sound way, restructuring processes that are necessary to respond to changing situations;

*socially*
- to explore and respect the ethical values in the different contexts where business activities are done;
- to overcome double standards (in international activities) and implement the same ethical, social and environmental standards

in the different countries and to demand the same commitment from the suppliers;

- to pay for raw material and primary goods above the costs of production;
- to offer multi-stakeholder dialogues on sensitive issues or in fields of conflicts;
- to eradicate discriminations based on gender, ethnic origin, race, religion, disability and culture in the workplace;
- to support efforts for broader representation of women in leading positions;

*politically*

- to balance private and public interests;
- to be willing to fulfil the obligations towards the different stakeholders, especially consumers (quality of products and transparency/truth of product information) and the state (paying taxes, respecting legal requirements);
- to be willing to strengthen laws and regulations where necessary, in order to respect values based on human rights and achieve ethical goals;

*environmentally*

- to respect sustainability as a long-term environmental, economic and social commitment;
- to have a sense of accountability to the different stakeholders including nature.

## 5. Responsible Political Leadership

*Responsible political leadership is not solely a matter of individual virtues but is closely linked to the community and the responsibility of those who elect political leaders.*

Responsible political leadership means:
*on the community/constituency level*

- to empower people to become subjects and active citizens in organic union with the community;
- to act in solidarity with other life-affirming groups and movements that strive for recognition and political participation;

- to promote and facilitate the emergence of agencies among the people and from below;
- to promote transparency as a regular institutional process that allows checks and balances of leadership;
- to be aware of the danger of corruption and to actively fight it;
- to promote a participatory political setting which allows the emergence of young leaders;
- to be accountable, beyond the patterns of democracy by delegation, by a binding representation;
- to promote peace, which presupposes a very careful use of the monopoly of organised violence as well as a commitment to eradicate the roots of non-peaceful states of affairs;
- to strengthen the autonomy of the social political reality, which implies the promotion of freedom;

*on the level of the leader*

- to have a sense of, and for, spirituality, which presupposes the acceptance of the limitation and of the decentralisation of all political power;
- to be self-critical (especially in a Christian perspective where human finitude is acknowledged in a basic way);
- to foster life-affirming aims expressed through social movements;
- to keep promises;
- to network between groups and movements.

## 6. Responsible Media Leadership

*The media have a great potential to influence people's ideologies, interests and priorities in life. The use and misuse of the media is directly linked with the quality of life enjoyed by individuals in a civil society. Consumers must be equipped with the ability and the perspective to understand and use the media critically.*

Responsible media leadership means:

- an interest to develop a critical holistic perspective to read, interpret and understand the media;
- to provide media education for people at all levels;
- to raise awareness about the role the media play in shaping people's lives;

- to provide education, support and training to journalists in order to enhance their skills and their commitment to defend the interests of the economically, socially, politically weak;
- to affirm the role and the significance of the whole range of media (including non-conventional media) for effective communication;
- to use mass media to connect peoples, cultures, traditions and religions and affirm human communities;
- to use computer-based communication technologies such as the internet to promote 'real', rather than 'virtual' human communities.

# CONTRIBUTORS

## Editors

### Stückelberger, Christoph

Prof. Dr. Theol., *1951. Founder and chairperson of Globethics.net. Director of the Institute for Theology and Ethics of the Federation of Swiss Protestant Churches in Berne, Switzerland. Professor of Ethics at the University of Basel, Switzerland. Reformed pastor. Director of the Swiss protestant development organisation 'Bread for all' (1993-2004). Author of various books on economic ethics, environmental ethics, peace ethics. Regular visiting professor in developing countries.

Themes: business ethics, environmental, peace and justice issues, bioethics.

Recent publications: *Global Trade Ethics. An Overview*, WCC Publications: Geneva, 2003 (in reprint, available in German, English, French, Chinese); with Mugambi, Jesse K.N. (eds), *Responsible Leadership. Global Perspectives*, Nairobi: Acton Publishers, 2005.

Web: www.sek-feps.ch; www.christophstueckelberger.ch
E-mail: stueckelberger@globethics.net

### Mugambi, Jesse K. N.

Prof. Dr. Phil. & Rel. Studies, *1947. Professor of Philosophy and Religious Studies at the University of Nairobi, Kenya. Professor Extraordinarius at the University of South Africa in Pretoria. Member, World Council of Churches Working Group on Climate Change. Trustee, Kenya Rainwater Association. Founder of Action Publishers, Nairobi. Has a long and wide experience in teaching, ecumenical relations, research and publication.

Themes: theology, philosophy, education and communication.

Recent publications: *Christian Theology and Social Reconstruction*, Nairobi: Acton Press, 2003; with Stückelberger, Christoph (eds), *Responsible Leadership. Global Perspectives*, Nairobi: Acton Publishers, 2005.

Web: www.acton.co.ke
E-mail: info@acton.co.ke; jmugambi@iconnect.co.ke

## Authors [1]

### Anderson-Rajkumar, Evangeline

Prof. Dr. Theol., *1963. Professor in Women's Studies, United Theological College in Bangalore, India. President of the Association of Theologically Trained Women of India.

Themes: gender, caste, poverty, ecology and development.

Recent publications: 'Politicising the Body: Towards Asian Feminist Christology', in: *Asian Journal of Theology*, April 2004; 'Skin, Body and Blood. Explorations in Dalit Hermeneutics', in: *Religion and Society*, June-September 2004.

Web: www.womenutc.com

E-mail: uctevangline@gmail.com

### Andrade, Paulo

Prof. Dr. Theol., *1958. Professor of Ethics at the Pontifical Catholic University of Rio de Janeiro, Brazil.

Themes: philosophy and ethics, political ethics.

Recent publications: 'Militância e Crise de Subjectividade', in: Leonardo Boff *et al.*, *Fé e Política. Fundamentos*, 2004, pp. 111-121; 'Reflexões teológicas sobre a relação Fé e Política', in: *Atualidade Teológica*, Year VIII, 2004, fasc. 18, pp. 358-380.

Web: www.puc-rio.br

E-mail: paulof@rdc.pu-rio.br

### Asante, Emmanuel

Prof. Rev., *1950. Former President of Trinity Theological Seminary of Legon, Ghana. Currently: Head of Department of Religious Studies, Faculty of Social Sciences, Kwame Nkrumah University of Science and Technology in Kumasi, Ghana.

Themes: family ethics, religious ethics.

Recent publications: *Topics in Old Testament Studies*, Accra: SonLife, 2005; *Germs From the Preachers Pedestal. A Collection of Sermon and Talks*, Accra: SonLife, 2005.

E-mail: asanteema@hotmail.com

### Dierckxsens, Wim

Dr., *1946. Senior researcher at the Ecumenical Research Department – Associación Departamento Ecuménico de Investigaciones (DEI) in San José, Costa Rica, and member of the World Forum for Alternatives (WFA).

Themes: globalisation, trade ethics.

Recent publications: 'La transición hacia el postcapitalismo: el socialismo del siglo XXI', Panamá/Caracas: Ruth Casa Editorial/ Monte Avila, 2006 (available in Italian); with Tablada, Carlos, *Guerra global, resistencia mundial y alternativas*, Panamá: Ruth Casa Editorial, 2004 (4th edition), and *El ocaso del capitalismo y la utopía reencontrada*, Bogotá: Editorial Desde Abajo, 2003 (available in French: Paris, 2006).

Web: www.dei-cr.org
E-mail: mariwim@racsa.co.cr

## Dimitriadis, Nikos
PhD candidate, *1974. Student at the Faculty of Theology, Aristotle University in Thesssaloniki, Greece.
Themes: ecumenical relations and interreligious dialogue.
Web: http://users.auth.gr/nikosdim
E-mail: nikosdim@theo.auth.gr

## Ferencz, Árpád
Dr. Theol., *1972. Associated Teacher at the Protestant Theological Institute, Department of Ethics in Cluj, Roumania. PhD (2003) in Dogmatics on Karl Barth. Parish pastor in Romania.
Themes: Reformed theology, ecclesiology, bioethics, interreligious dialogue.
Publications: in Hungarian language.
Web: www.proteo.kereszteny.hu
E-mail: arpad720822@yahoo.de

## Gathaka, Jephthah
B. Theol., *1948. Anglican Priest. Executive Director of the Ecumenical Centre for Justice and Peace (ECJP) in Nairobi, Kenya. Former Director of the Justice, Peace and Reconciliation Programme of the National Council of Churches of Kenya.
Themes: social and economic issues.
E-mail: ecut@nbnet.co.ke

## Hadsell, Heidi
Prof. Dr. Theol., *1950. Professor of Social Ethics and President of Hartford Seminary, USA. Themes: environmental ethics, economic ethics, interreligious encounters and ethics, the public voice of the churches.
Recent publications: *Public Theology* (in preparation); 'Environmental Movements as Forms of Resistance', in: Stone, Ronald/Stivers, Robert (eds), *Resistance and Theological Ethics*, Lanham, MD: Rowman & Littlefield, 2004.
Web: www.hartsem.edu/centers/hadsell
E-mail: hadsell@hartsem.edu

**Hansen, Guillermo**
Prof. Dr., *1963. Professor of Systematic Theology and Ethics, Chairperson of the Department of Systematic Theology and Director of Post-Graduate Studies at ISEDET University, Buenos Aires, Argentina. Pastor of the United Evangelical Lutheran Church.
Themes: issues relating to Christian theology and late-modernity, ethics and globalisation, science and theology.
Recent publications: 'Reasoning through Theology. The Encounter with the Sciences in Times of Cultural and Social Fragmentation', in: *Studies in Science and Theology* 10, 2005/6; 'El método transdisciplinar y la vocación biopolítica de la teología', in: *Cuadernos de Teología* XXIV, 2005; 'Neoliberal Globalization. A *Casus Confessionis?*', in: Karen Bloomquist (ed.), *Communion, Responsibility, Accountability. Responding as a Lutheran Communion to Neoliberal Globalization*, Geneva: Lutheran World Federation, 2004.
E-mail: hansen@fibertel.com.ar

**Hoppe, Hella**
Dr. rer. pol., *1970. *Senior Economic Affairs Officer* at the Institute for Theology and Ethics (ITE) of the Federation of Swiss Protestant Churches (FSPC) in Berne, Switzerland.
Themes: global economy, economic ethics, gender ethics.
Recent publications: with Christoph Stückelberger, *Globalance. Perspectives chrétiennes pour une mondialisation à visage humain*, Berne: FEPS, 2005; with Floro, Maria, *Engendering Policy Coherence for Development. Gender Issues for the Global Policy*, Berlin/New York: Friedrich Ebert Stiftung, 2005; with Dolfsma, Wilfred, 'Global Gender Division of Labour', in: O'Hara, Philip (ed.), *Global Political Economy and the Wealth of Nations. Performance, Institutions, Problems and Policies*, London/New York: Routledge, 2004, pp. 188-207.
Web: www.sek-feps.ch
E-mail: hella.hoppe@sek-feps.ch

**Kasongo, Muteho**
Prof. Dr., Professor of Social Ethics in the Université Libre des Pays des Grands Lacs (ULPGL) in Goma, Democratic Republic of Congo. Vice Dean of the Theological Faculty, Coordinator of the Comité d'Ethique/Head of the Department of Ethics.
Themes: gender ethics, comparative religions ethics.
E-mail: kambmut@yahoo.com

**Kim, Un Hey**
Prof. Dr. Theol., *1963. Graduate of Seoul Women's University (B.A.) and of the Presbyterian Theological Seminary (M.Div.) in Korea, and of Drew Seminary in Carmel, NY (Th.M.) and from Clare-

mont Graduate University in California (PhD) in the USA. Presently full time instructor for Christianity and Culture at the Presbyterian College and Theological Seminary in Seoul, Korea.

Themes: feminist ethics, ethics and culture and theology.

E-mail: lifeempty1216@hanmail.net; changeself@hanafos.com

## Kobia, Samuel M.

Dr. Theol., *1947. M.A. in Urban Planning at MIT/Boston, PhD in Theology and Religious Science. Methodist pastor. Former General Secretary of the National Council of Churches in Kenya. General Secretary of the World Council of Churches since 2004. Author of various books on political ethics such as: *The Quest for Democracy in Africa* (1993).

Recent publications: *The Courage to Hope. The Roots for a New Vision and the Calling of the Church in Africa*, Geneva: WCC Publications, 2003; *Called to the One Hope*, Geneva: WCC Publications, 2006.

Web: www.wcc-coe.org

E-mail: sam.kobia@wcc-coe.org

## LenkaBula, Puleng

Dr., teaches political and economic ethics, feminist/womanist/ African women's ethics at the department of Systematic Theology and Theology of the University of South Africa in Cape Town. Just completed her doctoral degree in Ethics.

Themes: bioprospecting, biodiversity and intellectual property rights and their impacts on Africa and on biodiversity, gender/economic and social justice.

Recent publications: 'Justice and Reconciliation in Post-Apartheid South Africa. A South African Woman's Perspective', in: *International Review of Mission* 94(372), 2005, pp. 103-116; 'The Social and Ethical Implications of Article 27 of the Agreement on Trade Related Aspects of Intellectual Property Rights (TRIPS) on African communities, biodiversity and indigenous knowledge', in: *Journal of Theology for Southern Africa*, Cape Town: South African Council of Churches, 11 October 2005.

Web: www.unisa.ac.za

E-mail: lenkap@unisa.ac.za

## Lind, Christopher J.L.

Prof. Dr., Senior Fellow at Massey College, University of Toronto in Toronto, Canada. Former Director, Toronto School of Theology, University of Toronto (2003-2006). Former President of St. Andrew's College in Saskatoon, SK and St. Stephen's College in Edmonton, AB. Former Professor of Church & Society, St. Andrew's College (1985-2003).

Themes: ethics & economics, professional ethics, practical ethics, contextual theology.

Recent publications: 'Keeping and Sharing. Confidentiality in Ministry', in: *Journal of Pastoral Care and Counselling*, Volume 60:1-2, Spring-Summer 2006; *Something's Wrong Somewhere. Globalization, Community and the Moral Economy of the Farm Crisis*, Halifax, NS: Fernwood, 1995.

E-mail: christopher.lind@utoronto.ca

## Machasin, Muhammad

Prof. Dr., *1956. Professor history of Islamic Studies at the State Islamic University Sunan Kalijaga in Yogyakarta, Indonesia. Teaches as well history of Islamic cultures, history of world religions, Islamic theology and Islamic history at (state) Gadjah Mada University, Protestant Duta Wacana University, Catholic University Sanata Dharma and a private university (all in Yogyakarta, Indonesia). Has been active in organising and promoting interfaith encounters. Vice head of Nahdatul Ulama Consultative Board in Yogyakarta (1997-2006).

Recent publications: *Al-Qdadii Abd Al-Jabbâr, Mutasyabih al-Qur'an*. Dalih Rasionalitas al-Qur'an (on Abd al-Jabbar's discussion on the problem of ambiguous passages of the Koran), Yogyakarta: LKIS, 2000; *Islam Teologi Aplikatif* (Applied Theology of Islam), Yogyakarta: Alif, 2003; *Muhhamadiya and Nahdiatul Ulama in the Reformation Era*, Cleverainga Lectures, Jakarta: KITLV, 2004.

E-mail: mmachasin@yahoo.com

## Ondji'i Toung, Richard

Dr. Theol., *1964. General Secretary of the Interdisciplinary and Interreligious Center of Ethical Research (CIIRE) in Yaoundé, Cameroon. PhD on the Contribution of Economic Ethics related to debts and poverty eradication in Central Africa (2004). M.A. in Economics and in International Relations. Pastor.

Themes: economic ethics, family ethics, ethics of international financial systems.

E-mail: revondjii@yahoo.co.uk

## Sachs, Jeffrey

Prof. Dr., *1954. Economist, Professor and Director of the Earth Institute at Columbia University in New York. United Nations special adviser, Head of the UN Millennium Project (to half world poverty by 2015). Chairperson of the World Health Organisation's commission for macro-economy and health.

Themes: mainly the causes of poverty, the role of rich country policies, and the possibilities for a poverty-free future

Recent publication: *The End of Poverty. Economic Possibilities for Our Time*, New York, NY: Penguin Group 2005.
Web: www.earth.columbia.edu
E-mail: sachs@columbia.edu

### Shashkin, Pavel

Dr. Phil., *1976. PhD in Philosophy, Master of Law. Political scientist, staff member of the Department for External Church Relations of the Moscow Patriarchate.

Themes: economy, political and legal issues, international and European law.
Web: www.mospat.ru
E-mail: brute@mospatr.ru

### Silantyev, Roman

Executive Secretary of the Interreligious Council of Russia.
Theme: contemporary Islam in Russia
E-mail: r.silantiev@mail.ru

### Walz, Heike

Dr. theol., *1966. Professor of Systematic Theology at the Universitarian Institute ISEDET in Buenos Aires, Argentina, where she is Coordinator of the Forum for Gender and Theology. Serving as ecumenical coworker of Mission 21, evangelical mission agency in Basel, Switzerland. Pastor of the Evangelical Church of the Palatinate in Germany (EKD).

Themes: gender ethics, gender studies in theology, intercultural theology.

Recent publication: *'… nicht mehr männlich und weiblich…'? Ekklesiologie und Geschlecht in ökumenischem Horizont*, Frankfurt: Lembeck, 2006.
E-mail: walz@isedet.edu.ar

### Wandja, Afumba

Prof. Rev., *1947. Christian Ethics Professor at the Protestant University in the Democratic Republic of Congo (DRC). Academic Dean, Protestant University, DRC. Pastor of a French-Swahili local Church of the United Methodist Church of the DRC.

Themes: peace and reconciliation, biodiversity ethics, comparative religions ethics

Recent publications: 'Les rapports entre parents et enfants à la lumière du Commandement d'honorer ses parents', in: *Revue Congolaise de Théologie Protestante* 13, 1999; 'Essai d'un discours pastoral et éthique de l'Eglise sur la paix et la réconciliation', in: *Revue de la Faculté de Droit* 3, 2003.
E-mail : afumbalbert@yahoo.fr

**Walder, Anne**

Lic iur., *1964. Senior Social Affairs Officer at the Institute for Theology and Ethics (ITE) of the Federation of Swiss Protestant Churches (FSPC), Bern, Switzerland.

Themes: family ethics, diaconal and social work of the churches.

Recent publication: with Annette Wisler Albrecht, *Informaternité:... pour harmoniser maternité et activité rémunérée*, Berne: Confédération des syndicats chrétiens de Suisse, 2000.

Web: www.sek-feps.ch

E-mail: anne.walder@sek-feps.ch

**Walker, Peter**

B.Sc. in Environmental Sciences, and Ph.D. (1981) in Soil from Sheffield University, UK. Director of the Feinstein International Center at Tufts University, USA. Spent many years with the International federation of the Red Cross and Red Crescent Societies, including a period as head of Regional Delegation for Southeast Asia.

Themes: mainly natural disasters, including international strategic policy on mitigation, prevention and response, but also development of indigenous knowledge and famine early warning systems, role of military forces in disaster relief, etc.

Recent publications: 'Cracking the Code. The Genesis, Use and Future of the Code of Conduct', in: *Disasters Journal*, Vol. 29, Issue 4, December 2005, pp. 323-326; with Wisner, Ben, 'Katrina and Goliath. Why the Greatest Military and Economic Power in the World Did Not Protect New Orleans', in: *Humanitarian Exchange*, Number 32, December 2005, pp. 46-48.

Web: http://fic.tufts.edu

E-mail: peter.walker@tufts.edu

**Widyamatdja, Josef P.**

Rev., *1944. Executive Secretary of Faith Mission and Unity Christian Conference of Asia (CCA) in Chiangmai, Thailand.

Themes: globalisation, peace and justice issues.

Recent publications: *Building Spirituality and Culture of Peace for All*, India: Christian Conference of Asia, 2003; *Re-routing Mission. Towards a People's Concept of Mission and Diakonia*, India: Christian Conference of Asia, 2004; *Asia Africa Spirit and Struggle Amid Globalization*, India: Christian Conference of Asia, 2005.

E-mail: henduk@yahoo.com

**Wijaya, Yahya**

Prof. Dr. Theol., *1955. Professor of Ethics and Director of Postgraduate Studies at Duta Wacana Christian University in Yogyakarta, Indonesia. Pastor.

Themes: business ethics, intercultural ethics, political ethics.

Recent publications: *Iman atau Fanatisme?(Faith or Fanatism?)*, Jakarta: BKP, 1997; *Business, Family and Religion. A Public Theology in the Context of the Chinese-Indonesian Business Community*, Oxford, etc.: Peter Lang, 2002.

Web: www.ukdw.ac.id

E-mail: yahyawijaya@ukdw.ac.id

### Wisner, Ben

Research associate at the Environmental Studies Program at Oberlin College, USA and at the Crisis States Research Centre of the Development Studies Institute (DESTIN) of the London School of Economics, and at the Benfield Hazard Research Centre, University College in London. Vice-chair of the Earthquakes and Megacities Initiative, vice-chair of the International Geographical Union's Commission on Hazards and Risks, and a research coordinator for the United Nations University's project on urban disasters. He is also an advisor to the emergency-response program of the American Friends Service Committee.

Themes: society-environment relations

Recent publication: *At Risk. Natural Hazards, People's Vulnerability and Disasters*, London: Routledge, 2004 (2nd edition).

E-mail: ben.wisner@oberlin.edu; bwisner@igc.org

### Zhu, Rachel Xiaohong

Dr. Phil., *1970. Associate Professor at the Department of Philosophy of Fudan University in Shanghai, China and Secretary for Religious Studies Program at the Christian Studies Center. Themes: religion and society, the social role of churches in China, science of religions, business ethics.

Recent publication: contribution to Kwang-sun Suh, David/ Meuthrath, Annette/Hyondok, Choe (eds), *Charting the Future of Theology and Theological Education in Asian Contexts*, Delhi: Indian Society for Promoting Christian Knowledge (ISPCK), 2004.

Web: www.fudan.edu.cn/english

E-mail: rachelbs1@hotmail.com

NOTE

[1]   Most authors are participants in the Globethics.net network; their e-mail addresses and other informations can also be found on www.globethics.net. Recent publications include works related to ethics only.

This printer has a green label guaranteeing
environmentally-friendly printing procedures.

Dépôt légal 3ᵉ trimestre 2007 - n° 4558

N° d'impression : 205310

L'impression et le façonnage de cet ouvrage
ont été réalisés à l'Imprimerie LUSSAUD
85200 FONTENAY-LE-COMTE